THE ESSENTIAL
FOOTBALL FAN

THE ESSENTIAL FOOTBALL FAN

The Definitive Guide to Premier and Football League Grounds

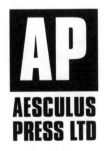

AESCULUS
PRESS LTD

www.aesculus-press.com

Cover design by Ashley Shaw

All material is copyright of Aesculus Press Limited 2004

Aesculus Press Limited
PO Box 5276
Swadlincote
Derbyshire
DE11 9ZT

Typeset on an Apple Macintosh
by Acer Designs, Manchester
(0161 881 3074)

Printed and bound in Great Britain by Ashford Colour Press Ltd.,
Gosport, Hampshire

ISBN: 1-904328-22-9

INTRODUCTION

Welcome to the second edition of the Essential Football Fan. Based on the acclaimed website www.footballgroundguide.co.uk, the book covers every ground in the Premier League, the Coca Cola Football Leagues, the Cup finals venue and The Millennium Stadium. Not only has this second edition been revised and updated for the new season, but it is now in colour so that we can all fully enjoy some of the great photos of the respective stadiums. However, to keep costs down, the book has had to be trimmed slightly and this means that unlike the first edition, the Conference National League has not been included this time.

The book follows on from the success of the first edition and inside you will find a host of information useful to the travelling supporter. Not only are there practical details, such as directions to the grounds, car parking etc., but also includes other information to make your day more enjoyable, such as pub and food recommendations. The Guide has been compiled based on not only my personal visits to the grounds, but also the feedback of thousands of supporters who have visited them in recent seasons, giving an all-around independent view. Without this feedback, this book would not have been possible, so a big thank you to everyone who has contributed.

Although I have strived to make sure that every detail is as much up to date as possible, things can change over the course of a season - for example, a pub will close or another open, so please bear this in mind. I hope you find this guide useful and informative. But remember this is only a guide and should be treated as such. If you find that things have changed or you feel that you can provide better directions or add useful additional information, then please feel free to e-mail me at duncan@footballgrounds.net. Remember this guide is for football fans by football fans, so feel free to have your say. Wherever possible, I'll strive to include your comments in future editions.

Also look out for the companion guide to this book: 'The Essential Scottish Football Fan', covering the grounds of the 42 Scottish League teams and Hampden Park.

ABOUT THE AUTHOR

My father first took to me to see a game when I was aged six in 1970 at Villa Park. The memories from that visit have always stayed with me. It was a cold winter's day, made a lot warmer by nearly 60,000 fans crammed into the ground for a league cup semi-final against Manchester United. The atmosphere was intense and I was soon hooked on attending games. But it was not Aston Villa but Birmingham City that became my love and I was soon a regular at St Andrews. As a teenager, I started to go to Birmingham away games and my fascination with different football grounds really began.

Since then it's me craning my neck trying to see more of a ground, after glimpsing a floodlight pylon in the distance, from a car or train window. These stadiums are just so different from any other type of building you would come across. Plus when you add the fans, a football game, the atmosphere, then they take on a magic all of their own. Having visited all 92 Premier and Football League grounds in England and Wales, the websites and books have given me further impetus to visit even more

grounds than I originally had ever envisaged. I now have a fascination for the last surviving old grounds and stands, as well as marvelling at the new structures that seem to be built every year.

I hope you enjoy the book and that it will improve your away trips, as well as perhaps whetting your appetite to visit a ground that you hadn't thought about visiting before.

Duncan Adams
August 2004
Duncan Adams (left) with Derek Allan, Brighton Football Club Secretary on completing visits to all 92 grounds at Withdean Stadium.

Special Thanks

To Han van Eijden for his continual support and his wealth of football knowledge over the years. To Ian Dewar, an exiled Nottingham Forest fan in Canada, for rewriting parts of the Guide so that it became immensely more readable. To Owen Pavey for providing a number of great photographs, as well as Colin Peel, Lee Roberts, Neil Shenton, Tim Rigby and Richard Hooper for their contributions. To Thomas Mapfumo, of European Football Statistics, for providing the average attendance information - please visit his website at www.european-football-statistics.co.uk. I am also indebted to Simon Inglis and his book 'The Football Grounds Of Great Britain' for some of the historical information contained within this Guide. And lastly to my wife Amanda, for her unquestioning support and patience in my ground visiting travels and putting this book together..

www.footballgroundguide.co.uk

LEGAL NOTICE & DISCLAIMER:

CONTENTS

PREMIERSHIP

CHAMPIONSHIP

LEAGUE ONE

LEAGUE TWO

HIGHBURY, ARSENAL

Ground Name: Arsenal Stadium
(but still known to many fans as Highbury)
Capacity: 38,500 (all-seated)
Address: Avenell Rd, Highbury,
London, N5 1BU
Main Telephone No: 0207-704-4000
Main Fax No: 0207-704-4001
Ticket Office: 0207-704-4040
24 Hour Ticket Info: 0207-704-4242
Stadium Tours: 0207-704-4100
Pitch Size: 110 x 71 yards
Club Nickname: The Gunners
Home Kit Colours: Red & White
Official Website: www.arsenal.com
Unofficial Websites:
Arsenal Land: www.arsenal-land.co.uk
Arseweb: www.arseweb.com
Jack Kelsey Fan Club:
www.arsenalarsenal.co.uk
Arsenal World: www.arsenal-world.net
German Gunners: www.arsenalfc.de
Tipperary Gunners: www.tipperary-
gunners.freeservers.com

WHAT'S THE GROUND LIKE?

The ground has greatly improved in recent
years with the redevelopment of both ends
of the stadium. In particular, the
replacement of the open terrace Clock End
with a superb stand has kept the famous
clock and hence some character. These
developments have made Highbury one of
the best grounds in the country. However
the roof at the Clock End (also known as the
South Stand) doesn't cover the front rows of
seats, so pray it doesn't rain. The Clock End
is divided between home and away fans. The
other end, the famous North Bank, has also
been redeveloped with a large two-tiered
stand. Both sides, the East and West Stands,
are older and similar in design, having both
been built in the 1930s. Each has a large
bottom tier, with an upper tier partly
overhanging the lower. There are two large
video screens that sit in opposite corners of
the ground.

FUTURE GROUND DEVELOPMENTS

Arsenal have commenced with the
construction of a new stadium at Ashburton
Grove, about a five minute journey from
Highbury. The 60,000 capacity stadium has
been designed by the same company who

designed Stadium Australia. From the plans I have seen, it looks simply stunning, with an interesting roof design similar to Stade De France in Paris. The Club hope to kick off in the new stadium for the start of the 2006/07 season. It is intended that Highbury will be re-developed for housing, although the existing East and West stands will be preserved.

WHAT'S IT LIKE FOR VISITORS?

Away fans are mostly housed in one corner of the Clock End (South Stand) where up to 1,700 fans can be accommodated. If demand requires it, then an additional 944 seats can be made available in the lower tier of the West Stand. I have been to Arsenal on a couple of occasions and have always been impressed with the ground itself. I did not experience any problems on my visits and have had a couple of pleasant days out. My only slight criticism is that the ground is not as atmospheric as some other grounds in the Premier. The delicious 'Football's Famous

Chicken Balti Pie' (£2.60) is available inside the ground.

WHERE TO DRINK

Mark Long recommends the 'Twelve Pins' (formerly the Finsbury Park Tavern) near Finsbury Park Tube Station. 'Normally a good mix of home and away fans and about a ten minute walk from the ground'. Whilst David Hurst adds: 'The Drayton Arms, near where the away coaches are parked, is popular with away supporters'.

GETTING THERE & WHERE TO PARK

Leave the M1 at Junction 2 and onto the A1, following the signs for City (Central London). Keep going on the A1 for around six miles, until you see Holloway Road Tube Station. Take the third left-hand turn after the tube station, called Drayton Park. Go down this road and then turn right into Aubert Park and then left into Avenell Road. Street parking, although be wary of a residents

only parking scheme in operation around the ground. It perhaps may be better to park further out of London around a tube station and get the tube to the ground.

By Train/Tube

I have always gone by train/tube to Highbury. The nearest underground station is Arsenal, which is on the Piccadilly line and is only a few minutes walk from the North Bank. However, the queues at the station at the end of the game can be horrendous. Other tube stations in walking distance of the ground are Finsbury Park (where there is also a railway station, served by frequent trains to Kings Cross, Potters Bar and Stevenage), on the Piccadilly Line and Highbury and Islington on the Victoria Line

LOCAL RIVALS

Tottenham Hotspur.

ADMISSION PRICES

East and West Stands
Upper Tier Centre blocks: Adults £68
Upper Tier Next to Centre blocks: Adults £50
Upper Tier Wing blocks: Adults £44
Lower Tier Centre blocks: Adults £36
Lower Tier Wing blocks: Adults £33
North Bank Stand
Upper Tier Centre block: Adults £51
Upper Tier Wing block: Adults £42.50
Lower Tier Centre block: Adults £42.50
Lower Tier Wing block: Adults £33
Lower Tier Outer Wing block: Adults £28
Clock End (South) Stand
All Lower Tier areas: Adults £33
Family Enclosure (Members Only)
Adult - Lower Tier Centre block: £36
Adult - Lower Tier Wing Block: £33
Senior Citizens: £14.50
Cannon Club: £14.50
Junior Gunners: £13
Away Fans:
Clock End (South Stand): Adults £33,
Concessions £16.50
West Stand: Adults £33, Concessions £16.50

PROGRAMME & FANZINES

Official Programme: £2.50.

The Gooner Fanzine: £2.
Up The A**e Fanzine: £1.

RECORD ATTENDANCE

73,295 v Sunderland
Division One, March 9, 1935.

AVERAGE ATTENDANCE

2003-2004: 38,079 (Premier League).

STADIUM TOURS

The Club offer stadium tours, which also allow you entrance into the Arsenal Museum in the North Bank Stand. The tours, which must be booked in advance cost: Adults £8 and £4 for concessions, or there is a family ticket available (for two adults and two children) which costs £20. Further discounts are available for group bookings. The tour is available on most weekdays and it is advisable that you book well in advance of your visit. To book a place, call the club on 020-7704-4504 or email: tours@arsenal.co.uk.
The museum can be visited separately, but it is only open to those not on a stadium tour on Fridays (9.30am-4pm) and matchdays. The cost of entry to the museum is Adults £4 and £2 concessions.

DID YOU KNOW?

Arsenal Football Club began life in the south-east London suburbs of Woolwich and Plumstead when a group of predominantly Scottish workers at the Woolwich Arsenal Armament Factory decided to form the Dial Square football team in late 1886.

VILLA PARK, ASTON VILLA

Ground Name:	Villa Park
Capacity:	43,000 (all-seated)
Address:	Villa Park, Trinity Rd, Birmingham B6 6HE
Main Telephone No:	0121-327-2299
Main Fax No:	0121-322-2107
Ticket Office:	0121-327-5353
Ticket Office Fax:	0121-328-5575
Stadium Tours:	0121 327 2299
Club Nickname:	The Villans
Pitch Size:	115 x 72 yards
Home Kit Colours:	Claret & Blue
Official Website:	www.avfc.co.uk

Unofficial Websites:
Heroes & Villains:
www.heroesandvillains.net
Independent Supporters Association:
www.avisa.co.uk
Villa Talk: www.villatalk.com
Holteenders.com: www.holteenders.com
(Rivals Network)

WHAT'S THE GROUND LIKE?

Three sides of the ground have been rebuilt in recent years, making it one of the better in the League. The Holte End is a large two-tiered structure, opened in the 1994/95 season and holds 13,500 supporters. The other end, the North Stand, is older (built in the late 1970s), but still modern looking. This is two-tiered, with a double row of executive boxes running across the middle. On one side of the pitch is the Doug Ellis stand, which again is two-tiered and is roughly the same height as the other two stands. Opposite is the three-tiered Trinity Road Stand, complete with a row of executive boxes. Although many fans were disappointed to see the old Trinity Road Stand go, I think its replacement gives the ground a more overall balanced look, because the new stand, although the largest at Villa Park, has roughly the same roof level as the other three sides. There are also two large video screens installed in opposite corners of the ground. An unusual feature is that between the Trinity Road & Holte End Stands is a pavilion type structure that was built at the same time as

the Trinity Road. This three-tiered building is used for corporate hospitality. On the other side of the Holte End is another similar looking structure that is used for police control. The only disappointment with Villa Park is that the corners of the ground are open; however there are plans to fill in the corners at the North Stand end of the ground
(see below).

FUTURE GROUND DEVELOPMENTS

The Club have received planning permission to extend the North Stand. This will involve the 'filling in' of the corners to either side of the North Stand. However there are currently no firm timescales as to when this will take place. When completed the capacity of Villa Park will be increased to 51,000.

WHAT'S IT LIKE FOR VISITORS?

Away supporters are housed in the lower tier of the North Stand where up to 3,000 fans can be accommodated. If demand requires it, then part of the Doug Ellis Stand can also be allocated to away fans. A visit to Villa Park is normally an enjoyable experience with a good atmosphere being generated within the ground. Please note that most fans tend to frequent the refreshment area and toilets that are right by the turnstile entrance to the away end. There is, in fact, another refreshment area and toilet block at the back on the other side of the North Stand (on the new Trinity Road Stand side), which tends to be quieter. 'Football's Famous Chicken Balti Pie' (£2) is available inside the ground. Also just inside the entrance, there is a programme hut from which not only is the current match programme available, but also a selection of older programmes are for sale, usually including a number involving the away side.

Now, as I support the other team in Birmingham (and no it isn't Solihull Borough!), it has been suggested that I am biased against Villa Park. Well all I can say is that I have been to the ground on a number

of occasions and in fact, I can now claim to have sat in every stand, so that just shows you how unbiased I really am!

WHERE TO DRINK

There are a number of pubs in the vicinity of Villa Park, but most of them on matchdays are either members only or have bouncers on the door. However, Dave Cooper recommends the following for away fans: 'The Cap and Gown (formerly The Witton Arms), is not a bad pub, to which half the pub is given to away fans (there is even a separate entrance for visiting fans). It is only two minutes walk from the away entrance, right on Witton Island. Otherwise there is the Harriers, which is on Broadway, near to the school of the same name. It is ten minutes walk from the ground and you can usually find street parking in this area'. If you arrive a bit earlier, then you may wish to visit the historic Barton Arms, located about a 15 minute walk away on High Street Aston (A34). This is one of Birmingham's finest pubs, with superb Victorian decor, serving Oakham ales and Thai food also on offer. Please note that alcohol is not available in the away end.

GETTING THERE & WHERE TO PARK

The ground can be seen from the M6, if you are coming from the North side of Birmingham. Leave the M6 at Junction 6 and take the slip road signposted Birmingham (NE). Turn right at the island (the fourth exit), the ground is well signposted from here. However to be on the safe side, turn right at the second set of traffic lights (there is a derelict pub on the corner) on to Aston Hall Road. This road will take you down to the ground. Street Parking (although don't be surprised if you are approached by kids wanting to 'mind your car').

By Train
Take the short train journey from Birmingham New Street (around 10-15 minutes) to either Aston or Witton station. Witton station is nearer to the away end and is only a few minutes walk from the ground. Turn left out of the station exit and continue down to a roundabout. Turn left at the

roundabout into Witton Lane and the entrance to the away section is down this road on the first corner of the ground that you reach. Aston station is a ten minute walk away from the ground. Extra trains are laid on to the ground on matchdays.

LOCAL RIVALS

Birmingham City, West Bromwich Albion and Wolverhampton Wanderers.

ADMISSION PRICES

Listed in the following order
Adult, Over 65, Under 16, Student

Trinity Road
Upper Centre
£29, £15, £13, £22
Upper Wings
£26, £14, £13, £19
Middle Centre
£29, £15, £13, £22
Middle Wings
£26, £14, £13, £19
Lower Centre
£24, £13, £13, £18
Lower Wings
£23, £13, £13, £17
Family Section
£17, £9, £7, £17

Doug Ellis
Upper Centre
£29, £15, £13, £22
Upper Wings
£26, £14, £13, £19
Lower Centre
£24, £13, £13, £18
Lower Wings
£23, £13, £13, £17

Holte End
Upper Centre
£26, £14, £13, £19
Upper Wings
£24, £13, £13, £18
Lower Centre
£23, £13, £13, £17
Lower Wings
£23, £13, £13, £17

North Stand
Upper Centre
£26, £14, £13, £19
Upper Wings
£17, £9, £7, £17

Away Fans
North Stand (Lower)
£23, £13, £13, £17

PROGRAMME & FANZINES

Official Programme: £2.50
Heroes & Villans Fanzine: £1.20
Holy Trinity Fanzine: £1

RECORD ATTENDANCE

76,588 v Derby County
FA Cup 6th Round, March 2nd, 1946.

AVERAGE ATTENDANCE

2003-2004: 36,622 (Premier League).

STADIUM TOURS

Tours are available on each Sunday except matchdays. The cost, including lunch overlooking the pitch is: Adults £19.95 and £9.95 for under 16s. Tours can be booked on 0121-327-5353 (and then selecting the events option).

DID YOU KNOW?

The site, on which Villa Park was built in 1897, was the mid-Victorian Aston Lower Grounds amusement park.

BIRMINGHAM CITY, ST ANDREWS

Ground Name: St Andrews
Capacity: 30,016 (all-seated)
Address: St Andrews Ground, Birmingham B9 4NH
Main Telephone No: 0121-772-0101
Main Fax No: 0121-766-7866
Ticket Office No: 0121-202-5333
Pitch Size: 115 x 75 yards
Club Nickname: The Blues
Home Kit Colours: Royal Blue & White
Official Website:
www.bcfc.com
Unofficial Websites:
Keep Right On: www.keeprighton.co.uk
Tired & Weary: www.tiredandweary.com

WHAT'S THE GROUND LIKE?

Approximately three-quarters of the ground has been rebuilt since the mid 90s. One large single-tiered stand, incorporating the Tilton Road End and Spion Kop, completely surrounds half the pitch and has replaced a former huge terrace. At the back of the Spion Kop Stand, which runs along one side of the pitch, are a row of executive boxes, as well as a central seated executive area which also incorporates the Directors 'box'. The other new stand, the Railway End, was opened in February 1999. It is a large two-tiered stand, unusual in having quite a small top tier, called 'The Olympic Gallery', which overhangs the lower tier. Again there is a row of executive boxes in this stand, housed at the back of the lower tier. Only one 'old' stand (it was built in the early 1960's), the Main Stand, now remains of the former St Andrews. This is a two-tier stand running along one side of the pitch, with a row of executive boxes across its middle.

FUTURE GROUND DEVELOPMENTS

The Club are in talks with Birmingham City Council about the feasibility of building a new 60,000 capacity stadium on the East side of the city. It is believed that if the scheme were to proceed, the design would be based on the Melbourne Dome in Australia and will feature a retractable roof. The stadium would be used for a number of other sporting events such as athletics as well as football. In view of this, the club have, for the time being, shelved the proposed £12m redevelopment of the present Main Stand, which would have increased the overall capacity of St Andrews to around 36,500.

WHAT'S IT LIKE FOR VISITORS?

Away supporters are housed on one side of the Railway Stand's lower tier where the normal allocation is 3,000 tickets, but this can be increased to around 4,500 for cup games. There are Birmingham fans housed above the away supporters, as well as to the other side of the stand (fans are separated by plastic netting). The facilities and the view from this stand are pretty good. There is the normal array of food on offer, such as pies, burgers and rollover hot dogs, plus a deeper version of the 'Chicken Balti Pie' (£2) by Wrights pies. Outside the ground just across the road from the entrance to the away section is a 'Big W' outlet which has a reasonably priced café inside. There is also a McDonald's a short walk away, going back towards the city centre. It is worth bearing in mind that a certain section of Birmingham fans are particularly passionate about their club and this can make for an intimidating atmosphere for away supporters. I would advise as a precaution to keep your club colours covered around the ground or in the city centre.

John, a visiting Burnley fan, informs me: 'The beer inside the ground was drinkable and the Balti pies were delicious! On the downside, the seat I had been allocated was in Row 21 seat 002 which was right up against the wall. I've had more legroom on a package tour flight to the Canaries! What really annoyed me were a small section of the City fans who spent the entire game screaming abuse and gesturing to the away fans'.

Alan Sexton, a visiting West Ham supporter, adds: 'The ground itself is three-quarters of the way to being a top class stadium but desperately needs a new Main Stand. If this is built, joining with the Tilton Road and Railway Stands. then St Andrews will be one of the best, if not the best, ground in the Midlands. Atmosphere-wise it was the best ground I have visited all season for sheer volume before and during the game. As for the concourses, they left little to be desired and were extremely crowded, the scrum to try and get a pie was not for the faint hearted'.

Well, having watched the Blues since 1972, I can honestly say that I have almost seen it all. The good, the bad and the ugly. The atmosphere at some games can be electric, at others virtually non existent. The Club itself has come on a great deal under the ownership of David Sullivan and the Gold Brothers and the stadium has been transformed. The crowd, when on form, can still give a great rendition of the Blues anthem 'Keep Right On To The End Of The Road'.

WHERE TO DRINK

The pubs near to the ground can be quite intimidating for away supporters and are not recommended. Best to drink in the city centre and get a taxi to the ground (about £4). Or if you are coming by car, you can stop on the way at the Gosta Green or The Sacks Of Potatoes at Aston University. These pubs are about a ten minute drive from the ground on matchdays (see directions below). If coming by train then either drink in the city centre or, if walking up to the ground, you may care to stop at the Anchor Pub on Bradford Street, renowned for its range of real ales on offer, and named Birmingham 'CAMRA Pub Of The Year' on more than one occasion. Although there are a number of Blues fans that frequent the pub, they tend to be of the CAMRA bearded variety and therefore as long as you don't turn up mobbed handed, you should be okay. The pub is situated just behind Digbeth coach station. Otherwise alcohol is served within the ground.

GETTING THERE & WHERE TO PARK

Leave the M6 at Junction 6 and take the A38(M) (known locally as the Aston Expressway) for Birmingham City Centre. Continue past the first turn off (Aston, Waterlinks) and then take the next turn off, for the Inner Ring Road.

Turn left at the island at the top of the slip road and take the Ring Road East, signposted Coventry/Stratford. (For the Gosta Green Pub turn right at the first traffic lights and the pub is over the bridge on your left and The Sacks Of Potatoes further up on the right). Continue along the ring road for two miles, crossing straight across three islands. At the fourth island (there is a large McDonald's on the far left-hand corner), turn left towards Small Heath. Birmingham City's ground is about a quarter of a mile up this road on your left. The ground is well signposted on the Inner Ring Road.

There is a car park at the ground but this is for pass holders only. There is, though, plenty of street parking off the left-hand side of the ring road, either around the small park at the third island you cross or along the road next to and behind the BP garage before the fourth island. Bear in mind that if you arrive after 1.30pm these areas are likely to be already full. There are some local schools and businesses that offer parking facilities for around £3-£4.

By Train

The nearest station is Bordesley, which is about a ten minute walk from the ground, but it is only served by trains from Birmingham Snow Hill. If you arrive at New Street Station in the city centre, either walk to Snow Hill (ten minutes) take a taxi (about £4) or embark on the 20-minute walk to the ground.

As you come onto the concourse of New St station, bear to the left of the escalators and through the glass doors. Walk down towards to the end of the Station Service Road. Cross to the other side of the road at the bottom (where there is a new shopping centre) turn right and follow the purple pedestrian signs for Digbeth Coach Station. These will lead you to a descending flight of stairs at the side of the shopping centre on your left and then going down a road with the Markets on your right and a large church on your left. Follow this road around to the right and then take the next left which will take you up to the main dual carriageway. Turn right along the dual carriageway, passing Digbeth Coach Station on your right and the impressive looking Crown Pub on your left. Cross over the dual carriageway to the Crown pub side of the road and continue walking away from the city centre. You will come to a fork in the road where you want to bear left going underneath a railway bridge. Passing the Clements Arms on your left, just continue straight down this road, crossing a large roundabout (with a McDonald's over on one corner). The entrance to the away section is further up the road on your left.

Otherwise you can take the following buses from the city centre: Nos 96, 97, 58 and 60. The 97 and 98 can be found in Carrs Lane in the city centre. As you come off the platform and onto the station concourse, go straight up the escalators in front of you. At the top of the escalators, turn left and keep in that direction so that you leave the shopping centre by going down a long ramp. Turn right at the bottom of the ramp into New Street and continue to the bottom. Then turn left into the High St and, just past Marks & Spencers on the right, is Carrs Lane. Turn into Carrs Lane and the bus stops are down on the left by the church.

LOCAL RIVALS

Aston Villa, West Bromwich Albion and Wolverhampton Wanderers.

ADMISSION PRICES

Adults: £32-£40
Concessions: £16-£20

PROGRAMME & FANZINES

Official Programme: £2.50
Made In Brum Fanzine: £1
Zulu Fanzine: £1

RECORD ATTENDANCE

66,844 v Everton
FA Cup 5th Round, February 11, 1939.

AVERAGE ATTENDANCE

2003-2004: 29,076 (Premier League).

DID YOU KNOW?

In 1886, the Club created history when they became the first football club to become a limited liability company, when Small Heath FC Ltd was created.

BLACKBURN ROVERS, EWOOD PARK

Ground Name: Ewood Park
Capacity: 31,367 (all-seated)
Address: Blackburn, Lancashire, BB2 4JF
Main Telephone No: 08701-113-232
Main Fax No: 01254-671-042
Ticket Office: 08701-123-456
Pitch Size: 115 x 76 yards
Club Nickname: Rovers
Home Kit Colours: Blue & White
Official Website: www.rovers.co.uk
Unofficial Websites:
Rovers Interactive: www.roversactive.co.uk
Blackburn Supporters: www.brfc-supporters.org.uk

WHAT'S THE GROUND LIKE?

The ground is quite impressive, having had three new large stands built during the 90s. These stands are at both ends and at one side of the ground. They are of the same height and of roughly similar design, being two-tiered and having a row of executive boxes as well as similar roofs. The ends are particularly impressive, both having large lower tiers. The only downside is the open corners, although there is a superb Sony Jumbotron screen at one corner by the away end, which shows an excellent pre-match programme and the teams emerging from

dressing rooms and onto the pitch. There is also an electric scoreboard at the Darwen End of the ground. The Riverside is the only undeveloped stand, running down one side of the pitch. This is a smaller single-tiered stand which is not as pleasing to the eye as its modern counterparts. It also contains a fair number of supporting pillars and is partly covered (to the rear). Just to highlight how much the ground has changed, this was at one time the 'best' stand at Ewood Park. One other interesting feature of the ground is the fact that the pitch is raised. This means that players have to run up a small incline, whilst taking throw-ins and corners. Outside the stadium, behind the Blackburn End, there is a statue of former club owner Jack Walker.
Future Ground Developments
There are plans to redevelop the Riverside Stand, but there are no firm time scales as to when this is likely to take place. The proposed new stand will increase the capacity to around 40,000.

WHAT'S IT LIKE FOR VISITORS?

Away fans are housed at the Darwen End where the facilities provided are good. However, the spacing between the rows of seats leaves a lot to be desired, being quite tight. The Darwen End is shared with home supporters, but if demand requires it, the whole of the stand can be made available. Normally the away allocation is for three-quarters of the stand, at just under 4,000 tickets, which are split between the whole of the upper tier and part of the lower tier (with the lower tier being allocated first). If you have not bought a ticket in advance, then you need to buy one from the away supporters' ticket office at the ground as you can't pay on the turnstiles. The ticket office is located on the corner of the Darwen End and the Jack Walker Stand.

Alcohol is available on the concourse as well as the normal range of pies (including the delicious 'Football's Famous Chicken Balti Pie' at £1.90), burgers, hot dogs and chips. If you are looking to eat something prior to entering the ground, then there is a baker in Bolton Road selling hot pies from one of its windows. Across the Bolton Road, by the home end is a McDonald's, which I noticed had a walk through service for fans! I found the Blackburn fans both friendly and helpful, which coupled with the relaxed stewarding has made it, so far for me, four pleasant visits to Ewood Park.

WHERE TO DRINK

The Fernhurst is really known as the 'away supporters pub'. It is on the Bolton Road (A666) just across from the ground at the away supporters end (Darwen End). You can also park at the Fernhurst pub for £3, but you will be delayed getting away after the game. It is a spacious pub with Sky Sports being shown on a large screen. With a restaurant area to its rear and a large function room upstairs. On my last visit the pub had even put up a number of signs welcoming the fans of the visiting team, which was a nice touch. Most other pubs that I came across in the area had large signs outside showing that they were for home fans only. Alcohol is also served within the ground.

Andrew Kennedy, a visiting Sunderland supporter, adds: 'I would also recommend the Golden Cup pub just up Bolton Road from the Fernhurst (going away from the ground). It is on the small side but had a good mix of home and away supporters on my visit'. This pub is a good 10-15 minute walk away from the Fernhurst, going uphill. A little closer but in the same direction is the Bear Hotel which also has a bar.

If you are arriving at Mill Hill station, then you might want to give the Navigation pub a try. It is a Thwaites pub which sits on one side of a canal

and on my visit had a good mix of home and away supporters. It is about a five minute walk away from the station. As you exit the station, turn left and just keep straight on up the road in front of you. As you approach a bridge going over the canal, the pub can be seen just over on the right.

GETTING THERE & WHERE TO PARK

From The North:
Use Motorway M6 to junction 30, to the M61 - leave junction 9 then onto the M65 towards Blackburn - leave the M65 at Junction 4 (A666) and follow signs towards Blackburn. Ewood Park is about one mile down the road on the right-hand side.

From The South:
Use Motorway M6 to junction 29 then onto the M65 towards Blackburn. Leave the M65 at Junction 4 (A666) and follow signs towards Blackburn. Turn right at the first set of traffic lights and Ewood Park is about 1 mile down the road on the right hand side.

From The East:
Use Motorway M62 onto M66/A56, then onto the M65, head towards Blackburn - leave the M65 at Junction 4 (A666) and follow signs towards Blackburn. Turn right at the first set of traffic lights and Ewood Park is about 1 mile down the road on the right-hand side.

Various private car parks are available around the ground, costing in the region of £3. If you want to get away reasonably quickly after the game (the roads immediately around Ewood are closed off for crowd safety for around 30mins after the game) then, as you come down the hill on the A666, you will pass a Total garage on your left. Turn right at the next traffic lights and down on your left there are some industrial units where you can park for £3. After the game, turn left out of the car park so that you are going away from Ewood, turn right at the second mini roundabout and this will take you back up to the M65.

By Train
Blackburn station is at least a couple of miles from the ground and hence a good 20-25 minute walk. Consider a taxi instead, or as Dave Grest suggests: 'Get a Darwen bound bus from stand M, outside of the railway station. It costs £1 one way and you really can't miss the ground'. Blackburn station is served by trains from Manchester and Leeds.

Tony Durkin adds: 'The main doors to the

railway station face the bus station from where you can take either a Number 1, 3 or 225 bus (the latter goes from Stand N) bus to Ewood. To walk to the ground turn left at those main doors and go straight on towards Darwen Street. Turn left and you will reach a major junction over which runs a railway bridge (Darwen Street Bridge), which is impossible to miss. Crossing over the road as soon as you turn left onto Darwen Street will be a help, as when you get to the junction you need to follow the road towards Bolton and Blackburn Royal Infirmary. It is called Great Bolton Street after the bridge and then becomes Bolton Road. Follow this road for just over a mile (passing the Infirmary on your left and the canal on the right). After you go under another railway bridge and pass Kwik-Save supermarket on your right, the ground is on your left just after you pass the Aqueduct pub (home fans only).

Closer to the ground is the small station of Mill Hill, which is a 10-15 minute walk away. This station is served by local trains running between Blackburn and Colne. Blackburn station is only a three minute ride away from Mill Hill. From the platform at Mill Hill go up the steps, turn left and take the first road on the left (it is called Parkinson Street and runs parallel with the rail line). Follow this to its end, turn right (by the Stakes Hall pub) into Albert Road. This road twists and bends a few times, but follow it round and you will end up going under an aqueduct which carries the Leeds-Liverpool Canal over the road. As you go under that, you will see the ground coming up ahead of you, on the left just after the junction with Bolton Road.

LOCAL RIVALS

Burnley, Bolton, Preston, Manchester United, and Manchester City.

ADMISSION PRICES

Like a number of Clubs, Blackburn operate a match category policy (A & B) whereby the ticket prices cost more for the most popular games. Category B prices are shown below in brackets.
Home Fans:
Jack Walker Stand (Upper Tier Central): Adults £34 (£30). No Concessions.
Jack Walker Stand (Upper Tier Outer Wings): Adults £30 (£26), Senior Citizens £18 (£14). Juniors £10 (£5)
Jack Walker Stand (Lower Tier Central): Adults £31

(£27). Senior Citizens £18 (£14). Juniors £10 (£5)
Jack Walker Stand (Lower Tier Outer): Adults £23 (£18). Senior Citizens £18 (£14). Juniors £10 (£5)
Jack Walker Stand (Lower Wing Block W06 Near Blackburn End): Adults £28 (£24). Senior Citizens £18 (£14). Juniors £10 (£5)
Jack Walker Stand (Lower Wing Block W01 Near Darwen End): Adults £20 (£15). Senior Citizens £15 (£12). Juniors £10 (£5)
CIS Riverside Stand (Central): Adults £28 (£24). Senior Citizens £18 (£14). Juniors £10 (£5)
CIS Riverside Stand (Inner Wings): Adults £23 (£18). Senior Citizens £18 (£14). Juniors £10 (£5)
CIS Riverside Stand (Outer Wings): Adults £20 (£15). Senior Citizens £15 (£12). Juniors £10 (£5)
Blackburn End: Adults £28 (£24). Senior Citizens £18 (£14). Juniors £12 (£5)
Darwen End (Lower Tier): Adults £28 (£24). Senior Citizens £18 (£14). Juniors £10 (£5)
Away Fans:
Darwen End: Adults £28 (£24). Senior Citizens £18 (£14). Juniors £10 (£5)

PROGRAMME & FANZINE

Official Programme: £2.50.
4000 Holes Fanzine: £1.

RECORD ATTENDANCE

62,522 v Bolton Wanderers
FA Cup 6th Round, March 2, 1929.

AVERAGE ATTENDANCE

2003-2004: 24,376 (Premier League).

STADIUM TOURS

The Club offer 90 minute tours of the ground, which are run on weekdays all year round. The tour costs: Adults £3.50 and Concessions £2. There is also a family ticket available, priced at £10 for two adults and two children. Tours can be booked on 08701-123-456.

DID YOU KNOW?

Blackburn's first home game was played at Oozehead Ground, near St Silas' School in Preston New Road in 1876.

BOLTON WANDERERS

BOLTON WANDERERS, REEBOK STADIUM

Ground Name: Reebok Stadium
Capacity: 28,723 (all-seated)
Address: Burnden Way, Lostock, Bolton, BL6 6JW
Main Telephone No: 01204-673-673
Main Fax No: 01204-673-773
Ticket Office: 0871-871-2932
Ticket Office Fax: 0871-871-8183
Team Nickname: The Trotters
Pitch Size: 105 x 68 metres
Home Kit Colours: White With Navy Trim
Official Website: www.bwfc.co.uk
Unofficial Websites:
Wanderers Way: www.wanderersways.com
London Whites: www.londonwhites.co.uk
Scottish Supporters Club:
www.bwfcscotland.co.uk
BWFC4U: www.bwfc4u.co.uk
This Is Lancashire:
www.thisislancashire.co.uk/lancashire/bolton/wanderers/

WHAT'S THE GROUND LIKE?

For those who visited the old Burnden Park, be prepared to visit a different world. The stadium, which was opened in 1997 and built by Birse Construction, is simply stunning and can be seen for miles around. The design is space-age in appearance and is unlike anything else in the country. Each stand has a conventional rectangular lower tier, with a semi-circular upper tier above. This is then topped with some diamond shaped floodlights that sit above the supporting tubular steel supporting structure. The ground is completely enclosed and has a large video screen in one corner, which replays goals from the game. This gives you an opportunity to cheer a goal at least three more times after it has been scored. One unusual feature of the ground is that the teams emerge from separate tunnels at either side of the halfway line.

WHAT'S IT LIKE FOR VISITORS?

Away fans are housed in the two-tiered South Stand at one end of the ground, where up to 5,000 supporters can be accommodated, although the normal allocation is nearer 3,000. The lower tier is shared with home supporters, but the upper tier is given entirely to away fans. Alex Smith adds: 'Away fans should note that the bottom rows of the lower tier are not covered by the roof and therefore you may get wet if it rains'. Whilst Paul Kelly warns: 'The stewards at the Reebok can be a bit overzealous, often throwing out fans for little reason. My advice to away fans is do not even think about celebrating a goal by going further forward than the front row. They'll have you even if you're just on the bit of track behind the adverts. Also you may be told to sit down during the game, take heed and do so. Fans have been removed who persistently stand up during the game'.

I went to the old Burnden Park a couple of times and I did not find it the most welcoming of grounds for away supporters. However, I am pleased to report that things are a lot more relaxed at the Reebok. I was particularly impressed with the stadium and for the first time in this country, I felt I could have easily been sitting in a comparable stadium in the United States. The refreshment facilities are superb, complete with overhead televisions to keep you amused. I wish that other clubs would copy the way that supporters in the Reebok are served. There are proper queuing barriers and exit lanes. One person takes the order and deals with the money, whilst another prepares your order at the same time. Simple when you think about it, and it is just a pity that other clubs seem to think that supporters enjoy the lottery of being in the scrum that develops around the refreshment kiosk. If the stadium was bigger, it would easily be voted the best in England, but with a capacity of under 40,000, it is just too small for this accolade. A 125 room hotel has been built behind the away end of the ground, 19 of which have views of the pitch. I just wonder if hotel guests occupying these rooms may at some time put on their own half-time show!

WHERE TO DRINK

Steve Openshaw recommends the Bromilow Arms: "From the M61, go past the stadium on your left, move into the right-hand filter lane and turn right at the traffic lights into Lostock Lane; go past the Barnstormers pub on your right and the Bromilow Arms is further down on the left. Good ale, friendly atmosphere, free car park and is only a ten minute walk from

ground". I personally visited this pub before a game and I was well impressed with the warm welcome and the good mix of home and away fans. The small pub has a country feel and serves good real ale and food from a lunchtime snack menu. All in all, it was a gem!

Mike Clarkson has informed me that: 'Although the local pubs do indicate 'Home Only', as long as you don't have away team colours on, you should not have any problems. Try the Middlebrook Tavern on the Middlebrook Retail Park (Reebok Stadium is on the Middlebrook Retail estate), Old Orleans or even the micro brewery at the ten pin bowling alley. There are also plenty of eating outlets on the Retail Park: KFC, Burger King, Pizza Hut and a Bolton Wanderers themed McDonald's as well as several other themed restaurants. At the ground is Café '58 (celebrating our last FA cup win) and inside the usual pies, burgers and beer'. There is also the Beehive Pub near to the ground where you can park your car as well (see below). Otherwise alcohol is served within the ground.

GETTING THERE & WHERE TO PARK

From The South:
M6 to Junction 21a, take eastbound M62 leaving at Junction 12. Follow signs for M61 (Bolton/Preston) and leave the M61 motorway at Junction 6. The ground is visible from this junction and is clearly signposted.
From The North:
M6 to Junction 29 and take the M65 towards Blackburn. Leave the M65 at junction two and join the M61 towards Manchester. Leave the M61 at Junction 6. The ground is visible from this junction and is clearly signposted.
John Walsh adds: 'Because of traffic congestion on the M60 (formerly M62) caused by the Trafford Centre, I would recommend that supporters travelling from the South take the North directions above. It is about 10 miles further but can save 30 minutes and a lot of frustration!'

There is a car park at the ground, but wait for this, it costs £5! Plus on my last visit the cars in the away section of the car park were packed in like sardines, meaning that away fans leaving early (my team had just been stuffed!) couldn't get a quick getaway as there were cars blocking them in. However, a lot of the surrounding industrial estate units offer cheaper parking. Gary Lovatt adds: 'On the parking front, a handy little idea is to park at the Beehive pub which is on the roundabout (half a mile past the stadium coming from the motorway) where you pay £5 per car but get it all back at the bar. I also recommend you try their cajun chicken baguette!' To get to the Beehive, leave the M61 at Junction 6 and drive down towards the stadium. Then continue straight on past the stadium and the Beehive pub is situated at the next roundabout, on Chorley New Road.

By Train
Horwich Parkway railway station serves the stadium, with regular trains from Bolton's main station. Horwich Parkway is only a few minutes walk from the stadium.

LOCAL RIVALS

Manchester United, Bury, Blackburn, Preston and, from a little further a field, Tranmere Rovers.

ADMISSION PRICES

Bolton operate a four category system of ticket pricing (A+, A, B, C) whereby the most popular matches will cost more to watch than the least popular ones. The highest category (A+) ticket prices are shown below, with the lowest category (C) ticket prices shown in brackets.
Home Fans*:
East & West Stands (Upper Tier):
Adults: £38 (£29), Senior Citizens & Students: £27 (£20), Juniors: £21 (£14)
East & West Stands (Lower Tier):
Adults: £35 (£25), Senior Citizens & Students: £25 (£17), Juniors: £16 (£10)
North & South Stands (Upper & Lower Tiers):
Adults: £30 (£21), Senior Citizens & Students: £23 (£16), Juniors: £16 (£10)
Family Area:
1 Adult + 1 Junior: £42 (£26), 2 Adults: + 2 Juniors: £84 (£52)
Away Fans:
South Stand (Upper & Lower Tiers):
Adults: £30 (£21), Senior Citizens & Students: £23 (£16), Juniors: £16 (£10)
* Club members can receive substantial discounts on some of these ticket prices. The senior citizen concessions apply to over 65s.

PROGRAMME & FANZINES

Official Programme: £2.50
White Love Fanzine: £1
Tripes & Trotters Fanzine: £1

RECORD ATTENDANCE

At The Reebok:
28,353 v Leicester City
Premier League, December 28, 2003.
At Burnden Park:
69,912 v Manchester City
FA Cup 5th Round, February 18, 1933.

AVERAGE ATTENDANCE

2003-2004: 26,795 (Premier League).

DID YOU KNOW?

The Wanderers were originally known as Christ Church when they were formed in 1874 by Sunday School teacher, Thomas Ogden, one of the 12 founder members of the Football League.

CHARLTON ATHLETIC, THE VALLEY

Ground Name:	The Valley
Capacity:	26,875 (all-seated)
Address:	Floyd Road, Charlton, SE7 8BL
Main Telephone No:	020-8333-4000
Main Fax No:	020-8333-4001
Ticket Office:	020-8333-4010
Ticket Office Fax:	020-8333-4011
Ground Tours:	020-8333-4010
Pitch Size:	112 x 73 yards
Team Nickname:	The Addicks
Home Kit Colours:	Red & White
Official Website:	www.cafc.co.uk

Unofficial Websites:
Addicks Online: www.addicksonline.co.uk
Goodbye Horse Fanzine:
www.goodbyehorse.com
Forever Charlton: www.forever.charlton.net
Charlton Memorabilia:
www.lungrot.fsnet.co.uk/index.html
Net Addicks: www.netaddicks.com (Rivals
Network)

WHAT'S THE GROUND LIKE?

The construction of the North Stand has transformed the ground. What was a single-tier separate stand is now a large two-tiered affair, extending and completely enclosing the North East and North West corners. The redevelopment of this area of the ground was completed in 2002 and in total houses 9,000 fans. Both sides have also been redeveloped in the mid 1990s and anyone who saw the derelict Valley a few years back now wouldn't believe their eyes. The West Stand on one side is a good sized two-tiered stand, whilst opposite, is the smaller single-tiered East Stand, where the vast open terrace, reputedly the country's biggest, was located until demolished in the 1990s. There is a row of executive boxes that run across the back of this stand and it has a television gantry suspended beneath its roof. The older South Stand, behind the goal, is given to away supporters and now looks out of place in its smart surroundings. On one side of this is a police control box. The stadium doesn't have any floodlight pylons as such, but has rows of small floodlights running across the tops of the stands. The stadium is overlooked by a block of flats beyond the South Stand and it is not uncommon to see fans out on their balconies watching most of the game for free.

FUTURE GROUND DEVELOPMENTS

George Packman informs me: 'The Club have revealed that they intend to increase the capacity of the Valley to over 40,000. The first phase of the scheme would see an additional tier added to the East Stand, which would increase capacity to just over 30,000. This would be followed by the redevelopment of the Jimmy Seed (South) Stand, which would be replaced with a similar looking structure to the existing North Stand, resulting in the Valley becoming totally enclosed and boosting capacity to 37,000. Lastly, a third tier could be added to the new South Stand at a later stage, meaning that the Valley would have a final capacity of 40,600. Approval for the scheme is needed though from Greenwich Council'.

WHAT'S IT LIKE FOR VISITORS?

Away fans are housed in the Jimmy Seed (South) Stand at one end of the ground, which is slightly raised above pitch level, making for a generally good view. Up to 3,000 away fans can be accommodated in this end. However, if the visiting team are unlikely to sell their full allocation of 3,000 tickets, then this end may be shared with home fans. This stand, being older than the rest of the ground, looks somewhat tired and for those used to other modern premiership grounds, may find it somewhat of a shock.

Peter Inwood, a visiting Leeds fan, adds: 'There is one solitary supporting column in the entire ground and guess where it is? Right in the middle, behind the goal, in the away supporters end. Very annoying it is as well. However, I would commend the stewards, who took a relaxed attitude to the away supporters standing throughout the match, although expect to be searched on the way in'. Otherwise the height between rows is good and the stand quite steep, keeping you fairly close to the playing action. There are refreshment areas on either side of the stand (not just by the entrance turnstiles).

I was quite impressed with the atmosphere at the Valley and I can see why many away fans see it as one of their favourite away days to the capital. The Charlton fans are clearly passionate about their team, but in a non-intimidating way. I had a pleasant day out and would go again. I was particularly impressed with the loud P.A. system that played some great music before the game started. It is worth noting that you can only gain entrance to the ground by ticket, which you have to buy from a ticket booth beforehand.

WHERE TO DRINK

Simon Phillips informs me that 'The Antigallican', a big pub near Charlton station, seems to be the favourite haunt of away supporters. However, it can get very busy and this is not helped by the local police not allowing fans to drink outside. Colin Gilham recommends the 'Rose of Denmark' on Woolwich Road. The pub not only allows away supporters but absolutely welcomes them. They have a photo display on the wall of fans from visiting clubs that have frequented the pub this season. Please note that this is a home supporters' only pub after the game. To find these pubs, come out of Charlton station and turn left into Charlton Church Lane and the Antigallican pub is down on the right hand corner. If you continue down to the T-junction with the Woolwich Road and turn left, you will reach the Rose of Denmark further down on the left.

There is also the Charlton Liberal Club, to which away fans are welcome on payment of a small entry fee. This is more spacious, less busy and has a large screen television. The club can be found by turning right out of Charlton station and walking 300 yards up the hill on the left-hand side of the road, past the row of shops. The club is a five minute walk from the away end. Alternatively alcohol is available in the away end before kick off, but strangely not at half-time.

GETTING THERE & WHERE TO PARK

Leave the M25 at Junction 2 and follow the A2 towards London. When the A2 becomes the A102(M), take the A206 towards Woolwich and you will come to the ground on your right. If you cross over the Thames you have gone too far.

There is street parking, but due to a local residents parking scheme, not in close vicinity to the ground or Charlton railway station.

Colan Hyde informs me of the following car parks that are available on match days: Thames Barrier visitor centre (cost £5) and the Westminster Industrial Estate (Warspite Road, off Woolwich Road, behind the Million Hare pub, cost £5).

By Train/Tube
The ground is in walking distance of Charlton railway station, which is served by Charing Cross and London Bridge mainline stations. On Saturdays, there are also services from Cannon Street station.

Colin Gilham says: 'Come out Charlton station into Charlton Church lane (all exits lead onto this road) and turn right and cross over to the other side. Take the next left into Floyd Road and then right into Valley Grove for the away section entrance'.

Darryl Chamberlain adds: 'Although Charlton station is very close to the Valley, many people will find it easier to take the (far more reliable) tube, using the Jubilee Line to get to North Greenwich station and then take a short ride on buses 161, 472 or 486 to get to the ground'.

LOCAL RIVALS

Millwall, Crystal Palace and West Ham.

ADMISSION PRICES

Home Fans:
Adults: £20-£35
OAPs/Under 18s: £20-£25
Under16s: £15-£20
Away Fans:
Adults: £20-£35
OAPs/Under 18s: £20-£25
Under 16s: £15-£20

PROGRAMME

Official Programme: £2.50.

RECORD ATTENDANCE

75,031 v Aston Villa
FA Cup 5th Round, February 12, 1938.

AVERAGE ATTENDANCE

2003-2004: 26,293 (Premier League).

DID YOU KNOW?

In the 1970s, Charlton boasted the largest ground in the League, with a capacity of some 66,000 fans.

CHELSEA, STAMFORD BRIDGE

Ground Name: Stamford Bridge
Capacity: 42,449 (all seated)
Address: Fulham Road, London, SW6 1HS
Main Telephone No: 0870-300-1212
Main Fax No: 020-7381-4831
Ticket Bookings: 0870-300-2322
Ticket Enquiries: 020-7915-2951
Stadium Tours: 0870-603-0005
Pitch Size: 113 x 74 Yards
Club Nickname: The Blues
Home Kit Colours: Royal Blue With White Trim
Official Website: www.chelseafc.co.uk
Unofficial Websites:
Blue And White Army –
www.chelsea.rivals.net (Rivals Network)

WHAT'S THE GROUND LIKE?

The ground has been transformed in recent years with three sides being rebuilt. The completion, at one side of the pitch, of the impressive looking West Stand in 2001, means that Stamford Bridge is now the largest league ground in London. A far cry from the Stamford Bridge of old, which was largely open with one huge three-tiered stand, the East Stand, being at one side of the pitch. This stand, opened in 1973, has been retained and the developers have taken advantage of the fact that the 'old' Stamford Bridge was oval shaped and stretched the new stands right around the ground filling the corners, so that the ground is enclosed. Both ends are two-tiered, with the North Stand now renamed the Matthew Harding Stand in memory of the man who did so much to help transform the Club. The new West Stand is a superb looking three-tiered affair having a row of executive boxes running across its middle.

WHAT'S IT LIKE FOR VISITORS?

Away fans are located in the lower tier of the East Stand, where up to 3,000 supporters can be accommodated. If the visiting Club declines the full allocation, then 1,500 tickets are reserved for part of the lower tier, towards the Matthew Harding Stand side of the East Stand. For Cup games, the allocation can be increased to 5,200 by also reserving the lower tier of the Matthew

Harding Stand to away fans. The delectable 'Football's Famous Chicken Balti Pie' (£2.50) is available inside the ground.

I have received reports of the stewarding being quite strict at Stamford Bridge, with fans being ejected for not sitting down etc. so be on your best behaviour. And even though you may have paid quite a high price for your match ticket, don't be surprised if you end up with a poor view, especially if you are seated beneath the overhang of the middle tier. I personally did not experience any problems on my visit, but it is worth bearing in mind that the Chelsea fans are passionate about their club and this can make for an intimidating atmosphere. However, as with the general improvement in football, away fans are more tolerated nowadays at Stamford Bridge. Please also note that Stamford Bridge now has a no smoking stadium.

WHERE TO DRINK

The pubs near the ground can be quite partisan, so I would recommend getting a drink somewhere on the journey there. Gordon, a visiting Newcastle fan, adds: 'There are quite a few pubs on the Kings Road that are okay as long as you don't break into a chorus about your team!' Ross

Mooring also tells me: 'The best (well, least partisan) pub for away fans is the Slug and Lettuce outside Fulham Broadway train station situated a few minutes walk from the ground. It's an upmarket pub with a good security and police presence outside on matchdays. Very full but rarely any trouble. Away fans though should avoid the Sofa Bar. Alcohol (Budweiser) is available inside the ground but it is a bit pricey, even for Londoners!' Johan van Oosten recommends the White Horse Pub near Parsons Green Station which is excellent.

GETTING THERE & WHERE TO PARK

Leave the M25 at Junction 15 and take the M4 towards London, which then becomes the A4 up to Hammersmith. Carry on over the Hammersmith flyover and after a further one and half miles, take the turning towards Earls Court. Continue past Earls Court station and down the one-way system until you reach the junction with Fulham Road. At this junction, turn right at the traffic lights and after about half a mile, you will see the ground on your right. A number of local resident schemes are in operation around the ground, so you may well end up having to park some way from the ground itself. Thanks to Andy Harris for providing the directions.

By Tube

The nearest tube station is Fulham Broadway which is on the District Line. Take a tube to Earls Court and, if necessary, change for a Wimbledon bound tube.

LOCAL RIVALS

Fulham, Arsenal, Tottenham and from a little further afield, Leeds and Manchester United.

ADMISSION PRICES

Home Fans:
West Stand Upper Tier: Adults: £48, No Concessions
West Stand Lower Tier: Adults: £43, No Concessions
West Stand Executive Seats: Season Tickets Only
Shed End Stand Upper Tier: Adults: £43. No Concessions
Shed End Stand Lower Tier Family Section: Season Tickets Only
Matthew Harding Upper Tier: Season Tickets Only
Matthew Harding Lower Tier: Adults: £38, OAPs: £24, Juveniles: £16.
East Stand Upper Tier: Adults: £43, No Concessions
East Stand Middle Tier: Season Tickets Only
East Stand Lower Tier: Adults: £40, OAPs: £24, Juveniles: £16.

Away Fans:
East Stand Lower Tier: Adults: £40, OAPs: £24, Juveniles: £16.

PROGRAMME & FANZINES

Official Programme: £3.
Chelsea Independent Fanzine: £1.50.
CFCUK Fanzine: £1.

RECORD ATTENDANCE

82,905 v Arsenal
Division One, October 10, 1935.

AVERAGE ATTENDANCE

2003-2004: 41,234 (Premier League).

STADIUM TOURS

The Club offer tours of the ground, which are available three times a day, except matchdays and bank holidays. The tour lasts for around 75 minutes and costs: Adults £8 and Concessions £5. There are also family tickets available which offer a discount on these prices. To book your tour call Chelsea World Of Sport on 0870 603 0005.

DID YOU KNOW?

When Chelsea were elected to the Football League Division Two, they were the only team to be admitted to the League without having kicked a ball.

GOODISON PARK, EVERTON

Ground Name: Goodison Park
Capacity: 40,260 (all-seated)
Address: Goodison Road,
Liverpool, L4 4EL
Main Telephone No: 0151-330-2200
Main Fax No: 0151-286-9112
Ticket Office: 0870-442-1878
Ground Tours: 0151-330-2277
Pitch Size: 112 x 78 yards
Club Nickname: The Toffees
Home Kit Colours: Royal Blue & White
Official Website: www.evertonfc.com
Unofficial Websites:
Toffee Web: www.toffeeweb.com
Blue Kipper: www.bluekipper.com
When Skies Are Grey:
www.whenskiesaregrey.com (Rivals Network)

WHAT'S THE GROUND LIKE?

Looking from the outside, Goodison, with its tall stands seems huge. The crowds filling the narrow streets around the ground on matchday make you feel that you are going back in time to when the outside of every football ground appeared like this. However, that's Goodison's problem. Apart from the newish Park Stand (which has an electric scoreboard on its roof), the rest of the ground looks tired. Yes the ground is still large, but it needs modernising.

For example, there are lots of supporting pillars (but to be fair at least the Club don't sell tickets directly behind them) and the ground just looks as if it has seen better days.
Nevertheless, unlike some new grounds, Goodison oozes character and the three-tiered Main Stand is still an impressive sight. There are two large video screens at opposite corners of the ground.

A unique feature of the stadium is a church which sits just beyond one corner of the ground (selling teas and snacks at reasonable prices, plus upstairs it normally hosts a small programme fair on matchdays, except Sundays). If you have time before the game, look out for the statue behind the Park Stand which is a tribute to the legend that was Dixie Dean. After all these years, the Everton team still come out to the theme tune of the old police series, Z-cars.

FUTURE GROUND DEVELOPMENTS

After pulling out of the King's Dock Redevelopment Scheme, the Club have confirmed their desire still to move to a new stadium by announcing talks with a number of developers about the possibility of building a new 55,000 seated stadium at Central Docks on the bank of the River Mersey. The scheme could cost as much as £500m to implement and the Club, amongst other issues, are exploring the possibility of leasing the new stadium, rather than owning it directly.

WHAT'S IT LIKE FOR VISITORS?

Away fans are located in one corner of the two-tiered Bullens Road Stand, which is at the side of the pitch, where just over 3,000 away fans can be accommodated. If you can, try to get tickets for the upper tier as the view from the lower tier can be quite poor. In the rear of the lower tier there are a number of supporting pillars that can hinder your view, the seating is of the old wooden type and the gap between rows is tight. The front of the lower tier is a lot better having newer seats and no supporting pillars to contend with. Some visiting clubs elect to take a lower allocation than the 3,000 on offer. If this applies then only the lower tier is given to away fans. The facilities within the stand are basic and it is really showing its age. However, away fans can generate some noise from this stand, making for a great atmosphere. If you are a neutral supporter, I would sit in the Park Stand, where the view is good and the facilities excellent. I have enjoyed a couple of good days out at Goodison. The atmosphere was relaxed and friendly, with both sets of fans mixing freely before the game.

On a poignant note, if you do happen to notice some flowers lying around the perimeter of the pitch, this is because the ashes of a number of supporters have been interned around it.

WHERE TO DRINK

I found a moderately busy pub called the Anfield Hotel. I guess with a name like that a lot of Evertonians boycott the place! To find this pub, walk up to Walton Lane (the A580 dual carriageway) from the ground. Turn left and take a ten minute walk down Walton Lane, passing Walton police station. As you go under a bridge, the pub is a short distance down the next road on your left. Tom Hughes adds: 'The city centre is usually the best bet for a pre-match drink. There are hundreds of pubs available ranging from designer types to real-ale and sawdust bars. The pubs nearest to Lime Street Station are best avoided with the exception of the big-House (the Vines) next to the Adelphi which is worth a visit. Nearer Goodison 'The Hermitage' (a friendly pub, 5-10 minutes walk up Walton Lane and under the bridge) on Queens Drive is also okay'. Peter Bennett suggests the following: 'Pubs on Walton Lane or The Spellow and Wilnslow Hotel outside Goodison are recommended. The only pub that away fans should avoid is The Royal Oak.' Stuart Roberts adds: 'Away fans are always made welcome in the Netley (which is where the internet Evertonians drink) which is easy to get to. To find the pub, walk to the Everton Megastore at one corner of the ground and then go down the road that runs between the Megastore and Stanley Park. At the bottom of the road on the right-hand side, you will come to the Netley. Don't be discouraged by the outward appearance. It may look a dive -in fact it is a dive! - but it's a very friendly place where you'll be made welcome'. Otherwise there is the 'Stanley Park' aka 'The Blue House' pub on Langham Street and, as a last resort, alcohol is served in the away section of the ground.

GETTING THERE & WHERE TO PARK

Follow the M62 until you reach the end of the motorway (beware of a 50mph speed camera about a quarter of a mile from the end of the motorway). Then follow the A5058 towards Liverpool. After three miles, turn left at the traffic lights into Utting Avenue (there is a McDonald's on the corner of this junction). Proceed for one mile and then turn right at the corner of Stanley Park into Priory Road. Goodison is at the end of this road. If you arrive early (around 1pm) then there is street parking to be found around Walton Lane. Otherwise park over towards Anfield or in Stanley Park itself (the entrance to the car park, which costs £6, is in Priory Road).

By Train
Kirkdale station is the closest to the ground (just under a mile away) and can be reached by first getting a train from Liverpool Lime Street to Liverpool Central and then changing there for Kirkdale.

On exiting from Kirkdale Station turn right and then cross the railway bridge. You will see a pub opposite called the 'Melrose Abbey', which is a recommended watering hole. Walk up Westminster Road, alongside the pub, for about 400yds and you'll see the Elm Tree pub. Turn left at the pub into Goodall Street and walk up to the end of the road, crossing the junction with Carisbrooke Road and into Harlech Street. At the end of Harlech Street you will reach the main County Road (A59). Cross over County Road at the traffic lights and then proceed down Andrew Street. At the top of Andrew Street you can see St Lukes Church in the corner of the ground.

The main railway station in Liverpool is Lime Street which is over three miles from the ground and is really too far to walk (although it is mostly downhill on the way back to the station), so either head for Kirkdale station or jump in a taxi.

Thanks to Geoff Barnes for providing the directions from Kirkdale Station.

LOCAL RIVALS

Liverpool.

ADMISSION PRICES

Home Fans:
Main Stand: Adults* £30, Under 16s £20
Main Stand Top Balcony: Adults* £27, Under 16s £16
Family Enclosure: Adults*£27, Over 65s £18 Under 16s £16
Bullens Stand (Upper Tier): Adults* £29, Under 1's £20
Bullens Stand (Lower Tier): Adults* £25, Over 65s £18, Under 16s £16
Bullens Stand (Lower Tier Paddock At Front): Adults* £27, Under 16s £16
Gwladys Street (Upper Tier): Adults* £27, Juniors £16
Gwladys Street (Lower Tier): Adults* £24, Juniors £16
Park Stand: Adults* £28, Juniors £18
Away Fans
Bullens Stand (Upper Tier): Adults* £29, Under 16s £20
Bullens Stand (Lower Tier): Adults* £25, Over 65's £18, Under 16s £16
Bullens Stand (Lower Tier Paddock At Front): Adults* £27, Under 16s £16

* For fixtures against Liverpool and Manchester United, the ticket price quoted above is

increased by £3. Over 65s and under 16s, prices remain unchanged.

PROGRAMME & FANZINES

Official Programme: £2.70
Satis Fanzine: £1
Speke From The Harbour: £1

RECORD ATTENDANCE

78,299 v Liverpool
Division One, September 18, 1948.

AVERAGE ATTENDANCE

2003-2004: 38,837 (Premier League).

STADIUM TOURS

Tours of the ground are available at a cost of: Adults £8.50, Concessions £5, or there is a family ticket available (2 adults + 2 children) at £20. Tours take place daily except Saturdays and some matchday Sundays. Call the club on 0151-330-2277 to book.

DID YOU KNOW?

During the late 19th Century, Everton played matches at their Anfield Ground before moving onto their new Goodison ground in 1892. A certain other team in Liverpool took up residence at their old ground.

LOFTUS ROAD STADIUM, FULHAM

Ground Name: Craven Cottage
Capacity: 22,000 (all-seated)
Address: Stevenage Road,
London, SW6 6HH
Main Telephone No: 0207-893-8383
Main Fax No: 0207-384-4715
Ticket Office: 0870-442-1234
Ticket Off. Fax No: 0207-384-4810
Team Nickname: The Cottagers
Home Kit Colours: Black & White
Official Website: www.fulhamfc.com
Unofficial Websites:
Fulham Web: www.fulhamweb.com
Fulham Supporters Club:
www.fulhamsc.com

WHAT'S THE GROUND LIKE?

After ground sharing with QPR for the last couple of seasons, Fulham have at long last returned to Craven Cottage, their home since 1894. Promotion to the Premier League in 2001 meant that Craven Cottage, in order to comply with Premier League rules, would have to become an all-seated stadium. The

Club were allowed one season's grace to do this, but with the Club unable to gain the necessary permissions (including a lot of objections from local residents) to totally redevelop Carven Cottage into a modern 30,000 all seated stadium, the Club took the decision to vacate Craven Cottage and look for a new site to build. The search for a suitable site has so far come to nothing and, much to the delight of Fulham fans, the Club decided to return to Craven Cottage and upgrade it to an all-seated ground.

Both ends were mostly large open terraces and this is where most of the work has taken place. These have been replaced by two large all-seated covered stands that look fairly similar in design. They both though have some supporting pillars, which is disappointing, and to one side they have a separate three storey structure that looks like it will be used to house corporate executive boxes. On one side of the ground is the Stevenage Road Stand, that previously had terracing at the front, but has now been made all-seated. The stand was originally designed by Archibald Leitch (who designed a number of football grounds and stands in the early part of the 20th century) and was opened in 1905. Considering its age, it can be forgiven for having a number of supporting pillars. It does though have a fine looking gable on its roof labelled Fulham Football Club. Opposite is the only stand not to see any major changes through this current burst of redevelopment. This stand, which sits on the banks of the Thames, is the aptly named Riverside Stand, all-seated and covered. Opened in 1972, it is slightly raised above pitch level. Also saved from the redevelopment is the famous Craven Cottage, which overlooks the ground from one corner, between the Stevenage Road Stand and Putney End. It looks somewhat misplaced, being more reminiscent of a small cricket pavilion rather than something found at a football ground, but it does add to the overall character. An unusual feature is that the teams enter the field from one corner of the ground, by the Cottage. A disappointment is having the fabulous old floodlights removed and replaced by a nondescript modern set.

FUTURE GROUND DEVELOPMENTS

Although the Club have returned to Craven Cottage and have spent a lot on the ground redevelopment, it is still their intention to move to a new 30,000 capacity stadium if a suitable site can be found.

WHAT'S IT LIKE FOR VISITORS?

Away fans are housed to one side of the new Putney End Stand, on the river side of the ground. The stand will be shared with home supporters, with away fans being allocated around 3,000 seats, which is just under half of the overall capacity of this stand. If required, an additional block of seating of around 500 seats can also be made available in the Riverside Stand. One huge benefit which the new Putney End stand has over the old terrace is that it has a roof. I once got soaked just as the game kicked off on the old terrace on a bitterly freezing December day and then watched as the rain turned to sleet, so you can say that this

particularly pleases me!

On a nice summer day, this is one of my favourite grounds. From the walk from the tube station through a park, to having a pint overlooking the Thames, this can be quite an enjoyable experience. I have been there on four occasions and never had any problems. My only grumble was the rather large police presence outside the ground (including mounted police and dog handlers) before and after the game – you would have thought they were expecting a riot. On one of my visits, the Birmingham Fans were chanting to the Fulham fans, "you only sing when you're rowing!"

WHERE TO DRINK

Some of the pubs near the ground have been designated home supporters only, so most away fans now use the pubs South of the River (across Putney Bridge). The Dukes Head is recommended, which has nice views overlooking the River Thames and does good food. It is a Youngs pub with a cosmopolitan atmosphere as it is located next to a number of rowing clubs. Allow 20 minutes to walk from the pub to the ground. David Frear adds: 'The Crabtree on Rainville Road (10 minutes from the ground) welcomes all away supporters and as a Fulham season ticket holder I can tell you that as long as you don't watch your football at Loftus Road, you can be assured of a warm welcome'. Andrew Johnson recommends the Kings Head, on Fulham High Street, to be one of the nearest to the ground and always popular with away fans.

GETTING THERE & WHERE TO PARK

From the North M1:
Thanks to Robert Donaldson, a visiting Stockport County fan, for providing the following directions: 'At the end of the M1, turn right (west) onto the A406 (North Circular) and follow it towards Harrow for nearly 4.5 miles. Turn left (east) onto the A40 heading into London (passing close to Loftus Road and after a little over 4 miles turn right (west) onto the A402 for just about 350 yards. Here you turn left (south) along the A219 for a little over half a mile. This brings

you into Hammersmith where you turn right onto the A315 and then after just 130 yards or so turn left (south) back onto the A219. Follow this road for a little over a mile and the ground down the side streets off to your right.

From the South M25:

Leave the M25 at Junction 10 and take the A3 towards Central London. After around eight miles, leave the A3 at the turn off for the A219. Take the A219 towards Putney. Continue straight on this road, down Putney High Street and across Putney Bridge. You will see the ground on your left.

Parking is possible on the streets around the ground but there are council parking meters there now, so make sure you bring some change (£1 per hour), and early arrival is advised.

By Tube

The nearest station is Putney Bridge, which is on the District Line. The ground is about a 15 minute walk. Turn left out of the station and then just follow the other supporters. You get a nice pleasant walk through Bishops Park along the riverbank to the ground (note that the park is closed after evening games).

LOCAL RIVALS

Chelsea, QPR and Brentford.

ADMISSION PRICES

Fulham operate a four category system of ticket pricing (A+, A, B, C) whereby the most popular matches will cost more to watch than the least popular ones. The highest category (A+) ticket prices are shown below, with the lowest category (C) ticket prices shown in brackets.

Home Fans:

Riverside Stand (Centre): Adults: £44 (£35), Over 65s/Students: £34 (£25), Juniors: £22 (£17)

Riverside Stand (Wings): Adults: £38 (£32), Over 65s/Students: £28 (£22), Juniors: £19 (£16)

Riverside Stand (Outer Wings): Adults: £34 (£28), Over 65s/Students: £24 (£19), Juniors: £17 (£14)

Stevenage Road Stand (Centre): Adults: £38 (£32), Over 65s/Students: £28 (£22), Juniors: £19 (£16)

Stevenage Road Stand (Wings): Adults: £34 (£28), Over 65s/Students: £24 (£19), Juniors: £17 (£14)

Stevenage Road Stand (Outer Wings): Adults: £32 (£26), Over 65s/Students: £22 (£18), Juniors: £16 (£13)

Hammersmith End: Adults: £32 (£26), Over 65s/Students: £22 (£18), Juniors: £16 (£13)

Putney End: Adults: £32 (£26), Over 65s/Students: £22 (£18), Juniors: £16 (£13)

Away Fans:

Putney End: Adults: £32 (£26), Over 65s/Students: £22 (£18), Juniors: £16 (£13)

PROGRAMME & FANZINE

Official Programme: £2.50.
One F In Fulham Fanzine: £2.

RECORD ATTENDANCE

49,335 v Millwall
Division Two, October 8, 1938.

AVERAGE ATTENDANCE

2003-2004: 16,342 (Premier League).

DID YOU KNOW?

The Club was originally formed in 1879 as 'Fulham St Andrews' Cricket and Football Club.

ANFIELD, LIVERPOOL

Ground Name: Anfield
Capacity: 45,362 (all-seated)
Address: Anfield Road,
Liverpool, L4 0TH
Main Telephone No: 0151-263-2361
Main Fax No: 0151-260-8813
Ticket Office: 0870-220-2151
Ground Tours: 0151-260-6677
Pitch Size: 110 x 75 yards
Club Nickname: The Reds
Home Kit Colour: All Red
Official Website: www.liverpoolfc.tv
Unofficial Websites:
Kop Talk: www.koptalk.com
Liverpool Mad: www.liverpool-mad.co.uk
(Footy Mad Network)
This Is Anfield: www.thisisanfield.com
Red & White Kop: www.redandwhitekop.net

WHAT'S THE GROUND LIKE?

Walking up to the ground alongside Stanley
Park, I have to say that, from a distance,
Anfield is not particularly impressive. Inside
though, the ground is wonderful and only the
most critical of visitors would find fault with it.
The famous Kop Terrace at one end of the
ground has been replaced by a huge stand
designed to emulate the old Kop, hence it's
odd shape (kind of semi-circular) and single
large tier. The other end, the Anfield Road

Stand, part of which is given to away
supporters, is the most recent addition to the
ground. It has boosted not only the overall
capacity of the stadium, but has given Anfield
a more balanced and enclosed feel as all
corners are now filled. On one side of the
stadium is the large, two-tiered Centenary
Stand, where the front tier legroom is the
tightest I have ever known. Opposite is the
Main Stand, the oldest in the ground and
looking its age with a number of supporting
pillars. This stand has a TV gantry suspended
beneath its roof. In the corner between the Kop
and Centenary stands is an electric scoreboard,
which surprise, surprise, shows the match
score in bright red letters.
Around the outside of the ground, there are
the Bill Shankly Gates on Anfield Road. These
wrought iron gates have the legendary
Liverpool phrase 'You'll Never Walk Alone'
displayed above them. There is also a statue of
the great Shankly near the Club shop. Also
along Anfield Road, there is the moving
memorial to the victims of the Hillsborough
disaster, which always has flowers adorning it.

FUTURE GROUND DEVELOPMENTS

Steve Edwards reports: 'The Club have applied
for planning permission to build a new 60,000
all-seated stadium to be located in nearby

Stanley Park. The stadium would retain the Anfield name and cost in the region of £80m to build. It is hoped that Liverpool can kick off the 2006/07 season in their new home'.

WHAT'S IT LIKE FOR VISITORS?

Away fans are located in the Anfield Road Stand at one end of the ground, where just under 2,000 seats are available, although this can be increased for Cup games. This stand is also shared with home supporters, some of whom will be sitting in the small seated tier above the away fans. Malcolm Dawson, a travelling Sunderland supporter says: 'Try to avoid getting tickets sold as restricted view for the rear rows of the Anfield Road Stand as it can be difficult to see the goals with people standing up in front of you'.

Kimberly Hill adds: 'Restricted view doesn't even begin to describe what it was like. The Wolves fans insisted on standing so it was like trying to watch the game through a letterbox!' The facilities within the stand are not bad. There is a Ladbrokes betting outlet and the refreshment kiosks sell a wide variety of burgers, hot dogs and pies, including a 'Scouse Pie' at £1.80.

I have always found it to be a good day out at Anfield, getting the feeling that you are visiting one of the legendary venues in world football. This is enhanced with the teams coming out to 'You'll Never Walk Alone' reverberating around the ground, with the red and white scarves and flags of the fans displayed across the Kop, at the beginning of the match. The atmosphere is normally great, so sit back and enjoy the experience.

WHERE TO DRINK

The Arkles pub near to the ground (see directions by car), is known as the away fans pub, but as can be expected, it can get extremely crowded. If you arrive early, a better bet may be to take the 10 minute walk across Stanley Park to the pubs near Goodison. The Spellow, Wilnslow Hotel and Stanley Park (aka the Blue House) are all recommended.

Brian McIlwrick informs me: 'I got to the ground at around 1.30pm and decided to enter the away end early, only to find that they don't serve alcohol to away fans. Be warned!'

GETTING THERE & WHERE TO PARK

Follow the M62 until you reach the end of the motorway (beware of a 50mph speed camera about a quarter of a mile from the end of the motorway). Then follow the A5058 towards Liverpool. After three miles turn left at the traffic lights into Utting Avenue (there is a McDonald's on the corner of this junction). Proceed for one mile and then turn right at the Arkles pub for the ground. If you arrive early (around 1pm) then there is street parking to be found. Otherwise it as an idea to park in the streets around Goodison and walk across Stanley Park to Anfield, or you can park in a secure parking area at Goodison itself which costs £6.

By Train
Kirkdale station is the closest to the ground (just under a mile away) and can be reached by first getting a train from Liverpool Lime Street to Liverpool Central and then changing there for Kirkdale.

On exiting from Kirkdale Station turn right and then cross the railway bridge where you'll see a pub opposite called the 'Melrose Abbey', (which has been recommended). Walk up Westminster Road, alongside the pub and continue until passing the Elm Tree pub. Follow the road around the right-hand bend and then turn left into Bradwell Street. At the end of Bradwell Street you will come to the busy County Road (A59). Cross over this road at the traffic lights and then go down the road to the left of the Aldi superstore. At the end of this road you will reach the A580 Walton Lane. You should be able to see Goodison Park over on your left and Stanley Park in front of you. Cross Walton Lane and enter Stanley Park following the footpath through the park (keeping to the right), which will exit into Anfield Road and the away end. Or bear right down Walton Lane and then turn left down the road at the end of Stanley Park for the ground. Thanks to Jon Roche for providing these directions.

The main railway station in Liverpool is Lime Street which is over three miles from the ground and is really too far to walk (although it is mostly downhill on the way back to the station), so either head for Kirkdale station or jump in a taxi. Craig Hochkins adds: 'You can catch various buses from the bus station which is seven minutes walk away from the train station and is well signposted. Either the 17a 17b 17c or the 26 will drop you right outside the ground at a cost of about a £1. The buses are run by Arriva and the journey takes about 15 to 25 minutes depending on traffic'.

LOCAL RIVALS

Everton and Manchester United.

ADMISSION PRICES

The Club operate a category system, so that ticket prices vary with the opposition being played. The categories; A & B are shown in brackets:

Home Fans:
Main Stand: Adults: (A) £30, (B) £28
Centenary Stand: Adults: (A) £30, (B) £28
The Kop: Adults: (A) £28, (B) £26,
The Kop Family Ticket: 1 Adult: (A) £28, (B) £26, + up to 2 Children
(each child charged at half adult price ticket)
Anfield Road Stand: Adults: (A) £30, (B) 28
Anfield Road Family Ticket: 1 Adult: (A) £30, (B) 28 + up to 2 Children
(each child charged at half adult price ticket)
OAPs All Stands: (A) £21-£22.50, (B) £21-£19.50

Away Fans:
Anfield Road Stand:
Adults: (A) £30, (B) 28
OAPs & Juniors: (A) £15, (B) £14

PROGRAMME & FANZINES

Official Programme: £3
The Liverpool Way Fanzine: £2
Red All Over The Land Fanzine: £1.50

RECORD ATTENDANCE

61,905 v Wolverhampton Wanderers
FA Cup 4th Round, February 2, 1952.

AVERAGE ATTENDANCE

2003-2004: 42,706 (Premier League).

STADIUM TOURS

The Club offer tours of the ground which operate on a daily basis, except Bank Holidays and matchdays. There is also a museum at the ground and the club offer combined tour and museum tickets as well as individual museum entrance. The costs are:
Ground Tour & Museum:
Adults: £9, Children & OAPs £5.50Museum Only:
Adults: £5, Children & OAPs £3
   For details of family tickets and for making tour bookings call: 0151 260 6677.
   The Club also offer combined tour, museum and lunch packages, with lunch being taken in one of the executive boxes in the Centenary Stand. The cost of this is: Adults £28.95, Under 14s £18.95, Under 8s £12.95, Under 5s £7.95.

DID YOU KNOW?

The one end of Anfield was renamed the Spion Kop in 1906 after the battle of Spion Kop and later it became known as 'the Kop'. This was the hill in present day South Africa where Boer guerrillas had inflicted a heavy defeat on the British army in 1900. Many of the men killed were from the Northwest of England so the name was especially poignant. Other grounds around the country also renamed some of their terraces after the Spion Kop, such as St Andrews in Birmingham and Hillsborough in Sheffield.

CITY OF MANCHESTER STADIUM

Ground Name:	City Of Manchester Stadium
Capacity:	48,000 (all-seated)
Address:	Sportcity, Rowsley St, Manchester M11 3FF
Main Telephone No:	0161-231-3200
Main Fax No:	0161-438-7999
Ticket Office:	0870-062-1894
Ticket Office Fax:	0161-438-7810
Team Nicknames:	The Blues or Citizens
Pitch Size:	116.5 x 78 yards
Home Kit Colours:	Sky Blue & White
Official Website:	www.mcfc.co.uk

Unofficial Websites:
Unofficial Man City: www.uit.no/mancity/
MCFC Stats: www.mcfcstats.com
Blueview:
http://manchestercity.rivals.net/default.asp?sid=91
4 (Rivals Network)
Reddish Blues: www.reddishblues.com

WHAT'S THE GROUND LIKE?

After playing at Maine Road for 80 years, the Club moved to the new City Of Manchester Stadium in August 2003. It was originally built for the Commonwealth Games, held in 2002. After that event it was agreed Manchester City would become the new tenants, thus incurring the envy of clubs who would also relish the chance to gain such a wonderful stadium. The Club have spent £20m in refitting costs, so that it is now more of a football ground rather than an athletics stadium.

The running track has been removed and the stands extended further downwards (adding a further 10,000 seats to the capacity) so that the spectators are closer to the playing action.

The stadium has a bowl design and is totally enclosed. Both stands on either side of the pitch are virtually identical, being semi-circular in shape, three-tiered with a row of executive boxes running across the stands between the second and third tiers. The ends are smaller in size, being two-tiers high, again with a row of executive boxes, but this time running across the back just below the roof. Both of these ends are of the more traditional rectangular design. The second tier around the stadium slightly overhangs the lower. The roof runs continuously around the stadium stretching up over the stands and down to the ends, creating a spectacular effect. There is a perspex strip just below the roof and the spectator areas, allowing light to reach the pitch. The upper tiers are steeper than the lower, ensuring that fans are kept close to the playing action. Iain Macintosh says: 'An interesting feature of the new stadium is the operable louvers in each of the four corners. These are located at either end of the level three seating in the East and Colin Bell stands. These are closed when in use, but when the stadium is unoccupied, they are opened to allow the wind to blow through the enclosed bowl, which helps keep the grass pristine'. There is also a small basic electric scoreboard in one corner of the stadium, in between the East and Key 103 stands, adjacent to the upper tier of the away fans section '.

Peter Llewellyn adds: 'Many City fans still call their new home Eastlands, when it didn't have an official name. Some have suggested The Blue Camp, others New Maine Road but officially it's The City of Manchester Stadium. Unlike many other stadiums and stands, there are no letters across the seats, so there is nothing like MCFC spelt out across them'.

Man City get my vote for the weirdest looking mascots in the league. Whilst most clubs have elected to re-create some furry creature, Man City have as their mascots a pair of aliens called 'Moonchester' and 'Moonbeam'.

WHAT'S IT LIKE FOR VISITORS?

The stadium is certainly less intimidating for away fans than Maine Road ground and from the outside it looks simply spectacular. However, I think because it looks so good from the outside the expectations are raised somewhat; when you actually enter inside, you are a little disappointed as it does not match the exterior, looking somewhat bland in comparison.

Away fans are located in one side of the Key 103 (South) Stand at one end of the ground, in both the upper and lower tiers, where up to 3,000 fans can be accommodated (4,500 for cup games). The view of the action is pretty impressive although the legroom is a little tight. The facilities are also quite good with spacious concourses, large plasma flat television screens showing the game and a good selection of food

on offer, including chips and the delicious 'Football's Famous Chicken Balti Pie' (£2.20) as well as the alternative vegetarian option. Also on offer is a 'pie and a pint' for £4.

Atmosphere within the new ground is sadly lacking compared to Maine Road, but I'm sure this will develop in time. I did hear one good rendition of the Man City fans anthem 'Blue Moon' though on my visit. My only real complaint was the lack of distance between the home and away supporters. Only a few seats and a row of stewards stood in-between the two sets of fans, which led to a lot of unpleasant baiting between the two. And of course it was always the away fans who were adjudged to be causing the problems by the stewards (although I'm sure that if I visited on another occasion I probably would have seen the same Man City fans baiting in the same manner) and this led a number of away fans on my visit being escorted out of the stadium. At the end of the game, fans are kept apart immediately outside via a large fence which is erected by the police, which seems to lead to a lot of exchanges of unpleasant abuse. Some away fans have suggested that it may be best to keep colours covered on making your way back to your transport. Please note that smoking is only permitted within the stadium on the concourses themselves and not at your seat.

Away fans visiting the stadium are not issued with a paper ticket, but a plastic one instead that is slightly larger than a credit card. To enter the stadium you have to hold the plastic ticket up against a sensor which then allows entry. Most away fans seemed quite confused by this on my

visit but there were plenty of stewards on hand to help resolve problems. Peter Llewellyn adds: 'If you are an adult trying to get into the stadium using a concession ticket (OAP or child) the stewards will know and you'll be ejected'.

WHERE TO DRINK

There are not many pubs around the stadium and the few available are predominantly for home support. However, 'The Stanley' (aka Sports Bar) pub does let in away fans in small numbers. It is about a 10 minute walk from the stadium, just set back from the main A6010 (Pottery Lane), going towards Ashburys train station. The easiest way to find it is to locate the large Asda store behind one side of the stadium (there is also a McDonald's outlet next door to the store, plus there is a café located inside) and on facing the superstore turn right and proceed down the main road and you will come to the pub on the left. It does cost £1 for adults to enter the pub (they even stamp your hand as if you were entering a night club) but children are at least admitted free. Inside there is a large screen showing SKY Sports, good service and a good mix of home and away support. Otherwise drink in the centre of Manchester before the game or alcohol is available inside the stadium (lager £2.40, cider £2.40, John Smiths bitter £2.30). Chris Fogarty adds: 'Away fans should avoid the Queen Victoria and Crossroads pubs at the bottom of Grey Mare Lane'.

GETTING THERE & WHERE TO PARK

The stadium is located in the north-east of Manchester.

From the South M6:
Leave the M6 at Junction 19 and follow the A556 towards Stockport and then join the M56 going towards Stockport. Continue onto the M60 passing Stockport and heading on towards Ashton Under Lyne. Leave the M60 at Junction 23 and take the A635 towards Manchester. Branch off onto the A662 (Ashton New Road) towards Droylsden/Manchester. Stay on the A662 for around three miles and you will reach the Stadium on your right.

From the M62:
Leave the M62 at Junction 18 and then join the M60 Ashton Under Lyne. Leave the M60 at Junction 23 and take the A635 towards Manchester. Branch off onto the A662 (Ashton

New Road) towards Droylsden/Manchester. Stay on the A662 for around three miles and you will reach the Stadium on your right.

Iain Macintosh informs me: 'I find this route an easier one to the ground: leave the M60 at Junction 24 and take the A57 (Hyde Road) towards Manchester. Turn right onto the A6010 (Pottery Lane). There are quite a number of unofficial car parks on both sides of Pottery Lane, costing around £5 per car. Pottery Lane becomes the Alan Turing Way and goes right past the stadium on your left'.

Car Parking:
There is little parking at the stadium for supporters and there is a residents only parking scheme in the streets near to it, which extends about a mile out from the stadium. It means parking further away and then walking. Some unofficial car parks have sprung up mostly charging around £5 per car. Peter Llewellyn tells me: 'The road links are busy even on non-matchdays so make sure you allow plenty of time. The stadium is part of Sportcity so car users should follow the brown Sportcity signs until near the stadium'.

By Train
The closest train station is Ashburys which is a short five minute train ride away from Manchester Piccadilly Station. The stadium is about a 10 minute walk away from Ashburys station. As you come out of the station turn left and after proceeding up the road you will come to the stadium on your left.

Otherwise if you have time on your hands, then you can embark on the 20-25 minute walk from Piccadilly Station to the stadium. At the bottom of the main station approach turn right into Ducie Street. At the end of the road turn right onto Great Ancoats Street. Cross over the road, then the canal and turn left into Pollard Street - this is well marked as a walking route to Sportcity. Continue straight along Pollard Street which leads onto the A662 Ashton New Road and you will come to the stadium on your left."

An alternative way from the station is to go over the bridge to platform 13/14 (trains from Liverpool and some Transpennine trains come in here anyway) and exit down the steps to Fairfield Street. Turn left at the exit and left again under the railway (Travis Street continuing into Adair Street), left at the end and right into Pollard Street (then as above).

Alternatively you can get a taxi from Piccadilly

Station (around £4.50) or a bus from Piccadilly Gardens. Go down the main approach from the station, then along London Road to Piccadilly Gardens; normal service and special matchday buses leave from the right-hand side of the square (between Lever Street and Oldham Street) - 70p each way. 216 and 217 are the main service buses, but 185, 186, 230, 231, 232, 233, 234, 235, 236, 237,X36 and X37 also go from the city centre to the stadium (and 53 and 54 from the city's ring road). On the return, the special buses leave from Ashton New Road just across from the away end.

Thanks to Steve Parish for providing the above directions and bus information.

LOCAL RIVALS

Manchester United.

ADMISSION PRICES

Like a number of Clubs, Manchester City operate a category system (A, B & C) for matches, whereby the most popular matches cost more to watch.
Home Fans:
Colin Bell Stand (level 2 middle tier): Adults: £36 (A) £32 (B) £28 (C), No Concessions.
Colin Bell Stand (levels 1 & 3): Adults: £34 (A) £30 (B) £26 (C), No Concessions.
East Stand: Adults: £34 (A) £30 (B) £26 (A), Concessions: £19 (A) £18 (B) £17 (C)
North Stand; Adults: £28 (A) £25 (B) £21 (C), Concessions: £14 (A) £12 (B) £11 (C)
Key 103 (South) Stand: Adults: £28 (A) £25 (B) £21 (C), Concessions: £14 (A) £12 (B) £11 (C)
Family Stand: Adults: £25 (A) £22 (B) £18 (C), Concessions: £12 (A) £11 (B) £10 (C)
Away Fans:
Key 103 (South) Stand: Adults: £28 (A) £25 (B) £21 (C), Concessions: £14 (A) £12 (B) £11 (C)

Please note that tickets have to be purchased in advance and are not on sale on the day of the game.

PROGRAMME & FANZINES

Official Programme: £2.50.
King Of The Kippax Fanzine: £2.
Chips 'N' Gravy Fanzine: £1.
City Till I Cry Fanzine: £1.50.

RECORD ATTENDANCE

At The City Of Manchester Stadium:
47,304 v Chelsea
Premier League, February 28, 2004.
At Maine Road:
84,569 v Stoke City
FA Cup 6th Round, March 3, 1934.

AVERAGE ATTENDANCE

2003-2004: 46,834 (Premier League).

STADIUM TOURS

The Club offer tours on most days. Costs: Adults £7.50 and concessions £4.50. Tours must be booked by calling the ticket office on 0870-062-1894.

DID YOU KNOW?

When Ardwick FC became Manchester City in 1894, the colours were Cambridge blue and sky blue.

OLD TRAFFORD, MANCHESTER

Ground Name:	Old Trafford
Capacity:	67,721 (all-seated)
Address:	Sir Matt Busby Way, Manchester, M16 0RA
Main Telephone No:	0870-442-1994
Main Fax No:	0161-868-8804
Ticket Office (Sales):	0870-442-1999
Ticket (Enquiries):	0870-442-1994
Stadium Tours:	0870-442-1994
Club Nickname:	The Red Devils
Pitch Size:	116 x 76 yards
Home Kit Colours:	Red, White & Black.
Official Website:	www.manutd.com

Unofficial Websites:
Red11.Org: www.red11.org
M-U-F-C: www.m-u-f-c.co.uk
ManUMyView: www.manumyview.co.uk
Red Issue: www.redissue.co.uk (Footy Mad Network)
Heatons Heros: www.heatonsheroes.co.uk
United We Stand: http://manchesterunited.rivals.net/ (Rivals Network)

WHAT'S THE GROUND LIKE?

Old Trafford is the largest league ground in England. What has made it so special is having the stands envelop the corners, making the stadium completely enclosed. The ground has seen much development in recent years, with three stands each having an additional tier added. Both ends, which look almost identical, are now large two-tiered stands. Each is steep, with a large lower tier and smaller upper tier. The three-tiered North Stand at one side of the ground is the largest capacity stand of any League ground in England. These redeveloped stands dwarf the older Main (South) Stand on the opposite side. This stand is single-tiered, with a television gantry suspended below its roof. All the stands have a row of executive boxes at the back of the lower tier.

The ground looks a little imbalanced with the Main (South) Stand, looking somewhat out of place with its larger newer neighbours. However, in my opinion, the best views of the ground are from the front of this stand and from the away section, as you look out upon the three newer, larger sides. Still, if this Main Stand was to be redeveloped in the same manner as the others and the corners of the ground filled, then it would probably be the envy of Europe.

Unusual aspects of the ground include the raised pitch and the teams entering the field from the corner of the Main Stand. On either side of the North Stand are two impressive looking electric scoreboards. Outside the ground is the Sir Matt Busby Statue fronting the impressive green glassed East Stand facade. There is also a clock and plaque in remembrance of the Munich disaster.

FUTURE GROUND DEVELOPMENTS

The Club have announced that they are looking into ways of expanding Old Trafford's capacity. Ideally they would like to redevelop the South Stand, but with the proximity of a railway line behind this stand it is not economically feasible to do so. However, it is likely that the Club will at some stage increase the capacity to 75,000, by filling in the north-east and north-west corners. This will be done by adding an additional tier to link the North Stand with the East and Stretford Ends. No firm timescales have been announced as to when this might take place, but it is likely to be sooner rather than later.

WHAT'S IT LIKE FOR VISITORS?

Away fans are located in one corner of the ground, taking up part of the East and South stands. The view from the away sections is excellent and up to 3,000 away supporters can be accommodated. Fans are normally searched on the way into the ground by the stewards and once inside there are a number of refreshment kiosks. These sell a range of pies and other refreshments, plus alcohol is normally available (although at a recent England game there was none on sale). The away fans section is set back from the pitch as there is a disabled area to its front. The legroom between rows is a little tight, but the good thing is that the away fans can really make some noise from this part of the stadium. On my last visit, I felt the stewards and police were a little heavy-handed leading to some ugly confrontations with some of the away fans, especially when it was announced that away fans were to be kept behind for a short period of time after the game had finished.

As you probably know, Old Trafford is billed as the 'Theatre Of Dreams' and is certainly one of the best grounds in the country. However, if you have never been there before, be prepared to be a little disappointed, as reality will probably not meet your pre-conceived expectations. Getting tickets for Man Utd home games is pretty difficult even if you are a member of the club, so make sure you have tickets before you travel.

WHERE TO DRINK

Most of the pubs around the ground operate members only schemes and/or are for home fans only. On my last couple of visits I have had a drink at the Quadrant pub which had a mixture of home and away fans and a couple of handy Chinese/Chippies nearby. The pub is about a 10-15 minute walk away from Old Trafford, in the direction of the Cricket Ground (see tip for parking below for more info). Andy Syborn adds: 'Away fans are okay

to drink in the Bridge at Sale. It is two stops from Old Trafford on the Metro (about an eight-minute journey)'. Alternatively alcohol is normally served within the ground, although for some games the Club opt not to sell any.

GETTING THERE & WHERE TO PARK

From the South:
Leave the M6 at Junction 19 and follow the A556 towards Altrincham. This will lead you onto the A56 towards Manchester. Keep on the A56 for six miles and then you will come to see Sir Matt Busby Way on your left. The ground is half a mile down this road on your left, although on matchdays this road may well be closed to traffic.

From the North:
Leave the M6 at Junction 30 and take the M61 towards Bolton. At the end of the M61, join the M63. Leave the M63 at Junction 4 and follow the A5081 towards Manchester. After about two miles you will reach Sir Matt Busby Way on your right for the ground.

From The West:
Follow M56 until its end and then take the M60 (W&N) as for Trafford Centre. At Junction 7 leave M60 and take the A56 towards Stretford. Stay on the A56 for 2.1 miles then you will see Sir Matt Busby Way on your left. The ground is half a mile down this road on your left, although on matchdays this road may be closed to traffic. Thanks to Brian Griffiths for providing these directions.

Parking:
There are lots of small private car parks near to the ground, otherwise it is street parking. Peter Bennett suggests parking at Old Trafford Cricket Ground (cost £5). Try to arrive early (before 1pm) as if you arrive later, it takes ages leaving the car park after the game. Paul Taylor a visiting Newcastle fan adds: 'The stadium is quite close to the Trafford Centre (a large shopping and leisure/entertainment complex). You can park there for free (even when it's closed) and then take Bus number 250 to the stadium (for times use the GMPTE web site). However, you can't get the bus back, you have to walk. Buses don't go near Old Trafford after matches. The walk takes about 20 minutes'.

Alternatively:
Park in Altrincham town centre and take the Metrolink to the ground (20 minutes). Some pubs, such as the Bricklayers Arms in Altrincham town centre, will allow parking for the afternoon, as long as you enjoy a pre-match drink (they also do good

food). Kevin Dixon-Jackson tells me: 'You can get the Metrolink to Old Trafford from Ladywell Halt, in Eccles, where there is also free secure parking. You can reach Eccles from the M60 (take the Carrington spur J8 A6144(M)) or M602 Motorway (leave at the first junction for Eccles), turn right, and right again at the lights, onto Eccles New Road. Secure parking is immediately on your right. You are only 200 yards away from the drinking capital which is Eccles town centre!'

My Tip For Parking and Getting Away After The Game:
Going along the A56, as the stadium emerges in front of you, follow the signs for Old Trafford Cricket Ground, which means that you will bear off the A56 to the right. At the end of the park on your left and before you reach the Cricket Ground, turn right into Great Stone Road. Just over the hill you will see a pub called the Quadrant, which is next door to a chip shop. There is plenty of street parking in this area, up to around 1.15-1.30pm. You are only a 10 minute walk away from the ground. The Quadrant pub itself, I found okay to have a drink in. After the game, head away from Old Trafford (keeping the Quadrant pub on your left) along the side streets. You will reach the A5145 (Edge Lane). Turn right down here and you will eventually join up again with the motorway and avoid all the traffic jams on the A56. This worked brilliantly for me after an England game and I was back in Birmingham shortly after 6.45pm.

By Train/Metrolink
Old Trafford has both its own railway station next to the ground and a Metrolink station which is located next to Lancashire County Cricket Club on Warwick Road, which leads up to Sir Matt Busby Way. Both stations are served by Manchester Piccadilly mainline station. Thanks to Mark Embling for providing this information.

Chris Kilcourse adds: 'The Metrolink also has another branch line going to Eccles from Manchester City Centre. There are two stops to leave the tram - Pomona and Exchange Quay. These are on the opposite (Salford) side of the ground - probably a quieter line on Matchdays. Pomona is the closest to the ground, only a short walk away and closer than Lancashire CC. Exchange Quay is the one to use for return journeys as the trams get full and may not stop at Pomona going back'.

LOCAL RIVALS

Manchester City, Liverpool and, from a little further a field, Leeds United.

ADMISSION PRICES

Please note that home section tickets are normally made only available to members of the club, which are then allocated by a ballot system (unless you want to buy a corporate hospitality ticket). Tickets rarely make general sale, although it does sometimes happen (especially in the early rounds of domestic and European Cup competitions), so it is worth checking. There always seems to be a number of ticket touts operating around the ground, but I dread thinking how much they would be asking for a ticket.

Home Fans*:
Adults: £26-£34, Concessions: £13-£17.
Away Fans:
Adults: £29, Concessions: £14.50.
Concessions apply to Over 65s and under 16s.
*Please note that Club members are eligible for a discount on the above prices.

PROGRAMME & FANZINES

Official Programme: £3.
Red Issue Fanzine: £2.

RECORD ATTENDANCE

Record Attendance (for Old Trafford):
76,962 - Wolves v Grimsby
FA Cup Semi Final, March 25, 1939.
Record Attendance (for a United Game):
70,504 v Aston Villa
Division One, December 27, 1920.

AVERAGE ATTENDANCE

2003-2004: 67,641 (Premier League).

STADIUM TOURS

The Club offer tours, which are available daily (except matchdays and the day before a European game). The tour also includes a visit to the Club Museum and costs: Adults £8.50, Under 16s & over 65s: £5.75. Discount family tickets are available. To book your tour, call the Club on 0870 442 1994.

DID YOU KNOW?

That Old Trafford has the largest stand in at any ground in the League, with 26,000 seats available in the North Stand.

RIVERSIDE STADIUM, MIDDLESBROUGH

Ground Name:	Riverside Stadium
Capacity:	35,100 (all-seated)
Address:	Middlesbrough, Cleveland, TS3 6RS
Main Telephone No:	01642-877-700
Main Fax No:	01642-877-840
Ticket Office:	01642-877-745
Ticket Office Fax:	01642-877-843
Stadium Tours:	01642-877-730
Club Nickname:	Boro
Pitch Size:	115 x 75 yards
Home Kit Colour:	All Red
Official Website:	www.mfc.co.uk

Unofficial Websites:
Fly Me To The Moon:
http://middlesbrough.rivals.net/default.asp?sid=892 (Rivals Network)
Southern Supporters Club: http://mss.org.uk

WHAT'S THE GROUND LIKE?

The stadium was only opened in August 1995 and is light years away from the old Ayresome Park. It has been further improved with the filling in of the two corners. This means that the Riverside is now totally enclosed, vastly improving its overall feel. The West Stand is slightly larger than the other three sides, which makes the appearance somewhat imbalanced. Although it looks great from the outside (especially so at night, when illuminated and visible from miles around), inside it is somewhat bland. It seems to lack character,

but I'm sure this will develop in time. Outside the main entrance you will find a pair of statues dedicated to two former Boro greats: George Hardwick and Wilf Mannion.

What's It Like For Visiting Supporters?
Away supporters are housed in the South Stand at one end of the stadium, which is shared with home supporters (with the obligatory 'no-mans' land in between). Up to 3,450 fans can be accommodated in this area. I was quite impressed with the facilities inside the ground and the view from the away section is excellent. One thing to point out is that there is very little in the way of pubs or eating establishments nearby, so you will need to head into the town centre for these (see recommendations below). Please also note that smoking is not permitted in the seated areas of the ground. Normally a friendly day out.

WHERE TO DRINK

Chris Taylor recommends Doctor Browns, a 10 minute walk from the ground at the bottom of Corporation Road, in the city centre. This pub serves real ale, has SKY TV and, on my last visit, had a good mix of home and away fans, both inside and outside of the pub. On the corner opposite the pub is also a sandwich bar, which was doing a brisk trade in, amongst other things, trays of roast potatoes and gravy. To find this pub: if you were standing outside the stadium with the main entrance behind you, head over to your left and turn right down the road, going under a bridge. A little way down this road on your left, there is an underpass (there is usually some programme and fanzine sellers standing by its entrance). Go down through the underpass and as you emerge on the other side, turn right and go down the road and through another underpass. You will emerge in a small retail park (there is a McDonald's over on your right), which you walk through unto you come to a main road. Turn right along this road and you will see the Doctor Browns pub over on your left.

Mike Barron, a visiting Wolves adds: 'You have to mention the Tuxedo Royale strip bar - it's the big white ship located opposite the stadium on the River Tees. It's £1 to get in and then it's £1 a pint before 1.30pm and then £2.20 a pint thereafter with free strippers. Away fans can get admittance if not wearing colours'. Otherwise, there is a bar at the back of the away stand within the ground (£2.50 per pint).

GETTING THERE & WHERE TO PARK

It is quite easy to find. Just follow the A66 (signposted Teeside from the A1) past Darlington's new ground and on into Middlesbrough. Carry on up the A66, through the centre of Middlesbrough and you will pick up signs for the Riverside Stadium. Although there is no parking available directly at the

stadium itself, there are a number of private parks (mostly on waste land) nearby.

Jerry Hill adds: 'I would suggest that away fans should follow the route marked "away coaches" from the A66, as this passes many private car parks along the river, all priced at £4'. Bear in mind though that if you do park at one of these car parks, then it may take 45 minutes or so after the game, before you can exit them. Otherwise, as the stadium is only about one mile from the town centre, you could also consider parking in a long stay car park in the town centre (about a 15-20 minute walk away from the ground). Robert Wells informs me: 'The retail area around the McDonald's near to the Doctor Browns pub is free on Saturdays. I found this out on a visit this season. To reach it, simply go past the exit for Riverside on A66, then take the next exit at the Gala bingo and cinema complex. Head for this complex and the parking is on your left'.

By Train
The ground is also walkable from Middlesbrough train station, which is on Albert Road. This station is not on a main line and is served by trains from Darlington.

If you come out of the main entrance, turn left onto Zetland Road. Then left again into Albert Road and proceed under the railway bridge. Turn immediately right into Bridge Street East, going past the Bridge pub (not recommended for away fans) and then take the next right into Wynward Way. The stadium is down this road. If you come out of the rear station entrance, turn right onto

Bridge Street East. Go Straight past the Bridge pub and then take the next right into Wynward Way for the ground.

Thanks to Glenn Brunskill for providing the directions.

LOCAL RIVALS

Sunderland and Newcastle United.

ADMISSION PRICES

Home Fans
West Stand Upper Tier: Adults: £39,
Concessions: £26
West Stand Lower Tier: Adults: £34,
Concessions: £17
East Stand Upper Tier: Adults: £37,
Concessions: £23
East Stand Lower Tier: Adults: £34,
Concessions: £17
North Stand: Adults: £30, Concessions: £17
South Stand: Adults: £30, Concessions: £17

Away Fans:
South Stand: Adults: £30, Concessions: £17

PROGRAMME & FANZINES

Official Programme: £2.50.
Fly Me To The Moon Fanzine: £1

RECORD ATTENDANCE

For The Riverside Stadium:
35,000 England v Slovakia
Euro 2004 Qualifier, June 11, 2003.
For A Middlesbrough Game At the Riverside
34,814 v Newcastle United
Premier League, March 5, 2003.
For A Middlesbrough Game At Ayresome Park:
53,536 v Newcastle United
Division One, December 27, 1949.

AVERAGE ATTENDANCE

2003-2004: 30,398 (Premier League).

STADIUM TOURS

The Club hold weekly tours of the stadium on most weekdays plus Sundays. The tours cost £5 for adults and £2 for senior citizens and children. Tours must be booked in advance on 01642-877-730.

DID YOU KNOW?

When the Riverside Stadium opened in 1995, it was the largest new football ground stadium to have been built in England since the Second World War.

NEWCASTLE UNITED

ST JAMES' PARK, NEWCASTLE

Ground Name: St.James' Park
Capacity: 52,193 (all-seated)
Address: St. James' Park, Newcastle-upon-Tyne NE1 4ST
Main Telephone No: 0191-201-8400
Main Fax No: 0191-201-8600
Ticket Office: 0191-261-1571
Pitch Size: 110 x 73 yards
Club Nickname: The Magpies or The Toon
Home Kit Colours: Black & White
Official Website: www.nufc.co.uk
Unofficial Websites:
NUFC.com: www.nufc.com
Howay The Toon: www.howaythetoon.com
Tyne Talk: www.tyne-talk.tk (Sports Network)
Talk Of The Tyne: www.talkofthetyne.com
(Rivals Network)

WHAT'S THE GROUND LIKE?

The ground has largely been rebuilt in recent years and is unrecognisable from the St James' Park of old. On approaching the ground, it looks absolutely huge, as it appears to have been built on raised ground. I particularly liked St James' Park as it is totally enclosed and has a great atmosphere. With the completion of the additional tier to the Milburn and Leazes (Sir John Hall) Stands, the capacity has been increased to over 52,000. These stands have a huge lower tier, with a row of executive boxes and a smaller tier above. This development has created the largest cantilever structure in Europe and has a spectacular looking roof, which allows natural light to penetrate (and hence is good for the pitch). However the ground now looks somewhat imbalanced with one half of the ground being significantly larger than the other two sides.

WHAT'S IT LIKE FOR VISITORS?

Away fans are housed in the Sir John Hall Stand in the North West corner of the ground, in the very top tier of the stand (the photo above was taken from this area). Up to 3,000 fans can be accommodated in this section for Premiership games and a larger allocation is available for cup games. Be warned though that it is a climb of 14 flights of stairs up to the away section and that you are situated quite far away from the pitch. So if you are scared of heights or have poor eye sight then this may not be for you. On the plus side you do get a wonderful view of the whole stadium, plus the Newcastle skyline and countryside in the distance. Also the legroom and height between rows are the best that I have come across and the facilities on offer are pretty good. The concourse is spacious and there is a fair selection of pies and burgers on offer, all served in Newcastle United branded packaging (which made me wonder if their sales were affected when playing Sunderland!). There are also televisions on the concourse, showing the game being played live, with separate refreshment areas which serve alcohol, again in Newcastle United branded plastic glasses. Beware that most games are sold out in advance and trying to get tickets can be extremely difficult. So don't travel unless you have one.

Jeremy Gold, a visiting Leyton Orient supporter, adds: 'The visitors' section is on level seven at the top of the stand. The view is a long way from the pitch, although it is still good. If you suffer from vertigo, don't go! The stewarding at the game I went to was fairly strict. However, people were being warned against gesturing before they were thrown out. Unfortunately some people didn't take the hint and about five or six made the long trip back down the 14 flights of stairs!'

The atmosphere in St James' Park can be electric and it is certainly one of the best footballing stadiums in the country. I personally found the Geordies friendly and helpful and a trip to Newcastle can be one of the better away trips in the Premier League.'

WHERE TO DRINK

The ground is one of the few in the country that is literally right in the centre of the city. You are only a few minutes walk from the main shopping areas of Newcastle. There are plenty of bars to choose from in the city centre, but most away fans tend to favour the pubs opposite and around Newcastle Railway Station. The 'A Head Of Steam' 'The Lounge' and 'O'Neills' are all recommended, but some

of these bars only admit fans if colours are covered and none of them allow children. Alternatively there is 'Idols' which has strippers and is popular with both home and away fans. Alcohol is also served within the ground.

GETTING THERE & WHERE TO PARK

At the end of the A1(M) continue on the A1 and then the A184 towards Newcastle. Continue along this road, bearing left onto the A189. Continue over the River Tyne on the Redheugh Bridge, from which the ground can be clearly seen. Carry on straight up the dual carriageway (St James Boulevard). This leads directly to the Gallowgate end of the ground. As the ground is so central, there are a number of pay and display car parks in the vicinity.

By Train

Newcastle Central Railway Station is half a mile from the ground and takes 10-15 minutes to walk.

Thanks to Ian Kavanagh for providing the following directions: 'Come out of the station, across the two zebra crossings and head right onto Grainger Street. Follow this road up to the second set of traffic lights (at Pizza Hut). This will see you at the top of the Bigg Market - Drinker's Paradise! You should have met a throng of black and white shirts by now, but failing that, bear left onto Newgate Street and follow the road all the way around to the roundabout with Gallowgate. Following this road all the way round which will lead you straight to St James Park and the away fans' section'.

Andrew Saffrey adds: 'If you're feeling lazy, you can get buses 36, 36B, 71, 87 or 88 from Berwick Street (across the road from the station), up to the ground. The fare should be about 50p'. Claire Stewart informs me: 'You can also get the metro from inside the train station up to the ground, which has its own 'St. James' Park" stop. Go on the metro from the railway station to Monument Metro Station where you need to change trains to go to St James Park. You can also walk up to the ground from Monument Station. It's pretty easy to find and if you do happen to get lost, then just follow the black and white crowd!'

By Air

Newcastle Airport is located seven miles from the City Centre. The easiest way to get into Newcastle is to go by the Metro transit system.

The airport has its own Metro station which is situated next to the passenger terminal. There are frequent departures to the City Centre and the journey is 23 minutes. This costs £2 for a single ticket or £3 return (£3.80 at peak periods). Change at Monument Metro Station for a metro to St James Park Station.

LOCAL RIVALS

Sunderland and Middlesbrough.

ADMISSION PRICES

Due the large number of season ticket holders, there are only around 2,500 tickets available to home fans for each game (more if the away team do not take up their full allocation). These tickets are normally go on sale at 9am on the Monday, two weeks before a home game (but check with the Club for precise details of sales dates). There are also a number of 'Executive Seats' available for each game, but obviously they are priced accordingly.

Home Fans:
Milburn Stand (Platinum Club): Adults £47, Senior Citizens £40, no further concessions.
Milburn Stand (Bar 1892): Adults £46, Senior Citizens £40, no further concessions.
Milburn Stand (Sovereign Club): Adults £44, Senior Citizens £36, No further concessions.
Milburn Stand (Black & White Club): Adults £44, Senior Citizens £38, no further concessions.
Milburn Stand (Level 7): Adults £35, Senior Citizens £28, Juniors £18.
Milburn Stand (Paddock): Adults £34, Senior Citizens £28, Juniors £17.
East Stand & Paddock: Adults £34, Senior Citizens £28, Juniors £17.
Sir John Hall Stand (Sports Bar): Adults £42, Senior Citizens £36, no further concessions.
Sir John Hall Stand (including corners): Adults £28, Senior Citizens £24, Juniors £15.
Sir John Hall Stand (Level 7): Adults £25, Senior Citizens £22, Juniors £15.
Newcastle Brown (Gallowgate End) Stand: Adults £28, Senior Citizens £24, Juniors £15.
Family Enclosure: Adults £20, Senior Citizens £17, Juniors £7.

Away Fans:
Sir John Hall Stand: Adults: £28, Senior Citizens £24, Juniors £15.

PROGRAMME & FANZINES

Official Programme: £2.50.
The Mag Fanzine: £2.
True Faith Fanzine: £1.50.

RECORD ATTENDANCE

68,386 v Chelsea
Division One, September 3, 1930.

AVERAGE ATTENDANCE

2003-2004: 51,966 (Premier League).

DID YOU KNOW?

St James' Park is the oldest ground in the North East with football first being played there in 1880.

FRATTON PARK, PORTSMOUTH

Ground Name: Fratton Park
Capacity: 20,101 (all seated)
Address: Frogmore Road,
Portsmouth, PO4 8RA
Main Telephone No: 02392-731204
Main Fax No: 02392-734129
Ticket Office: 0871-230-1898
Ticket Office Fax No: 0871-230-1899
Team Nickname: Pompey
Pitch Size: 115 x 73 yards
Home Kit Colours: Blue, White & Red
Official Website: www.pompeyfc.co.uk
Unofficial Websites:
Pompey Till I Die: www.pompeytillidie.com
Pompey Online: www.pompeyonline.com

WHAT'S THE GROUND LIKE?

A few seasons back, a new covered home end
was completed, bringing a vast improvement
on the previous open terrace. It is a good sized
single-tiered stand and is called the TY Europe
Stand (previously known as the Fratton End)
and is the tallest stand at the ground. The
opposite end, the Inter-cash Milton End, is
uncovered and open to the elements. It is all-
seated and is given to away fans. There is a
small moat in front of this area. Both side
stands are two-tiered and originally had

terracing at the front, which has now been
replaced with seating. The South Stand dates
back to the 1920s and is starting to show its
age. However, it still has some character with
an old fashioned looking media gantry perched
on its roof and raised team dugouts at its front.
Opposite, the North Stand looks somewhat
plain and functional. Both the North and South
Stands are two-tiered and have a number of
supporting pillars. The ground is completed
with a superb looking set of tall floodlights that
were first used in 1962.

If you get a chance to wander around the
outside of the ground beforehand then make
sure to go down to the home end to look at
the mock Tudor facade in Frogmore Road that
is now partly used as a club shop, but still
overlooks the entrance to the Fratton End (TY
Europe Stand).

FUTURE GROUND DEVELOPMENTS

Steve Edwards informs me: 'Portsmouth have
almost finalised contracts for the redevelopment of Fratton Park. The new ground
will be built on the present site (although the
pitch will be rotated 90 degrees) and will have
an initial capacity of 28,000 (rising to 35,000
at a later stage). Planning permission has been

granted and Barr Construction have won the contract to build it. The cost of the scheme is £26m and it is hoped that work will commence at the end of the current season'.

WHAT'S IT LIKE FOR VISITORS?

With the Inter-cash Milton End being uncovered and having been one of those former terraces that have been converted to all-seating, it is not one of the better stands in which to view a game. The facilities are not particularly great and the legroom is tight. The sight of portaloos as you go through the turnstiles does little to raise enthusiasm and it has to be said that it is probably the worst away stand in the Premiership. However, once you put all that to one side (if you can) then at least Fratton Park is a proper looking football ground, with a great atmosphere (which is helped by a drummer and bell ringer in the home end). So sit back and enjoy it as such grounds are now becoming few and far in between with the advent of new stadia being built.

The Inter-cash Milton End can accommodate just over 3,000 supporters but this is divided between home and away support, with the normal allocation for away supporters being around 2,000. On my last visit, the end was split between home and away fans, but praise to the home support who got behind their team but in a non-intimidating way towards the away fans. Fans were literally separated by a netted area only three seats wide, but there were no problems whatsoever. The delicious 'Football's Famous Chicken Balti Pie' (£2.20) is available inside the ground. Please note that the Club no longer allow smoking in the seated areas of the ground.

Chris Saunders, a visiting Middlesbrough fan, adds: 'It terms of facilities the ground is light years away from Premiership standard, but the atmosphere is electric with the legendary 'Play Up Pompey' echoing around the ground. The Portsmouth fans are a great bunch and made me most welcome. If you are feeling hungry then there are a McDonald's and KFC across the road from the ground. As mentioned the Inter-cash Stand doesn't have a roof, so if you are going, take a coat just in case it rains and some sunglasses if it is sunny, and if it's really sunny also bring sunblock!'

WHERE TO DRINK

On my last visit I went to the Good Companion pub, which is on the main A2030 about a five minute walk away from the ground. It is a large pub serving Gale real ales and had a good mix of home and away support. I also noticed that it was doing a brisk business in food. Martin Hewitt recommends the Devonshire (two minutes walk from the ground) and the Harvester but advises away fans to avoid the Milton Arms, Shepherds Crook and the Newcome Arms. Whilst Ian Pratt recommends the Brewers Arms which is 'always popular with away fans'.

Graham Fewster, an exiled Pompey fan Down Under, adds: 'A pub I would recommend is the Connaught Arms. Popular with home and away fans, they serve a good selection of draught beers as well as some great pasties. The pub is located at the junction of Penhale and Guildford Road, which is roughly 200 yards away from Fratton Road but the walk is somewhat longer. But it is worth it take it from me!'

Otherwise drink in Portsmouth City Centre or down at Southsea before the game. Remember Portsmouth is still a major naval port and hence some of the pubs can get quite rowdy at weekends.

GETTING THERE & WHERE TO PARK

Go along the M27 (ignoring the M275 turn off for Portsmouth town centre) and continue on to the A27. At the junction with the A2030 turn right towards Southsea/Fratton and just continue straight along the A2030 and eventually you will see the ground in front of you, just slightly to your left. There is a large car park behind the TY Europe Stand, but this is for home supporters only. So it is mostly street parking for away fans. This is best found on the right-hand side of the A2030 before you reach the Good Companion pub.

By Train

The nearest local train station is Fratton, which is a 10 minute walk away. Portsmouth train station is at least a 25 minute walk away. On arrival at Fratton by train you pass the ground on the left. Fratton station has a footbridge as the only way out. At the top of the stairs from the platform turn left onto the footbridge (from which you can see the floodlights of Fratton Park) and exit into Goldsmith Avenue. (Note that if the gate on the footbridge is closed you need to turn right on the footbridge and exit via Platform 1, turn left as you exit the station, walk 30 metres and go back over the footbridge to Goldsmith Avenue.) Turn left along Goldsmith Avenue and walk about half a mile passing straight around a small roundabout (by the Pompey Centre). Then turn left into Frogmore Road and the entrance to the TY and South stands is 100m ahead. For the Milton End stay on Goldsmith Avenue for another 100m and turn left into Apsley Road. The entrances to the Milton End are 100m ahead.

Thanks to Peter Coulthard for providing the directions.

LOCAL RIVALS

Southampton.

ADMISSION PRICES

Matchday tickets are only available in the Intercash Milton End for both home and away supporters. The Club operate a category system of ticket pricing (A & B) whereby the most popular games cost more to watch. Tickets prices are shown below with category B prices shown in brackets:
Adults: £30 (£26)
OAP's: £22 (£18)
Juniors: £19 (£16)

PROGRAMME & FANZINE

Official Programme: £3.
True Blue Fanzine: £1.

RECORD ATTENDANCE

51,385 v Derby County
FA Cup 6th Round, February 26, 1949.

AVERAGE ATTENDANCE

2003-2004: 20,108 (Premier League).

DID YOU KNOW?

That the South Stand was designed by the famous football ground architect Archibald Leitch and was opened in 1925.

STADIUM OF LIGHT, SUNDERLAND

Ground Name:	Stadium Of Light
Capacity:	48,300 (all-seated)
Address:	Stadium Of Light, Sunderland, SR5 1SU
Main Phone Number:	0191-551-5000
Main Fax No:	0191-551-5123
Ticket Office:	0191-551-5151
Ticket Office Fax No:	0191-551-5150
Stadium Tours:	0191-551-5055
Team Nickname:	The Black Cats
Pitch Size:	105 x 68 metres
Home Kit Colours:	Red & White
Official Website:	www.safc.com

Unofficial Websites:
Ready To Go: www.readytogo.net
Supporters Club (Heart Of England Branch):
http://users.tinyonline.co.uk/malcolm.dawson/index.html
RedandWhiteBarmy: http://sunderland.rivals.net (Rivals Network)
One Sunderland: www.onesunderland.com

WHAT'S THE GROUND LIKE?

The Club moved to the new stadium from Roker Park in July 1997. It is totally enclosed and is the largest new football ground so far to be built in England. The stadium itself is truly magnificent and I would say that it is one of the best (if not the best) stadiums in England. It is composed of two three-tiered stands (at one end and one side of the pitch), whilst the others are two-tiered. Unfortunately, sitting at the back of the highest tiers means a limited view of the majority of the stadium, hence the feeling of being a bit cut off. The West Stand also has a row of executive boxes (which you can sit outside if you wish). There is a large electronic scoreboard at either end. You really have to experience not only the stadium but also the occasion that is Sunderland to believe it. Away fans are housed at one end of the stadium, in the two-tiered Metro FM (South) Stand.

Currently, with half the stadium being larger than the other, it looks a little imbalanced from the away end. However, looking at the larger stands, one feels that if the Club added a tier to the remaining sides an even more remarkable stadium would emerge.

FUTURE GROUND DEVELOPMENTS

Kevin Davis informs me: 'The Club have secured planning permission to add another 7,200 seats to the Metro FM (South) Stand, which would take the capacity to 55,000. The Club have not yet confirmed when they will go ahead with this. If they then proceed to add another tier to the McEwans Stand, then the final capacity would be around 64,000'. However with the Club now back in Division One and with attendances falling, these plans have been put on hold.

WHAT'S IT LIKE FOR VISITORS?

If you can only get to one stadium this season, then go to this one. I found the stadium almost overwhelming, the PA system deafening (especially when the classical piece Dance Of The Knights from Prokofiev's Romeo and Juliet is played before the players come on to the pitch at the start of the game and Republica's Ready To Go, as the teams come out of the tunnel) and the Sunderland supporters are exceptionally friendly (I was even given a Sunderland shirt by one supporter!). But bear in mind you are not allowed to smoke or swear inside the stadium. If you persist with either you may find yourself being ejected from the ground! The delicious 'Football's Famous Chicken Balti Pie' (£2.20) is available inside the stadium.

WHERE TO DRINK

There are bars inside the ground but they get really crowded. I would recommend the William Jameson (Wetherspoons pub) in the centre of town for a drink before or after the game, as it has a great atmosphere. Graham Dutton recommends the new Yates's bar opposite Wetherspoons, whilst Maurice Perry informs me: 'Try Idols on High Street West, in the City Centre, which has good beer and scantily clad barmaids and dancers. Away fans are welcome'. Whilst Jason Adderley, a visiting West Brom fan, adds: "The Albion pub, on Victor Street, is a five minute walk from the ground, with some parking nearby. I've used this pub the last three times I've visited Sunderland with West Brom. Always friendly and the landlord even puts on complimentary snacks after the game. Otherwise there is a chippy a couple of doors away. An all round top boozer'.

GETTING THERE & WHERE TO PARK

Exit the A1 at the Durham/Sunderland exit and take the A690 towards Sunderland. After about eight miles, turn left onto the A19, signposted for the Tyne Tunnel. Stay in the left-hand lane and take the Sunderland slip road onto the bridge over the River Wear. Turn right onto the A1231 following the signs for Sunderland. Go straight over four roundabouts into Sunderland. Then go through two sets of traffic lights and you will see the Stadium car park on your right, about a mile after the traffic lights. However

there is only limited parking at the ground, so alternatively, you can park in the City Centre and walk to the ground (about 10-15 minutes). The traffic for a couple of miles around the ground was solid when I went so allow plenty of time for your journey.

There is also a Park & Ride scheme in operation on matchdays, free for both home and away supporters. This is situated at Sunderland Enterprise Park, which is well signposted just off the A1231. Buses run every five minutes, for 90 minutes before kick off and continue after the game until everyone has gone.

By Train/Metro

Chris Rutter informs me: 'Sunderland train station in the City Centre is walkable from the stadium (around 15 minutes). From the station, exit between WH Smith and the bakery. Turn left and walk down High Street West and then turn left again and walk up Fawcett Street to the Wear Bridge. From here you can see the stadium as it is on raised ground. Simply cross the bridge and turn left into Millennium Way, opposite the Wheatsheaf pub (home fans only). The away turnstiles are located on the side of the ground which is straight ahead".

Ashley Smith adds: 'A new Metro train service has started running to Sunderland with two new stations: Stadium of Light and St. Peters, both serving the stadium. The metro provides regular and rapid transport from both Newcastle and the South of Sunderland. Both new stations are only a few minutes walk from the stadium, although away supporters should alight at St Peters Station as that is closest to their entrance. This provides an alternative to the regular rail services. Please note though that after the game, the Stadium of Light metro station only operates Northbound (i.e. towards Newcastle) and St Peters metro station only operates Southbound (i.e. towards Sunderland centre).

By Air

The nearest airport is Newcastle which is located 24 miles away. However the journey is pretty straightforward as both the Stadium Of Light and Newcastle Airport are both served by the Metro transit system. There are frequent departures to Sunderland and the journey time is just under an hour. Change at South Gosforth Metro Station for a metro to the Stadium Of Light Station.

LOCAL RIVALS

Newcastle United and Middlesbrough.

ADMISSION PRICES

Home Fans:
West Stand & Premier Concourse (Centre): Adults:

£24, No Concessions
West Stand & Premier Concourse (Wings): Adults:
£24, Under 16s: £17
Fosters Stand (Centre): Adults: £24, No
Concessions
Fosters Stand (Wings): Adults: £24, Under 16s:
£17
Carling Stand: Adults: £24, No Concessions
Metro Fm Stand: Adults: £22, Under 16s: £17
Concession Corners: Adults: £18, Concessions:
£13, Under 16s: £8
Away Fans:
Metro Fm Stand: Adults: £24, Under 16s: £17

PROGRAMME & FANZINES

Red & White Review Official Programme: £2.50
A Love Supreme Fanzine: £2
Sex & Chocolate Fanzine: £1.50
The Wearside Roar Fanzine (TWR): £2

STADIUM TOURS

The Club offer regular tours of the stadium.
These cost £6 for adults and £4 for concessions.
A family ticket (2 adults + 2 children) is
also available at £18. For tour times and
availability ring the tour hotline on 0191 551
5055.

RECORD ATTENDANCE:

At The Stadium Of Light:
48,353 v Liverpool
Premier League, April 13, 2002.
At Roker Park;
75,118 v Derby County
FA Cup 6th Round Replay, March 8, 1933.

AVERAGE ATTENDANCE

2003-2004: 27,120 (Division One).

DID YOU KNOW?

Malcolm Dawson informs me: 'The Stadium of
Light was so named for two reasons. Firstly, it is
built on the site of the former Monkwearmouth
Colliery and the name was chosen to reflect the
heritage of the area and honour the men who
worked in the region's collieries. In fact outside
one corner of the stadium is a giant Miners
Lamp. Secondly, the name was also chosen as
to 'illuminate' the way ahead for the Club'.
Geoff Hall adds: 'Part of the story about the
naming of the stadium was because at the top
of the former colliery lift a sign read 'Into the
Light'. SAFC wanted links to the industrial
history of the place, hence the stadium name.
The gates on the west side of the ground have

'Into the Light' written on them to recall this
fact'.

WHITE HART LANE, TOTTENHAM

Ground Name: White Hart Lane
Capacity: 36,214 (all-seated)
Address: Bill Nicholson Way, 748 High Rd, Tottenham, London, N17 0AP
Main Telephone No: 020-8365-5000
Main Fax No: 020-8365-5005
Ticket Office: 0870-420-5000
Ticket Office Fax: 0870-420-5001
Stadium Tours: 020-8365-5056
Team Nickname: Spurs
Pitch Size: 110 x 73 yards
Home Kit Colours: White & Navy Blue
Official Website: www.spurs.co.uk
Unofficial Websites:
The Spur: www.thequake.com/thespur.html
Northern Spurs: www.northernspurs.co.uk
Top Spurs: www.topspurs.com
The Spurs Web: www.thespursweb.com (Rivals Network)
My Eyes Have Seen The Glory: www.mehstg.co.uk

WHAT'S THE GROUND LIKE?

I have always been a great fan of White Hart Lane, ever since my first visit way back in 1987. It has always been one of my favourite grounds in London to visit. In recent years it has virtually been rebuilt, making it one of the best in the country. The ground is totally enclosed which really adds to its overall look and can make for a great atmosphere. Both ends have huge Jumbotron video screens, built into the roof, which are a unique feature. All the stands are two-tiered with a row of executive boxes/concourse and are of roughly the same height, giving the ground a well balanced look. Only the East Stand on one side has a couple of large supporting pillars, otherwise there are no obstructions to your view. A TV gantry is also suspended from beneath the roof of this stand, whilst on top a gold coloured Cockerel sits proudly. Another unusual feature of the stadium is the Police Control Box that is suspended underneath the roof in the south-west corner of the ground, it looks like some kind of UFO!

FUTURE GROUND DEVELOPMENTS

Steve Edwards informs me: 'Haringey Council have now approved plans for the redevelopment of the East Stand at White Hart Lane. When completed, this will increase the capacity of White Hart Lane to 50,000. However, the Club will not go ahead with the redevelopment until the Government improve transport links around the stadium. The Club have even mooted that if the transport situation is not adequately resolved, then they will leave the Lane and possibly move to the new Wembley Stadium that is currently being built'.

WHAT'S IT LIKE FOR VISITORS?

Away fans are housed in one corner of the ground in between the South and West Stands, where up to 2,900 supporters, if demand requires it, can be accommodated in the lower and upper tiers. If you have a ticket for the upper tier then prepare yourself for quite a climb to reach the away area. You are though rewarded with a great view of the action from this section and the legroom is ample. The facilities in this new-ish stand are also above average. On the downside there is little space between the away and home fans. As you would expect there is plenty of banter between the two, but the stewards tend to take a tougher line on the away support. On my last visit a number of fans were ejected from the ground and there were repeated warnings to away fans to remain seated. One strange aspect of sitting in the upper tier is that you have the Police Control Box directly above you, where a number of uniformed faces can be seen peering down on the away fans. The delicious 'Football's Famous Chicken Balti Pie' (£2.20) is available inside the ground. I have always quite enjoyed my trips to Tottenham. White Hart Lane is excellent and the atmosphere generally good, although it is wise to exercise caution around the ground and you may consider keeping colours covered.

WHERE TO DRINK

Dave Thomas, a visiting Birmingham City fan tells me: 'We found a nice little boozer up a side road called the Antwerp. Popular with both home and away fans, it is highly recommended. To find it, take a right turn when you come out of White Hart Lane Station and then right onto the main High Road. You go past the ground on your left and then go right into Church Road. Walk down the road going under a bridge and the pub is on the left opposite a park. There are bouncers on the door but there's no problem getting in. Richard Crouch recommends The Park right by Northumberland Park station. This is a small comfortable pub which is about a 10 minute walk along Park Lane from the away end. Also the Bricklayers Arms (no away colours) is also recommended. Carsie, a Spurs fan from Belfast, adds: 'I would suggest the Three Compasses which is situated in Queen Street (behind Middlesex University), which is a five minute walk from White Hart Lane Station'. Inside the ground, alcohol is served in the refreshment areas. This is in the form of plastic bottles of Carlsberg at £2.50 per 500ml bottle.

GETTING THERE & WHERE TO PARK

Leave the M25 at Junction 25 and take the A10 towards Enfield. Continue on the A10 through Enfield and at the roundabout with the Northern Circular (A406), turn left onto the A406 (Sterling Way). Turn right into Fore Road (the A1010) which becomes the High Road and you will come to the ground on your left. Sharon Genge adds: 'If you arrive around midday, you can park at the local schools which are very easy to find. For £5 you can park until 6pm which is ample time to get back to the car after an afternoon match'.

The Editor of My Eyes Have Seen The Glory Fanzine adds: 'There is another way to get to the ground avoiding the A10 and A406. When you come off the M25, take the A10 turning and then turn left at the first set of lights. This takes you into Bullsmoor Lane. Follow the road through until a busy crossroads with traffic lights. Go straight over and then you are on Meridian Way (A1055). This road takes you straight down to Tottenham. Just keep going straight (over roundabouts and traffic lights and past the site at Picketts Lock) until you pass Tesco's on the left-hand side. After going through the traffic lights at this store go through the next set and turn right at the lights after those (Sedge Road). If you park around this area you will be able to get away fairly quickly and will be close to Northumberland Park station (as mentioned by others) and conveniently located for The Park Pub which is right next to the station. There is also a lot of tow-away zones directly around the ground, so check the parking restrictions before you leave your car or you might face a trip to Wood Green (not recommended at the best of times) and a £100 bill to get your car back!'

By Train

The nearest tube station is Seven Sisters which is on the Victoria Line. However, the ground is about 20 minutes walk, but there are plenty of buses running up Tottenham High Road to the stadium. The nearest railway station is White Hart lane, which is served by Liverpool Street Station. Richard Crouch adds: 'The best station to get to White Hart Lane from is Northumberland Park. Come out of the station and cross the road and you are in Park Lane. It is a 10 minute stroll to the ground'.

LOCAL RIVALS

Arsenal.

ADMISSION PRICES

At the time of going to print, matchday prices for the 2004/05 season were yet to be confirmed. Prices below are for last season.

In common with most Clubs, Tottenham operate a category system (A,B & C) for matches whereby tickets cost more for the most popular matches (category A). Concessions are also normally only available in the North Stand to Club Members, apart from some matches which are deemed by the Club to be family matches where Senior Citizens and Under 15s can purchase tickets at half the adult price, in the South Stand.

Home Fans:

West Stand Upper Tier: Season Tickets Only
West Stand Lower Tier: Adults £55 (A), £46 (B), £37 (C)
East Stand Upper Tier: Adults £55 (A), £46 (B), £37 (C)
East Stand Upper Tier (Restricted View): Adults £50 (A), £42 (B), £34 (C)
East Stand Lower Tier: Adults £45 (A), £38 (B), £33 (C)
East Stand Lower Tier (Restricted View): Adults £40 (A), £34 (B), £30 (C)
South Stand Upper Tier: Adults £40 (A), £34 (B), £30 (C)
South Stand Lower Tier: Adults £35 (A), £29 (B), £25 (C)
North Stand Upper Tier: Adults £40 (A), £34 (B), £30 (C) Senior/Junior Member: £20 (A), £17 (B), £15 (C)
North Stand Lower Tier: Adults £35 (A), £29 (B), £25 (C) Senior/Junior Member: £18 (A), £15 (B), £13 (C)
Disabled: £35 (A), £29 (B), £25 (C)

Away Fans:

South Stand Upper Tier: Adults £40 (A), £34 (B), £30 (C)
South Stand Lower Tier: Adults £35 (A), £29 (B), £25 (C)
Normally no concessions are made available to away fans, but check with your own Club first.

PROGRAMME & FANZINES

Official Programme: £3
One Flew Over Seaman's Head Fanzine: £2 - published 5 times a season.
Cock A Doodle Do Fanzine: £2.
My Eyes Have Seen The Glory Fanzine: £2

RECORD ATTENDANCE

75,038 v Sunderland
FA Cup 6th Round, March 5, 1938.

AVERAGE ATTENDANCE

2003-2004: 34,876 (Premier League).

STADIUM TOURS

Tours of the ground are normally run on weekdays and non-match Saturdays. The tours cost: Adults £7.50, Concessions £4.50. Ring 0208-365-5056 to book.

DID YOU KNOW?

The familiar white shirts and navy blue shorts were adopted in 1898 in respect to Preston North End and stuck ever since.

WEST BROMWICH ALBION

THE HAWTHORNS, WEST BROMWICH

Ground Name: The Hawthorns
Capacity: 27,877 (all-seated)
Address: Halfords Lane,
West Bromwich,
West Midlands,
B71 4LF
Main Telephone No: 0121-525-8888
Main Fax No: 0121-524-3462
Ticket Office Fax No: 0121-524-3466
Ticket Office: 0121-525-8888
Team Nickname: The Baggies
Pitch Size: 115 x 74 yards
Home Kit Colours: Navy & White
Official Website: www.wba.co.uk
Unofficial Websites:
Baggies.Com: www.baggies.com
Unofficial West Brom: www.westbrom.com
WbaUnofficial.com:
http://westbromwichalbion.rivals.net (Rivals
Network)
Baggies World: www.baggiesworld.co.uk
(Sport Network)
Disabled Supporters Club: www.wba-dsc.co.uk

WHAT'S THE GROUND LIKE?

With the completion of the East Stand in 2001,
the Club had achieved its objective in
completely rebuilding the Hawthorns and
making it a modern stadium. Not only has the
ground received a much needed face lift, but it
is now totally enclosed and all-seated. The East
Stand is an impressive, large single-tiered
stand, which has been well integrated with the
rest of the ground. It has a row of executive
boxes running along the back, and to each
side of the stand the previous open corners
have been filled with corrugated sheeting.
There is a thin supporting pillar on each side of
the stand to support the corner structures. This
stand, which is well set back from the pitch,
has been designated as a no smoking area. On
the other side is the relatively new but smaller
Halfords Lane Stand, stretching around two
corners of the ground. The Home end, The
Apollo 2000 Stand (Birmingham Road) is large,
covered, and quite steep. At the other end,
away fans are housed in the Smethwick end,
which is also a relatively new stand. Two new
video screens have been installed at opposite
corners of the ground, one at the Smethwick
End side of the East Stand and the other in the
opposite corner of the Halfords Lane Stand.

An interesting feature of the ground is that in
one corner of the ground (between the East
Stand and Birmingham Road End) you will
notice, perched up on a wall, a large Throstle
standing on a football. This has been kept over
from the previous stand (it used to sit above
the clock on the half-time scoreboard) and
maintains the links with tradition. Outside the
ground on the same corner is the recently
erected 'Jeff Astle Memorial Gates' in tribute to
the legendary striker.

FUTURE GROUND DEVELOPMENTS

The Club have completed the purchase of the

Woodman Pub, which sits outside the corner of the ground, between the Apollo 2000 and East Stands. This has led to speculation that the Club will redevelop this area so that the ground capacity can be raised to over 30,000.

WHAT'S IT LIKE FOR VISITORS?

Away fans are housed on one side of the Smethwick End, where the normal allocation is 3,000 seats. This means that this stand is shared with home supporters. For Cup games, the whole of this stand can be allocated to away fans, raising this figure to 5,200. The facilities and the view of the pitch in the Smethwick end are okay, although the legroom is a little cramped. I have been to the Hawthorns on a number of occasions and have always found it to be a fairly friendly place. The only thing against a visit in terms of a day out is a nearby pub for away fans, meaning that most elect to drink inside the ground instead. Considering that the concourse at the back of the Smethwick End is pretty small in comparison to its overall capacity, it has then an uncomfortable feel, especially when there is a large away support.

Thankfully the West Brom team no longer emerge to that annoying 1960s tune 'The Liquidator' (although it is still played before the game starts). They had been playing it for so many years that some opposing fans have made up a set of lyrics to go with it! Look out for the West Brom Mascot called 'Baggie Bird' who does a good job of entertaining the away fans before the game. This even involves going in goal and challenging players to take a shot! One tip on finding your seat in this stand is to remember that although your ticket is marked with the letter of the row, say Row B or Row LL, the plates indicating the row in the stand read B1 or LL1. As you would expect, a number of fans get confused by the addition of the number 1 and start to wander around the stand looking for their seat. You have been warned!

WHERE TO DRINK

Huw Morris, a West Brom fan, recommends The Vine, which is about 20 minutes from the ground. From Junction 1 off the M5 turn left towards West Bromwich town centre (opposite direction to the ground). Take the first left into Roebuck Street. The Vine is down on the left. You can also street park in this area and walk to the ground. If you continue towards West Bromwich going over a small mini roundabout, then on the right just before the lights is the Desi Junction pub. This Asian run pub does an excellent 'Balti Buffet'. For £4.95 per adult you can each as much as you like

and I found the food to be pretty good. The buffet is available all day on a Saturday and you can wash it down with a pint of Cobra beer. Alcohol is also available within the ground (on my last visit £2.30 for a can of Carling or Worthington), along with the delicious 'Football's Famous Chicken Balti Pie' (£2.20).

GETTING THERE & WHERE TO PARK

The ground is located on the A41 (Birmingham-West Bromwich Road). If approaching from outside the area, the ground is about half a mile from Junction 1 of the M5. On leaving the M5 take the A41 towards Birmingham, the ground is on your right. Beware though of speed cameras on this stretch of the A41. Street parking or alternatively there are a few private matchday car parks at some local industrial units near the ground or at Hawthorns station which costs £4.

By Train/Metro

The closest stations are The Hawthorns which is about five minutes walk from the ground and Smethwick Rolfe Street, which is about a 15 minute walk. The Hawthorns is served by a metro service from Birmingham Snow Hill station, whilst Smethwick Rolfe Street is served by local trains from Birmingham New Street. The metro service takes eight minutes to the Hawthorns from Birmingham Snow Hill and trains run every 15 minutes.

LOCAL RIVALS

Wolverhampton Wanderers, Birmingham City and Aston Villa.

ADMISSION PRICES

Home Fans:
East Stand (Upper Tier): Adults £33, Over 60s: £17, Under 16s: £15
East Stand (Lower Tier): Adults £33, Over 60s: £17, Under 16s: £15
Halfords Lane Stand: Adults £33, Over 60s: £17, Under 16s: £15
Apollo 2000 (Birmingham Road) Stand: Adults £28, Over 60s: £15, Under 16s: £13
Smethwick End: Adults £28, Over 60s: £15, Under 16s: £13
Away Fans:
Smethwick End: Adults £28, Over 60s: £15, Under 16s: £13

PROGRAMME & FANZINE

Official Programme: £3
Grorty Dick Fanzine: Great read and a bargain at 70p! (If you wonder what a Grorty Dick is, it is a Black Country food dish!)

RECORD ATTENDANCE

64,815 v Arsenal
FA Cup 6th Round, March 6, 1937.

AVERAGE ATTENDANCE

2003-2004: 24,765 (Division One).

DID YOU KNOW?

In terms of feet above sea level, The Hawthorns is the highest ground in the League.

BOLEYN GROUND, WEST HAM

Ground Name: Boleyn Ground
(but still known by fans as Upton Park)
Capacity: 35,647 (all-seated)
Address: Green St, Upton Park, London, E13 9AZ
Main Telephone No: 020-8548-2748
Main Fax No: 020-8548-2758
Ticket Office: 0870-112-2700
Pitch Size: 112 x 72 yards
Club Nickname: The Hammers or Irons
Home Kit Colours: Claret & Blue
Official Website: www.whufc.co.uk
Unofficial Websites:
Knees Up Mother Brown: www.kumb.com
West Ham Online: www.westhamonline.net
Unofficial West Ham:
http://whufc.4mg.com/whufc.htm
West Ham Mad: WestHammersFC.com (Footy Mad)

WHAT'S THE GROUND LIKE?

On one side of the ground is the impressive looking Dr Martens Stand that was opened in 2001. This large two-tiered stand has a capacity of 15,000. Its most striking feature can only be seen externally, where an elaborate facade comprising of two castle turrets has been built around the reception entrance area. The turrets have been

modelled on those appearing on the club crest. It is nice to see a Club actually trying to instil some character into a new stand. It currently sits a fair distance from the side of the pitch as this is intended to be moved 15 metres West, if and when the rest of the ground is redeveloped. Opposite is the smaller two-tiered East Stand. This older stand was opened in 1969. Both ends are large, smart, two-tiered stands. An electronic scoreboard is in one corner. Just outside is a handsome statue of England Captain Bobby Moore, holding aloft the World Cup Trophy which England won in 1966. The statue shows Moore being hoisted aloft by fellow West Ham players Geoff Hurst and Martin Peters with Everton defender Ray Wilson.

FUTURE GROUND DEVELOPMENTS

Building of a new East Stand plus extensions to the existing Bobby Moore and Centenary Stands have been postponed by the Club. The developments would have taken the capacity of Upton Park to 40,500 but have now been put on ice pending financial backing.

WHAT'S IT LIKE FOR VISITORS?

Away fans are housed in one end, in the lower

tier of the relatively new North Stand (also known as the Centenary Stand). The usual allocation for away supporters is 2,200 but, if demand requires, they can be allocated the whole of the lower tier of the North Stand, where up to 3,600 supporters can be accommodated. The ground is compact, with the fans seated close to the pitch. This, coupled with the passionate support of the West Ham faithful, can make for a vibrant atmosphere. However this can be intimidating for away supporters, so exercise caution around the ground. I personally enjoyed my visit and it is certainly not as bad as it was a few years ago. The West Ham fans can still give rendition of their club anthem 'I'm forever blowing bubbles....'. Inside the ground the delicious 'Football's Famous Chicken Balti Pie' (£2.20) is available.

WHERE TO DRINK

I have been advised by a number of supporters that most of the pubs around the ground are quite partisan and are for home supporters only. The Boleyn Pub, on the corner near to the ground, plus the Greengate, Wine Bar, Village and The Central pubs on Barking Road should all be given a wide berth by away fans. Kevin Hosking adds: 'Probably the best option for away fans is the Wetherspoons outlet called Millers Well which is opposite East Ham Town Hall. It is though about a 20 minute walk along Barking Road (although it may be an idea to travel to East Ham tube station before the game, go to the pub and then walk to the ground). Another good option is the Denmark Arms also on the Barking Road near the East Ham

Town Hall. This is a large pub which shows all live football games'.

GETTING THERE & WHERE TO PARK

From the M25:
Travel to M25 Junction 27, and go on to the M11 southbound. Follow the M11 south until it divides to join the A406 (North Circular Road). Take the left-hand fork signposted A406 South. Do not follow the signs for the City.

The end of the motorway joins the A406 from the left, creating a four lane road for a short distance. You need to be in one of the outside two lanes (this can be tricky if traffic is heavy). Proceed south (dual carriageway with slip roads) passing the junctions for Redbridge and Ilford.

Leave the A406 at the Barking junction. At the roundabout at the bottom of the slip road, turn right taking the third exit towards East Ham (Barking Road). Proceed West along Barking Road through several sets of traffic lights until you have passed the lights at East Ham Town Hall (big red Victorian building on the left just before the lights). Three-quarters mile further, you pass the ground on your right (behind a parade of shops, including the Hammers Shop). At the next lights (Boleyn Arms Pub on right-hand corner), turn right into Green Street. The main entrance to the ground is 200 yards on your right. Thanks to Gareth Howell for providing the directions.

On Saturday matchdays, parking is very restricted with little or nothing off-road. The best areas to look for spaces are roads left of Barking Road, once you are past the lights at East Ham

Town Hall. Andy Wright suggests: 'You can park at Newham General Hospital, where there is a pay and display car park, which costs £1.50 for four hours or £3.50 for six. To find the hospital: From Barking Road, passing the ground on your right, after a few traffic lights turn left into Prince Regent Lane (Newham General is signposted at the lights), the hospital is just up this road and is about a 15 minute stroll from the ground'.

Rob Wells adds: 'As a season ticket holder who travels to home games from Nottingham, I can offer an alternative route from the M11 to avoid the nightmare of Barking Road on a Saturday. After leaving the M11 on the A406, take the exit for A12 signposted Stratford. Stay on this road taking the underpass to the Green Man roundabout, which is a major junction. Then take the A11, again signposted Stratford. After about three miles, turn left onto the A112 signposted East Ham, through Plaistow. Carry on over the junction with Barking Road (A124). Third left after this junction is Glen Road, which takes you to the aforementioned Newham Hospital for parking. I find this journey a lot easier, although not recommended for midweek matches as the traffic gets too heavy'.

Alex Stewart suggests an alternative route: 'Come off the M25 at J29 and take the A127 to Upminster. Park at Upminster tube station (£1 for the day) and for £3.50 you can get a return ticket to Upton Park which will get you there in less than 25 minutes'.

By Train/Tube
The nearest tube station is Upton Park which is on the District, plus the Hammersmith and City Lines. The station is a short walk from the ground. Please note that West Ham tube station is nowhere near the ground. Steve Cook adds: 'The queue at Upton Park tube station after the game can be horrendous. You are better off going for a couple of pints and letting the queues die down. There are plenty of pubs along Plaistow High Road which are only a 5-10 minute walk from the stadium and as long as visitors are well behaved, they are made more than welcome'.

Andrew Saffrey adds: 'Forest Gate station is about 25 minutes walk from Upton Park and it's much less busy than Upton Park Station after the final whistle. It is served by local Great Eastern trains from Liverpool Street. Turn right out of the station, then left at the corner next to the pizza shop into Hampton Road. Walking down Hampton Road, turn first right into Richmond Road, a small street with traffic calming and lots of roundabouts. Go straight down this road and this eventually becomes Green Street. Then for the long walk down Green Street which has lots of shops and takeaways before arriving at Upton Park.

LOCAL RIVALS

Chelsea, Millwall, Tottenham and Charlton.

ADMISSION PRICES

Home Fans:
Adults: £24-£35
Concessions*: £12-£17.50
Category B prices are shown in brackets:
Away Fans:
Adults: £24
Concessions: £12
 * Juniors who are also Club members can gain a further discount on matchday prices.

PROGRAMME & FANZINES

Official Programme: £3
On The Terrace Fanzine: £2
Over Land And Sea: £2

RECORD ATTENDANCE

42,322 v Tottenham Hotspur
Division One, October 17, 1970.

AVERAGE ATTENDANCE

2003-2004: 31,167 (Division One).

DID YOU KNOW?

That the Club was formed as a works team called Thames Ironworks in 1895. Thames Ironworks were a firm of ship builders and the hammer tool was used by many a ship yard worker. The Club therefore has the nicknames 'Irons' and 'Hammers'.

JJB STADIUM, WIGAN

Ground Name: JJB Stadium
Capacity: 25,000 (all-seated)
Address: Robin Park, Newtown, Wigan WN5 0UZ
Main Telephone No: 01942-774-000
Main Fax No: 01942-770-477
Ticket Office: 0870-1122-552
Pitch Size: 110 x 60 metres
Team Nickname: Latics
Home Kit Colours: Blue with White & Green
Official Website: www.wiganlatics.co.uk
Unofficial Websites:
The Cockney Latic: www.cockneylatic.co.uk
(Rivals Network)
Ye Olde Tree & Crown:
www.yeoldetreeandcrown.34sp.com

WHAT'S THE GROUND LIKE?

For those of you who have visited Springfield Park but not yet seen the JJB Stadium, prepare to enter a different world. Saying the JJB is superb would be an understatement, it is truly magnificent. It opened in 1999 and is similar in design to Huddersfield's McAlpine Stadium, having both been built by the same company. However the JJB stadium is different in that the stands are rectangular (compared to the semi-circular at Huddersfield) and both ends have the supporting steel girders suspended from beneath the roof, rather sitting above the stand itself. The four stands are of roughly the same height and there is an electric scoreboard above the Adidas Stand, on one side of the stadium. The stadium is not totally enclosed, all corners being open. There is plenty of legroom between the rows of seats and the views of the pitch were excellent. The stands seem to rise up quite steeply and do sit back a fair distance from the pitch. Apparently the pitch utilises some sort of new type of grass - on my visit the pitch was immaculate.

The East Stand (Adidas Stand) on one side of the ground has a capacity of 8,178 and is where the away fans are housed. Opposite is the West Stand and this has a capacity of 6,022. The South Stand at one end of the ground holds 5,400 and the opposite North Stand has the same capacity. The stadium is shared with Wigan Warriors Rugby League Club.

WHAT'S IT LIKE FOR VISITORS?

Away fans are located in part of the Adidas (East Stand) at one side of the pitch. Normally, half this stand is allocated (around 4,000 seats), but if required the whole stand can be given to away supporters. I was thoroughly impressed with the stadium and found the Wigan supporters to be genuinely hospitable and knowledgeable about their football. The stadium has been designed so that even a few supporters can really make some noise, which makes for a good atmosphere. My only criticism was that the ground seemed a bit short on catering facilities, which led to long queues and with no queuing system, resulting in a free for all scrum at the counter!

Huw Illingworth adds: 'Although the facilities are exemplary I thought the ground and the atmosphere on my visit were somewhat soulless. Especially considering that the football club normally only fill a third of the stadium capacity'.

Of interest outside the ground is Robins Park, where Wigan play their reserve games and athletics meetings are held. There is quite a sizeable stand on one side of the Park, which was better than a lot that I have seen at other grounds around the country. A thoroughly pleasant day out and I would say that it is likely to be one of your better away trips this season.

WHERE TO DRINK

Jeff Taylor informs me: 'A new bar called Champions has recently opened and is directly opposite the main entrance to the JJB stadium. There is also a pub called the Red Robin a couple of minutes from the ground opposite the Cinema Complex. Both bars welcome peaceful visiting supporters'.

John Heeley from Wigan adds: 'I can happily recommend paying a visit to The Orwell at Wigan Pier before going to the stadium. It is an award winning pub with a good selection of traditional ales and regular guest beers. The food is also good. The pub is situated on the canal side and a short walk from the pub along the canal will take you to the ground. It is also only five minutes walk from both the train stations'. Having visited the Orwell myself, I can certainly echo the above comments. If you follow the A49 into Wigan from the motorway, you will pass the pub on your right. Otherwise alcohol is available inside the ground.

GETTING THERE & WHERE TO PARK

From The South:
Leave the M6 to Junction 25 then take the A49 to Wigan. After two miles you will reach a junction that has a McDonald's on your right. Turn left into Robin Park Road and continue into Scot Lane. The ground is down Scot Lane on your right.

From The North:
Leave the M6 at Junction 26 and follow the signs for Wigan town centre (this road meets the A49) then turn left into Robin Park/Scot Lane where – as above! - the ground is down Scot Lane on your right.

Car Parking:
There is plenty of free car parking at the stadium, although as you may expect there may be quite a delay in getting out after the game.

Thanks to Steve Booth for providing the directions above.

By Train
Wigan's central railway stations are a good 20 minute walk from the ground. So either take a taxi or break up the journey with a few pub stops on

the way! On exiting from either station, head under the railway bridge and keep to the right. Follow the road (A49) making sure you stick to the right for around 10 minutes. You should pass the Seven Stars Hotel and then pass under a second railway bridge. The Robin Park complex and the JJB Stadium should then be visible. Turn down Robin Park Road and you are there.

LOCAL RIVALS

Manchester City, Preston North End, Bolton Wanderers and Burnley.

ADMISSION PRICES

Home Fans:
West Stand: Adults: £17, Concessions: £12, Under 5s: Free
South Stand: Adults: £14, Concessions: £10, Under 5s: Free
North Family Stand: Adults: £14, Concessions: £10, Under16s: £4, Under 14s: £2, Under 5s: Free
Away Fans:
East Stand: Adults: £17, Concessions: £12

PROGRAMME & FANZINE

Matchday Programme: £2.50
Cockney Latic Fanzine: £1

RECORD ATTENDANCE

At JJB Stadium:
20,069 v West Ham United
Division One, May 9, 2004.
At Springfield Park:
27,526 v Hereford United
FA Cup 2nd Round, December 12, 1951.

AVERAGE ATTENDANCE

2003-2004: 9,483 (Division One).

DID YOU KNOW?

That Wigan played their first ever game in the Football League on August 19, 1978.

BRIGHTON & HOVE ALBION

WITHDEAN STADIUM, BRIGHTON

Ground Name: Withdean Stadium
Capacity: 7,053 (all-seated)
Club Contact Address: 8th Floor, Tower Point, 44 North Road, Brighton, BN1 1YR
Main Telephone No: 01273-695-400
Main Fax No: 01273-648-179
Ticket Office: 01273-776-992
Team Nickname: The Seagulls
Pitch Size: 110 x 75 yards
Home Kit Colours: Blue & White
Official Website: www.seagulls.co.uk
Unofficial Websites:
Flying High: www.bhafc.cjb.net
North Stand Chat: www.northstandchat.com
Albion Album: www.albion-album.co.uk
London Supporters: www.seagullsoverlondon.com
Brighton Fans: www.brightonfans.com

WHAT'S THE GROUND LIKE?

Brighton returned to the South Coast in 1999 after the nonsense of playing at Gillingham for two seasons. Brighton's original Goldstone Ground was closed in 1997 having been the Club's home since 1902. It is still hoped that the Club will move to a new purpose built ground in Brighton, but this process is taking longer than anyone expected, so for the time being Brighton will continue to play at the Withdean Athletics Stadium.

The initial impression of the stadium is of its picturesque surroundings, set into a hillside and mostly surrounded by woodland. One end is unused for spectators, increasing the rural look. This end is completely open, whilst the other has a couple of small temporary stands erected at either side of it, which are uncovered and therefore open to the elements. The pitch is surrounded by an athletics running track, hence the supporters are set back from the field. Although this type of multi-purpose stadium is popular on the Continent, this is the only current example in the Football League. The teams enter the field from one corner, which is unusual, making their way across some strange looking footbridges from the changing rooms. On one side of the ground, a temporary stand has been erected. This, the South Stand, has a capacity of 4,500 seats and has been designed by McAlpine and the views of the game are generally good. Opposite is the smaller North Stand, with a capacity of 1,500. This has a large Pavilion type building located behind it, which looks quite out of place at a football ground. The South Stand is raised above pitch level and uncovered, whilst the North Stand is partly covered (to the rear).

FUTURE GROUND DEVELOPMENTS

Although planning permission has been given for a new 22,000 capacity stadium at Falmer on the outskirts of Brighton, the scheme is now subject to a public enquiry, the results of which will not be available until later on in 2004. However, a report by a local planning inspector submitted to Brighton & Hove Council has indicated that the scheme should not go ahead. The Deputy Prime Minister John Prescott has the final decision on the new stadium plan and Brighton fans are now petitioning him to give the green light for construction to begin.

WHAT'S IT LIKE FOR VISITORS?

Away fans are housed in the north-east corner of the stadium, in a small temporary' stand, more reminiscent of the structures at golf's British Open than a football ground. This seated stand is uncovered, and depending on away numbers, may also be shared with Brighton supporters. Some green netting is used to separate the two sets of fans. The away capacity is between 400-800 seats, which could cause some hassle obtaining tickets for some visiting supporters. Also, as Brighton have a good following, games are all ticket and the majority sell out, so get a ticket before you travel! As you would expect from such an open stadium, the atmosphere is fairly flat. However, the Brighton supporters really try hard to get behind their team and this creates a good atmosphere. The fans also make the most of the temporary nature of the stands by making quite a large din by stamping their feet on the metal floor. The open nature of Withdean makes a visit daunting on a cold wet day.

Justin Long informs me: 'At the end of the game, a rocket went off from behind where the Brighton fans sat in the large temporary stand. This, it was explained to me, was done by a Brighton fan nicknamed "The Rocketman" and apparently he does it at every game. He watches the game by climbing trees and lets off a rocket if they score and at the end, if Brighton have won. Apparently, a couple of seasons back, Zamora got a hat-trick and he let off 3 rockets all at once. One landed on the pitch, still alight and the Club have been trying to catch him ever since but with no luck! Apparently, he has become a bit of a local legend'.

I had a fairly enjoyable day out at the stadium. This was my last ground visited of the current 92 and the Club were most accommodating in allowing me to have my photo taken on the pitch before the game. Special thanks to Club Secretary, Derek Allan, for his hospitality.

WHERE TO DRINK

Mark Collins tells me that: 'The Sportsman, at the rear of the North Stand, is now open on matchdays, though expect it to be crowded'. Otherwise Peter Hodd suggests the Preston Brewery Tap, located one mile south of the stadium, on the main A23 that is football friendly, but very crowded. Outside Brighton Mainline Station there are a number of excellent pubs. Please note that alcohol is not served within the stadium.

GETTING THERE & WHERE TO PARK

The stadium is located two miles from the town centre and is just off the London Road (A23). There is no parking allowed within a mile of the ground, due to matchday restrictions in place around the stadium (one of the conditions that was agreed for allowing Brighton to play there). Kevin Ditch tells me that: 'There is an excellent park and ride scheme which is available about one mile north of the ground, at Mill Road. Given that 90 per cent of away fans come from the north and travel down the M23/A23, this is the ideal site, as it is right next to the main road'. Colin Peel adds: 'I found the Park and Ride scheme to be brilliant; I got back in my car after the game in time for the start of Sports Report!'. Remember that your match ticket includes a park and ride ticket for either the train or bus.

By Train
The nearest railway station is Preston Park which is

about a 10-15 minute walk from the ground. The station is served by trains from London Victoria, Kings Cross and London Bridge (it is cheaper to travel from the latter two). On coming out of the station and walking down to the bottom of the hill, turn left along the A23 for the stadium or right for the Preston Brewery Tap pub. After the game, there is a football special waiting which takes you back along the short journey to Brighton. I chose to do this by parking in the city centre and then getting the train (it only takes five minutes) to Preston Park. This way you get the chance to sample the pubs around the station!

LOCAL RIVALS

With a lack of other league clubs in the area, Brighton fans have focused on Crystal Palace.

ADMISSION PRICES

Home Fans:
North Stand: Adults £22, Senior Citizens: £15, Under 16s: £14
North East Stand: Adults £21, Senior Citizens: £15, Under 16s: £14
South Stand: Adults £22, Senior Citizens: £15, Under 16s: £14
South East Stand: Adults £21, Senior Citizens: £15, Under 16s: £14
South West Stand: Adults £21, Senior Citizens: £14, Under 16s: £13
Away Fans:
Adults £21, Senior Citizens: £15, Under 16s £14.
Please note that as part of the restrictions imposed on the Club when playing at Withdean, no match tickets will be on sale on the day of the game. All match tickets must be bought in advance.

PROGRAMME & FANZINE

Official Programme: £2.50.
One F In Falmer: £1.

RECORD ATTENDANCE

At the Goldstone Ground:
36,747 v Fulham
Division Two, December 27, 1958.

AVERAGE ATTENDANCE

2003-2004: 6,248 (Division Two).

DID YOU KNOW?

That the Withdean ground was opened in 1936 and has served, amongst other things, as a Davis Cup tennis venue, a mortuary during the war, an athletics arena, a boxing venue, and a zoo!

TURF MOOR, BURNLEY

Ground Name: Turf Moor
Capacity: 22,546 (all-seated)
Address: Harry Potts Way, Burnley, BB10 4BX
Main Telephone No: 0870-443-1882
Main Fax No: 01282-700-014
Ticket Office: 0870-443-1914
Pitch Size: 115 x 73 yards
Nickname: The Clarets
Shirt Sponsors: Hunters
Home Kit Colours: Claret & Blue
Official Website:
www.burnleyfootballclub.com
Unofficial Websites:
London Clarets: http://surf.to/londonclarets
Accrington Clarets: www.accringtonclarets.co.uk
Clarets Mad: www.clarets-mad.co.uk (Footy Mad Network)
Claret Flag: www.claretflag.com (Rivals Network)

WHAT'S THE GROUND LIKE?

Half the ground was rebuilt in the mid-90s, much improving the overall look of Turf Moor. The two new stands, The Jimmy McIlroy and James Hargreaves stands, are particularly impressive at one end and one side of the ground. Both are large two-tiered stands, complete with a row of executive boxes. Both were built on two large former terraces, one of which was uncovered. The other two older stands are smaller, single-tiered and, as usual when surrounded with new stands, look worse than they actually are.

FUTURE GROUND DEVELOPMENTS

The Club are looking to purchase the adjacent Cricket Club, which would allow the redevelopment of the Cricket Field Stand to take place. The Football Club are proposing to build a two-tiered stand that would have a capacity of 7,000. However, this is dependent on finding a suitable site for the Cricket Club to relocate to. The old recreation ground in Fulledge had been proposed as a possibility, but plans were scrapped due to opposition from local residents. Therefore the redevelopment of the Stand has been put on hold, pending finding an alternative ground for the Cricket Club. If the Club are unable to relocate the Cricket Club, then they may increase the capacity of Turf Moor by adding a second tier to the Bob Lord Stand. Thanks to Dave Watson for providing the information.

WHAT'S IT LIKE FOR VISITORS?

Away fans are housed in the covered Lookers Stand (formerly the Cricket Field Stand, named because there is a cricket field behind it) at one end of the ground. This stand accommodates 4,125 supporters. Burnley are generally a well supported club and there is normally a good atmosphere; however, this can sometimes become quite intimidating for the away supporter making his way around the ground, so exercise your discretion.

WHERE TO DRINK

Tony Moore recommends the 110 Club on Yorkshire Street near the ground. This private club allows away supporters in for a nominal admission fee (20p). The club serves good reasonably priced food and children are also welcomed. They also offer a Claret & Blue bitter at only £1.10 per pint. Matthew Harrison suggests: 'The Sparrow Hawk Hotel, which is around five minutes walk away from the ground, serves good beer and food and is fine for away supporters'.

Paul Hanson adds: 'Another place I could recommend is the Queen Victoria Public House. The away fans are always directed and encouraged to park in one location, by the side of the Burnley fire station. Pass there, away from the football ground, and proceed for about 100 yards where you will find the entrance to the Queen Victoria (Brewers Fayre establishment). The ground is no more than 10 minutes walk away. Away fans visit regularly wearing their colours'. Pete Mitton also recommends the Cricket Club: 'The clubhouse at the Cricket Club (you can also park there) is open on matchdays and visitors are always made welcome (wearing colours), which is ideal as it is right next door to the ground'. Andrew Woodhall sent in this comment about the Cricket Club bar that he overheard from a visiting Gillingham fan: "Two pints of Theakstons, a bowl of pie and peas and a cigar....and still change from a fiver!" Whilst Mark Elliott informs me: 'The Woodman Inn on Todmorden Road (about a half a mile up the road from the ground) is a small and friendly enough place for away supporters, providing they are sensible and don't mind a bit of banter, plus the pub has a large screen which shows Sky Sports'.

Ian Pilkington advises: 'The Turf Hotel on Yorkshire Street and pubs in the town centre should be avoided. Colours are best covered up in and around the centre of town'.

GETTING THERE & WHERE TO PARK

Leave the M6 at Junction 29 and onto the M65. Leave the M65 at Junction 10 and follow signs for Towneley Hall. This road eventually goes past the ground. There is a car park designated for away fans at the cricket ground right next door. Otherwise, street parking.

BY TRAIN

There are two train stations that are in walking distance of Turf Moor – Burnley Central and Burnley Manchester Road. Central station is around a 20 minute walk from the ground and is mostly served by local trains. Manchester Road is a 15 minute walk and is served by the faster express service. Walking directions from both are as follows:

Manchester Road:
On leaving the station, cross the main road towards the cinema. The ground should be clearly visible in the distance straight ahead. Turn left and progress down Centenary Way, a dual carriageway (A682) that you cannot miss, going downhill towards the ground. A few minutes walk down this road will bring you to a roundabout where you should turn right under the canal bridge into Yorkshire Street (A671). Continue down this road and you will reach Turf Moor on your left, with the away stand the first to be reached. Thanks to Rob Quinn for providing the directions and station information.

Central Station:
Walk out of the station and across the road down towards a small retail area including Fads and Halfords Cycles. You will reach the inner ring road (A679), where you turn left and after about 200 yards you will reach a set of traffic lights. Turn right at the lights into Church Street (A682). Continue down Church Street until you reach a large roundabout at which you turn left under the canal bridge into Yorkshire Street (A671). Continue down this road and you will reach Turf Moor on your left, with the away stand the first to be reached. Thanks to Paul Hanson for providing the directions.

LOCAL RIVALS

Blackburn Rovers, Preston North End, Bolton Wanderers, and Blackpool.

ADMISSION PRICES

Home Fans:
Bob Lord Stand Adults: £19, Concessions: £12, Juniors: £9.50
James Hargreaves (Upper) Adults: £19, Concessions: £12, Juniors: £9.50
James Hargreaves (Lower) Adults: £17, Concessions: £11, Juniors: £8.50
Jimmy McIlroy (Upper) Adults: £17, Concessions: £11, Juniors: £8.50
Jimmy McIlroy (Lower) Adults: £16, Concessions: £10, Juniors: £8
Away Fans:
Lookers Stand: Adults: £19, £17, Concessions: £11, Juniors: £8.50

PROGRAMME & FANZINE

Official Programme: £2.50.
Bob Lord's Sausage Fanzine: £1.

RECORD ATTENDANCE

54,775 v Huddersfield Town
FA Cup 3rd Round, February 23, 1924.

AVERAGE ATTENDANCE

2003-2004: 12,541 (Division One).

DID YOU KNOW?

That Burnley have not always played in their famous claret and blue. The first colours were black and yellow stripes earning the club the nickname "Hornets".

NINIAN PARK, CARDIFF

Ground Name: Ninian Park
Capacity: 20,000
Address: Sloper Road, Cardiff, CF11 8SX
Main Telephone No: 02920-221-001
Main Fax No: 02920-341-148
Ticket Office: 0845-345-1400
Pitch Size: 110 x 70 yards
Team Nickname: The Bluebirds
Home Kit Colours: All Blue with White Trim
Official Website: www.cardiffcityfc.co.uk
Unofficial Websites:
Bluebirds Online: www.bluebirdsonline.com
Valley Rams: www.valleyrams.com
A Sleeping Giant: www.ccfcsleepinggiant.com
(Rivals Network)

WHAT'S THE GROUND LIKE?

The ground at long last is having an uplift after the arrival of the present Chairman, Sam Hammam. The John Smiths Grange End is a large former open terrace that now has a roof installed. This end is shared between home and away supporters. Opposite is the Spar Family Stand. This small, covered, all-seated stand has a number of supporting pillars running across the front. The overall appearance of this stand has changed recently, with the roof repainted with a large advert for the Clubs sponsors, Redrow. On one side of the ground is the Popular Bank Stand. This has a raised seating area to its rear and terracing at its front. There are a couple of supporting pillars in the seated area, whilst the roof does not cover the front terrace. Painted onto the roof is a huge advert for a local discount store. On the other side of the ground is the Grandstand. This two-tiered stand is covered and all-seated and

again has some supporting pillars. The ground also benefits from having some striking floodlight pylons at each corner of the ground.

FUTURE GROUND DEVELOPMENTS

The Club have submitted plans to Cardiff Council to build a 60,000 capacity stadium at Leckwith, opposite Ninian Park. The site, which currently houses a small athletics stadium, would be redeveloped at a cost of around £100m. Initially, a 30,000 capacity stadium would be built which could then be expanded to 60,000 if required. The scheme could also see the building of a hotel and a retail park. Sam Hammam has hinted that the new stadium may be named after St David, the Patron Saint of Wales. The existing athletics stadium would be relocated and Ninian Park would be sold for housing.

WHAT'S IT LIKE FOR VISITORS?

Away fans are housed on one side of the John Smiths Grange Terrace at one end of the ground. Around 1,000 away fans can be accommodated in this covered area, but this can be increased if demand requires it (maximum 2,000). Strangely, this area has a mix of seating to the front and terrace to the rear. This end is also shared with home supporters with the obligatory 'no-mans' land in-between. This consists of a fence, netting to prevent missiles being thrown and on top of the fence a sign which reads 'Cardiff City accept no liability for any damage caused by the non-drying security paint on the top of this fence'. So if you see someone with blue hands, you know where they have been! I personally did not experience any problems when I went, but it is worth bearing in mind that the Cardiff fans are passionate about their Club and this can make for an intimidating atmosphere. I would recommend that colours be kept covered up around the ground and in the adjacent car parks.

Scott Chapman, a visiting Plymouth Argyle supporter, adds: 'I found Cardiff to be particularly intimidating. There were a large amount of police on duty and away fans had to receive a police escort out of the ground after the game had ended. Not the most pleasant of away trips last season.'

WHERE TO DRINK

Dan Portillo recommends The Lansdowne, on Lansdowne Road. The owner (Roger) is a Cardiff City nut and the pub has wall-to-wall memorabilia. But most importantly, it is frequented by 'proper' City fans and visiting fans are safe there to enjoy a beer or two and a chat with the locals before the game. Mike Dibble recommends the Cornwall Hotel, which is also a pub. It's a 5-10minute walk from the ground and stands in Cornwall Street (taxi £2.50 from Central station). As Mike says: 'I use the Cornwall pre-match and have never witnessed any trouble over the last five or so years I have frequented it. Away fans are left to enjoy a trouble free pint. It has the usual variety of beers on tap including Brains and has a useful Chinese/chippy directly opposite for a munch.'

GETTING THERE & WHERE TO PARK

To avoid driving through the centre of Cardiff, leave the M4 at junction 33 and take the A4232 towards Cardiff/Barry. Keep on the A4232 towards Cardiff and then leave the dual carriageway at the B4267 exit signposted 'Cardiff (Leckwith) Athletics Stadium'. Follow the signs for the stadium and after about half a mile you will see Ninian Park over on your right. There is a huge car park at the ground.

By Train
The nearest train station is Ninian Park Halt, which is only a couple of minutes walk from the ground. This station is on a local line which is served by trains from Cardiff Central. Alternatively, as Barry Hodges informs me: 'Grangetown station is around a 10-15 minute walk away from Ninian Park and is served by fairly frequent trains from Cardiff Central that continue onto Penarth or Barry Island. On leaving Grangetown station turn left, cross the main road and then turn right into Sloper road for the ground'.

LOCAL RIVALS

Swansea City and from a little further away, Bristol City.

ADMISSION PRICES

The Club operate a category scheme (A & B)

whereby the most popular matches cost more to watch. Category B prices are shown in brackets.
Home Fans:
Grandstand Upper Centre: Adults: £27 (£25), Concessions: £23 (£21)
Grandstand Upper Wings: Adults: £24 (£22), Concessions: £22 (£20)
Grandstand Lower: Adults: £23 (£21), Concessions: £20 (£18), Under 10s: £14 (£12)
Popular Bank Seating (Centre): Adults: £22 (£20), Concessions: £18 (£16)
Popular Bank Seating (Wings & Back): Adults: £21 (£19), Concessions: £17 (£15)
Popular Bank Terrace: Adults: £18 (£16), Concessions: £12 (£10)
John Smiths Grange End Terrace*: Adults: £21 (£19), Concessions: £16 (£14)
Spar Family Stand: Adults: £20 (£18), Under 15s/OAPs: £12 (£10), Under 10s: £10 (£8)
Away Fans:
John Smiths Grange End: Adults: £21 (£19), Concessions: £16 (£14)
The Club offer discounts of up to £3 on game tickets if bought prior to matchday. Concessions apply to OAPs and Under 16s.
* Please note that only members of the Club can purchase tickets for this area.

PROGRAMME & FANZINES

Official Programme: £2.50
Thin Blue Line Fanzine: 50p
Barmy Army Fanzine: 70p
Ramzine Fanzine: £1

RECORD ATTENDANCE

For Ninian Park:
61,556 Wales v England
October 14, 1961.
For A Cardiff Match:
57,893 v Arsenal
Division One, April 22, 1953.

AVERAGE ATTENDANCE

2003-2004: 15,569 (Division One).

DID YOU KNOW?

That the ground was named after Lord Ninian Crichton Stuart who guaranteed to pay the annual rent on the new ground in 1910.

HIGHFIELD ROAD, COVENTRY

Ground Name:	Highfield Road
Capacity:	23,627 (all seated)
Address:	King Richard St, Coventry, CV2 4FW
Main Telephone No:	024-7623-4000
Main Fax No:	024-7623-4099
Ticket Office Enquiries:	024-7623-4020
Ticket Booking Line:	024-7657-8000
Club Nickname:	The Sky Blues
Pitch Size:	110 x 75 yards
Home Kit Colours:	Sky Blue & White
Official Website:	www.ccfc.co.uk

Unofficial Websites:
Lets All Sing Together: www.letsallsingtogether.com
Gary Mabbutt's Knee:
http://coventrycity.rivals.net/default.asp?sid=885
(Rivals Network)

WHAT'S THE GROUND LIKE?

Although the ground is beginning to show its age, it is still an enjoyable place to watch football as the crowd is close to the playing action. The stadium used to have a large open terrace at one end and this has been replaced by the East Stand, which is single-tiered with a couple of supporting pillars. The other end is a two-tiered stand that has an upper shelf which partly overlaps the lower tier. The upper tier has supporting pillars. One side, the North Stand, is a two-tiered stand again with some supporting pillars which could obstruct your view. Away supporters are housed in one side of this stand. On the other side of this stand is the single-tiered Britannia Tyres (Main) Stand, which has a row of executive boxes running across the top of the seating area. All four stands are of fair size and are of

roughly equal height. The ground, although only having one corner totally filled with seating, feels quite enclosed as the stands are close together. On one side of the ACE Resources West Stand is a strange looking three storey structure, used for corporate hospitality. On the stand's other side is an electric scoreboard. The ground does not have any floodlight pylons, instead having lights attached to the roofs of the stands.

Chris Hyams informs me: 'You may be interested to know that Highfield Road was the first League ground to experiment with all-seating in the early 1980s'.

FUTURE GROUND DEVELOPMENTS

Thanks to Coventry City Council, who pledged £21m to the Coventry Arena Development, the Club will now be moving to a new stadium in which they hope to kick off the 2005/06 season. The Arena Development will not only include a new 32,000 all-seated stadium for the Sky Blues, but also a retail development and railway station. Work has already begun at the site of a former gasworks in the Foleshill area of Coventry and the white steelwork has begun to be erected, which can be seen not too far away from Junction 3 of the M6. The new stadium will be owned by Coventry City Council and leased back to the Club. Highfield Road has now been sold and will be redeveloped for housing, but will not be vacated by the Club until the new stadium is open. The new stadium is to be called the 'Jaguar Arena' under a corporate sponsorship deal

WHAT'S IT LIKE FOR VISITORS?

Away fans are located on one side of the pitch, in

the North Stand. Just over 4,000 away fans can be accommodated on one side of this stand, next to the ACE Resources West Stand. Away fans occupy both the upper and lower tiers of this stand, with tickets to the upper tier normally sold first. There is one supporting pillar in the upper tier which may obstruct your view. Legroom is quite tight in this area and the general facilities are really showing their age. I have been to Highfield Road on a number of occasions and have not experienced any problems. However, my only real criticism is that the ground sometimes lacks atmosphere. This is generally because for most games it is only two-thirds full. The delicious 'Football's Famous Chicken Balti Pie' (£2) is available inside the ground.

WHERE TO DRINK

The traditional haunt of the away fans, the Sky Blue Tavern, is no longer in business, so you will need to travel further afield to get a pint. Merv Williams recommends the Rose and Crown on Walsgrave Road. Benn Nunn informs me: 'The best decent pubs near the ground (and they are few and far in-between) are the Rose and Woodbine in Barras Green, just to the north-east of the ground, and the Biggin Hall Hotel on Binley Road, which is the main road approaching the ground from the East'. Whilst Steve Browett adds: 'I would recommend the Hastings on Clay Lane. It is about a five minute walk from the ground. It's a Bass House which has separate bars for home and away supporters, who are always made welcome'.

GETTING THERE & WHERE TO PARK

Leave the M6 at Junction 3. Take the A444 towards the City Centre. Go across four islands and at the fifth one turn right (signposted Football Ground). Turn left at the next island, follow the road around to the right and at the next island bear to the left. The ground is a short distance down this road on the right. Street parking.

By Train
The ground is a good 20 minute walk from Coventry train station. Thanks to Paul McKay for providing the following directions to the ground: 'Come out of the station and walk straight ahead, using the series of subways and bridges which go over the ring road towards the City Centre. These take you to the Bull Yard (a small park/garden) next to Warwick Road. Carry on up the ramp past HMV and the banks and when you see Cathedral Lanes and the Lady Godiva tent, turn right. Go down this road passing the Council House (on the left) and the old Odeon (on the right). You then walk under the ring road. This is now Gosford St. Keep on this road until the traffic lights of Sky Blue Way, where you cross over into Walsgrave Road. Then depending on which stand

you are in, take either the first, second, or third on your left where you will see the mighty Highfield Road stadium in front of you. If you see something else, then without wishing to state the obvious, you may have gone the wrong way!'

LOCAL RIVALS

Aston Villa, Leicester City, Birmingham City, West Bromwich Albion, and Wolverhampton Wanderers.

ADMISSION PRICES

Home Fans:
Britannia Tyres (Main Stand): Adults: £22, Senior Citizen: £11, Junior £6.50
North Stand: Adults: £19,   Senior Citizen: £9.50, Junior £6.50
East Stand: Adults: £19,   Senior Citizen: £9.50, Junior £6.50,
ACE Resources West Stand: Adults: £16, Senior Citizen: £8, Students £10.50, Junior £6.50
West Stand: Adults: £15, Students £10, Senior Citizen: £7.50, Junior £6
Away Fans:
North Stand: Adults: £19,   Senior Citizen: £9.50, Junior £6.50.

PROGRAMME & FANZINES

Official Programme: £2.50
Twist & Shout Fanzine: £1

RECORD ATTENDANCE

51,455 v Wolverhampton Wanderers
Division 2, April 29, 1967.

AVERAGE ATTENDANCE

2003-2004: 14,816 (Division One).

DID YOU KNOW?

That the sky blue club colour was introduced in 1889. The city used to be a major good producer of coloured materials, especially sky blue. There is an old expression 'As true as Coventry Blue'.

CREWE ALEXANDRA

ALEXANDRA STADIUM, CREWE

Ground Name: Alexandra Stadium
(but still known to a lot of fans as Gresty Road)
Capacity: 10,066 (all-seated)
Address: Gresty Road, Crewe,
Cheshire, CW2 6EB
Main Telephone No: 01270-213-014
Ticket Office: 01270-252-610
Main Fax No: 01270-216-320
Pitch Size: 112 x 74 yards
Team Nickname: The Railwaymen
Official Website: www.creweAlex.net
Unofficial Websites:
www.crewealex.co.uk (Rivals Network)

WHAT'S THE GROUND LIKE?

The building of the £6m pound Air Products Stand
(formerly known as the Railtrack Stand) in 1999
changed forever the look and feel of the ground.
Before, it had always been small and homely, but
the addition of the Air Products Stand has drastically
changed the overall scene. The stand, which sits
proudly along one side of the pitch, is a single-tier
cantilever holding just under 7,000 people. It looks
huge compared to the other stands and must be at
least three times the size of the old Main Stand.
Considering that the overall capacity of the ground
is just over 10,000, one can understand how the Air
Products Stand dominates Gresty Road. The other
three separate stands are roughly of the same
height, but are rather small. So much so, that a
number of footballs are shot out of the ground
during a game. The newest of these smaller stands is
the Advance Personnel Stand (previously known as
the Gresty Road End). This replaced a former open

terrace and seats around 900. An unusual feature is
the absence of dugouts. Instead, the teams are given
a section of seating at the front of the Air Products
Stand. You will also notice that the pitch is slightly
raised above ground level.

FUTURE GROUND DEVELOPMENTS

At some point in the future, the Club hope to
replace the Blue Bell BMW Stand (formerly
known as the Popular Side) with a new two-tiered
stand, which will also contain executive boxes.

WHAT'S IT LIKE FOR VISITORS?

Away fans are housed in the Blue Bell BMW
Stand at one side of the ground. The whole of this
stand is given to away supporters and houses
1,680 fans, though if required the Charles Audi
Family Stand can also be allocated to away fans.
Entrance to the away stand is by ticket only (no
cash is accepted at ironically some of the oldest
turnstiles I have ever seen at a League Ground).
Tickets need to be purchased from the ticket
booth next to the supporters' club at the entrance
to this stand. Please also note that alcohol is not
available in this stand.
Under Dario Gradi, Crewe continue to play
some attractive football and the games that I
attended were no exception. It is amazing in this
day and age to think that he has now managed
Crewe for 20 years. I found Crewe to be relaxed
and friendly, making for a good day out. However,
the addition of the Air Products Stand has made
the ground atmosphere a little flat, even with the

efforts of the Crewe supporters (including a drummer) in the Advance Personnel Stand, to boost it. There is a popular fish and chip shop just outside the stadium, the smell of which, early in the game, wafts across the ground.

WHERE TO DRINK

If you get there reasonably early before the game, the supporters' club at the ground allows small numbers of away fans in. There are also a several pubs within walking distance of the ground. The pick of these is probably the Brunswick on Nantwich Road (same road as the train station). Although the pub does not look that welcoming with a number of bouncers on the door, once inside you will find a nice mix of home and away supporters. Jim Alex recommends 'The Barrel' further along on Nantwich Road. There are also a couple of handy fish & chip shops located along this road.

GETTING THERE & WHERE TO PARK

Leave the M6 at Junction 16 and take the A5020 towards Crewe. Follow this road right into Crewe. At the roundabout junction with the A534, Nantwich Road, turn left. Gresty Road is down past the Railway Station on the left. Just before you reach this island you will see a sign pointing to the right, which displays 'Away Supporters On Street Parking'. This directs you to an industrial estate on the right of the road (you will also see the Volkswagen dealership, L C Charles on the front of it). It takes about 15 minutes to walk to the ground from here.

By Train
The ground is only a few minutes walk from the train station. As you come out of the Railway Station turn left and Gresty Road is down the road on your left.

LOCAL RIVALS

Port Vale, Stoke City and Wrexham.

ADMISSION PRICES

All Areas Of The Ground:
Adults: £17, OAPs: £13.50, Students: £5.50, Juniors: £4.50
Discounts on these prices (in some cases up to £2) are available to Club members purchasing tickets in advance of matchday

PROGRAMME & FANZINE

Official Programme: £2
Super Dario Land Fanzine: £1

RECORD ATTENDANCE

20,000 v Tottenham Hotspur
FA Cup 4th Round, January 6, 1960.

AVERAGE ATTENDANCE

2003-2004: 7,741 (Division One).

DID YOU KNOW?

That the Club took their name after the town and the then Princess Alexandra.

CRYSTAL PALACE, SELHURST PARK

Ground Name: Selhurst Park
Capacity: 26,309 (all-seated)
Address: Selhurst Park, London,
SE25 6PU
Main Telephone No: 0208-768-6000
Ticket Office: 0208-771-8841
Fax No: 0208-771-5311
Team Nickname: The Eagles
Pitch Size: 110 x 74 yards
Home Kit Colours: Red & Blue
Official Website: www.cpfc.co.uk
Unofficial Websites:
Holmesdale Online: http://holmesdale.cjb.net/
Red n Blue Army: www.rednbluearmy.com
Bulletin Board Services: www.cpfc.org

WHAT'S THE GROUND LIKE?

Both ends of the ground have had new stands constructed in recent years, much improving the overall look of the ground. The two-tiered Holmesdale Road Stand is at one end and is where the bulk of home supporters congregate. This stand has a large lower tier, with a smaller upper tier that overhangs it. The stand looks impressive and has a large curved roof, as well as windshields on either side of the upper tier. Opposite is the Whitehorse Lane Stand. This is unusual in having a single tier of seating, with a double row of executive boxes above them. A

video screen perches on the roof, which somehow doesn't look as if it was originally meant to be fitted there. This stand has now been renamed the 'Croydon Advertiser Family Stand'. One side is the large, covered, single-tiered Arthur Wait stand, while on the other side the Main Stand is also single-tiered. Both stands are now beginning to show their age; for example, both have wooden seating and a number of supporting pillars and the Main Stand has a row of small floodlights perched on its roof. The Arthur Wait Stand has a TV gantry suspended beneath its roof. Michael Clement says: 'To add a bit of razzmatazz at the beginning of games, the Club now play a programme of loud music as the teams emerge onto the pitch'. This includes playing 'Glad All Over' by the Dave Clarke Five, which is enthusiastically joined in by the Palace fans.

FUTURE GROUND DEVELOPMENTS

'There were plans to redevelop the Main Stand, with a similar looking stand to the current Holmesdale Road Stand. However due to the opposition of local residents, these plans have been put on ice. The Club may now have to look for a site on which to build a new stadium', says Michael Clement.

CRYSTAL PALACE

WHAT'S IT LIKE FOR VISITORS?

On the whole, Crystal Palace is a fairly relaxed ground to visit and you are unlikely to encounter any problems, except perhaps getting stuck in traffic on the way to the game! Away fans are located in one corner of the Arthur Wait Stand near to the Holmesdale Road End, where just over 2,000 away supporters can be accommodated. Nikita, a visiting Gillingham fan, adds: 'If you are seated towards the rear of the stand then you will find that you are sitting on old wooden seats and there is very little legroom'.

On my last visit there was a particularly good atmosphere within the ground. I was impressed with the Palace fans, who clearly were passionate about their Club, but in a non-intimidating manner to away fans. In fact there was plenty of good banter going on between the two sets of supporters. Within the Arthur Wait Stand, there are plenty of refreshments available, including burgers (£2) and chips (£1), however, please note that alcohol is not served to away fans. Also if you do happen to visit the gents, watch out for the small downward flight of steps to the toilets. I almost went flying!

WHERE TO DRINK

Opposite Thornton Heath Railway Station there is a Wetherspoons pub, popular with both home and away supporters. It is about a 15-minute walk from here to the ground (as you come out of the pub turn right and follow the other fans). There are plenty of kebab and chip shops available enroute to the ground.

Phil Moore recommends the following pubs around Selhurst Park, where on the whole, away fans are tolerated: 'Good news for real ale lovers is that Palace is surrounded by more CAMRA listed pubs than ever, I think there are four or five in the 2004 Good Beer Guide. Not to mention the two new Wetherspoon outfits'.

Around Selhurst Railway Station:
Two Brewers - Gloucester Road
From the station cross the road using the zebra crossing and turn right (heading away from ground). Gloucester Road is third on the left. Comfortable cottage type pub. Small public bar,

Shepherd Neame ales on sale - rare outside Kent.
Clifton Arms - Clifton Road
Turn left out of the station and take the third road on the left. This is the nearest pub to the stadium. A big Victorian corner pub well known for high quality of ales. Selection changes weekly. Three or four bitters always on. Drawback: due to its popularity, away fans will only be admitted if they turn up early. After 1:30pm, it's Palace season ticket holders only past the doorman.

Around Thornton Heath Railway Station:
The Railway Telegraph - Brigstock Road
From the station, cross the road (zebra) and turn right. The pub is 100 yards down this road. A spacious Youngs house. Firm favourite with away fans. There's also a Wetherspoon' s pub directly opposite the station.

Around Norwood Junction Railway Station:
The Alliance - Station Road (by clock tower)
A gem. Usually two real ales. Narrow shape of bar does means it can get crowded when waiting for service. Bar staff are friendly.
Wetherspoon - South Norwood High Street
A few doors down from the Alliance. Standard Wetherspoon's fare.
The Ship - South Norwood High Street
From the station, turn right at the Clock Tower into the High St. Continue down to cross roads with Portland Road. Cross with care and carry on for another 100 metres. The Ship is a free house with three to four real ales and ciders. Has wooden floor, juke box SKY TV. Very noisy.
The Portmanor - Portland Road
From the station, turn right at the Clock Tower into the High St. Continue down to cross roads with Portland Road. At crossroads turn right heading downhill under the railway bridge. You can't miss the pub. Do not be put off by garish disco decor as this place serves great beers. Usually three real ales. There are banks of TVs behind the bar that are continuously screening football.

Alternatively alcohol is served inside the ground.

GETTING THERE & WHERE TO PARK

Leave the M25 at Junction 7 and follow the signs for the A23 to Croydon. At Purley, bear left onto the A23 at its junction with the A 235 (to Croydon). You will pass roundabouts and junctions with the A232 and A236 as you pass Croydon, after which the A23 bears left at Thornton Heath (at the Horseshoe pub roundabout). Here you must go straight over, into Brigstock Road (B266), passing Thornton Heath Station on your left and bearing right onto the High Street. At the next mini roundabout (Whitehorse Road/Grange Road), go left into Whitehorse Lane. The ground is on your right.

Thanks to Richard Down for providing the alternative directions: 'An alternative route for fans coming from the North is to leave the M25 at Junction 10 and follow the A3 towards London. After about ten miles you will reach the Tolworth roundabout at which you turn right onto the A240 towards Epsom. After about three miles turn onto the A232 towards Sutton. Follow the A232 through Sutton and Carshalton and just before reaching Croydon, turn left onto the A23 north towards Thornton Heath' where the A23 bears left at Thornton Heath (at the Horseshoe pub roundabout). Here you must go straight over, into Brigstock Road (B266), passing Thornton Heath Station on your left and bearing right on to the High Street. At the next mini roundabout (Whitehorse Road/Grange Road), go left into Whitehorse Lane. The ground is on your right.

There is plenty of street parking in the area. Please note that the traffic can be pretty bad on Saturdays even without football traffic, so make sure you allow yourself some extra time to make the journey.

By Train

The nearest railway stations are Selhurst or Thornton Heath which are served by London Victoria main line station, Clapham Junction, London Bridge (every 30 mins) and East Croydon (every 15 mins). You can also use Norwood Junction station which is served by Victoria, but is a little further away. It is then a 10-15 minute walk to ground. Note that Crystal Palace station is nowhere near the ground.

If you are coming from outside London, it may be an idea to purchase a 'Travelcard' at the first tube station you encounter (or some train operators also allow you to add this onto your train ticket) and tell the clerk that you want a 'Travelcard' that will cover you as far as Selhurst or Thornton Heath. The card then allows you unlimited travel on the tube and trains within the London travel zone and avoids having to buy a ticket for each leg of the journey.

LOCAL RIVALS

Charlton Athletic, Millwall and, a little further away, Brighton and Hove Albion.

ADMISSION PRICES

Executive Area/Directors Box: Adults: £55, Concessions: £39
Main Stand: Adults: £40, Concessions: £24
Croydon Advertiser Family Stand (Whitehorse Lane Stand): Adults: £30, Concessions: £16
Holmesdale Stand (Gallery): Adults: £40, No Concessions
Holmesdale Stand (Upper): Adults: £35, Concessions: £16
Holmesdale Stand (Lower): Adults: £35, Concessions: £16
Arthur Wait Stand (Including Away Fans): Adults: £35, Concessions: £21

Please note that members of the official Crystal Palace supporters club and Junior Eagles Club can receive a £2 discount on these ticket prices.

PROGRAMME

Official Programme: £2.50.

RECORD ATTENDANCE

51,482 v Burnley
Division Two, May 11, 1979.

AVERAGE ATTENDANCE

2003-2004: 17,344 (Division One).

DID YOU KNOW?

Palace, wearing blue and white at the time, were a working men's team, founded by employees at the Crystal Palace in 1861.

PRIDE PARK STADIUM, DERBY

Ground Name:	Pride Park Stadium
Capacity:	33,597 (all seated)
Address:	Pride Park Stadium,
	Derby, DE24 8XL
Main Telephone No:	0870-444-1884
Main Fax No:	01332-667540
Pitch Size:	105 x 68 metres
Club Nickname:	The Rams
Shirt Sponsors:	Marstons Pedigree
Home Kit Colours:	Black & White
Official Website:	www.dcfc.co.uk

Unofficial Websites:
The Rams: www.therams.co.uk
Popside Message Board: www.popside.com

WHAT'S THE GROUND LIKE?

The ground is a big, handsome change from the old Baseball Ground, which was the former home of the Club since 1895. The new stadium was opened by Her Majesty the Queen in 1997, and is totally enclosed with all corners being filled. One corner has executive boxes, giving the stadium a continental touch. The large Toyota West Stand, which runs down one side of the pitch, is two-tiered, complete with a row of executive boxes. The rest of the ground is smaller in size than the West Stand, as the roof drops a tier to the other sides, making it look unbalanced. It is a pity that the West Stand could not be replicated throughout the rest of the stadium as this would have made it truly magnificent.

WHAT'S IT LIKE FOR VISITORS?

Away fans are located at one end of the stadium in the Cawarden (South) Stand, where the allocation is normally 3,000, although this can be increased to 4,800 if demand requires it. I have thoroughly enjoyed my visits to Pride Park. The stadium and the facilities within it are superb. The PA system is almost better than you would experience in a cinema and queuing for a beer behind the stands reminded me of being at a theme park, as you are able to watch television screens as you wait. The Derby supporters are passionate about their team and this, coupled with the stadium design, makes for a great noisy atmosphere. I found the Derby supporters friendly and did not experience any problems at all. The delicious 'Football's Famous Chicken Balti Pie' (£2) is available inside the ground, as well as burgers, hot dogs and chips. The game is shown live on these screens, with commentary, so that you don't have to miss a thing while waiting for your half-time cuppa. There is also a Ladbrokes betting outlet. Please note that you have to buy a match ticket before entering the stadium from the lottery office adjacent to the away turnstiles.

WHERE TO DRINK

There are a couple of pubs opposite the station, such as the Merry Widows, that tend to be the favourite haunts of away supporters. However, unless you are going to arrive mob-handed, then it is probably best to turn right out of the station and make your way down to The Brunswick or Alexandra Hotel. Both these pubs have a railway theme, serve a great range of real ales and offer a selection of filled rolls. Although they both have bouncers on the doors, away fans are normally let in as long as there is no singing. There are bars at the back of the stands (£2.50 a pint), however they do get quite crowded.

GETTING THERE & WHERE TO PARK

From the M1, exit at Junction 25 and take the A52 towards Derby. The ground is signposted off the A52 after about seven miles. Stephen Wilson informs me: 'The away fans car park is signposted from the A52. It is the car park of the Derby Tertiary College. There is a £4 charge and it is about a 10 minute walk to the stadium (walk back out of car park onto the main road (Pride Park Way), cross over railway bridge and the stadium is straight ahead)'. Otherwise it may an idea to park in the centre of town and then walk to the ground. Whilst Kenny Lyon adds: 'Perhaps a better place to park for all fans is the cattle market car park. This costs £2 and is about 5-10 minutes walk from the ground and is just off the A52. To get there, go past the normal turning for the stadium and go up to the 'pentagon roundabout'; take the first turning off there and then take the next left - you then drive about 300 yards back on yourself, passing it on your left as you drive along the A52'.

By Train
The ground is about 15 minutes walk from Derby railway station and is signposted. As you exit, turn right and at the bottom of the road turn right again and follow the crowd.

LOCAL RIVALS

Nottingham Forest and Leicester City.

ADMISSION PRICES

Home Fans
Adults: £17-£32
Concessions: £6-£17
Away Fans
Adults: £17-£27
Concessions: £6-£14

Derby operate a category system for pricing match tickets, with the most popular games costing more to watch. It will mean that for most games the lowest ticket prices quoted above will not be available. Please also note that the Club offer a £2 discount on adult tickets and a £1 discount on concession tickets if purchased prior to matchday.

PROGRAMME

Official Programme: £2.50.

RECORD ATTENDANCE

At Pride Park;
33,597 England v Mexico
Friendly, May 25, 2001.
For a Derby game at Pride Park:
33,378 V Liverpool
Premier League, March 18, 2000
At the Baseball Ground;
41,826 v Tottenham Hotspur
Division One, September 20, 1969.

AVERAGE ATTENDANCE

2003-2004: 22,330 (Division One).

DID YOU KNOW?

That Derby County sported the Derbyshire County Cricket Club's colours of amber, chocolate and pale blue in their earliest days.

KINGSTON COMMUNICATIONS STADIUM, HULL CITY

Ground Name: Kingston Communications Stadium
Capacity: 25,504 (all-seated)
Address: The Circle, Walton St, Hull, HU3 6HU
Main Telephone No: 0870-837-0003
Main Fax No: 01482-304-882
Ticket Office: 0870-837-0004
Ticket Office Fax: 01482-304-923
Team Nickname: The Tigers
Pitch Size: 114 x 78 yards
Home Kit Colours: Amber & Black
Official Website: www.hullcityafc.net
Unofficial Websites:
Amber Nectar: www.ambernectar.com
Hull City Online: www.hullcity.com (Footy Mad)
Tigers Cooperative: www.tigersco-op.org.uk
Three O'Clock At Kempton:
www.thekempton.com
City Independent: www.cityindependent.com
(Rivals Network)
Southern Supporters: www.hcss.org.uk

WHAT'S THE GROUND LIKE?

The Kingston Communications Stadium (commonly referred to as the KC Stadium) was opened in December 2002. It cost almost £44m to build, by Birse Construction and is home to both Hull Football and Rugby League Clubs. I'm

not a fan of most of the bland new grounds, but the KC Stadium is an exception to this rule. Built in a parkland setting, it can be seen for some distance around and will undoubtedly win awards for its impressive design.

The stadium is totally enclosed, with the West Stand being around twice the size of the other three sides. The roof rises up and curves around the West Stand, giving the stadium an interesting look. Inside, the curves continue as each of the stands slightly bow around the playing area, drawing the eye to sweep panoramically around them. Each stand is single-tiered, apart from the two-tiered West Stand. This stand also has a row of executive boxes running across its middle. There is an electric scoreboard at the North End of the stadium, where the Police Control Box is also situated. The pitch looked in excellent condition on my visit in January, plus under soil heating has been installed. The P.A. system within the stadium is also excellent. All told, this a stadium that would not look out of place in the Premiership.

FUTURE GROUND DEVELOPMENTS

The stadium has been built in such a way that at some stage, an additional tier could be added to the East Stand. It is also possible to add another 2,000 seats at each end of the ground by moving the retaining wall back over the concourse. These developments would raise the capacity to over 30,000.

WHAT'S IT LIKE FOR VISITORS?

Away fans are located in the North Stand End of the ground, where up to 4,000 supporters can be housed, although the normal allocation is half that number. As you would expect a visit to the KC Stadium is far pleasanter than it was to the old Boothferry Park. The facilities available are good, plus there is not a bad view of the playing action to be found anywhere (although you are a little set back from the pitch). On the concourse alcohol is available, plus burgers, pies etc. including the delicious 'Football's Famous Chicken Balti Pie' (£2.20). I found the atmosphere to be good within the stadium, but unfortunately there is an element of Hull support that feel the need to berate away supporters throughout the game. This, coupled with the fact that there are no pubs nearby that welcomes away fans, means that although it is a truly magnificent stadium it is still not the greatest of days out.

Please note that the stadium has been designated a no smoking and a no standing area. The latter decree does seem a little ridiculous. This has led to some unpleasant confrontations between away fans and stewards, so you have been warned. You can though smoke on the concourses but not at your seat.

WHERE TO DRINK

There are a number of pubs within a few minutes walk of the stadium, but these are all designated as being for home supporters only. Most local fans still seem to be heading for pubs situated around Boothferry Park. These are best avoided by away fans, particularly the Silver Cod pub. Alcohol is served within the ground (lager £2.30 a pint, bitter £2.20), otherwise you can head for the nearby City Centre, where there are plenty of pubs to be found. David Jenkin, a visiting Exeter fan, recommends the Sandringham pub, near to Hull main station, in the City Centre. On his visit, the pub was both friendly and welcoming.

Robert Walker adds: 'If you are walking to the stadium from the City Centre, there are several pubs on Spring Bank, including the Editorial and the Tap and Spile. Or there is the Admiral of the Humber (a Wetherspoons outlet) on Anlaby Road near Hull Paragon Railway Station'. Whilst Keith Brown informs me: 'Behind Paragon station is another pub called the Yorkshireman, which was okay'.

GETTING THERE & WHERE TO PARK

The stadium is fairly close to the old Boothferry Park ground, but slightly nearer to the town centre, which is three-quarters of a mile away. If you used to approach the old ground down Anlaby Road, pass the ground on your right, go under the railway bridge, and at the second set of traffic lights, turn left into Walton Street and you're there.

From The West:
Leave the M62 at Junction 38 and join the A63, towards Hull. Stay on the A63 and the stadium is clearly signposted (KC Stadium) as you approach Hull. About one mile from the centre of Hull, leave the A63 (also signposted for the Hull Royal Infirmary) and take the second exit at the roundabout. Turn left at the lights and then over the flyover, right at the next lights and the ground is down on the right.

From The North:
Leave the A164 at the Humber Bridge Roundabout and take the first exit into Boothferry Road. The stadium is three miles down this road on the left.

Car Parking
There is no available parking as such for away supporters at the ground. Although there is a Park & Ride facility signposted off the A63 (shared with home supporters), most fans opt to park in one of the many town centre car parks and then walk to the stadium. Chris Bax adds: 'It is perhaps easiest to park at the Infirmary (clearly signposted from the A63) where it is only £1.50 for 4 hours (£2.50 for 8). It's a 10-15 minute walk to the ground from there'.

Robert Walker adds: 'The most convenient car park in the City Centre is the Pryme Street multi-storey car park, which is open to 7.30pm. Leave the A63 at the Myton Street exit and head North towards the City Centre. You will pass Paragon station on your left. At the next traffic lights turn right into Spencer Street and then immediately left into Prospect Street and follow the road around to the right into Pryme Street. The car park entrance is on the right. There is also an NCP car park at the end of Pryme Street and Council surface car parks off Freetown Way. To walk to the stadium, cross over Ferensway and walk along Spring Bank. Turn left onto Derringham Street by Polar Bear pub and then right onto walkway to the stadium'.

Please note that some residential areas near the stadium have been made residents only parking zones, so don't park there as you may well end up with a parking fine. John Womersley adds: 'There is some street parking less than five minutes walk away. Leave the A63 at the Humber Bridge Roundabout and take the first exit into Boothferry Road. Pass Boothferry Park and forward onto Anlaby Road towards the Hull Royal Infirmary. You will pass the KC Stadium on your left. Go over the flyover and turn right at The Eagle pub into Coltman Street, then take the

second right into Cholmley Street then fourth right into the Boulevard. There are many side streets without parking restrictions. To get to the ground, simply walk to the top of the Boulevard and go up the pedestrian walkway to the stadium. To get home, simply go the other way down the Boulevard, then left into Hessle Road. After a quarter mile, you'll come to a roundabout which takes you onto the A63 (Clive Sullivan Way) and M62.

By Train
The stadium is a 15 minute walk from Hull Paragon station. Exit on the North (bus station) side of the station and follow the signed pedestrian route to the stadium via St. Stephens Square, St. Stephens Street and Londesborough Street. Thanks to Robert Walker for providing the train information.

LOCAL RIVALS

Scunthorpe United, York City, Grimsby Town, Lincoln City and Leeds United.

ADMISSION PRICES

The Club operate a category system (A & B) for ticket prices, whereby the more popular matches cost more to watch. Category B prices* are shown below in brackets.
Home Fans:
De Vries West Stand: Adults: £19 (£18), Concessions: £13 (£12)
De Vries West Stand Family Section: Adults: £16 (£15) OAPs: £13, (£12) Juniors: £9 (£8)
East Stand: Adults: £18 (£17), Concessions: £10 (£10)
East Stand Family Section: Adults: £15 (£14) OAPs: £10 (£9), Juniors: £8 (£7)
MKM South Stand: Adults: £17 (£16), Concessions: £10 (£9)
South Stand Family Section: Adults: £15 (£14) OAPs: £10 (£9), Juniors: £8 (£7)
Away Fans:
North Stand: Adults: £17 (£16), Concessions: £10 (£9)
  * Please note that category B priced tickets must be purchased in advance of matchday. If tickets are not purchased prior to matchday, then the category A price will be charged on the day of the category B match instead.
  Students and the unemployed can buy adults tickets for the home areas at a discounted rate providing that they are purchased prior to matchday and that the necessary proof is shown (i.e current NUS card/UB40/photographic ID). Tickets for the family areas (and at a ratio of at least one child to every two adults) must also be purchased prior to matchday.

PROGRAMME

Official Programme: £2.50.

RECORD ATTENDANCE

At The Kingston Communications Stadium:
23,495 v Huddersfield Town
Division Three, April 24, 2004.
At Boothferry Park:
55,019 v Manchester United
FA Cup 6th Round, February 26, 1949.

AVERAGE ATTENDANCE

2003-2004: 16,847 (Division Three).

DID YOU KNOW?

That Hull City are the only league team with two previous grounds, The Boulevard and Boothferry Park, still in existence.

PORTMAN ROAD, IPSWICH

Ground Name:	Portman Road
Capacity:	30,300 (all seated)
Address:	Portman Road, Ipswich, IP1 2DA
Main Telephone No:	01473-400-500
Main Fax No:	01473-400-040
Ticket Office:	01473-400-555
Pitch Size:	112 x 70 yards
Team Nickname:	Blues or Tractor Boys
Home Kit Colours:	Blue & White
Official Website:	www.itfc.co.uk

Unofficial Websites:
Pride Of Anglia: www.prideofanglia.co.uk
Those Were The Days: www.twtd.co.uk (Rivals Network)
Ipswich Town MAD: www.ipswichtown-mad.co.uk (Footy Mad Network)
Tractor Boys: www.tractor-boys.com
Singing The Blues: www.stb-online.co.uk (Sport Network)

WHAT'S THE GROUND LIKE?

The overall look of the ground has greatly improved with the redevelopment of both ends in recent years. Both these ends, the Greene King (South) Stand and the North Stand, are similar in appearance and size, and dwarf the smaller older stands located on each side of the ground. Unusually, both ends have a larger upper tier which overhangs slightly the smaller lower tier. Both have windshields to either side of the upper tier and they are completed with some spectacular floodlights perched on their roofs. Both sides are much older stands and now look quite tired in comparison. On one side, the fair sized Britannia Stand is a two-tiered covered stand with a row of executive boxes running across its middle. Opposite is the smaller Cobbold Stand. Again it is two-tiered and has a row of executive boxes. However it is only partly covered, with the small lower tier of seating being open to the elements. Outside are two statues of the former Ipswich and England managers. One is of World Cup winner Sir Alf Ramsay and is located on the corner between the Cobbold and North Stand, while Sir Bobby Robson's statue is placed behind the Cobbold stand in Portman Road.

WHAT'S IT LIKE FOR VISITORS?

Away fans are placed in one corner in the upper tier of the Cobbold Stand at one side of the pitch. Up to 1,700 away supporters can be accommodated (or according to some - crammed in). An additional 400 seats are also made available in the Family Section of the Cobbold Stand, where further concessions are available. Although the views from this area are not too bad, the legroom is a little cramped and, as with the rest of the stand, the facilities are beginning to show their age. On the plus side, away fans really can make some noise, contributing to a really great atmosphere. The delicious 'Football's Famous Chicken Balti Pie' (£2.20) is available inside the ground.
I have always found this to be a friendly place and pleasurable day out even though I've never seen my team win there! On one occasion, I even

---

got accosted by some Ipswich fans, whilst coming out of the railway station, and ended up accompanying them on a pub crawl before the game. Overall, Portman Road is a good day out although it does seem to take an eternity to get there!

WHERE TO DRINK

Alas, the main away supporters' pub for many a year, the Drum & Monkey, has now closed down. So at the moment there is really only the Station Hotel near to the ground. This is located just outside the railway station and has been a traditional meeting place for away fans. Other pubs in the area, such as the Victoria, the Hare & Hounds and the Swan, are very much home pubs and are best avoided by away fans.

GETTING THERE & WHERE TO PARK

Follow the A14 around Ipswich until you see the turning for Ipswich (A137). Stay on this road and you will eventually see the ground on your left. Bill Leggate adds: 'There is extremely limited on-street car parking around the ground. There are, however, three car parks in Portman Road with a total of about 800 spaces. Two are pay and display and one is pay on admission. Early arrival is recommended to ensure a space close to the ground. There are several town centre car parks within 10 minutes walk, all of which are well signposted'.

By Train
The ground is only a quarter of a mile away from Ipswich train station. You will see it as you come into the station. Ipswich is served by trains from London Liverpool Street and Peterborough.

LOCAL RIVALS

Norwich City and Colchester United.

ADMISSION PRICES

The prices quoted below are for those tickets purchased prior to matchday. Tickets purchased on matchday can cost up to £2 more per ticket.
Home Fans:
Cobbold Stand (Upper Premium Seats): Adults: £42.50, OAPs: £32, Under 16s: £21
Cobbold Stand (Upper Centre): Adults: £29, OAPs: £18, Under 16s: £8.50
Cobbold Stand (Upper Wings): Adults £24, OAPs: £17, Under 16s: £8.50
Cobbold Stand (Lower Tier): Adults: £20, OAPs: £14, Under 16s: £5.50
Britannia Stand (Upper Premium Seats): Adults: £32.50, OAPs: £18, Under 16s: £17

Britannia Stand (Upper Centre): Adults: £29, OAPs: £18, Under 16s: £8.50
Britannia Stand (Upper Wings): Adults £25, OAPs: £18, Under 16s: £8.50
Britannia Stand (Upper Outer Wings): Adults: £24, OAPs: £17, Under 16s: £8.50
Britannia Stand (Family Area Upper Tier): Adults: £24, OAPs: £17, Under 16s: £5.50
Britannia Stand (Family Area Lower Tier): Adults: £20, OAPs: £14, Under 16s: £5.50
Greene King South Stand (Premium Seats): Adults: £35.50, OAPs: £26.50, Under 16s: £17
Greene King South Stand (Upper Tier): Adults: £25, OAPs: £18, Under 16s: £8.50
Greene King South Stand (Lower Tier): Adults: £20, OAPs: £14, Under 16s: £8.50
North Stand (Upper Tier): Adults: £25, OAPs: £18, Under 16s: £8.50
North Stand (Lower Tier): Adults: £20, No Concessions
Away Fans:
Cobbold Stand (Upper Wing): Adults: £24, Over 65s: £17, Under 16s: £8.50
    If demand requires it then additional seating can be made available in the lower tier at a reduced ticket price compared to the Upper Tier.

PROGRAMME

Official Programme: £2.50.

RECORD ATTENDANCE

38,010 v Leeds United
FA Cup 6th Round, March 8, 1975.

AVERAGE ATTENDANCE

2003-2004: 24,520 (Division One).

DID YOU KNOW?

That Ipswich claim to have been one of the first clubs to use goal nets in 1890.

ELLAND ROAD, LEEDS

Ground Name:	Elland Road
Capacity:	40,204 (all-seated)
Address:	Elland Road, Leeds, LS11 0ES
Main Telephone No:	0113-367-6000
Main Fax No:	0113-367-6050
Ticket Office:	0845-121-1992
Ticket Office Fax No:	0113-367-6055
Pitch Size:	117 x 76 yards
Club Nickname:	United
Home Kit Colours:	White With Blue & Yellow Trim
Official Website:	www.lufc.co.uk

Unofficial Websites:
To Ell And Back: www.toellandback.com (Rivals Network)
Leeds Fan Club Message Board:
www.leedsunitedfanclub.com

WHAT'S THE GROUND LIKE?

I first went to Elland Road in the mid 1980s. I remember being impressed as to how the two-tiered stands continued around the corners, giving that enclosed feeling, an essential ingredient of any great stadium. The only real let down was having one side a mixture of terrace and seating. I thought at the time if only they could fill that side... Well as we all know they have, but who could have dreamt of the giant of a stand that now sits proudly on this side. The East stand is simply huge, towering above the rest of the ground (it is at least twice the size of the other

stands) and has been quite well integrated into the stadium. However, the other stands now look a little tired in comparison. One of these, the West Stand, was renamed in March 2004 the John Charles Stand in honour of their former great player. There is an electric scoreboard in one corner of the ground between the South and John Charles Stands.

WHAT'S IT LIKE FOR VISITORS?

Apart from the visit of Manchester United and the odd cup tie or local derby, Leeds is a fairly enjoyable place to watch your football. However, if you are attending one of the former games, then exercise caution around the ground and the adjacent car parks. Away fans are located in the south-east corner of the South Stand at one end of the ground, where up to 1,800 fans can be accommodated. This allocation can be doubled if necessary by giving away fans the whole of this stand. Facilities within are fairly basic, the legroom limited, plus I saw a number of fans being ejected (without warning) for swearing. So be on your best behaviour.

WHERE TO DRINK

The nearest pub is the Old Peacock, situated behind the South Stand. It is a home supporters' pub which really should be avoided. A far better bet is the Dry Salters pub which is about a 10 minute walk from the ground. On my last visit, it had a good mix of home and away supporters, good priced real ale and large screen SKY TV. To find this pub start with the Old Peacock pub behind you, turn left and follow the road down to the very end. Pass the entrances to a number of car parks and go under a railway bridge. At the end of the road, turn left along the dual carriageway and the pub is a short way down tucked in on the left. Otherwise alcohol is served within the ground.

Just a few doors down from the Old Peacock pub is the United Fisheries chippy, which does brisk business on matchdays. There is also a McDonald's outlet across the road from the East Stand.

GETTING THERE & WHERE TO PARK

Elland Road is well signposted around the Leeds area and is situated right by the M621.
From The North:
Follow the A58 or A61 into Leeds City Centre, then follow signs for the M621. Join the M621 and after one and a half miles, leave the motorway at the junction with the A643. Follow the A643 into Elland Road for the ground. Go down Elland Road past the ground on your right and the Old Peacock pub on your left, where you will come to a couple of entrances to a number of large unofficial car parks (£3).
From The South:
Follow the Motorway M1 and then onto the M621. You will pass the ground on your left and then you need to take the next exit from the motorway and turn left onto the A6110 ring road. Take the next left onto Elland Road for the ground. Just as you go under a railway bridge there are several entrances to a couple of large unofficial car parks (£3). Surprisingly the traffic seemed to disperse quite well after the end of the game.

By Train
Leeds train station is around a 30 minute walk from the station, so probably best to either take a taxi or one of the shuttle buses that run from just outside the station to the ground. Ben Smith adds: 'The shuttle buses start running two hours before kick off and are probably a better idea than the long walk'.

LOCAL RIVALS

Bradford City, Huddersfield Town and from a little further a field Manchester United and Chelsea.

ADMISSION PRICES

The Club operate a category system, so that ticket prices vary with the opposition being played. The categories: B & C and CC (Carling Cup) are shown in brackets:
Home Fans
East & John Charles Stands:
Adults: £30 (B), £25 (C) £12 (CC), Concessions: £20 (B), £17 (C), £6 (CC)
Revie & South Stands + Quadrants:
Adults: £22 (B), £19 (C) £12 (CC), Concessions: £15 (B), £13 (C), £6 (CC)
Family Area:
Adults: £30 (B), £25 (C) £12 (CC), Concessions: £20 (B), £17 (C), £6 (CC)
Under 16s: £15 (B), £13 (C), £6 (CC)
Away Fans
South Stand: Adults: £22 (B), £19 (C) £12 (CC), Concessions: £15 (B), £13 (C), £6 (CC)

PROGRAMME & FANZINES

Official Programme: £3.
The Square Ball Fanzine: £1.
To Ell And Back: £1.

RECORD ATTENDANCE

57,892 v Sunderland
FA Cup 5th Round Replay, March 15, 1967.

AVERAGE ATTENDANCE

2003-2004: 36,666 (Premier League).

DID YOU KNOW?

That the South Stand was known commonly as the Scratching Shed until improvements in 1974 saw an impressive £500,000 new stand built, complete with 16 Executive Boxes.

WALKERS STADIUM, LEICESTER

Ground Name: Walkers Stadium
Capacity: 32,500 (all-seated)
Address: Filbert Way, Leicester, LE2 7FL
Main Phone Number: 0870-040-6000
Main Fax No: 0116-247-0585
Ticket Office: 0870-040-6000
Ticket Office Fax No: 0116-229-4404
Club Nickname: The Foxes
Pitch Size: 110 x 76 yards
Home Kit Colours: Blue & White
Official Website: www.lcfc.co.uk
Unofficial Websites:
For Fox Sake: www.forfoxsake.com
The Fox Fanzine: www.foxfanzine.com (Rivals Network)
FilbertStreet.Net: www.filbertstreet.net
The Cunning Fox: www.norfox.net
Independent Supporters Association:
www.lcisa.com
South Coast Foxes:
www.southcoastfox.netfirms.com

WHAT'S THE GROUND LIKE?

In August 2002 the club moved into its new home, only a stone's throw away from their old Filbert Street ground. The stadium was built by Birse Construction at a cost of £35m, is completely enclosed with all corners being filled with seating. The sides are of a good size, built in the same style and height. Running around three sides of the stadium, just below the roof, is a transparent perspex strip, which allows more light and facilitates pitch growth. On the remaining side is a row of executive boxes. Completely encircling the stadium and hanging from the roof itself is a collage of player images, along with adverts for the sponsors of the stadium, Walkers. There are also same basic looking (red LCD display) electric scoreboards at either end.

Like most new stadiums, this is functional but lacks character. I don't know whether I'm starting to suffer from new stadium fatigue having visited so many in the last few years, but to me it seemed somewhat bland looking both inside and out. However, it does have one redeeming feature - atmosphere. The acoustics are very good and both sets of supporters can really generate some noise, making for an enjoyable visit.

FUTURE GROUND DEVELOPMENTS

The stadium has been built in such a way that, if required, an additional tier could be built onto the East Stand. This would increase the capacity to just under 40,000.

WHAT'S IT LIKE FOR VISITORS?

Away supporters are housed in the north-east corner of the stadium, where just over 3,000 fans can be accommodated. The view of the playing action is good (although you are set well back from the pitch) as well as the facilities available. The concourse is comfortable and there is your normal range of hot dogs, burgers and pies available (including the Balti Chicken pie £2.20). However no alcohol is available in the away section (bitter and lager are both available in the home areas).

Paul Groombridge, a visiting Gillingham fan adds: 'From the far upper seats of the away section, the view was pretty good, though from there, you'd probably complain of being too far away from the action (I thought it was okay). One good thing about being at the top of the away section - you can use the plastic transparent panels as pretty good drums when singing!'

I have received a number of reports of away fans being treated somewhat heavy-handedly by the local constabulary around the stadium and of some even being 'frog marched' from the railway station to the ground. Although these measures may be deemed necessary in order to prevent violent disorder, is doesn't do much for the overall away day experience at Leicester.

WHERE TO DRINK

The ground is walkable from the city centre (15-20 minutes), where there are plenty of pubs to be found. Most of the pubs near the stadium are for home fans only. In particular, the Victory and Turnstile pubs should be avoided by visiting supporters and the Half Time Orange pub, located just over the road from the away end, is a members-only Leicester City bar.

Andy Jobson, a visiting Southampton fan, informs me: 'Probably the best bet for away fans is the Counting House pub on Freemens Common Road. It has a good mix of both sets of supporters with all the normal facilities on offer'. Beaumont Fox adds: 'This pub is located just off the Aylestone Road, past the Local Hero pub (home fans only) and the Mecca Bingo Hall. It does, though, exclude away supporters when the game is deemed to be a high profile one'. Peter Moss, a visiting Liverpool supporter, continues: 'On my last visit, the Counting House was only admitting home fans. I would like to recommend the Pride Of Leicester pub which is near to the Victory pub and Leicester Rugby Club. This was the nearest pub to the stadium that we could find for an away fan to drink in'.

For those arriving by train, The Hind pub across the road from the station serves a selection of real ales. Please note that alcohol is not served to away fans inside the stadium itself.

GETTING THERE & WHERE TO PARK

Leave the M1 at Junction 21, or if coming from the Midlands, follow the M69 until the end of the motorway (which meets the M1 at Junction 21).Take the A5460 towards Leicester City Centre. Continue on this road until you go under a railway bridge. Carry on for another 200 yards and turn right at the traffic lights into Upperton Road (signposted Royal Infirmary) and then right again into Filbert Street. The new stadium is visible just behind the old Filbert Street ground.

Allow yourself a little extra time to get to the ground as traffic does tend to get quite congested near the stadium. Plenty of street parking to be found (especially around the Upperton Road area), although as Greg Barclay warns: 'Don't double park as the traffic wardens tend to have a field day at every match'. Alternatively you can park at Leicester Rugby Club (£3) which is a 10 minute walk from the stadium.

By Train

The train station in the City Centre is walkable from the ground and should take you around 20-25 minutes. There is normally a heavy police presence around the station.

Thanks to Philip Draycott for providing the following directions from the station to the ground:

'Come out of the station, cross the road in front of the station and proceed to the left. Follow this around to the right and now you are walking with the main Central Ring Road (Waterloo Way) on your left. Keep this to your left as the pavement becomes a separate path and the road sinks down into a dip down to your left. A quick left and right to stay on the pathway as it crosses New Walk and you go down the left-hand side of New Walk Museum. The pathway rejoins the main road as pavement again and you see a small recreation ground (Nelson Mandela Park) on your right. Turn right into Lancaster Road and then cross the park to the crossings over the main road by the public lavatories. Head for the Victory pub opposite (not recommended for away fans), turn left across the front of the Leicester Royal infirmary. After the first right into Walnut St, you can see the stadium behind the old Filbert Street ground'.

LOCAL RIVALS

Derby County, Nottingham Forest and Coventry City.

ADMISSION PRICES

Leicester operate a three tier category system (A+,

A, & B) whereby admission prices are higher for the most popular games. Discounts on these prices are available to members of the Club (including Fox Cubs).

Home Fans:
West Stand (Centre):
Adults: £39 (A+), £34 (A), £29 (B)
Senior Citizens (60 years+) and Young Adults: (Under 22) £34 (A+), £29 (A), £24 (B)
Juveniles: £29 (A+), £24 (A), £18 (B)

West Stand (Wings):
Adults: £32 (A+), £27 (A), £22 (B)
Senior Citizens (60 years+) and Young Adults: (Under 22) £27 (A+), £22 (A), £20 (B)
Juveniles: £22 (A+), £17 (A), £17 (B)
Alliance & Leicester Stand (Premium Seats):
Adults: £37 (A+), £32 (A), £27 (B)
Senior Citizens (60 years+) Young Adults (Under 22): £32 (A+), £27 (A), £22 (B)
Juveniles: £27 (A+), £22 (A), £17 (B)
Alliance & Leicester Stand (Centre & Wings)
Adults: £34 (A+), £29 (A), £25 (B)
Senior Citizens (60 years+) and Young Adults (Under 22): £29 (A+), £24 (A), £21 (B)
Juveniles: £24 (A+), £19 (A), £17 (B)
BMI Baby Family Area

Adults: £32 (A+), £27 (A), £22 (B)
Senior Citizens (60 years+) and Young Adults (Under 22): £27 (A+), £22 (A), £20 (B)
Juveniles: £22 (A+), £17 (A), £17 (B)
Lineker and Fosse Kop Stands:
Adults: £32 (A+), £27 (A), £22 (B)
Senior Citizens (60 years+) and Young Adults (Under 22): £27 (A+), £22 (A), £20 (B)
Juveniles: £22 (A+), £17 (A), £17 (B)
Away Fans:
Adults: £32 (A+), £27 (A), £22 (B)
Senior Citizens (60 years+) and Young Adults (Under 22): £27 (A+), £22 (A), £20 (B)
Juveniles: £22 (A+), £17 (A), £17 (B)
In addition to these prices there may also this season be what the Club call 'fans fixtures'. For example, these will be typically League Cup games against lower opposition. Prices for these fixtures (all areas of the ground) are: Adults £15, Concessions £10, Juveniles £8.

PROGRAMME & FANZINES

Official Programme: £3
The Fox Fanzine: £1
When You're Smiling Fanzine: £1

STADIUM TOURS

The Club run tours on a daily basis (except matchdays). The cost is £3 per person (minimum five people or minimum charge of £15.00) or £2.00 per person (for group bookings over 20 people), £1.50 per person for schools, youth and charity groups, including cubs and scout groups (minimum 15 people). Call the Club on 0116 229 4496 to book.

RECORD ATTENDANCE

At Walkers Stadium:
32,148 v Newcastle United
Premier League, December 26, 2003.
At Filbert Street:
47,298 v Tottenham Hotspur
FA Cup 5th Round, February 18, 1928.

AVERAGE ATTENDANCE

2003-2004: 30,983 (Premier League).

DID YOU KNOW?

That the Club changed its name from Leicester Fosse to Leicester City in 1919.

KENILWORTH ROAD, LUTON

Ground Name:	Kenilworth Road
Capacity:	9,975 (all-seated)
Address:	1 Maple Road, Luton, LU4 8AW
Main Telephone No:	01582-411-622
Ticket Office:	01582-416-976
Main Fax No:	01582-405-070
Pitch Size:	110 x 72 yards
Team Nickname:	The Hatters
Home Kit Colours:	White & Black
Official Website:	www.lutontown.co.uk

Unofficial Websites:
Hatter Net: www.hatternet.com (Rivals Network)
Supporters Trust: www.trustinluton.com
Luton Town Mad: www.lutontown-mad.co.uk
(Footy Mad Network)

WHAT'S THE GROUND LIKE?

The Club have been talking about moving to a new stadium for some time now and hence investment in Kenilworth Road in recent years has been neglected. One side of the ground and one end are small and covered. A Luton fan once told me that the council would not let the club build any higher than the surrounding houses. The small end, The Oak Road Stand, is given to away supporters and this has a simple electric scoreboard on its roof. The other end is a large covered all-seated stand, which was originally a terrace. You can still see parts of the old terrace at the back of this stand. The small side of the ground (called the Bobbers Stand as entrance used to cost a Bob!) is predominantly filled with a

row of executive boxes and is so small that you can clearly see the houses behind it. Netting has been suspended between the floodlight pylons on its roof to reduce the number of footballs being kicked out of the ground. The other side, the Main Stand, is an older two-tiered covered stand. This stand is mostly wooden (therefore no smoking allowed) and is really beginning to show its age. The Main Stand only runs around two-thirds of the length of the pitch, with another newer structure bolted onto one end. This area is known as the New Stand and is used as a family area. An odd feature is the dugouts being located opposite the players' tunnel, resulting in quite a procession across the pitch.

FUTURE GROUND DEVELOPMENTS

Steven Tearle informs me: 'The Club are still considering moving to a new stadium near Junction 10 of the M1, with a capacity of 15,000. However, no formal time scales have been announced as to when this might take place'.

WHAT'S IT LIKE FOR VISITORS?

The entrance to the Oak Road Stand must be one of the most unusual in the country. After going down a rather small alleyway, the impression is of queuing to go into someone's house! Just over 2,000 supporters can be accommodated in this stand and even a small number of fans can really make some noise. The Luton fans, who like to sing, tend to congregate in the Main Stand immediately to the right of the away end, which can make for a good atmosphere. On the downside, there always feels to be a large police presence, which seems unnecessary for the majority of games. Also, there are a number of supporting pillars in this stand, which may hinder your view, plus the legroom is a little on the tight side. The refreshments are not bad though, with a good selection of pies and burgers available, including the excellent 'Football's Famous Chicken Balti Pie' (£2.20).

WHERE TO DRINK

Josephine Kingston recommends the Bedfordshire Yeoman on Dallow Road near to the ground. Josephine adds: "All away supporters are welcomed, except those from Watford!". To get to this pub, continue down Oak Road towards the official car park and then bear left following the road that goes behind the Main Stand. Continue to follow the road away from this stand and over a little bridge. On the left-hand side, you will see a chip shop (which always seems to do good business on matchdays) and over on the right you will see an alleyway. Go down this alleyway to the end and as you come out of it, the pub is on your right. It is medium sized, popular with home and away supporters. Francis Dunn adds: 'There is also the Nelson Flagship on Dunstable Road by Sainsbury's, which tends to be a bit quieter than the Bedfordshire Yeoman.' Please note that alcohol is not served to away supporters within the ground.

GETTING THERE & WHERE TO PARK

Leave the M1 at Junction 11 and take the A505 towards Luton. Go through one set of traffic lights and at the first roundabout, turn right into Chaul End Lane. At the next roundabout, turn left into Hatters Way. Whilst continuing down Hatters Way, the ground will be seen on your left, although it is not accessible from this road. At the end of Hatters Way turn left and start looking for street parking from here on (the ground will now be on your left).

By Train
Luton train station is a good 15 minutes walk away from the ground. From the station, turn left along the railway bridge, down the steps, and turn right along Bute Street which runs through the Arndale Shopping Centre. At the top of the centre, bear right along Dunstable Road. Kenilworth Road and the ground is on the left. Thanks to Tom Hunt for providing the directions.

LOCAL RIVALS

Watford.

ADMISSION PRICES

Home Fans:
Main Stand* (Upper Tier): Adults: £21, Concessions: £11.50
Main Stand* (Lower Tier): Adults: £17.50, Concessions: £10.50
Kenilworth Road End: Adults: £17.50, Concessions: £10.50.
Family Stand: 2 Adults + 1 Child £37, 1 Adult + 2 Children £32; each additional child: £8.
*Restricted view tickets are available in the Main Stand, priced Adults: £12, Concessions: £9
Concessions apply to over 60s, Under 16s and students (with valid NUS card).
Away Fans:
Adults: £17.50, Concessions: £10.50

PROGRAMME

Official Programme: £2.50.
Record Attendance
30,069 v Blackpool
FA Cup 6th Round Replay, March 4, 1959.

AVERAGE ATTENDANCE

2003-2004: 6,339 (Division Two).

DID YOU KNOW?

That Luton have pioneered amongst others things: identity cards for fans, the use of a plastic pitch and banning away fans from Kenilworth Road. It is interesting that none of these measures are still in use today.

THE DEN, MILLWALL

Ground Name: The Den
Capacity: 20,146 (all-seated)
Address: Zampa Road, London SE16 3LN
Main Telephone No: 020-7232-1222
Main Ticket Office: 020-7231-9999
Fax No: 020-7231-3663
Pitch Size: 105 x 68 yards
Team Nickname: The Lions
Home Kit Colours: Blue & White
Official Website: www.millwallfc.co.uk
Unofficial Websites:
House Of Fun: www.hof.org.uk
Millwall Online: www.millwallonline.co.uk
(Rivals Network)

WHAT'S THE GROUND LIKE?

The ground is a dramatic improvement from the dank and foreboding 'Old' Den and is quite smart looking. The new Den is made up of four fair sized two-tiered stands that are of the same height. The corners of the ground are open, apart from one corner where there is a large video screen. Steve Armstrong informs me: 'The stadium is used to film the Sky One Channel TV show Dream Team, which features an imaginary team

called Harchester United.'

WHAT'S IT LIKE FOR VISITORS?

Away fans are located at one end of the ground in the North Stand (usually in the upper tier only). Around 4,000 away fans can be accommodated in this end. Like the general improvement in football, a trip to Millwall is not as threatening as it once was. However, it is hardly a relaxing day out and I found the Den to be quite intimidating. The large police presence at the match I attended did nothing to dampen this feeling. I would advise that you exercise caution around the ground and not to wear club colours. The most popular method of travel for away fans to the Den is by official club coach. The police are well drilled in dealing with the coaches and once inside the ground you will generally find the stewards helpful and friendly.

WHERE TO DRINK

I wouldn't recommend drinking around the ground. There are bars at the back of the stands that serve alcohol as well as some decent food such as chicken and chips.

GETTING THERE & WHERE TO PARK

There are number of ways of getting to the ground but the most straightforward, if not the shortest in distance, is to follow the A2 into London from Junction 2 of the M25. The A2 actually passes the ground. Once you go past New Cross Gate tube station on your right, the ground is about a mile further on. The only awkward bit is about halfway in-between New Cross Gate and the ground where the road splits into two. Keep to the right following the signs A2 City/Westminster. You will come to the ground on your right. Street parking can be found on the small estate on your left just past the ground. There are no sizeable car parks around the ground (typical British planning!).

By Tube/Train
There are two tube stations that are about 15-20 minutes walk from the ground. Surrey Quays and New Cross Gate, both on the East London Line.

However, it is probably best to go by rail as South Bermondsey Railway Station is only a few minutes walk from the ground and there is now a direct walkway specifically built for away fans which takes you directly to the away end and back to the station afterwards. This has made the police's job of keeping rival supporters apart so much more manageable. If your team brings a sizeable following, an 'away fan' football special may be laid on from London Bridge. In these instances, the police are well drilled in getting away fans into the ground from the special train and safely away afterwards.

LOCAL RIVALS

West Ham United, Crystal Palace, and Charlton Athletic.

ADMISSION PRICES

Like a lot of clubs Millwall operate a category policy (1 & 2) whereby the most popular games cost more to watch. Ticket prices for category 2 games are shown in brackets:
Home Fans:
West & East Stands (Upper Tier) Adults: £26 (£23), Senior Citizens: £16 (£13), Juniors: £13 (£11)
West Stand (Lower Tier) Adults: £23 (£21), Senior Citizens: £14 (£11), Juniors: £10 (£8)
Cold Blow Lane (South) Stand Adults: £19 (£17), Senior Citizens: £12 (£10), Juniors: £10 (£7)
East Stand (Lower Family Enclosure): Season Ticket Holders Only
Away Fans:
North Stand (Away Fans): Adults: £19 (£17), Senior Citizens: £12 (£10), Juniors: £10 (£7)
Please note that discounts are available on the above home adult prices if you are a member of the Millwall Supporters Club. Also be aware that for certain matches the Club will only sell tickets for the home areas to members of the Club. So you may need to check this in advance, rather then just turning up on the day.

PROGRAMME & FANZINES

Official Matchday Programme: £2.50
No One Likes Us (NOLU) Fanzine: £1
The Lion Roars (TLR) Fanzine: £1
Tales From Senegal Fields Fanzine: £1

RECORD ATTENDANCE

At the Old Den; 48,672 v Derby County FA Cup 5th Round, February 20, 1937.
At the New Den, 20,093 v Arsenal FA Cup 3rd Round, January 10, 1994.

AVERAGE ATTENDANCE

2003-2004: 10,497 (Division One).

DID YOU KNOW?

That the owners of the JT Morton jam and marmalade factory in West Ferry Road formed the Club as Millwall Rovers in 1885.

CARROW ROAD, NORWICH CITY

Ground Name: Carrow Road
Capacity: 24,349 (all-seated)
Address: Carrow Road, Norwich, NR1 1JE
Main Telephone No: 01603-760-760
Main Fax No: 01603-613886
Ticket Office: 0870-444-1902
Team Nickname: The Canaries
Pitch Size: 114 x 74 yards
Home Kit Colours: Yellow & Green
Official Website: www.canaries.co.uk
Unofficial Websites:
German Canaries: www.german-canaries.de
Green & Yellow: www.greenandyellow.co.uk
On The Ball City: www.norwichcity-mad.co.uk
(Footy Mad Network)
Wrath Of The Barclay:
www.wrathofthebarclay.co.uk
Northern Canaries: www.northerncanaries.com
Yellow Army: www.yellowarmy.co.uk
Carrow Road: www.carrowroad.net
Stella Canaries: www.stellacanaries.com
Capital Canaries: www.capitalcanaries.com

WHAT'S THE GROUND LIKE?

Carrow Road has been virtually rebuilt since the early 90s, with all four sides of the ground

having new stands. The newest of these is the Jarrold South Stand at one side of the pitch which was opened in 2004. It is an impressive looking cantilever, single tier, all-seated stand, that can house up to 8,000 supporters. It is unusual in having not one, but three separate television gantries suspended beneath its largely perspex roof. The rest of the ground is also all seated and all stands are covered. Both ends look particularly smart, being large two tiered affairs, complete with a row of executive boxes. They also have a pair of large floodlight pylons protruding from their roof. On the remaining side is the Geoffrey Watling City Stand. This single tiered stand is smaller than both ends and houses, amongst other things, the Directors Box and Press Area. This stand extends around to meet the ends at both corners, giving the ground an enclosed look on that side.

FUTURE GROUND DEVELOPMENTS

Jason Smith informs me: 'The Club have commenced with filling in the corner between the new Jarrold South Stand and the Norwich and Peterborough (River End) stand. This will add a further 1,500 seats, raising overall capacity to 26,000. It is hoped that the lower tier of this stand will be open for the end of 2004, with it being fully opened in March 2005. The stand will also include a large area for disabled supporters. Planning permission has also been given for a hotel to be built on the other side of the Jarrold Stand.' Oliver Napthine adds: 'The new South Stand has been built in such a way that an additional tier can be added at a later stage if required. This development would increase the capacity to around 30,000'. Whilst Jon Springall comments: 'An additional tier could also be added to the Geoffrey Watling Stand at some stage (the foundations are already in place), which would further raise the capacity to around 35,000'.

WHAT'S IT LIKE FOR VISITORS?

Away fans are housed on one side of the new South Stand, on a side of the ground. As you would expect from a new stand, the facilities and view of the playing action are good. The normal allocation in this area is 2,500 fans although this can be increased further for cup games. If you are located at the very back of this stand then you can enjoy some fine views across the city. I found the Club to be particularly friendly and relaxed. I certainly would rate it as one of the better away days, even though it seems an eternity to get there. As Delia Smith is now on the board of Norwich City, the food available within the ground has been spruced up a fair bit. I haven't had the pleasure just yet, but I have been informed that it is pretty good. Please note that smoking is not allowed in the seated areas of the South Stand.'

Tom Jameson, a visiting Sheffield United fan, adds: 'I recently visited Carrow Road and found it to be a pleasant, relaxing atmosphere which made for a very enjoyable day out. We were the first away supporters to sit in the new South Stand, towards the right-hand side of the stand, towards the Barclay End. The stand is very modern, and offers a decent view of the action with plenty of legroom. One problem I did encounter was the tendency of the stewards to order away supporters to keep seated throughout the game. This led to our fans singing 'Sit down, if you hate Wednesday' instead of the usual 'Stand up, if you hate

Wednesday' and 'Sit down, stand up', which did not go down too well with the stewards who in my mind very harshly ejected one supporter from the stadium. So it is advisable to comply with the steward requests, although I did find it all rather annoying'.

WHERE TO DRINK

I found that the number of good pubs situated in between the train station and the ground were plentiful and friendly. In fact it almost ended up being a pub crawl before the match had begun! The traditional haunt of away fans for many years was the Clarence Harbour, but this alas is now making way for a housing development. Most fans now seem to be heading instead for the Ferry Boat pub which is only a five minute walk away from the ground. John Sheehan adds: 'The Ferry Boat was extremely welcoming to us as away supporters, as well as being family friendly'. Alternatively there is the 'Compleat Angler', which is by the river opposite the railway station (around 5-10 minutes walk from the ground)'.

Rob Emery tells me: 'Not far away from the ground and towards the City Centre a new leisure complex called the Riverside has opened. This has a number of drinking and eating establishments, including a Wetherspoons outlet. But it is predominantly an area for home supporters and most of the bars there will not admit or serve fans in away colours.' Whilst Nicholas Mead suggests: 'The Coach and Horses on Thorpe Road brews its own beer and is around a 15 minute walk from the ground'.

GETTING THERE & WHERE TO PARK

The ground is well signposted from the A11 and A47. From the southern bypass (A47) take the A146 into the city. At the traffic lights turn right and follow the outer ring road, which is left at the roundabout. Turn right at the next lights. Follow the inner ring road around to the right, over the river and the ground is on your right. If in doubt follow signs for the railway station until you get to the river (where the rail station is off to the left and the ground on your right).

David Clarke informs me that the best car park for away fans is Norfolk County Hall, which is well signposted on the left of the A146, as you follow signs towards the ground from the Southern Bypass. It is currently £2 and can hold about 2,000 cars and does usually fill up by 2pm for games where the away team bring loads of fans. Martyn Swan adds: 'It's advisable to get to the car park before 1pm if you want a decent spot, otherwise you may get stuck in spaces at the back, and it can then take ages at the end of the game to exit'.

By Train
The ground is walkable from Norwich train station. If you ignore all those wonderful pubs it should take you around 5-10mins to walk to the ground. From the station turn left and head for the Morrisons supermarket and you should see the ground behind that.

LOCAL RIVALS

Ipswich Town.

ADMISSION PRICES

The Club operate a match category policy (A, B, C) whereby the more popular matches cost more to watch. Category C prices are shown below in brackets. For certain games such as Carling Cup games, these ticket prices may be further reduced.
Home Fans*:
Geoffrey Watling City Stand (Centre): Adults: £30 (£21), No concessions.
Geoffrey Watling City Stand (Wings): Adults: £29 (£18), Concessions & Under 16s: £21 (£12), Under 12s: £11 (£6)
Jarrold Stand (Centre): Adults: £30 (£21), No concessions.
Jarrold Stand (Wings): Adults: £29 (£18), Concessions & Under 16s: £21 (£12), Under 12s: £11 (£6)
Norwich & Peterborough Stand (River End): Adults: £28 (£16), Concessions & Under 16s: £20 (£10), Under 12s: £11 (£6)
Barclay Stand:
Adults: £28 (£16), Concessions & Under 16s: £20 (£10), Under 12s: £11 (£6)
Coca Cola Family Area:
Adults: £27 (£15), Concessions £19 (£10), Under 16s: £10 (£5) Under 12s: £10 (£3)
Away Fans:
Adults: £29 (£21), Concessions & Under 16s:

£21 (£12), Under 12s: £11 (£6)
Concessions apply to senior citizens over 60 years of age and students in full-time education.
* A discount is available on these prices for Club members.

PROGRAMME & FANZINE

Official Programme: £2.50.
Y'Army Fanzine: £1.

RECORD ATTENDANCE

Record Attendance:
43,984 v Leicester City
FA Cup 6th Round, March 30, 1963.

AVERAGE ATTENDANCE

2003-2004: 18,987 (Division One).

DID YOU KNOW?

That until 1935, the Club's former ground was called 'The Nest' – an apt name for a team called the Canaries.

PLYMOUTH ARGYLE

HOME PARK, PLYMOUTH

Ground Name:	Home Park
Capacity:	20,922 (all-seated)
Address:	Plymouth, PL2 3DQ
Main Telephone No:	01752-562-561
Main Fax No:	01752-606-167
Ticket Office:	01752-562-562
Team Nickname:	The Pilgrims
Shirt Sponsors:	Ginsters
Home Kit Colours:	Green & White
Official Website:	www.pafc.co.uk
Unofficial Websites:	

Greens On Screen: www.greensonscreen.co.uk
London Supporters Club: www.pasalb.co.uk
Rub Of The Greens: www.rubofthegreens.com
(Rivals Network)

WHAT'S THE GROUND LIKE?

During 2001, Home Park was transformed with three sides of the ground being completely rebuilt. Both ends and one side of the ground have been replaced by single-tiered, covered all-seated stands. Most impressively, the corners between these stands have been filled so that the ground is totally enclosed on those sides. This just leaves just the Grandstand at one side of the pitch as the only remnant of the old Home Park. This classic looking stand dates back to the late 1940s and is partly covered, with seating at the rear and a large terrace at the front. Home Park is the most westerly and southerly League Ground in England.

FUTURE GROUND DEVELOPMENTS

The Club intend at some point to finish the ground by redeveloping the old Grandstand. It is

intended to build a multi-tiered stand with a capacity of 6,000 seats which will make the overall capacity of Home Park around 18,600. However at present the Club do not have the necessary finances to pursue this project.

WHAT'S IT LIKE FOR VISITORS?

Away fans are housed in the Barn Park End, which is now all-seated and covered. As you would expect from a new stand, the facilities and views of the playing action are both good. The normal allocation for this end is 1,300 seats, although this can be increased to 2,022 if demand requires it. On the downside though, I have received a number of reports of the stewarding being somewhat over zealous in the away end. One fan described Home Park as a '21st Century stadium, with 14th century stewarding' and on a number of occasions fans have been ejected from the ground, for merely standing up rather than remaining seated during the game. So make sure you are on your best behaviour. Also be aware that smoking is not permitted in the seated area, only on the concourse behind the stand, which can get quite crowded. The delicious 'Football's Famous Chicken Balti Pie' (£2.20) is available inside the ground.

WHERE TO DRINK

I went to the Cherry Tree, which is a good 15-20 minute walk away from the ground: from the car park at the home end turn right and walk up the hill along the main road. At the large set of traffic lights at the top of the hill turn left and you can

PLYMOUTH ARGYLE

see the pub about 50 yards down on the right. Terry from Plymouth also recommends the Pennycomequick (great name!) if you are walking to the ground from the railway station. Dave Potham recommends the Britannia which is the closest pub to the ground and is a Wetherspoons outlet. However this pub is opposite the Embassy Club, best avoided by away fans. Otherwise alcohol is available within the ground.

GETTING THERE & WHERE TO PARK

Take the M5 to the south-west and at the end of the motorway continue onto the A38. On entering Plymouth, turn left onto the A386 (towards Plymouth). When this road splits into two, keep on the left-hand side (signposted Plymouth) and after about a mile you will see the ground on your left. It is well signposted 'Plymouth Argyle Home Park' on the way into Plymouth.

There is quite a large car park at the ground, which is free. It is operated on a 'first in before the game, first out after the game basis'. If you are last in, then on average it takes around half an hour to clear. The car park is normally full by 2.30pm on matchdays. There is some street parking if you drive past the ground, heading away from the city centre.

By Train

Plymouth railway station is about one and half a miles away, so either take a cab (£3) or embark on the 25 minute walk. As you come out of the station turn right and down the hill and under the railway bridge. Just keep walking straight along this road and you will soon see the floodlights of the ground in the distance.

LOCAL RIVALS

Exeter City and Torquay United.

ADMISSION PRICES

All Fans:
Tickets purchased prior to matchday:
Seating: Adults: £20, Concessions: £13, Children: £5
Terrace: Adults: £15, Concessions: £12, Children: £5
Matchday Prices:
Seating: Adults: £22, Concessions: £15, Children: £5
Terrace: Adults: £16, Concessions: £13, Children: £5

PROGRAMME & FANZINE

Official Programme: £2
Rub Of The Greens Fanzine: 50p

RECORD ATTENDANCE

43,596 v Aston Villa
Division Two, October 10, 1936.

AVERAGE ATTENDANCE

2003-2004: 12,654 (Division Two).

DID YOU KNOW?

That the original Grandstand at Home Park was destroyed during the war by German bombing.

PRESTON NORTH END

DEEPDALE, PRESTON

Ground Name: Deepdale
Capacity: 22,225 (all-seated)
Address: Sir Tom Finney Way,
Preston, PR1 6RU
Main Telephone No: 0870-442-1964
Main Fax No: 01772-693-366
Ticket Office: 0870-442-1966
Ticket Office Fax No: 01772-693-365
Team Nickname: The Lilywhites
Pitch Size: 110 x 77 yards
Home Kit Colours: White & Navy
Official Website: www.pnefc.net
Unofficial Websites:
Lilywhite Magic: www.lilywhites.net
Who's That Jumping Off The Pier?:
http://prestonnorthend.rivals.net/default.asp?sid=941
(Rivals Network)
Irish Supporters Club: http://homepage.eircom.net/~pne/

WHAT'S THE GROUND LIKE?

Three-quarters of the ground have now been
redeveloped in recent years, with some excellent
looking all-seater stands, complete with spectacular
looking floodlights. The three stands, at both ends and
at one side of the pitch, are of the same height and style
and are all large, covered, single-tiered. Each has a
likeness of a past player outlined on the seats and is
named after that player. Tom Finney, Bill Shankly and
now on the latest stand to be built, goalkeeping legend

Alan Kelly, makes a welcome change from the boring
letters (such as 'Holte End' - don't they know which
stand they are in?) outlined on most new stands. Only
one old stand remains now, the Pavilion Stand at one
side of the pitch. This was built in the 1930s and has
seating at the rear (capacity 1,000) and terracing to the
front (capacity 2,000). It is covered, but the roof does
not extend far enough to cover the terracing at the front.
There is also a TV gantry hanging precariously from its
roof, plus I noticed last time that a number of footballs
seem to get stuck up on the roof during the game.
Sometime during this season, a statue of Tom Finney is
to be unveiled outside the stadium.

FUTURE GROUND DEVELOPMENTS

John Kelly informs me: 'Planning permission has been
granted to build a two-tiered stand complete with a row
of executive boxes to replace the existing Pavilion Stand
and Paddock. However there have been no time scales
announced as to when this will take place. These
developments would result in an increased capacity of
around 30,000.'

WHAT'S IT LIKE FOR VISITORS?

Away fans are housed in the modern Bill Shankly Stand
at one end of the pitch. Normally, the allocation for
away fans is approximately half of this stand (3,000

seats) and it is shared with home supporters. However, for teams with a large away support, the whole end can be allocated, raising the allocation to 6,000.

The views of the playing action and facilities within this stand are excellent. The stand is particularly steep, meaning that fans are kept relatively close to the pitch. On the concourse there are TVs by the refreshment serving areas showing the game live and with the bars being open during the game, this is too much of a temptation for some. There is a wide range of food available including bacon rolls, burgers and even vegetarian 'butter' pies. I particularly enjoyed my last visit as the fans, stewards and even police all seemed to be fairly friendly and there was a good atmosphere being generated within the ground.

WHERE TO DRINK

David Higgerson informs me: 'One of the best pubs for away fans is the Toy Soldier, on the Deepdale retail park, just off the Blackpool Road (A5085). The retail park and pub are on the right just before Deepdale (look for the McDonald's sign) if you come off the M6 at junction 31'. The pub is quite large and is a Big Steak House type establishment and, like many such places, lacks atmosphere. However it was predominantly away fans that seemed to be present.

A better bet probably is The Sumners, just up the Tom Finney Way (used to be Deepdale Rd) from the ground. A good friendly atmosphere, with both home and away supporters mixing freely (although note that away fans are not admitted when there is a local derby. There is a good sized beer garden and car park at the pub. Sometimes the pub does charge for parking but this can be redeemed against a purchase at the bar. Good food is available and children are allowed in. James Pritchett provides the following directions to The Sumners: 'Make sure you go

towards Sainsbury's and away from the town centre and it should take five minutes. As you go past Sainsbury's, turn right at the lights and it is halfway up the hill, opposite another pub called the Garrison. It should be full, but friendly. The Garrison has recently been refurbished and welcome a mix of away and home support and are friendly towards families. It serves Theakstons on draught.

Paul Billington adds: 'In all honesty, visiting fans should avoid town centre pubs simply because the police will move you on quickly if they see you and most pubs will refuse to serve away fans. If you arrive by train, I would recommend the Vic and Station not for the decor but simple convenience. Another pub worth considering is The White Hart on Watling Road (approximately 500 yards east of Sumner's and the Garrison, up past Fulwood Barracks). It is another Scottish & Newcastle pub with sizzling platters and other such delights from an inexpensive and good quality menu. A good alternative if the others prove too busy. Ample car parking and children welcome'. Otherwise alcohol is served within the ground.

GETTING THERE & WHERE TO PARK

Leave the M6 at Junction 31 and follow signs Left for Preston. Go up a steep hill (often a police speed trap on the hill, so stick to 30mph) and follow the road down to a mini roundabout (speed camera by the BP garage on the left). At the roundabout with the Hesketh Arms turn right into Blackpool Road. Go straight on over three sets of lights and just before a fourth set, the ground appears set slightly back on the left. Parking is mainly in the streets surrounding the ground. Thanks to Ian, an exiled Birmingham City fan in Preston for the directions.

Mike Holroyd adds: 'As you turn right at the Hesketh Arms roundabout into Blackpool Road and then pass a park on the left, there is now another speed camera to

watch out for. The police also sometimes set up another mobile speed trap on the forecourt of the fire station on the left, so watch your speed. Plus as you near the ground don't be tempted to park up on the grass verges, you are likely to find after the game that you have been given a ticket for it!'

Kate Abbatt suggests: 'If you want to avoid the pre- and post-match traffic, here's a handy tip. Instead of leaving the M6 at Junction 31, carry on to Junction 31a signposted Preston East and Longridge (this is a limited junction as you can only leave northbound and join southbound.) Keep in the right-hand lane and go across the roundabout signposted Preston east, football ground and museum, across the next roundabout (Anderton Arms on your right) and then left at the next one. At the next lights, go right onto Watling Street. You will go past the White Hart and a row of shops. At the next lights by Fulwood Barracks, keep in the left-hand lane. You can either park in Sumners (turn left straight after the lights) or follow the road up to the big junction at Blackpool Road and the ground is on your left and take your chances with on-street parking. Sumners is better as you are the right side of the ground to get away quick after the game. Blackpool Road gets badly snarled up after games and the lights don't help it'.

By Train
Preston station is around a mile and a half from the ground and takes around 25 minutes to walk, although you will pass some good pubs on the way. Leave the Preston railway station via the main entrance and head right at the top of the drive. This is the main High Street. Continue along High Street, passing all the regular big name shops. Some good pubs and eateries can be found down side streets off the High Street, so if you have time, take a look. Try the Old Black Bull and Academy, the latter being about the last place on the High Street that will allow away supporters before you get to Deepdale.

Colours are not recommended around town. The High Street (or Church Street/Fishergate as its known) is about a mile long, and you will pass a church and a bike shop as you come to its end. Simply carry on walking along this street and when you reach the ring road, you head straight over the large traffic lights, heading towards a pub called the County Arms opposite the prison. Turn left along the road passing the County Arms (which is not recommended for away supporters) and continue along Deepdale Road. On the left is Tom Finney sports bar, a home fans only pub, but if you have no colours you may get in. The ground is now another half a mile in a straight line along this road. Thanks to Kevin Wrenn for supplying the directions and general information.

LOCAL RIVALS

Blackpool, Burnley and Blackburn Rovers.

ADMISSION PRICES

Home Fans*:
Sir Tom Finney Stand (Premium Area): Adults: £20, No

Concessions
Sir Tom Finney Stand: Adults: £18, Students/OAPs: £11, Under 16s: £6
Sir Tom Finney Stand (Family Area): Adults: £18, OAPs: £11, Under 16s: £4
Alan Kelly Town End: Adults: £17, OAPs: £11, Under 16s: £6
Bill Shankly Stand: Adults: £17, OAPs: £11, Under 16s: £6
Pavillion Stand: Adults: £17, Students/OAPs: £11, Under 16s: £6
Away Fans:
Bill Shankly Stand: Adults: £17, OAPs: £11, Under 16s: £6
* The Club also operate a scheme whereby under eight years old can be admitted free into some home areas of the ground.

PROGRAMME

Official Programme: £2.50.

RECORD ATTENDANCE

42,684 v Arsenal
Division One, April 23, 1938.

AVERAGE ATTENDANCE

2003-2004: 14,150 (Division One).

NATIONAL MUSEUM OF FOOTBALL

John Messner informs me: 'The Museum is located within the two new stands of Deepdale. The exhibits include a gallery on the history and development of the game in England, along with how it has played a role in the social history of the nation over the years. This gallery runs the length of the Tom Finney Stand. The Museum also features an interactive gallery where visitors can explore elements of the game including tactics, rules, equipment, and grounds. There is a Special Exhibitions Gallery whose first exhibition will be on Wembley Stadium. There are also a gallery charting the history of Deepdale and a gallery to feature art and other visual items from the Museum's vast collection'.

For visiting supporters attending a match, then please note that the Museum will be open until 2.30pm on Saturday matchdays and 7.30pm on evening matchdays. The museum is free to enter.

DID YOU KNOW?

That in 1888 Preston were founder members of the League and became the first team to achieve the League and Cup double, doing so at their first attempt.

QUEENS PARK RANGERS

LOFTUS ROAD, QUEENS PARK

Ground Name:	Loftus Road Stadium
Capacity:	19,148 (all-seated)
Address:	South Africa Road, London, W12 7PA
Main Telephone No:	020-8743-0262
Ticket Office:	0870-112-1967
Main Fax No:	020 749 0994
Pitch Size:	112 x 72 yards
Team Nickname:	The Superhoops
Home Kit Colours:	Blue & White
Official Website:	www.qpr.co.uk

Unofficial Websites:
qpr.org: www.qpr.org
qprnet.com: www.qprnet.com (Rivals Network)
Dave's QPR Website:
www.queensparkrangersfc.com
Loyal Supporters Association: www.qpr-lsa.co.uk

WHAT'S THE GROUND LIKE?

Loftus Road has a compact feel as the ground is totally enclosed, with supporters being close to the pitch. An unusual aspect is that all four stands are roughly the same height with their roofs meeting at all four corners with no gaps. The South Africa Road Stand, on one side of the ground, has a larger upper tier compared to the lower tier, with a row of executive boxes running across the middle. There are a couple of supporting pillars in this stand. The other side, the Ellerslie Road Stand, is single-tiered with a television gantry suspended below its roof. Both ends are similar looking two-tiered stands. There is a small electric scoreboard at the away end of the ground dividing the two tiers. The ground oozes character and there is

nothing similar in the league. However, Loftus Road is starting to look tired, having had little recent investment.

WHAT'S IT LIKE FOR VISITORS?

Away fans are situated in the two-tiered School End, where just over 3,000 fans can be accommodated. Normally only the lower tier is open (where 1,279 fans can sit), but if demand requires it, the upper tier (capacity 1,749) is also opened. Please note though that in the upper tier, there are 499 severely restricted view seats available, which are normally charged at half the usual price. In these seats, you have difficulty in seeing the goal at the School End, unless you stand up.

I must say that on my three visits, I have found the stadium lacking a little in atmosphere. Also the legroom between rows was a little tight. There is normally quite a large police and steward presence and you should expect to be searched before you enter the away end. However, on the plus side, I have never experienced any problems there as it is generally relaxed and friendly. Dan Markham, a QPR fan disagrees, with me: 'It is virtually impossible to have such a small compact enclosed stadium and not have a tremendous atmosphere. You are close to the pitch, close to the visiting fans and most importantly close to the action'. Another plus point was that the food that was served within the ground was quite good and the service prompt, although £2.50 for a slice of pizza seemed quite expensive.

Richard Wilson, a visiting Birmingham City supporter, adds: 'A word of advice for away fans.

They are often very slow at the turnstiles at Loftus Road. I would seriously suggest arriving half an hour before kick off or risk missing the start of the game'.

WHERE TO EAT & DRINK

Grant Donnohoè recommends the Springbok right by the ground (near the ticket office). Come out of White City Underground Station, go down the road right in front of the station – the Springbok is down on the left. Whilst Richard Wilson recommends The Green in Shepherds Bush. Exiting Shepherds Bush Underground Station, on the Hammersmith and City line, turn left out of the station and The Green is a short way down the road on the left. Otherwise there are plenty of pubs to choose from in Shepherds Bush. Please note that alcohol is not available in the away end.

On the eating front, David Frodsham adds: 'On my travels to many football grounds, I have yet to find a wider selection of foods available than on the Uxbridge Road. The cosmopolitan inner city means that you can almost eat your way around the world. From the normal range of cafés, burger bars, fried chicken outlets and chippies, there are Indian, Chinese and Thai outlets as well as Lebanese and Indian kebab shops, the latter selling donair kebabs made with Indian spices!

GETTING THERE & WHERE TO PARK

From The North/West:
At the end of the M40, take the A40 towards Central London. At the point where the A40 becomes the A40(M), turn off onto the A40 towards White City/Shepherds Bush and turn right into Wood Lane and then turn right into South Africa Road for the ground.
The nearby BBC car park in Wood Lane is now for pass holders only, so it is a case of trying to find some street parking.

By Train/Tube
I tend to use Shepherds Bush tube station, simply because there seems to be more pubs around this area. There are in fact two Shepherds Bush tube stations, one on the Central Line and the other on the Hammersmith and City line. The latter is nearer to the ground which is about a 10 minute walk. Leaving the tube station, turn right and the ground will come into view further down on the right. Michael Howard, a visiting Reading supporter, recommends: 'The White City Tube on Wood Lane (opposite the BBC Television Centre). It's nearer the ground and less people seem to use it on matchday'. Please note that Queens Park tube station is nowhere near the ground!

Jonathan Burt adds: 'The nearest train station to the ground is Kensington Olympia which can be accessed via Watford or Clapham Junction. It is normally much quicker to get to the ground this way rather than using the tube line as it really cuts down the journey time. Olympia station is about 20-25 minutes walk from the ground or about 10-15 minutes walk away from Shepherds Bush Green.

LOCAL RIVALS

Brentford, Fulham and Chelsea.

ADMISSION PRICES

Home Fans:
South Africa Road: Adults: £26, Concessions: £14
Ellerslie Road Stand: Adults: £23, Concessions: £13
Loftus Road Upper: Adults: £22, Concessions: £12
Loftus Road Lower: Adults: £22, Concessions: £12
East & West Paddocks: Adults: £19, Concessions: £11
Away Fans:
School End Stand: Adults: £22, Concessions: £12

PROGRAMME & FANZINE

Official Programme: £2.50
A Kick Up The R's Fanzine: £2

RECORD ATTENDANCE

35,353 v Leeds United
Division One, April 27, 1974.

AVERAGE ATTENDANCE

2003-2004: 14,785 (Division Two).

DID YOU KNOW?

That in total, QPR have changed grounds more often than any other League club, a staggering 17 times, using, 13 different venues. This does not even take into account the temporary use of Stamford Bridge in 1915 and Highbury in 1930.

MADEJSKI STADIUM, READING

Ground Name: Madejski Stadium
Capacity: 24,200 (all-seated)
Address: Bennett Road, Reading, RG2 0FL
Main Telephone No: 0118-968-1100
Main Fax No: 0118-968-1101
Ticket Office: 0118-968-1000
Team Nickname: The Royals
Pitch Size: 102 x 70 metres
Home Kit Colours: Royal Blue & White
Official Websites: www.readingfc.co.uk and www.backtheboys.com
Unofficial Websites:
Hob Nob Anyone?: www.royals.cx
Off At Eleven: www.offateleven.com (Rivals Network)
1871 Royals: www.sportnetwork.net/main/s253.htm

WHAT'S THE GROUND LIKE?

This stadium, opened in 1998, is absolutely fabulous and is light years away from the old Elm Park. It is purpose built on the very outskirts of Reading, close to the M4, and the complex even boasts a hotel attached to the back of the West Stand. So if you have plenty of money and don't fancy the journey home, or if miraculously you have pulled inside the ground ...

The stadium is of a fair size and is totally enclosed, with all four corners being occupied. Three sides are single-tiered, whilst on one side the West Stand is two-tiered, including a row of executive boxes. The ground has been designed with the supporters in mind as they are very close to the pitch and the acoustics are good. The stadium has recently a installed video screen on the south-east corner. The Madejski is easily one of the best stadiums in the Championship Division and wouldn't look out of place in the Premier League.

Named after Reading's multi-millionaire chairman, the stadium is shared with London Irish Rugby Club and was recently voted as having the best facilities for disabled supporters in the League.

FUTURE GROUND DEVELOPMENTS

Matthew Coggins informs me: 'The stadium has been built in such a way that an additional tier could be added at a later stage to the East, North and South Stands, increasing the capacity to a maximum of 40,000. However this would not be undertaken until the Club reach the Premier League'.

WHAT'S IT LIKE FOR VISITORS?

Away fans are located in one end of the stadium, in the Fosters Lager South Stand, where up to 4,500 can be accommodated (although the normal allocation is half that number). The facilities in this stand are excellent with plenty of legroom and the views of the pitch are superb. Away fans can really make some noise, so make the most of it. One little tip: buy your ticket in advance, as tickets sold on the day cost £2 more. I had a very pleasant day out at this wonderful stadium. A word of warning though: I have received a number of reports of over-zealous stewarding, so be on your best behaviour. Please also note that smoking is not allowed in the seated areas of the stadium.

WHERE TO EAT & DRINK

Apart from a Harvester on the road towards Reading, there are no pubs near the ground. So either drink in the town centre or alternatively there are bars at the back of the stands where Courage, Fosters (£2.40 per pint) and Guinness (£3 per pint) are on offer. James Days adds: 'I would recommend heading to Friar Street in the town centre where there are about 10-15 different bars and pubs to choose from, all pretty friendly'. However, I have been informed that not many of these town centre pubs allow fans in wearing colours. Next to the ground on a Retail Park are the following food outlets: McDonald's, KFC and Pizza Hut.

GETTING THERE & WHERE TO PARK

If you are travelling along the M4 from the west, you can see the stadium on your left. Leave the M4 at Junction 11, bear left on to the A33 relief road which leads you directly to the stadium. The Madejski Complex is well signposted from Junction 11.

There is a car park at the ground (£5) and at the nearby speedway track (£4). They hold about 2,000 cars between them. However, if you do not arrive in good time before the game, you may find that they are already full. Andy Charman adds: 'For big fixtures on Saturdays, the nearby car park belonging to Hewlett Packard (turn right at the first roundabout on the relief road) has also been opened up. It holds around 1,000 cars and costs £4 per car to park there'.

Mark Sugar adds: 'Don't park in the nearby Business Park unless there is an individual unit charging for matchday parking. You may find yourself with a parking ticket or even clamped if you do. The Club, in the interests of crowd safety, now prevent traffic from leaving the car parks, until 10 minutes after the final whistle'. Colin Haines informs me: 'You can also park at the Post House Hotel on Basingstoke Road. It costs £3 per car and although a 10-15 minute walk away from the ground, you may find it easier to get away, than some of the other car parks, after the game'.

If you want street parking, don't bear left onto the relief road as you leave Junction 11, continue straight on and you will pass a few roads on your right. Park in one of these and walk to the ground (10-12 minutes). I managed to get away with no problems after the game.

Alternatively the Club operate a Park & Ride scheme at Foster Wheeler at Shinfield Park. The return shuttle bus costs: Adults: £1.50, Children: 75p. From Junction 11 of the M4, take the B3270 towards Earley and then follow the signs to Football Car Park C.

By Train

Get the train to Reading mainline station and then the No 79 'Football Special' bus. The buses leave just down from the station. Once you come out of the main station entrance, turn right and they are about 200 yards down the road on the opposite side - there is normally one waiting. The fare is £2 return and takes about 15 minutes. Across the road from the station is the Firkin pub, which is good for a pint, but they don't allow you in wearing colours. Also nearby is Bar Oz, which has also been recommended to me.

Thanks to Richard Stephens and Phillip Bott their help with the railway bus information.

Paul Willems, a visiting Bristol City supporter, adds: 'The bus from the station is good provided that away fans do not cause any trouble. If you do, then the buses refuse to pick you up after the game. I have a bitter experience of this when the slowest police escort in history, by Thames Valley Police, got me back to the station at 7.30 pm!'

LOCAL RIVALS

Swindon Town, Oxford United and Wycombe Wanderers.

ADMISSION PRICES

Upper West Stand:
Adults: £24*, Concessions: £17*
All other areas (including away fans):
Adults: £21*, Concessions: £14*
* Discounts are available on these prices if tickets are purchased prior to matchday. Typically, away fans will pay £19 for an adult ticket and £11 for a concessions ticket purchased in advance of the day of the game.

PROGRAMME

Official Matchday programme:£2.50.

RECORD ATTENDANCE

At The Madejski Stadium:
24,107 v Chelsea
Carling Cup 4th Round, December 3, 2003.
At Elm Park:
33,042 v Brentford
FA Cup 5th Round, February 19, 1927.

AVERAGE ATTENDANCE

2003-2004: 15,095 (Division One).

DID YOU KNOW?

That the stadium was built on the site of an old rubbish tip.

BRAMALL LANE, SHEFFIELD

Ground Name: Bramall Lane
Capacity: 30,936 (all-seated)
Address: Bramall Lane, Sheffield, S2 4SU
Main Telephone No: 0870-787-1960
Main Fax No: 0870-787-3345
Ticket Office: 0870-787-1799
Club Nickname: The Blades
Home Kit Colours: Red, White & Black
Official Website: www.sufc.co.uk
Unofficial Websites:
Gallon Of Magnet: www.gallonofmagnet.cjb.net
Bladesmen: www.bladesmen.co.uk
We Are Blades: www.freewebs.com/bakersblades/
Greasy Chip Buttie: www.greasychipbuttie.co.uk
Supporters Club: www.suscwb.co.uk
The Blades Online: www.thebladesonline.com
(Rivals Network)

WHAT'S THE GROUND LIKE?

Bramall Lane has, in my opinion, been one of the most underrated grounds in the country. The construction of three large new stands, plus the filling in of two corners, makes it one of the best in the first division. Both sides of the ground are large single-tiered stands, as is the Kop at one end. The only disappointment with the latter is two large supporting pillars. Opposite is the Bramall Lane Stand, the oldest present, and where the away fans are housed. This stand is two-tiered and looks odd as it has two large supporting pillars in the upper tier. It also has an electric scoreboard, perched between the two tiers. Probably the smartest looking stand is the HFS Loans Stand at one side of the pitch. This single-tiered stand has the corners filled in by offices on one side and a family seated area on the other. At the back of the stand are a row of executive boxes and on its roof is a

small gable, reminiscent of when many older grounds featured them. The stadium is balanced with all four stands being of the same height.

Dave Croft adds: 'A lot of Blades fans sentimentally call the ground 'Beautiful downtown Bramall Lane', as a matchday announcer used to welcome the away fans with this description'.

FUTURE GROUND DEVELOPMENTS

Joel Beighton informs me: 'The Club have announced plans to build a leisure complex at the back of the Arnold Laver (South) Stand. This will include a casino, a new club shop, club museum and a health club'. This scheme is to link in with the previously announced scheme to build a hotel between the South Stand and Bramall Lane End. Part of the hotel would have a viewing area over the ground. Michael Hayes adds: 'The Club have also recently announced plans to build a corner of seats in-between the Kop and South Stands. This corner is going to be similar to the one recently built in-between the Kop and HFS Loans Stand. It will be slightly larger though and have 1,500 seats. These plans would raise Bramall Lane's capacity to 32,500'. However the Club are yet to announce when these works will commence.

WHAT'S IT LIKE FOR VISITORS?

Away fans are housed in the two-tiered Bramall Lane Stand at one end of the ground, where up to 5,200 supporters can be accommodated. However the normal allocation is 2,700 as only the upper tier is normally open. If demand requires it then the lower tier can be allocated as well. Please note that the front of the lower tier of this stand is uncovered, so if your team has a large away following, hope it doesn't rain! Chris Bax adds: 'Any tickets still available for the away end can be purchased from two dedicated away ticket windows just up from the turnstile entrances'. The delicious 'Football's Famous Chicken Balti Pie' (£2.20) is available inside the ground.

The United fans are particularly passionate and vocal about their Club. This makes for a great atmosphere at games, but also can make it somewhat intimidating for the away supporter. It was one of those grounds that by just listening to the crowd you could tell what was happening on the pitch. I found it quite amusing as having to go for a leak just before half time, I could hear the home crowd shout Goo-on as a Sheffield attack began. Then this got louder and louder as the United team got closer to the goal, Goo-on, Goo-on, Goo-On! and then the air turned blue as whoever it was missed the chance!

WHERE TO DRINK

The Sheaf House Pub and Railway Hotel are the closest pubs to the away supporters' entrance, but these are home fans pubs. George Donovan recommends the Golden Lion, just across the road and up the hill from the Sheaf House pub, about 50 yards from the away fans entrance. Richard Kirkland adds: 'About a 10 minute walk on Queens Road is the Earl of Arundel & Surrey which should be okay for visiting fans'. Otherwise, somewhat further along the road from the away end (about three-quarters of a mile past the B&Q on the left), is the Bridge pub which also has been recommended. Away fans though should avoid The Railway and Cricketers pubs on Bramall Lane.

Paul Webb, a visiting Birmingham City, fan adds: 'On a number of occasions we have visited the Norfolk Arms pub in the centre of Sheffield. It is by the Ibis Hotel and not far from the train station. A friendly, traditional pub with regulars that make you welcome. It's walkable to the ground, or the bar staff can order a taxi while you leave your car there'. If you are coming by train then Paul Kemp recommends The Howard which is opposite the train station.

GETTING THERE & WHERE TO PARK

From The North:
Leave the M1 at Junction 36 and follow the A61 into Sheffield. Follow the A61 into Sheffield passing Hillsborough Stadium on your right. Continue along the A61, which becomes the ring road around the western side of the city centre. You will eventually reach a roundabout at the junction with the A621. At the roundabout turn right onto the A621 Bramall Lane. The ground is a short way down on the left.

From The South:
Leave M1 at Junction 33 and take the A630 into Sheffield City Centre. On reaching the inner ring road

follow signs for A621 Bakewell, the ground is about a 1/4 of a mile the other side of the city centre. It is located on the A621 (Bramall Lane). Street Parking.

By Train
The ground is walkable from Sheffield mainline train station, (10-15 minutes). As you come out of the station, turn left at the island in front of the station and continue down this street to the ground.

LOCAL RIVALS

Sheffield Wednesday, Barnsley and Rotherham United.

ADMISSION PRICES

The Club operate a three-tiered system (A, B, C) of matchday ticket prices, whereby the most popular games cost more to watch. Category B & C prices are shown below in brackets.

Home Fans*:
South Stand: Adults: £24 (B £22) (C £12),
Concessions: £15 (B £12) (C £6)
HFS Loans Stand: Adults: £23 (B £21) (C £12),
Concessions: £14 (B £12) (C £6)
Streetwise Corner: Adults: £23 (B £21) (C £12),
Concessions: £14 (B £12) (C £6)
Hallam FM Kop: Adults: £20 (B £18) (C £12),
Concessions: £14 (B £12) (C £6)

Away Fans:
Bramall Lane Stand: Adults: £20 (B £18) (C £12),
Concessions: £14 (B £12) (C £6)
Concessions apply to under 16s and over 65s.
* Discounts are available on some of these prices to Members of the Club.

PROGRAMME

Official Programme: £2.50.

RECORD ATTENDANCE

68,287 v Leeds United
FA Cup 5th Round, February 15, 1936.

AVERAGE ATTENDANCE

2003-2004: 21,646 (Division One).

DID YOU KNOW?

The first football match at Bramall Lane took place in December 1862. The participating teams were Sheffield FC and another local side Hallam.

HILLSBOROUGH, SHEFFIELD WEDNESDAY

Ground Name: Hillsborough
Capacity: 39,859 (all-seated)
Address: Hillsborough, Sheffield, S6 1SW
Main Telephone No: 0114-221-2121
Main Fax No: 0114-221-2122
Ticket Office: 0114-221-2400
Ticket Office Fax: 0114-221-2401
Club Nickname: The Owls
Pitch Size: 115 x 75 yards
Home Kit Colours: Blue & White
Official Website: www.swfc.co.uk
Unofficial Websites:
London Owls: www.londonowls.co.uk
Owl Zone: www.owlszone.co.uk
AnzOwls: www.anzowls.com
Owls Online: www.owlsonline.com (Rivals Network)

WHAT'S THE GROUND LIKE?

Although the ground has not had the level of new investment some other clubs have recently received, it is still a beautiful ground oozing character. It has four large separate two-tiered stands, which are all covered. The South Stand, on one side of the ground, is the largest of the stands and is superb looking. Unfortunately, only one corner of the ground is filled (see picture below), between the West and North Stands. This area is uncovered. In the other corner is a small electric scoreboard.

Outside the ground near the main entrance is a memorial to the 96 fans who died at Hillsborough

in 1989, at the FA Cup Semi-Final between Liverpool and Nottingham Forest. The memorial is normally covered in flowers left by those who wish to pay their respects.

WHAT'S IT LIKE FOR VISITORS?

Away fans are normally placed in the upper tier of the West Stand (the Leppings Lane) end of the ground, where up to 3,700 away supporters can be accommodated. If there is a particularly large following (or for an FA Cup tie) then the corner above may also be made available, plus the lower tier of the West Stand. This can take the allocation up to 8,000. There are a number of supporting pillars in the West Stand, which could impede your view. Inside, the delicious 'Football's Famous Chicken Balti Pie' is available.

I had an enjoyable day out at Hillsborough, where I found the atmosphere around the ground to be relaxed. I thought the ground was certainly one of the best in the League, if not the country, in terms of setting and attractiveness. There was a continental feeling to the game, with a local band playing a number of tunes during the game that really got the crowd going. (This is the same band that has been adopted by the England Supporters' Club). Lee Hicklin adds: 'About a 100 yards down Leppings Lane there is a programme and football memorabilia shop, which is worth a visit'.

WHERE TO DRINK

Terry Potts recommends the Wadsley Jack on

Rural Lane. It's about a 10 minute walk (uphill!) from the visitors' end, going away from Sheffield Centre. Dave Reid informs me: 'If you continue up the road past the Wadsley Jack, there is the Rose & Crown pub which also welcomes away supporters'. Whilst Derek Hall, a visiting Hartlepool fan, adds: 'Another cracking pub is The Beehive, near the Wadsley Jack'. I also did pass a couple of pubs (the Norfolk Arms and The Red Lion) on the way into Sheffield on the A61 from the M1, where away fans were drinking. Bill Harris, a visiting Millwall fan, adds: 'I found an excellent pub called The New Barrack Inn on the A61 just before McDonald's on the way to the ground. Forget the exterior, inside the pub has some excellent decor and no juke boxes or fruit machines. Although on my own, I was made to feel very welcome and spent a good couple of hours talking football to the locals'. There is also the Horse & Jockey pub on Wadsley Lane going past the Park Hotel and about 300 yards further up on the right-hand side of the road. Just go down to the bottom of Leppings Lane, across Catch Bar Lane and then left into Middlewood Road and then a right into Wadsley Lane. It is about a 5-10 minute walk away and is the designated pub by the police for away fans.

GETTING THERE & WHERE TO PARK

Leave the M1 at Junction 36 and follow the A61 into Sheffield. Continue along the A61 for approximately eight miles. You will see Hillsborough Stadium on your right. This is not the shortest route to the ground, but this is definitely the easiest and avoids Sheffield City Centre. There is some street parking to be had if you arrive early, otherwise there are some unofficial car parks along the A61 that charge in the region of £2-£3.

Matthew Nicholls, a visiting Gillingham supporter, adds: 'I find it easier to park at Meadowhall shopping centre, just by Junction 34 of the M1, where you can park for free. I then take a yellow tram to Leppings lane, which costs less than £2 return and takes about 20 minutes'.

By Train
Sheffield Railway Station is situated in the town centre, two miles from the ground. Either get a taxi up to the ground or the bus station is a one minute walk from the station. Cross over at the pedestrian crossing and follow the signs. Head for the far side of the terminus. Bus no. 53 to Ecclesfield runs regularly to the ground. Jeremy Dawson informs me: 'If arriving by train, by far the easiest way to get to the ground is by tram. Leaving the station on a blue tram, you can either change to a yellow one in the city centre, which takes you to Leppings Lane (right by the ground), or stay on the blue one to Hillsborough, which is

a 10 minute walk to the ground'. Matt Wilcock adds: 'On matchdays, regular shuttle buses run from the road at the far side of the bus station. They are marked football'.

LOCAL RIVALS

Sheffield United, Leeds United, Rotherham United, Barnsley, Chesterfield and Doncaster Rovers.

ADMISSION PRICES

Home Fans*:
South Stand: Adults: £22, Concessions: £12
North Stand: Adults: £19, Concessions: £11
Kop End: Adults: £16, Concessions: £10
Family Enclosure: Adults: £16, Concessions: £9
Away Fans*:
West Stand: Adults: £19, Concessions: £11
 * Please note that a £1 discount is available on the price of these tickets if they are purchased prior to matchday.

PROGRAMME

Official Programme: £2.50.

RECORD ATTENDANCE

72,841 v Manchester City
FA Cup 5th Round, February 17, 1934.

AVERAGE ATTENDANCE

2003-2004: 22,336 (Division Two).

DID YOU KNOW?

That the Club are nicknamed 'The Owls' as the Hillsborough ground is situated in the Owlerton district of Sheffield.

FRIENDS PROVIDENT ST. MARY'S STADIUM

Ground Name:	Friends Provident St Mary's Stadium
Capacity:	32,251 (all-seated)
Address:	Britannia Rd, Southampton, SO14 5FP
Main Telephone No:	0870-220-0000
Main Fax No:	02380-727-727
Ticket Office Sales:	0870-220-0150
Ticket Office Enquiries:	0870-220-0155
Ticket Office Fax:	02380- 230-882
Stadium Tours:	0870-220-0170
Club Nickname:	The Saints
Pitch Size:	112 x 74 yards
Home Kit Colours:	Red & White
Official Website:	www.saintsfc.co.uk

Unofficial Websites:
Saints World: www.saintsworld.net
Saints Forever: www.saintsforever.com
Ultimate Saints: www.ultimatesaint.co.uk
Spanish Saints: www.spanishsaints.com

WHAT'S THE GROUND LIKE?

The Club moved from The Dell to the new St Mary's Stadium in 2001. In some ways this saw the Club returning to its roots as the Club was originally founded as 'Southampton St Mary's'. To be truthful the stadium looks, quite simply, superb. Although comparisons have been made with the Riverside in Middlesbrough, St Mary's is better as all sides are built in the same style and are of the same height. The stadium is completely enclosed, with all corners being filled with seating. There are also two superb looking screens sitting on the roofs at each end. Running around three sides of the stadium, just below the roof, is a transparent perspex strip, which allows more light into it and facilitates pitch growth. On the side of the stadium which does not have this, there is a row of executive boxes. The crowd are set well back from the playing action, as firstly there is a cinder track surrounding the playing surface and secondly the pitch itself must be the largest in the League (although the playing area does not use all of it).

WHAT'S IT LIKE FOR VISITORS?

Away fans are located in the Northam Stand at one end of the stadium, where normally up to 3,200 fans can be accommodated. For Cup games this allocation can be increased to 4,750. The view of the playing action and the facilities within this stand are excellent. Legroom is good, although the width of the seating seemed to be a bit narrower than other grounds (either that or I am putting on weight!). The concourse behind the stand features a Ladbroke's, has TVs which show the live action and a number of eating and drinking outlets. There are plenty of staff and the queues never seemed to get particularly long, which was a pleasant surprise. A range of Hollands Pies (£2) are on offer (to me, apart from the Shire Foods Balti Pie, these are the best range you can get), plus burgers (£2.50) and hot dogs (£2.50). There is also a 'Pie & Pint' outlet that, as the name suggests, only serves beer (£2.50 per pint) and pies. Perhaps they should rename it as 'Heaven'! Please note that smoking is not allowed within the seated areas of the stadium.

I thoroughly enjoyed my visit to St Mary's and would happily return. The stadium has (contrary to other reports) a great atmosphere and the facilities are first class. I particularly commend the Club for the friendliness of their staff, from the stewards to the catering staff. Even as I left the stadium, a steward wished me an enjoyable journey home! Considering that away supporters are almost treated with contempt at some other clubs, this was a refreshing change. Coupled with the relaxed attitude of the home supporters and the excellent facilities, they, in my opinion, make a visit to St Mary's one of the best days out in the League.

Phil Jones adds: 'There was an excellent view from all around the ground and the atmosphere was good. The one thing that struck me as being unique was that they have toilet facilities around the perimeter of the ground which are accessible prior to the turnstiles opening. Well done Southampton, it's the little touches like these, for the fans comfort and enjoyment of the day, which make all the difference'.

Colin Peel informs me that there is quite a good football memorabilia shop near the stadium on Old Northam Road called "The Football Shop", which is worth a visit.

WHERE TO DRINK

As most fans seem to end up in the City Centre before the game, there are plenty of pubs to choose from. Daren Wheeler recommends the following pubs: 'The Prince of Wales, The Bevois Castle and The Station as good friendly pubs for away fans. Ocean Village also has a lot of friendly drinking holes.

I found a good mix of home and away fans in a Wetherspoons Pub and The Standing Order in the City Centre. Remember though that the stadium is a good 20 minutes walk away. I also discovered a small pub called the Le Tissier Arms, which was only five minutes walk from the stadium. Although a predominantly 'home' pub, you seem to be able to get served there if you arrive fairly early or have colours covered (for some reason they started to refuse serving away fans nearer kick-off time). To find this pub, simply go to the corner of the stadium that has the Saints Superstore on it (between the Itchen and Chapel Stands) and then walk away from the stadium towards the City Centre, along the road that runs beside the river and you will come to the pub on your right. Chris Hayward recommends The Coopers Arms on Belvedere Road (5-10 minutes

walk away from the ground), good for both home and away supporters and is amongst the closest to the away coaches dropping off point in Britannia Road through local industrial estate.

Graeme Miles, a visiting Norwich supporter, adds: 'The Bevois Castle does a fantastic full English breakfast for £2 on Saturday matchdays. It is well worth a visit as it is very welcoming towards away supporters. If travelling by train, I would also recommend alighting at St Denys Station, as this is closer to the ground, and there are three pubs within a two minute walk (Bevois Castle is about 5-10 minutes from here) - The Dolphin, The Junction and also The South Western - which was recently voted the fourth best pub in Great Britain by CAMRA. Their selection of Real Ales is fantastic! Around the St Denys area, there is also plenty of street parking'. Otherwise alcohol is served within the ground.

GETTING THERE & WHERE TO PARK

There is hardly any parking available at the stadium for away fans (for home fans you can pay £5 for a car parking ticket in advance and park across the road from the stadium) and there are parking restrictions in force for the local area. Most fans seem to be just heading for the City Centre car parks and then embarking on the 15-20 minutes walk to the stadium. I did this and parked in an NCP car park, which cost £5. However, I should point out that after the game the roads around the City Centre become almost gridlocked. It took me over an hour to get away afterwards.

Alternatively, on my last visit I noticed a number of fans parking around the Marina area, which is 10 minutes walk to the ground. Parking in this area has the advantage that at the end of the game, you can avoid the City Centre gridlock by heading along the coast on the A3024 and then onto the M271/M27. Barry Sear tells me: 'I parked in Woolston where there is plenty of street parking and made the 15 minute walk from there to the ground over the Itchen toll Bridge. To get there, you leave the M27 at Junction 8 and follow the A3025 to Woolston. I was on the M27 within 10 minutes of getting back to the car'. Whilst Colin Peel informs me: 'I parked at NCP car park called "Bargate" at the junction of Palmerston Road and Houndwell Place. The cost was a mere £2 for 4 hours and it was only a 10-minute stroll to the ground'.

Gavin Ellis, a visiting Arsenal supporter, informs me: 'There is a free Park & Ride scheme in operation specifically for away supporters. This is situated just off junction 8 of the M27. The traffic in Southampton really made London look provincial and I'd definitely not recommend people driving into the centre'. John Josephs, a visiting Newcastle supporter, adds: 'After leaving the motorway at Junction 8 and heading towards Southampton, there are clear AA signs for the Visitors Park and Ride car park which is opposite a big Tesco superstore. Although it says pass holders only, this doesn't apply any more. They were checking match tickets at the entrance. I got there at about 6:00pm which was two hours before kick-off. There were six buses waiting but hardly any supporters. Once the bus was half-full, it left and 15 minutes later we were at the stadium. Afterwards the buses were waiting and although the police stop all cars after the match in a fairly wide area, the buses can still leave. Ten minutes later we were back at the car park and within five minutes I was on the M27 heading home. The car park is well organised with really friendly stewards and bus supervisors. I can recommend this to anyone.' Other fans have also recommended the park & ride to me, so on my last visit on a Saturday, I thought I would give it a try. I arrived at the Park & Ride at 11.45am to be informed that it didn't run before 1pm and then only if there were enough fans to fill the bus'. I didn't fancy hanging around so I left the car park and drove to St Mary's instead. However other fans that I spoke to arriving later found the service okay.

By Train

The stadium is located around one and a half miles away from Southampton station (where there is also quite a large car park), which should take about 30 minutes to walk. There is also a shuttle bus in operation taking fans from the station to the ground. This operates from the Blechynden Terrace bus stop outside the station.

Turn left out of the station's southern entrance and walk up Western Esplanade, which becomes Civic Centre Road. Remain on the Civic Centre Road and walk between the Civic Centre and the Marlands Shopping Centre. Eventually a crossroads is reached with the Nationwide Building Society on one corner and Lloyds Bank on another. Cross into New Road and follow this road across a park and past a college. Eventually you will reach a complex road junction with a number of traffic lights. Cross Kings Way into Northam Road and follow this road until you reach the ground on your right. There are signsl, which direct fans from the station to the ground.

Thanks to Scott Lydon, Jeff Manning and David Furnell for providing the directions.

LOCAL RIVALS

Portsmouth.

ADMISSION PRICES

The Club operate a category system (platinum, gold, silver and bronze) whereby tickets for the most popular games cost more. Prices listed below quote the bronze and gold prices.

Home Fans*:
Kingsland & Itchen Stands (Centre): Adults £28-£37, No Concessions.
Kingsland & Itchen Stands (Wings):
Adults: £25-£34, OAPs & Teenagers: £18-£26, Juniors: £12-£18.
Northam & Chapel Stands:
Adults: £25-£34, OAPs & Teenagers: £18-£26, Juniors: £12-£18.

Away Fans:
Northam Stand:
Adults: £25-£34, OAPs & Teenagers: £18-£26, Juniors: £12-£18.
* Members of the Club can qualify for a discount on these ticket prices.

PROGRAMME & FANZINE

Official Programme: £2.50.
Beautiful South Fanzine: £1.

RECORD ATTENDANCE

32,151 v Arsenal
Premier League, December 29, 2003.

AVERAGE ATTENDANCE

2003-2004: 31.699 (Premier League).

STADIUM TOURS

The Club offer tours of the stadium at a cost of:
Adults £6, Children (under 13) £3, Senior Citizens £1.50. A Family Ticket is also available at £15 (2 adults and 2 children). Tours need to be booked in advance on 0870 220 0170.

DID YOU KNOW?

That 103 years of history ended when on 26 May 2001 the Dell hosted its last ever game. Fitting that the last opponents, Brighton & Hove Albion, were the first ever opponents way back in 1898.

BRITANNIA STADIUM, STOKE

Ground Name: Britannia Stadium
Capacity: 28,218 (all-seated)
Address: Stanley Matthews Way,
Stoke On Trent, ST4 4EG
Main Telephone No: 01782-592-222
Main Fax No: 01782-592-221
Ticket Office: 01782-592-206
Ticket Office Fax: 01782-592-201
Pitch Size: 115 x 75 yards
Team Nickname: The Potters
Home Kit Colours: Red & White
Official Website: www.stokecityfc.com
Unofficial Websites:
Oatcake Fanzine: www.oatcake.co.uk (Rivals Network)
Stoke City Mad: www.stokecity-mad.co.uk (Footy MAD
Network)
Potters Underground: www.potters-und.co.uk
Stoke Fans For Action: www.stokecityfc.org.uk
Wheels In Motion: www.scwim.org.uk

WHAT'S THE GROUND LIKE?

The stadium opened in 1997, looks imposing from afar,
as is perched on a hill with hardly any buildings around
it. It looks good when lit up at night. A vast
improvement on the old Victoria Ground which has
now sadly been demolished. It is a fair sized stadium
comprising three separate stands, one of which extends
halfway around the ground. I'm a great fan of grounds
which are totally enclosed, so it is a shame that this
new ground has three open corners. Internally, I found
the stadium a bit lacking in character, however I'm sure
this will develop in time. In one corner of the ground
next to the away end is a large electric scoreboard. Tim
Green adds: 'Behind the Boothen End there are three
statues of the legendary former player Sir Stanley
Matthews, which were unveiled by Kevin Keegan'. The
Club also have an unusual looking blue coloured
mascot by the name of 'Pottermus', obviously this is
what happens to a hippo that visits the Potteries!

FUTURE GROUND DEVELOPMENTS

Stephen Armstrong informs me: 'If Stoke City gain

promotion to the Premier League, then the ground
capacity would probably be increased by filling in the
gap between the Boothen End and the John Smiths
Stand. This would take the capacity to over 30,000'.

WHAT'S IT LIKE FOR VISITORS?

Away fans are housed in the separate Big AM (South)
Stand at one end of the ground, where up to 4,800
supporters can be accommodated. The facilities and
view of the action from this stand are good. I was
personally quite disappointed with the inside of the
ground, it has this kind of 'McStadium' feel i.e. I could
have been in Middlesbrough's stadium of a few years
back and not really noticed much difference. Listen out
though for the Stoke anthem 'Delilah' being sung by the
home fans, they can still give a great rendition of that
Tom Jones classic. It is worth bearing in mind though
that Stoke fans are passionate about their club and this
can make for an intimidating atmosphere, so it is best to
keep colours covered around the ground.

WHERE TO DRINK

There is a distinct lack of pubs near the ground as it is
built away from other buildings. Therefore I would
recommend that you grab a drink on the way into
Stoke, which is probably advisable as Alan May informs
me: 'It is not recommended that any visiting supporters
drink in Stoke for safety reasons, however they are
usually welcome at the Staffordshire Knott in Handford
(from Junction 15 of the M6, take the A500 towards
Stoke and the pub is near to the junction with the A34).
Otherwise there is a bar at the back of the away end,
but this can get very busy.
  James Diamond says: 'There is a Holiday Inn and
Harvester Pub next to the ground. Car parking in the
Harvester car park is £3'. Colin Howard, a visiting
Tranmere fan, adds: 'The Harvester pub does not allow
fans to display colours inside the pub'. Otherwise also
close to the stadium is a Power League complex that
also has a bar, which does allow away fans, shows SKY
television and you can even park in their car park for
£4.

Kevin McPadden, the landlord of the Potters Bar, adds: 'We are prepared to offer our hospitality to all visiting teams en-route to the Britannia Stadium. We have a full menu of food and drinks available all day, children are welcome in a designated area, coaches welcome by appointment. The pub in Meir Park is approximately six minutes drive from the Britannia Stadium and is located on the A50 Uttoxeter/Stoke road. For further details please telephone 01782 395649 and ask for Kevin or Pat'.

GETTING THERE & WHERE TO PARK

Leave the M6 at Junction 15 and then go straight across the roundabout onto the A500 towards Stoke. As you see the stadium over on your right and some wasteland over on your left (where the old Victoria Ground used to be) turn right onto the A50 towards Uttoxeter. You will then pass the stadium on your right and then at the next island go around and comeback on yourself for the stadium entrance. Roger Davis informs me that: 'Visitors can purchase car park tickets for the stadium car parks from their own club at a cost of £4 per car'. Please note though that these tickets must be purchased in advance.

Matt Goldstraw adds: 'If you have a ticket for the official south car park, then after going onto the A500 towards Stoke from junction 15 of the M6, leave the A500 at the first junction and turn right at the large roundabout and onto the A34 towards Stafford. Go past a red petrol station and the Staffordshire Knot pub and after about a mile you will reach a small roundabout that on the right has the entrance to Trentham Awakes (previously known as Trentham Gardens). Turn left at the island and then continue straight up this road for about three miles. You will pass a golf club, a Toby Carvery, go over a railway bridge, over the canal and past an Esso garage. Then at a set of traffic lights, you will see an industrial estate on the right, and turn left on to Stanley Matthews Way for the stadium'.

Alternatively there are still some parking spaces at various commercial sites between the old Michelin Car park and the site of the old Victoria Ground. Bear in mind though that if you do park by the Victoria ground, allow a good 20 minutes to walk (mostly uphill) to the stadium. If you are intending to park in this area, then from Junction 15 proceed along the A500, passing the junction with the A34. The stadium will appear over on the right and the open site of the demolished Victoria ground will appear on your left. Leave the A500 at the next junction and turn left to go down to this area.

Andy Fenwick, a visiting Sunderland fan, adds: 'Don't be tempted to park on wasteland around the stadium; you may well end up as I did with a parking ticket waiting for you on your return'.

By Train

Stoke station is just under three miles from the stadium and really is too far to walk, so it is probably best to hire a taxi. Tim Rigby, a visiting Wolves fan, adds: 'There are some shuttle buses than run from Glebe Street in Stoke up to the Britannia Stadium, which depart every 15 minutes before kick off. There are return

buses after the game back to Glebe Street from behind the Sentinel (East) Stand'. Björn Sandström says: 'To catch this bus, turn right from the station and head down Station Road. At the bottom of Station Road at the traffic lights by the Roebuck Hotel, turn right to go along Leek Road (A52). Then go straight across the A500 dual carriageway and into Glebe Street which is straight across in front of you. You should then see the line of buses that will take you to the stadium. It is only about a five minute walk from the station'. The shuttle bus costs for a return ticket £2 Adults, £1.40 Children and £1 OAPs.

LOCAL RIVALS

Port Vale and Crewe Alexandra.

ADMISSION PRICES

Home Fans:
John Smith's Stand (Upper Tier):
Members: Adults: £21, Under 17s/OAPs: £13, Under 11s: £9
Non Members: add £4 membership fee to price stated above
John Smith's Stand (Lower Tier): Adults: £20, Under 17s/OAPs: £12, Under 11s: £9
Genesis Boothen End: Adults: £19*, Concessions: £12*
Sentinel (East) Stand: Adults: £19, Under 17s/OAPs: £12, Under 11s: £9
Family Area: Adults: £17, OAPs: £12, Under 17s: £10, Under 11s: £5.
Away Fans:
Big AM Stand: Adults: £19*, Concessions: £12*.
* A £2 discount is available on this price if the ticket is purchased prior to matchday.

PROGRAMME & FANZINES

Official Programme: £2.50
The Oatcake Fanzine: £1.20
A View To A Kiln Fanzine: £1

RECORD ATTENDANCE

At the Britannia Stadium:
28,218   v Everton
FA Cup 3rd Round, January 5, 2002.
At the Victoria Ground:
51,380 v Arsenal
Division 1, March 29, 1937.

AVERAGE ATTENDANCE

2003-2004: 14,425 (Division One).

DID YOU KNOW?

That the Boothen End at the Britannia Stadium was named after the famous stand of the same name at the Club's old Victoria Ground.

VICARAGE ROAD, WATFORD

Ground Name: Vicarage Road
Capacity: 22,100
Address: Vicarage Road, Watford, WD18 0ER
Main Telephone No: 01923-496-000
Main Fax No: 01923-496-001
Ticket Office: 01923-496-010
Team Nickname: The Hornets
Pitch Size: 115 x 75 yards
Home Kit Colours: Yellow & Black
Official Website: www.watfordfc.com
Unofficial Websites:
Rookery View: www.rookeryview.com
Independent Supporters Association:
www.geocities.com/wfcwisa
Blind, Stupid & Desperate: www.bsad.org
Glory Horns: www.gloryhorns.co.uk

WHAT'S THE GROUND LIKE?

The ground has had both ends redeveloped during the 1990s along with the front of the Rous stand. Both ends are large single-tiered stands, with some strange looking floodlights perched on the roof. There is just one side that lets the ground down. The East Stand is a mishmash of a couple of old stands and an open seated area in one corner. Otherwise there is a vast improvement from the Vicarage Road of old. Away supporters used to have a long walk to the away end as you had to walk around some allotments. However this is no longer the case, as away fans are now housed in the Vicarage Road Stand, previously the home end, at the opposite end of the ground. There is a large video screen in the corner between the Rous and Vicarage Road Stands. Vicarage Road is shared with Saracens Rugby Club.

FUTURE GROUND DEVELOPMENTS

James Dilley informs me: 'The Club plan to redevelop the East Stand, but have not announced any formal time scales The new single-tiered stand (capacity 4,500) will take a year to complete and will raise the capacity to around 23,000. The Club are also investigating the possibility of adding another tier to the Rous Stand and/or filling in the corners of the ground'.

WATFORD

WHAT'S IT LIKE FOR VISITORS?

Away fans are housed in the Vicarage Road Stand at one end of the ground. This stand is normally shared with home supporters (with the obligatory no-mans land in between), or if demand requires it the whole of this stand (capacity 4,500) can be given to away fans. I've always found this club friendly on my four visits and have never had any hassle, although at times there can be a heavy police presence around the ground and in the town centre. Inside the ground, the delicious 'Football's Famous Chicken Balti Pie' (£2) is available. On the first occasion that I visited Vicarage Road, I met a Watford supporter in a pub who gave me a free ticket to that night's game against Luton. I was also impressed with this chap as at the time he had visited 91 League grounds with Watford. Perhaps he was in some part my inspiration for doing the '92'.

WHERE TO DRINK

The ground is in walking distance of the town centre where, along the High Street, you will find a few pubs including a large Wetherspoons outlet called the Moon Under Water. Dominic Wade recommends Macs Bar in Fearnley Street, close to the ground. It is a small bar situated off Cassio Road and is clearly visible when taking the route to Vicarage Road from the town centre via Market Street. The pub is roughly a two minute walk to the away turnstiles. Rob Sterry adds: 'Away fans should avoid the Red Lion, outside the ground'.

GETTING THERE & WHERE TO PARK

I have in the past parked in the centre of town and walked down to the ground. As the stadium is central, it is difficult to miss, with the floodlights being clearly visible from some distance. Leave the M1 at Junction 5 and take the A4008 into Watford. If on nearing the town centre you can't see it on your left, just go around the inner ring road and you will soon spot it. There are also some private matchday car parks available at some industrial units near the ground.

By Train
The nearest station is Watford High Street, a 10 minute walk from the ground. However, you are likely to come into Watford Junction train station, which is about a 20 minute walk.
  Thanks to Albert Fuller for providing the following directions from Watford Junction to the ground: 'Leave the station and take the main road straight opposite Clarendon Road all the way over Ring Road at the lights, up to the High Street. Turn left and go past a Wetherspoon's (Moon under Water) on your right and then take the first right

after 100 yards into Market Street. Continue along again crossing Ring Road to a T-junction and then left at an excellent chip shop. Vicarage Road is the next right turn. Should take around 15-20 minutes to walk.

LOCAL RIVALS

Luton Town.

ADMISSION PRICES

The Club operate a two category system (A & B) for the ticket pricing of games:
Category A:
Upper Rous Stand: Adults: £25, No concessions
Other Stands Including Away End: Adults: £18, Concessions: £13
Family Area: Adults: £18, 2nd Parent: £10, 13-15 year olds: £5, 12 & under: £3

Category B:
Upper Rous Stand: Adults: £20, No concessions
Other Stands Including Away End: Adults: £16, Concessions: £11
Family Area: Adults: £16, 2nd Parent: £10, 13-15 year olds: £5, 12 & under: £3

PROGRAMME

Official Programme: £2.50.

RECORD ATTENDANCE

34,099 v Manchester United
FA Cup 4th Round Replay, February 3, 1969.

AVERAGE ATTENDANCE

2003-2004: 14,856 (Division One).

DID YOU KNOW?

After their spell at the West Herts Sports Ground at Cassio Road, where once they demolished Crouch End Vampires (sic) with a 14-1 scoreline, the move to Vicarage Road came in 1922.

WOLVERHAMPTON WANDERERS

MOLINEUX, WOLVERHAMPTON

Ground Name:	Molineux
Capacity:	29,400 (all-seated)
Address:	Waterloo Road, Wolverhampton, WV1 4QR
Main Telephone No:	0870-442-0123
Main Fax No:	01902-687-006
Ticket Office:	0870-442-0123
Ticket Office Fax No:	01902-687-003
Team Nickname:	Wolves
Pitch Size:	116 x 74 yards
Home Kit Colours:	Gold & Black
Official Website:	www.wolves.co.uk

Unofficial Websites:
The Wolves Site: www.thewolvessite.co.uk
Berlin Wolves: www.geocities.com/berlinwolves/
Supporters Trust: www.wolvestrust.co.uk
Wanderers Way: www.wanderersway.co.uk (Sport Network)
Wolf Message Board: www.the-wolf.co.uk

WHAT'S THE GROUND LIKE?

Molineux has been completely rebuilt in recent years, with the oldest stand, then called the John Ireland Stand (since renamed the Steve Bull Stand), being opened in 1979. Three other stands were then built in the early 1990s with the Jack Harris Stand the last to be completed in December 1993. The stadium itself is superb and is made up of four separate stands, complete with a couple of posh video screens in two corners, which show the game as it is being played. Both ends are large single-tiered stands (one of which the Stan Cullis Stand has a small clock perched on its roof), whilst both sides are two-tiered with a row of executive boxes along the middle. Both the side stands are unusual in being oval in shape, meaning

that those sitting on the halfway line are furthest away from the playing action. It is a pity that the stands do not go all the way around the ground (the corners of the ground are largely open) as this would make it a truly wonderful stadium. In one corner between the Jack Harris and Billy Wright Stands, there is a temporary seated stand, the green seats of which look out of place with the rest of the stadium.

What particularly impresses me about Molineux is that quality shows, getting the feeling that little expense has been spared in its construction. This is perhaps best summed up by the two statues that sit outside the ground. The impressive statue of Billy Wright is probably the finest football statue located at any ground in Britain. It is located outside the main entrance to the club offices, whilst another statue, this time of former player and manager Stan Cullis, sits behind the stand bearing his name.

FUTURE GROUND DEVELOPMENTS

Phil Painter informs me: 'Plans have been drawn up to increase Molineux's capacity to 43,000 by adding an additional tier to both ends of the ground, plus completely rebuilding the Steve Bull Stand'. The Club have purchased the necessary land to do this, but have also confirmed that the expansion will not begin until Wolves have established themselves in the Premier League'.

WHAT'S IT LIKE FOR VISITORS?

Away fans are normally housed on one side of the Jack Harris stand at one end of the ground, where around 2,000 fans can be accommodated. For games where there is a larger away following, then the away supporters are not given an 'end' as such, but are instead housed in the lower tier of the Steve Bull Stand which runs along the side of the pitch. Up to 3,200 away supporters can be accommodated in this area. Fans are sat quite far back from the playing area, which gives the illusion that the pitch is larger than at most other grounds. Musical delights at the ground include just before kick off, 'Hi, Ho, Silver Lining' with the crowd singing 'Hi, Ho, Wolverhampton! The catering facilities within the ground are pretty good, serving a good range of pies, hot dogs and burgers (£2.20). Pies include the delicious 'Football's Famous Chicken Balti Pie' (£2.20). Outside though it is advised that colours are kept covered around the ground and city centre (and that goes for your cars too). I have also heard of objects and other unmentionables being thrown down on away supporters from the upper tier of the Steve Bull Stand. The Club are trying to stamp this out, but it may be an idea to wear that 'lucky' cap if your team's fans are to be housed in this area!

WHERE TO DRINK

There are a number of pubs dotted around the ground, but they tend to be 'members only' for home fans. The Great Western, behind Wolverhampton train station has been recommended to me and I have enjoyed a good pint of real ale (Holdens & Bathams) there myself. However the pub is only really suitable for small numbers of away fans that are not wearing colours. Tim Rigby adds: 'To find this pub, turn right out of the train station entrance, walk along its frontage and go down through the new looking underpass. Then turn right and walk out of the old Low Level Station and it is in front of you on the opposite side of the road'. The Prince Albert, also nearby to the train station, should be avoided by away supporters. The ground is also in walking distance of the city centre where there are plenty of watering holes. However, some of them can be quite partisan so use your discretion and again covers should be covered.

GETTING THERE & WHERE TO PARK

From The South:
Leave the M6 at Junction 10 and take the A454 towards Wolverhampton. Continue to follow the A454 right into Wolverhampton (be wary of speed cameras on the A454). On reaching the traffic island that intersects with the ring road, turn right. As you approach the second set of lights, look for the signs for football parking. The ground is over the second set of lights on the right. Alternatively if you turn left into the City Centre, you may find a space in one of the many council run pay &

display car parks. The Civic Hall car park normally remains open for night matches.

From The North:
Leave the M6 at Junction 12 and take the A5 towards Telford and then turn onto the A449 towards Wolverhampton. On reaching the traffic island that intersects with the ring road, turn right. Then follow the directions as from South.

Thanks to Paul Judd, an exiled Wolves fan in Milton Keynes, for providing the directions.

By Train
The ground is walkable from the train station in the centre of the city (15 minutes). Leave the station and proceed straight on towards the town centre and as you reach the inner ring road turn right. Just follow the ring road as it continues in a circular pattern around to the left. Eventually you will see the Molineux on the right.

LOCAL RIVALS

West Bromwich Albion, Birmingham City and Aston Villa.

ADMISSION PRICES

Home Fans:
Billy Wright Stand: Adults: £26, Concessions: £16
Billy Wright (Family Enclosure): 1 Adult + 1 Under 17: £28
Additional Adult: £24, Additional Senior Citizen: £13, Additional Junior: £8
Steve Bull Stand: Adults: £24, Concessions: £13
Stan Cullis Stand: Adults: £20, Concessions: £12
Jack Harris Stand: Adults: £20, Concessions: £12
Away Fans:
Jack Harris Stand: Adults: £20, Concessions: £12
Steve Bull Stand: Adults: £24, Concessions: £13.
Concessions apply to over 65s and under 17s.

PROGRAMME & FANZINES

Official Programme: £2.50
Load Of Bull Fanzine: £1.50

RECORD ATTENDANCE

61,305 v Liverpool
FA Cup 5th Round, February 11, 1939

AVERAGE ATTENDANCE

2003-2004: 28,874 (Premier League).

DID YOU KNOW?

That Molineux has been their home ever since 1889.

OAKWELL, BARNSLEY

Ground Name:	Oakwell
Capacity:	23,009 (all-seated)
Address:	Grove Street, Barnsley, S71 1ET
Main Telephone No:	01226-211-211
Main Fax No:	01226-211-444
Team Nickname:	The Tykes
Pitch Size:	110 x 75 yards
Home Kit Colours:	Red & White
Official Website:	www.barnsleyfc.co.uk
Unofficial Websites:	

Copacabarnsley: www.copacabarnsley.co.uk
Barnsleyfc.net: www.barnsleyfc.net

WHAT'S THE GROUND LIKE?

Approximately three sides of the ground were redeveloped in the 1990s. On one side is the particularly attractive two-tiered covered East Stand running along one side of the pitch. Opened in March 1993, it has a capacity of 7,500. Opposite is the older West Stand, part of which dates back to 1904. It was made all-seated in the mid 1990s, but is only covered at the rear. On its roof is perched an ugly looking television gantry which obscures a probably more attractive gable. At the Pontefract Road End of the ground is an all-seated, covered stand for home supporters, which has a capacity of 4,500. The other end, the North Stand, was previously an open terrace, but

is now a relatively new single-tier covered stand, housing 6,000 supporters. This is the most recent addition to the ground, being opened in 1999, and has greatly enhanced the overall look of Oakwell. The North Stand is shared between home and away supporters. The amount of seats given to away supporters varies according to demand. An unusual feature of the ground is a purpose built stand for disabled supporters. This is a three floor structure that sits at the corner between the East and South Stands. There is also a new electric scoreboard at one corner of the North Stand on top of a newly constructed security control room.

FUTURE GROUND DEVELOPMENTS

Scott Kilner informs me: 'The club are looking to replace the old West Stand. It is anticipated that the new development will be more or less identical to the existing two-tiered East Stand. However no firm timescales have been set as to when this might happen'.

WHAT'S IT LIKE FOR VISITORS?

Away fans are housed in the new North Stand where the facilities are good. The normal allocation for away supporters is 2,000 although, if demand requires it, then the whole of this stand can be allocated (6,000). I found this club to be particularly friendly, from the car park attendant to the programme seller. Even the P.A. announcer had a sense of humour (although a little optimistic), when he announced that perhaps the visiting fans would like to come up again to see the next Barnsley home game, so that we could see a decent game of football! However, I have reports of fans getting hassle at Barnsley (especially in the town centre) and stewards acting a little heavy handedly, although I've never personally had any problems. It is advisable to keep colours covered especially around the town centre. The delectable 'Football's Famous Chicken Balti Pie' (£2.20) is available inside the ground.

WHERE TO DRINK

Drinking in the town centre is generally not recommended, especially near the bus and train Stations. Paul Sammon, a lifelong Tyke, recommends the Outpost on Sheffield Road. The pub is a 10 minute walk from the ground. Gary Holding, a visiting Blackburn supporter, adds: 'There was no alcohol on sale inside the ground for the away fans, but one minute away from the away end is the Metro Dome - an all-in-one leisure centre, which has a bar inside serving good food and ale'.

GETTING THERE & WHERE TO PARK

Leave the M1 at Junction 37 and take the A628 towards Barnsley. Stay on this road (the ground is well signposted) and you will eventually see the ground on your right. There is a fair sized car park located at the ground.

By Train
Barnsley railway station is about a 10 minute walk away. This station is served by trains running between Sheffield and Leeds.

From the train station, turn left away from the town centre and head towards the bridge that the dual-carriageway runs over. Go under the bridge and turn left up the slip road and then take the first road on the right and head towards the Metro Dome leisure complex at the top of the hill. Oakwell is now clearly visible. Thanks to Ian Ambler and Bryn Williams for providing the directions.

LOCAL RIVALS

Sheffield United, Sheffield Wednesday and Rotherham United.

ADMISSION PRICES

For the 2004/05 season, the Club have introduced a category system for ticket prices (A & B), whereby the most popular matches cost more to watch. Category B prices are shown in brackets.
Home Fans:
East & West Stands (Upper Tier): Adults: £20 (£18), OAPs/Juveniles: £11 (£10)
Barnsley Chronicle Family Area: Adults: £20 (£18), OAPs: £11 (£10), Juveniles: £7 (£6)
East & West Stands (Lower Tier): Adults: £19 (£17), OAPs/Juveniles: £10 (£9)
Pontefract Road End: Adults: £18 (£16), OAPs/Juveniles: £10 (£9)
Away Fans:
North Stand: Adults: £18 (£16), OAPs/Juveniles: £10 (£9)

PROGRAMME

Official Programme: £2.50.

RECORD ATTENDANCE

40,255 v Stoke City
FA Cup 5th Round, February 15, 1936.

AVERAGE ATTENDANCE

2003-2004: 9,620 (Division Two).

DID YOU KNOW?

That in 1897 Barnsley St Peters simplified its name to Barnsley FC and also dispensed with the brown and white striped shirts in favour of plain red ones.

BLOOMFIELD ROAD, BLACKPOOL

Ground Name:	Bloomfield Road
Capacity:	9,000 (all-seated)
Address:	Seasiders Way, Blackpool, Lancashire, FY1 6JJ
Main Telephone No:	0870-443-1953
Main Fax No:	01253-405-011
Pitch Size:	112 x 74 yards
Team Nickname:	Seasiders
Home Kit Colours:	Tangerine & White
Official Website:	www.blackpoolfc.co.uk
Unofficial Website:	

www.seasiders.net (Footy Mad Network)

WHAT'S THE GROUND LIKE?

In an ambitious move, the Club announced in 2000 their intention to redevelop Bloomfield Road, resulting in a new 16,000 all-seated stadium. Phase one of the project was completed in February 2002, with the opening of the new North and West Stands. Phase two, the rebuilding of the South and East Stands, is yet to commence.

The single-tiered West and North Stands are located at one side and at one end of the ground. They are impressive looking and the north-west corner between them has also been filled with seating so that this area of the ground is enclosed. At the back of the West Stand is a row of executive boxes. A personal gripe is that while understanding the Club's need for revenue, naming the West Stand 'The Pricebusters Matthews Stand' rather than just 'The Sir Stanley Matthews Stand', seems somewhat crass. Both the other sides of the ground have now been demolished. On the East side of the ground an open temporary 'golf style' seated stand has been erected to house away supporters, whilst the South end of the ground still awaits a new stand to be constructed.

FUTURE GROUND DEVELOPMENTS

After demolishing the old South Stand in 2003, the Club have yet to embark upon the building of its replacement. The stand would be similar to the North Stand and linked to the West Stand. It was scheduled to be open for the 2004/05 season but for various reasons, works are yet to commence. It is intended that once the South Stand has been completed then work would begin on the construction of a new East Stand. It is possible that work will begin on it sometime this season.

WHAT'S IT LIKE FOR VISITORS?

With delays to the building of the new South Stand, away fans will once again for this season find themselves being housed in a temporary stand on the Eastern side of the ground. The stand is more reminiscent of the type found at the 18th hole of the British Open Golf Championships, rather than at a football ground and has a capacity of 1,700. As you would expect from a temporary stand, the facilities are basic and the stand has no roof, leaving fans exposed to the elements. Dave Croston, a visiting Tranmere fan, adds: 'It was raining on our visit and the walkway in front of the away stand soon became a grey coloured quagmire, with large pools of water forming on it. I would suggest wearing heavy footwear on rainy days. There were inadequate small portacabin toilets and the food facilities were housed in a tiny wooden building with one narrow opening from which to get your food or beverage, and with only one person at a time being served, all added up to not a very pleasant experience'. However, the legroom is adequate and being housed close to the pitch, you do get a good view of the playing action. Remember to wrap up well in winter as the wind that comes off the Irish Sea can go right through you! On the whole though, I found the ground to be a welcoming one, I just hope they build that new South Stand soon!

WHERE TO DRINK

There are plenty of pubs in Blackpool town centre to choose from. Mike Latham recommends the Dunes pub on Lytham Road (Airport End). As he says: 'It serves the best pint of Boddies in the world!'. Steve Lumb adds: 'Another good pub is the Wetherspoons pub called the Auctioneer on Lytham Road, near Blackpool South Station. It's about 10 minutes walk to the ground and serves cheap beer and brilliant grub.' To get there, cross over the bridge by Blackpool South railway station (which you will pass on your left if you are coming into Blackpool on the M55), going towards the sea front (away from the ground). Turn right at the first set of traffic lights (at the Royal Oak pub) and the Auctioneer is a short distance down on the left.

GETTING THERE & WHERE TO PARK

Leave the M6 at Junction 32. Follow the M55 into the outskirts of Blackpool and continue straight along this road until you see the ground on your right. The ground is roughly located about halfway between the Pleasure Beach and the Tower and is about a quarter of a mile inland from the south shore. Large pay and display car parks are located just across the road from the ground (£1). Damian Feeney adds: 'It's worth bearing in mind that the car parking does increase during the holiday season to £3.20 for the required period. It runs from the Spring Bank Holiday until the end of the Illuminations. The canny can find street parking instead.'

By Train
The closest railway station to the ground is Blackpool South and is around a 10 minute walk away. However, fewer trains stop at this station with most calling at Blackpool North, which is around two miles away and therefore you may wish to jump in a cab to the ground.

LOCAL RIVALS

Preston North End and Burnley.

ADMISSION PRICES

Home Fans*:
Executive Area: Adults: £58.75, OAPs: £47, Under 18s: £41.25
Pricebusters Matthews (Centre): Adults: £19.50,

OAPs: £15, Under18s: £12
Pricebusters Matthews Stand (Wings): Adults: £17, OAPs: £13, Under 18s: £10.50
Pricebusters Matthews Stand (Outer Wings): Adults: £16, OAPs: £12, Under 18s: £9
Stanley Casino North West Stand: Adults: £16, OAPs: £11, Under 18s: £7
Classic Bathrooms North Stand Family Area: Adults: £16, OAPs: £11, Under 18s: £7 Under 11's £5
Floorline Direct North Stand*: Adults: £16, OAPs: £12, Under 18s: £9.
Away Fans*:
Adults: £16, OAPs: £11, Under 18s: £7
* A 50p discount per ticket on these prices is available if the ticket is purchased prior to matchday (excluding the Executive Area).

PROGRAMME & FANZINES

Official Programme: £2.50

RECORD ATTENDANCE

38,098 v Wolverhampton Wanderers
Division One, September 19, 1955.

AVERAGE ATTENDANCE

2003-2004: 6,326 (Division Two).

OTHER PLACES OF INTEREST

Blackpool is not Britain's premier seaside resort for nothing, so why not make a weekend of it? If you're feeling brave try the UK's largest and fastest roller coaster, 'The Big One' at the Pleasure Beach. I braved it, but was in shock afterwards! So much so that I had to seek out the Pleasure Beach bar for medicinal purposes. Only one word of caution, look at the other fixtures on the same day in Manchester/Bolton/Preston etc. as your game, because other away supporters attending these games will also be probably be heading to Blackpool after the game. So if there is a particular group of supporters from another club who you would rather avoid, my advice is to stay away.

DID YOU KNOW?

That the colour tangerine had been suggested by the then Director Albert Hargreaves (later club chairman) who was also an international referee. He had been refereeing an international game between Holland and Belgium when he recommended that the Dutch colours would suit Blackpool as being uniquely distinctive among English club colours.

FITNESS FIRST STADIUM, BOURNEMOUTH

Ground Name: Fitness First Stadium
Capacity: 9,600
(although the Club have a safety certificate for only 9,200 at the moment).
Address: Dean Court, Kings Park, Bournemouth, Dorset, BH7 7AF
Main Telephone No: 01202-726-300
Main Fax No: 01202-726-301
Ticket Office Enquiries: 01202-726-303
Ticket Booking Hotline: 0845-330-1000
Pitch Size: 105 x 78 metres
Team Nickname: The Cherries
Home Kit Colours: Red & Black
Official Website: www.afcb.co.uk
Unofficial Websites:
RednBlack: www.rednblack.net (Rivals Network)
Norwegian Supporters Club:
http://home.no.net/afcbnb

WHAT'S THE GROUND LIKE?

Anyone who visited the old Dean Court will not recognise the completely redeveloped ground. In a matter of months, the old ground was completely demolished and a new stadium built. This currently comprises three new stands, which are of roughly the same design and height and are quite smart looking, with the Main Stand having a row of executive boxes to its rear. Each is a covered single-tiered stand, with good views of the playing action and perspex wind shields at each side. The stand roofs have perspex panels, helping get more light to the pitch. They sit at each side of the pitch and at one end, which means that the South End of the ground is open. At the opening game against Wrexham on November 10, 2001, which was a sell out, a number of people were seen perched in trees behind the open end, watching the game for nothing! The corners of the ground are also open and these are home to some unusual looking

floodlights. The pitch has been rotated 90 degrees from its old position and if you ever visited the old ground, try figuring out where the old Brighton Beach End was located!

FUTURE GROUND DEVELOPMENTS

Paul Williams from the 'RednBlack' website informs me: 'All that is required now is to find funding for the missing fourth side and to build an extensive community building. Fans and local businesses have raised nearly £900,000 for the whole project so far and are planning to continue until the stadium is complete. There has also been quite a debate sparked recently by the Independent Supporters Association about whether this fourth side should be terracing or seated. If completed the overall capacity would rise to around 12,000'.

WHAT'S IT LIKE FOR VISITORS?

Away fans are located on one side of the East Stand, at one side of the pitch. The normal allocation for this area is 1,500, but this can be increased to 2,000 if required. The stand is shared with home supporters, offers a good view of the playing action and generates a good atmosphere. The facilities are okay and beer is served on the concourse as well as such delights as the delicious 'Football's Famous Chicken Balti Pie' (£2.20). On my visit, there were repeated calls over the tannoy for fans to sit down in the away section, with reminders that the stadium was an all-seated one. These got somewhat annoying to say the least. It can be argued that fans should sit down, but if everyone wants to stand, what is the problem?

Please also note that the stadium is a no smoking one, which met with cries of 'get your fags out for the lads' from the away support. (Note that the stewards will throw you out if you are caught smoking in the seated areas). Bournemouth is a nice seaside town, with good nightlife, so why not make a weekend of it?

WHERE TO DRINK

There is a bar behind the Main Stand, called the Cherry Tree, but this is for home supporters only.

There is one pub by the dual carriageway, called the Queens Park which is popular with both home and away fans. The pub shows SKY Sports and serves Ringwood real ale. On my visits it has been pretty relaxed, with home fans tending to congregate in the bar and the away fans in the lounge. To find this pub, simply walk away from the ground, on the road going from the main entrance to the stadium. At the end of the road turn left and the pub is a little way up on the left.

Joe Reynolds adds: 'Away fans are welcome in The Portman pub on Ashley Road, about 10 minutes walk away from the ground across Kings Park. It is a fairly spacious pub, serves good ale and food is available. It is normally a good pub with a friendly atmosphere'.

GETTING THERE & WHERE TO PARK

Follow the A338 towards Bournemouth. The ground is situated on the left of the A338 in the outskirts of Bournemouth. If you keep looking up to the left as you go into Bournemouth, you will eventually see the tops of the ground floodlights. At this point take the next exit off the A338 and turn left towards the ground. There is a large car park located at the ground. Alternatively, there is a council run car park, on the opposite side of the dual carriageway, which is handy for getting away quickly after the game.

By Train
The nearest train station is Pokesdown which is roughly a mile from the ground and is around a 15 minute walk. However, most trains arrive at Bournemouth Central, which is around a half hour walk to the ground. Either try to get a train to Pokesdown or grab a cab (£7-£8). If you do arrive at Pokesdown Station (which is served by trains from London Waterloo), then exit the station (there is only one exit) and turn right down the main Christchurch Road (A35). Proceed for about 400 metres and then turn right into Gloucester Road. Dean Court is located down the bottom of this road. Thanks to Andy Young for providing these directions.

If you arrive at Bournemouth Central, then leave the station by the South exit, thereby facing an Asda Supermarket. Turn left and walk down to the main Holdenhurst Road. Turn left (going away from the town centre) and then keep straight on along Holdenhurst Road for around 25 minutes, reaching the Queens Park pub (recommended by this Guide). Continue straight on past the pub until you reach a roundabout at which you turn right into Kings Park Drive. The ground is down the bottom of this road on the left. Alternatively you can

catch a yellow number 33 bus to the ground, normally a half hourly service. Come out of the station again by the South exit facing Asda and turn left until you get to a Texaco garage. There is a bus stop with shelter on the same side of the road. Ask the driver to be let off near Kings Park Drive. Please note that if you decide to use the same service coming back, take a yellow 34 bus as this is a circular service'.

LOCAL RIVALS

Portsmouth, Southampton, Brighton and from a little a further a field Reading.

ADMISSION PRICES

Home Fans*:
Main Stand (Centre): Adults: £21, Over 65s/Under 16s: £14, Junior Cherries: £14
Main Stand (Wings): Adults: £18, Over 65s: £11, Under 16s/Junior Cherries: £10
Main Stand (Family Area): Adults: £14, Over 65s: £7, Under 16s: £5, Junior Cherries: £4
North Stand: Adults: £15, Over 65s: £7, Under 16s: £6, Junior Cherries: £3
East Stand: Adults: £16, Over 65s: £8, Under 16s: £6, Junior Cherries: £4
Away Fans:
East Stand (Wings): Adults: £16, Over 65s: £8, Under 16s: £6.
* Students can also qualify for a generous reduction on the adult ticket price, providing that proof of student status can be shown.

PROGRAMME & FANZINE

Official Programme: £2.50
The 0844 To Waterloo Fanzine: £1.50

RECORD ATTENDANCE

8,809 v Sheffield Wednesday
League Division Two, September 16, 2003.
Before the ground was re-developed:
28,799 v Manchester United
FA Cup 6th Round, March 2, 1957.

AVERAGE ATTENDANCE

2003-2004: 6,863 (Division Two).

DID YOU KNOW?

That the Club changed the marvellously impressive name of Bournemouth and Boscombe Athletic to AFC Bournemouth for the very foresighted reason that they would be first in any alphabetical list of English Clubs, in front of Arsenal and Aston Villa. Editors and compilers however seem to have ignored the hint.

VALLEY PARADE, BRADFORD

Ground Name: Valley Parade,
Capacity: 25,136 (all-seated)
Address: Bradford, West Yorkshire, BD8 7DY
Main Telephone No: 01274-773-355
Ticket Office: 01274-770-022
Main Fax No: 01274-773-356
Club Nickname: The Bantams
Pitch Size: 113 x 75 yards
Home Kit Colours: Claret & Amber
Official Website:
www.bradfordcityfc.co.uk
Unofficial Websites:
City Gent: www.citygent.yorks.com
Boy From Brazil: www.boyfrombrazil.co.uk

WHAT'S THE GROUND LIKE?

The term 'a game of two halves' is often applied to a football game; in the case of Valley Parade, a stadium of 'two halves' comes to mind. The ground has been now been completely rebuilt since the mid 80s, but the initial impression is that one side is twice as big as the other. The Kop End (or now known as the Carlsberg Stand), is a relatively new two-tiered stand that is simply huge and looks quite superb. It once towered over the rest of the ground but the addition of an extra tier to the Sunwin Stand during 2001 has led to it meeting its once larger neighbour. With the corner between these stands also being filled, one has a truly impressive spectacle. The rest of the ground now looks rather out of place in the shadow of

their shiny neighbours. Away fans are housed in a small double decker type stand at one end, called the TL Dallas Stand. The other side, the Midland Road (East) Stand, is a single-tiered stand. There is also an electric scoreboard in one corner of the ground.

WHAT'S IT LIKE FOR VISITORS?

Away fans are housed in the TL Dallas Stand where 1,130 supporters can be accommodated. If possible, try to get tickets for the upper tier as the view of the action is far better. On the downside there are a number of supporting pillars which could well spoil your view. If demand requires it a section of the Midland Road (East) Stand can also be made available to away supporters. The delicious 'Football's Famous Chicken Balti Pie' (£2) is available inside the ground.

Look out for Bradford's mascot Lenny 'The City Gent'. A rather large man carrying a briefcase, umbrella and sporting a bowler hat, he is normally subjected to chants of 'Who ate all the pies?' from the away fans. In reply, he normally produces a large pie from his briefcase!

Having been a student in Bradford and having watched them win the old Third Division, I have a bit of a soft spot for this Club. Pleasingly I have found Bradford to have become rather friendlier towards away supporters in recent years. It is quite a good day out especially if you enjoy what the city has to offer. Make sure that you wrap up well unless the weather forecast is 80 degrees. This is because Bradford is situated at a bottom of a valley, down which a rather cold wind normally prevails.

WHERE TO DRINK

There are not that many pubs around the ground. However, there are a couple of hotels with bars, all about a 10 minute walk away. They are the Park and Cartwright hotels. Just continue to walk on the main road by the ground, away from the town centre and at the traffic lights where the entrance to the park is, turn right and you will see them in a row on your right. Also about a 10 minute walk away is the Corn Dolly, a good real ale pub on Bolton Road, but this has more of a home fan feel to it. Otherwise it is probably wise to drink in the centre or, if you are feeling adventurous, jump in a taxi and visit the Fighting Cock in Preston St or the New Beehive at the top of Westgate. Both of these pubs serve excellent real ale and are quite a mecca for CAMRA members. Darren Middleton recommends Haigys Bar on Lumb Lane whilst Jamie Morgan adds: 'A new pub/curry house has just opened called The Valley. It is on Manningham Lane, only a short distance past the ground'.

GETTING THERE & WHERE TO PARK

Leave the M62 at Junction 26 and take the M606 for Bradford. At the end of the motorway, keep to the right-hand lane and Valley Parade (Bradford and Bingley) is well signposted. Mostly street parking around the ground.

By Train
If going by train into Bradford Interchange, it is quite a walk to the ground (25 minutes). Either take a taxi (£3.50) or alternatively the bus station is located next to the train station (Bus Nos 622, 623, 626 or 662). Chris Hawkridge suggests: 'Supporters travelling via Leeds should catch the Leeds - Bradford Forster Square service (two trains per hour during the day) rather than those to Bradford Interchange. Forster Square is only 10 minutes walk from the ground'.

LOCAL RIVALS

Leeds United and Huddersfield Town.

ADMISSION PRICES

Home Supporters*:
Sunwin Stand: Adults: £18, OAPs: £12, Juveniles: £10
Sunwin Stand (Family Area):
1 Adult + 1 Child £20, Additional: Adult £15, OAP £12, Juveniles: £5

Midland Road (East) Stand: Adults: £18, OAPs: £12, Juveniles: £10
Carlsberg Stand: Adults: £18, OAPs: £12, Juveniles: £10
Away Supporters:
TL Dallas Stand: Adults: £18, OAPs: £12, Juveniles: £10
* Club Members can receive additional discounts on some on most of these prices.

PROGRAMME & FANZINE

Official Programme: £2.50
City Gent Fanzine: £1.50

RECORD ATTENDANCE

39,146 v Burnley
FA Cup 4th Round, March 11, 1911.

AVERAGE ATTENDANCE

2003-2004: 11,377 (Division One).

OTHER PLACES OF INTEREST

Bradford has some excellent curry houses such as the Kashmir in Morley Street and the Mumtaz in Great Horton Road to name but two. Omar Eliwi adds: 'The K2 Curry House on Lumb Lane, about five minutes walk from Valley Parade, serves great curries for under £4'. Whilst Jamie Morgan informs me: 'By far the very best place to have an authentic curry is the Shiraz on Oak Lane, 10 minutes walk away from the ground above where the Cartwright Hotel is (see where to drink). Three of you can eat for under £15, however the Shiraz is not licenced, the nearest off-licence is at the bottom of Oak Lane by the Cartwright Hotel'.

If you have time, the National Museum of Photography, Film & Television is worth a visit, if only to see one of the short films on its huge Imax cinema screen. The museum is free to visit, but the Imax costs £5.95 adults, £4.20 concessions (there are also some discounted family tickets available). The films are shown hourly, on the hour.

DID YOU KNOW?

That Bradford City is the only League Club in England to wear claret and amber.

GRIFFIN PARK, BRENTFORD

Ground Name:	Griffin Park
Capacity:	12,763
Address:	Braemar Road, Brentford, TW8 0NT
Main Telephone No:	0870-900-9229
Main Fax No:	020-8380-9937
Team Nickname:	The Bees
Pitch Size:	110 x 73 yards
Home Kit Colours:	Red, White & Black
Official Website:	www.brentfordfc.co.uk

Unofficial Websites:
Brentford Mad: www.brentford-mad.co.uk (Footy Mad Network)
Brentford Supporters Trust:
www.beesunited.org.uk
Griffin Park Grapevine: www.griffinpark.org
Brentford Always: www.brentfordalways.org

WHAT'S THE GROUND LIKE?

The Ealing Road Terrace, at one end of the ground, is a large open terrace given to away supporters. The other end, The Brook Road Stand, a strange affair, is a small double-decker stand that has seating on the first tier and terracing below. It is known affectionately by the Brentford fans as the 'Wendy House' and after a campaign by local supporters, this stand now no longer

houses away fans. Both sides of the ground are far better. One side is the all-seated Braemar Road Stand, but unfortunately it has a number of supporting pillars. Opposite is the all-seated and covered New Road Stand. The ground is shared with London Broncos Rugby League Club.

FUTURE GROUND DEVELOPMENTS

The Club announced in November 2002 their intention to sell Griffin Park and move to a new stadium at a site less than a mile away. The new stadium has a proposed capacity of around 25,000 and the Club are still seeking planning permission for this.

WHAT'S IT LIKE FOR VISITORS?

After being housed in the Brook Road Stand for the past few seasons, away fans now find themselves back at the other end in the open Ealing Road Terrace, where up to 2,200 supporters can be accommodated. This end is uncovered so it is difficult for the away fans to make their presence felt. Plus be prepared to get soaked when it rains. A better bet may be to try getting one of the 600 seats allocated to away supporters in Block A of the Braemar Road Stand. Although there are several supporting pillars which may hinder your view, the facilities in this stand are good. And unless your team has a large following, you can move seats to avoid the intrusion of the pillars. The delicious 'Football's Famous Chicken Balti Pie' (£2.20) is available inside the ground. I had an enjoyable visit and didn't experience any problems.

WHERE TO DRINK

Brentford is famous for being the only ground in England that has a pub at every corner of the ground. If you are feeling thirsty, get there early and have a pint in all four. They are the Royal Oak (a small locals pub), The Griffin (serves Fullers real ale), The Princess Royal and The New Inn, with the latter being the favoured pub for away supporters. Jim Prentice adds: 'Besides the corner pubs, another favourite is the Waggon and Horses. This pub is in easy reach of the ground, especially by alighting at Kew Bridge station, just before Brentford on the Waterloo - Reading line'. Whilst Roger Stamp informs me: 'Probably the best real ale pub in Brentford is the Magpie & Crown which is only five minutes walk from the ground, on Brentford High Street. The pub has four real ales on tap and welcomes both home and away supporters'.

GETTING THERE & WHERE TO PARK

Leave the M4 at junction 2 and take the A4, going around Chiswick Roundabout so that you end up coming back on yourself. Continue along the A4 and at the first roundabout take a left onto Ealing Road. The ground is located about half a mile down this road on your right. Street parking.

BY TRAIN/TUBE

The nearest train station is Brentford, which is around five minutes walk from the ground. This station is on the London Waterloo to Reading line, which normally runs every 15 minutes on Saturday afternoons. To get from the station to the ground, exit onto Station Road. Take the first right into Orchard Road, right again into Windmill Road and then first left into Hamilton Road which leads into New Road and the ground.

Caleb Johnstone-Cowan informs me: 'The nearest underground station to the ground is South Ealing, which is on the Piccadilly Line. This tube station is around a 15 minute walk from the ground, down Ealing Road'. Mick Hubbard adds: 'Finding the ground is easy enough though - you simply turn right out of the tube station and just go straight down Ealing Road, taking your life in your hands to cross the A4 at the bottom'! Otherwise, as you come out of the station, cross

over to the other side of Ealing Road and catch a number 65 bus down to the ground.

LOCAL RIVALS

Queens Park Rangers and Fulham.

ADMISSION PRICES

Home Fans*:
Braemar Road Stand: Adults: £17, OAPs: £12, Juniors: £3
Brook Road Stand: Adults: £17, OAPs: £12, Juniors: £3
New Road Stand: Adults: £17, OAPs: £12, Juniors: £3
Brook Road Stand (Terrace): Adults: £13, OAPs: £7, Juniors: £3
Away Fans:
Braemar Road Stand (Seating- Block A): Adults: £17, OAPs: £12, Juniors: £3
Ealing Road Terrace: Adults: £13, OAPs: £7, Juniors: £3
  * Students and the unemployed can buy adults tickets for the home areas at a discounted rate providing that they are purchased prior to matchday and that the necessary proof is shown (i.e current NUS card/UB40/photographic ID).

PROGRAMME & FANZINES

Official Programme: £2
Thorne In The Side Fanzine: £1
Hey Jude Fanzine: £1
Beesotted: £1

RECORD ATTENDANCE

39,626 v Preston North End
  FA Cup 6th Round, March 5, 1938.

AVERAGE ATTENDANCE

2003-2004: 5,592 (Division Two).

DID YOU KNOW?

That the surrounding land was formerly owned by the Griffin Brewery, hence the ground name, Griffin Park.

ASHTON GATE, BRISTOL CITY

Ground Name: Ashton Gate
Capacity: 21,479 (all-seated)
Address: Ashton Road,
Bristol, BS3 2EJ
Main Telephone No: 0117-963-0630
Ticket Office: 0870-112-1897
Main Fax No: 0117-963-0700
Team Nickname: The Robins
Home Kit Colours: Red & White
Official Website: www.bcfc.co.uk
Unofficial Websites:
The Incider: www.theincider.com
BristolCityNet: www.bristolcitynet.co.uk (Rivals
Network)
Love Of Bristol City: www.loveofbristolcity.tk

WHAT'S THE GROUND LIKE?

The Atyeo stand at one end of the ground is a
handsome, covered all-seated single-tiered stand.
It was opened in 1994, replacing a former open
terrace and made a great difference to the overall
look of the ground. At the other end is the smaller,
covered Wedlock Blackthorn Stand housing the
away supporters. On one side, is the two-tiered
GWR Dolman Stand, with the lower tier used as a
family area. Opposite, the Brunel Ford Williams
Stand is an older looking single-tiered stand, with
several supporting pillars. A small band resides in
one corner of the Atyeo Stand which on occasions
helps to boost the atmosphere.

FUTURE GROUND DEVELOPMENTS

A scheme for a new 30,000 capacity stadium
adjacent to the M49, which would have been

shared by Bristol City and Bristol Rovers, plus
Bristol Rugby Club, has recently been scrapped.
This may mean that the Club will instead re-
instate plans to redevelop Ashton Gate. This will
involve the rebuilding of three sides of the
ground, resulting in an increased capacity of
around 30,000. The Williams Stand will be the
first to be redeveloped increasing the capacity to
23,500. Next will be the Wedlock Stand (taking
the capacity to 26,000) and then finally the
Dolman Stand. Planning permission has already
been granted for the new stands, but when the
work will commence is anybody's guess.

WHAT'S IT LIKE FOR VISITORS?

Away supporters are housed at one end in the
Wedlock Blackthorn Stand, where the normal
allocation is 2,800. If required, this can be
increased to 5,500. The acoustics are excellent, so
even a small number of away fans can generate
some noise. The facilities are pretty standard, plus
there are a number of supporting pillars running
across the front, which could impair your view.
The delicious 'Football's Famous Chicken Balti
Pie' (£2.20) is available inside the ground. A day
out at Bristol City, in line with the general
improvement in football, is now far more
enjoyable for away fans than it once was.

WHERE TO DRINK

Derek Hall, a visiting Hartlepool fan, informs me:
'The Robins pub is definitely the best pub for
away fans. It is very friendly and is situated only a
few minutes walk away from the away end'.

Whilst Alex Webber recommends the Pumphouse and the Nova Scotia by the waterfront, but adds that pubs nearer to the ground, such as the Hen & Chicken, The Wedlocks and The Rising Sun, should be given a wide berth. Please note that alcohol is not available to away fans inside the ground.

GETTING THERE & WHERE TO PARK

Leave the M5 at Junction 18, travel along the Portway (A4) following signs for the Bristol Airport/Taunton (A38), over the swing bridge (Brunel Way), branching left into Winterstoke Road, and you will see the ground on your left. There is some limited parking available directly behind the away end which costs £5, otherwise try street parking.

By Train
The nearest railway station is Bristol Temple Meads, which is at least two miles from the ground and hence too far to walk, so best to get a taxi. Neil Le Milliere, a visiting Exeter City supporter, adds: 'Don't try and walk it from the station unless you really have to and then allow at least three-quarters of an hour for the journey'. Chris Davis says: 'There are buses which leave from behind the Atyeo Stand at the end of the game which go to the centre of Bristol and Temple Meads Station at a cost of 50p. Although predominantly for home fans, away fans can also use them'.

LOCAL RIVALS

Bristol Rovers, Cardiff City and some fans consider Swindon Town to be local rivals.

ADMISSION PRICES

The Club operate a category system whereby different ticket prices are charged according to the opposition being played. The prices shown below are for the highest category matches. Lower category matches receive a £1 discount on these prices.

HOME FANS:

Atyeo Stand: Adults: £16, OAPs: £13, Under 19s/Students: £11, Under 16s: £5
Dolman Stand/Family Enclosure: Adults: £18, OAPs: £14, Under 19s/Students: £11, Under 16s: £5
Williams Stand: Adults: £18, OAPs: £14, Under 19s/Students: £11, Under 16s: £5
'Platinum Seating': Adults: £23, OAPs: £17, Under 19s/Students: £14, Under 16s: £8
Away Fans:

Wedlock Stand: Adults: £16, OAPs: £13, Under 19s/Students: £11, Under 16s: £5

PROGRAMME & FANZINES

Official Programme: £2.50
One Team In Bristol Fanzine: £1.20
Cider'ed Fanzine: £1

RECORD ATTENDANCE

43,335 v Preston North End
FA Cup 5th Round, 1935.

AVERAGE ATTENDANCE

2003-2004: 12,864 (Division Two).

OTHER PLACES OF INTEREST

If you're into historical ships then the first steamship, the SS *Great Britain*, is moored at the historic docks. The area around the docks is quite pleasant with some good pubs. Pete Smith adds: 'The Clifton Suspension Bridge that overlooks Ashton Gate is quite an amazing sight. It was originally designed by Brunel and it goes over the Avon Gorge. As it is very high up, the views are superb'.

DID YOU KNOW?

That the Club were once nicknamed 'The Garibaldians', so called on account of the red shirts worn by the followers of the Italian revolutionary Garibaldi.

RECREATION GROUND, CHESTERFIELD

Ground Name: Recreation Ground
Capacity: 8,504
Address: Saltergate, Chesterfield, S40 4SX
Main Telephone No: 01246-209-765
Ticket Office No: As Above
Main Fax No: 01246-556-799
Pitch Size: 113 x 71 yards
Team Nickname: The Spireites or Blues
Home Kit Colours: Blue & White
Official Website: www.chesterfield-fc.co.uk

Unofficial Websites:
Spirezine: www.spirezine.co.uk (Rivals Network)
Chesterfield Supporters Society:
www.cfssweb.co.uk

WHAT'S THE GROUND LIKE?

At one end is the Spion Kop, a covered terrace for home supporters. Opposite is the small, open Cross Street End terrace. The covered Main Stand is medium sized and unusual in having its seating area raised above the pitch, thus there are a number of stair wells at the front of the stand leading up to the seats. There are a number of supporting pillars in this stand, which could restrict your view. This stand dates back to the 1930s and could really do with at least a lick of paint, as from the outside it looks very rusty in parts. The other side, the Compton Street Side, had a lot of work carried out during 2002 and this

former terrace has now been made all-seated. This stand is partly covered (to the rear) and has a row of supporting pillars. It has an unusual television gantry perched on its roof.

FUTURE GROUND DEVELOPMENTS

Andy Ford informs me: 'The Club held a ballot of fans earlier this year to vote on whether to move to a new stadium or stay and redevelop Saltergate. The fans narrowly voted in favour of moving to a new 10,000 capacity stadium, to be sited at the old greyhound track at Brimington, two miles away from Saltergate. However, whether the Club can actually raise the funds needed to build it remains to be seen'.

WHAT'S IT LIKE FOR VISITORS?

Away fans are primarily housed in the Cross Street Terrace at one end of the ground, where 1,400 fans can be accommodated. This area is uncovered and open to the elements, so be prepared to get wet. Additionally. away supporters are also given 450 seats in the covered Main Stand. Please note that the seats allocated to away fans in the Main Stand are in fact wooden benches and the facilities in this stand are pretty poor and, like the ground, are showing their age. On the plus side, Chesterfield is a pleasant town with plenty of eating and drinking places within easy walking distance of the ground. Although normally a relaxed and friendly day out, the local constabulary often have a high presence and regularly film supporters before, during and after games, which I found to be intrusive. Inside the ground, the delicious 'Football's Famous Chicken Balti Pie' (£2.20) is available.

WHERE TO DRINK

The Barley Mow in Saltergate is worth a visit as they have scantily clad barmaids (complete with blue & white CCFC mini skirts) serving the beer. This once, it was a pleasure to wait at the bar to be served! Tricia Hastings recommends the Market Tavern in the town centre, which apparently is a good real ale outlet.

GETTING THERE & WHERE TO PARK

Leave the M1 at Junction 29 and take the A617 towards Chesterfield. On reaching the edge of the town centre go straight across the first roundabout and then the next, passing the famous Chesterfield Church with the crooked spire on your left. As the road divides, keep to your left, going around an open car park. This road leads into Saltergate where you will pass the Barley Mow pub on your left and the Town Hall car park, before reaching the ground on your right.

I parked in the Town Hall council car park on Saltergate (£2.40 for four hours) and walked the relatively short distance (five minutes) to the ground. There seemed to be plenty of other car parks in the town centre to choose from.

By Train
Chesterfield railway station is walkable from the ground and takes around 10 minutes. Just follow the road out of the station (Corporation Street), and go straight across a big roundabout and you will find yourself on Saltergate. The ground is on your right. Thanks to Kevin Finney for providing the directions.

Please note that I have received reports of police rounding up away fans arriving at the station and escorting them directly to the ground. So you may want to bear this in mind if you intend travelling by rail.

LOCAL RIVALS

Mansfield Town, Rotherham United and the Sheffield clubs.

ADMISSION PRICES

Home Fans*:
Main Stand (Executive Area): Adults: £24, No Concessions
Main Stand (centre): Adults: £18, Over 65s/Under 16s: £12
Main Stand (wings): Adults: £16, Over 65s/Under 16s: £10
Compton Street Stand: Adults: £15, Over 65s/Under 16s: £9
Family Area: Adults: £14, Over 65s: £10, Under 14s: £4
Kop Terrace: Adults: £14, Over 65s/Under 16s: £7
Away Fans*:
Main Stand (wings): Adults: £16, Over 65s/Under 16s: £10
Cross Street Terrace: Adults: £14, Over 65s/Under 16s: £7
* For certain high profile games, ticket prices will increased by a further £2.

PROGRAMME

Official Programme: £2.50

RECORD ATTENDANCE

30,986 v Newcastle United
Division Two, April 7, 1949.

AVERAGE ATTENDANCE

2003-2004: 4,331 (Division Two).

OTHER PLACES OF INTEREST

Chesterfield is famous amongst other things for its church with a large crooked spire. It is near the town centre and clearly visible.

DID YOU KNOW?

That in the 1892-93 season, Chesterfield's first team sported a most unusual outfit of patriotic shirts with a large Union Flag.

LAYER ROAD, COLCHESTER

Ground Name:	Layer Road
Capacity:	6,200
Address:	Layer Road, Colchester, Essex, CO2 7JJ
Main Telephone No:	0845-330-2975
Main Fax No:	01206-715-303
Team Nickname:	The U's
Pitch Size:	110 x 70 yards
Home Kit Colours:	Blue & White
Official Website:	www.cu-fc.com
Unofficial Websites:	

ColUOnline: www.coluonline.com (Rivals Network)
Swedish Supporters Club: www.barside.com

WHAT'S THE GROUND LIKE?

At one end is the small, covered Layer Road End terrace. Opposite, the Clock End is another small but newer covered all-seater stand. It is a strange affair, having more rows of seats on one side of the stand than the other. It also has a number of supporting pillars that run across the front of it. The Main Stand on one side is partly covered (to the rear) and has seating in the middle and terracing to either side. The other side is a mostly covered terrace, which runs about two thirds of the length of the pitch, with terracing to one side. The ground unfortunately has a number of supporting pillars in various stands, which may obstruct your view.

FUTURE GROUND DEVELOPMENTS

Chris Firminger informs me: 'Plans have recently been on display to the general public, showing for the first time an artist's impression of the eagerly

awaited proposed 10,000 capacity stadium at the Cuckoo Farm site just off the A12 in Colchester. The new ground will have four covered sides with approximately 30 hospitality boxes, decent parking facilities and a direct link road from the A12. It has the same designers as the McAlpine Stadium in Huddersfield. If things go according to plans, then Colchester could be playing at their new ground for the start of the 2005/06 season'.

WHAT'S IT LIKE FOR VISITORS?

Visitors are housed in the small Layer Road End, where at least there is cover and in keeping with the rest of the ground, a few supporting pillars. Either half or all of this terrace is given to away supporters, dependant on numbers. Around 650 supporters can be accommodated in this area and can really make some noise. A small number of seats (196) are also made available to away supporters, but unusually they are at the opposite end to the away terrace in the Clock End. The delicious 'Football's Famous Chicken Balti Pie' (£2.20) is available inside the ground. Colchester has a fair number of army barracks situated in the vicinity of the town and you normally don't have to go far to see signs of the military presence.

WHERE TO DRINK

Jonathan Hull writes: 'For a drink near the ground, try the Dragoon in Butt Road which is on the way to the ground, almost opposite the police station. It is in the Campaign For Real Ale guide, serves good ales and does a mean chilli on matchdays. It is full of Col U fans but of the friendly real ale drinker variety'. There is also the Drury pub at the top of Layer Road, which is generally okay for away fans, unless it is a high profile match, such as a local derby, or where there has been a bit of history between the two clubs.

GETTING THERE & WHERE TO PARK?

The ground is situated one mile south of the town centre. Thanks to Richard Lay for providing the following directions:

From The North:
Leave the A14 at Ipswich and join the A12. On approaching Colchester do not take the first turn off but continue on the A12 towards London and take the Halstead/Cambridge turn off. At the top of the slip road, turn left and continue along Essex Yeomanry Way, then left at the roundabout into London Road. Proceed for just over three-quarters of a mile to the traffic lights (MFI store on your right). Turn right at the lights and follow this road until you reach its end where a pub (Leather Bottle) is on left. Turn left and follow until traffic lights at Boadecia Way, three-quarters of a mile, where you turn right. Go to its end and then turn left - this is Layer Road and the ground is about a quarter mile on left.

From The South:
Leave the M25 at junction 28 and head east. Leave the A12 before you reach Colchester at the Halstead/Cambridge turn off. Turn right at the top of the slip road and continue along Essex Yeomanry Way, left at roundabout into London Road. Then as above.

Richard also informs me: 'Parking is easiest in Boadecia Way or in one of the side roads to the right and this will leave about a 5 - 7 minute walk to the ground'. As for car parking, David Battson adds: 'There is a small unofficial car park about 200 yards from the ground. There is also a Park and Ride scheme which is well signposted (situated at Sobroan barracks). Cost for the unofficial car park is £2.50 per car and holds between 50 to 100 cars. The Matchday Park and Ride is slightly larger and is £2 per car. However, the buses can be every 20 minutes or so'.

By Train
Colchester railway station is really too far from the ground to walk, so best to jump in a taxi, which should cost about £5. If you arrive early and decide to walk to the ground (crossing through the town centre) then it should take about 40 minutes.

LOCAL RIVALS

Ipswich Town, Southend United, Gillingham and a little further away, Peterborough, Northampton, Cambridge and Wycombe.

ADMISSION PRICES

Home Fans*:
Main Stand (Seating): Adults: £18, Concessions: £11
Clock End (Seating): Adults: £18, Concessions: £11
Barside Terrace: Adults: £15, Concessions: £9
Family Area: Adults + 1 Child Under 12: £15, Additional Under 12: £4
Away Fans*:
Clock End Seating: Adults: £18, Concessions: £11
Layer Road End Terrace: Adults: £15, Concessions: £9
 * Please note that a £2 discount is available (except for under 12s in the family area) if tickets are purchased prior to matchday.

PROGRAMME

Official Programme: £2.50

RECORD ATTENDANCE

19,072 v Reading
FA Cup 1st Round, November 27, 1948.

AVERAGE ATTENDANCE

2003-2004: 3,536 (Division Two).

DID YOU KNOW?

That in 1937 Colchester United took over Layer Road, which had been the home of Colchester Town since 1909.

DONCASTER ROVERS

THE EARTH STADIUM, DONCASTER

Ground Name: The Earth Stadium
(but still known to many fans as Belle Vue)
Capacity: 10,550 (1,157 seated)
Address: Bawtry Road, Doncaster,
DN4 5HT
Main Telephone No: 01302-539-441
Fax No: 01302-539-679
Team Nickname: Rovers
Home Kit Colours: Red & White
Official Website:
www.doncasterroversfc.co.uk
Unofficial Websites:
Rovers On The Net: www.roversonthe.net
YAURS: www.yaurs.com
Doncasterrovers.co.uk:
www.doncasterrovers.co.uk
Belle Vue Chat: www.confguide.com/donny.mpl

WHAT'S THE GROUND LIKE?

The ground itself looks a little tired, but with
promotion back to the Football League in 2003,
some much needed improvements have taken
place. The ground is largely open, with both ends
being open terracing. On one side is the old
covered Main Stand, with seating to the rear and
terracing to the front and at either side. It runs
about half the length of the pitch and straddles the
halfway line. It seems to be a fairly old wooden
structure, with a number of supporting pillars
along the front. Opposite, the Popular Side is a
small covered terrace with a TV gantry perched
on its roof. During the closed season, 10
executive boxes were constructed behind
the Town End and in one corner of the ground.
Belle Vue is currently shared with Doncaster
Dragons Rugby League team.

FUTURE GROUND DEVELOPMENTS

Doncaster Council have sanctioned a proposal to
build a new 15,000 capacity stadium at a cost of
around £20m. The new stadium will be home to
the Doncaster Rovers Football Club, Doncaster
Dragons Rugby League Club and Doncaster Belles
Ladies Football Club. The proposed site is
adjacent to a lake, at the back of which has
recently been renamed Lakeside Village (the old
Yorkshire Outlet shopping centre), which is about
a mile and half South from the present Belle Vue
ground. Construction is due to start in December
2004 and it is hoped that it will be completed in
March 2006.

WHAT'S IT LIKE FOR VISITORS?

Away fans are housed in a portion of the old Main
Stand. This consists of 241 seats, plus a portion of
the terrace to the side and at the front of the
stand, which houses a further 876 away fans.
There are a number of supporting pillars at the
front that could spoil your view, plus part of the
terrace adjacent to the Main Stand is also
uncovered. I had a fairly uneventful day out at
Belle Vue, with no problems being experienced.

WHERE TO DRINK

Andy Liney informs me: 'The Club has its own
supporters' bar called the Viking Sports Bar, with
the entrance situated in the main car park near
the away end. Away fans are admitted for a day
membership fee of £1'. David Rose adds: 'There is
a bar in the bowling alley next to the View

DONCASTER ROVERS

Cinema, which is situated behind the ground'. Otherwise there are two pubs in short walking distance from the ground: The Park Hotel on Carr House Road and the Rockingham Hotel on Bennethorpe Road.

GETTING THERE & WHERE TO PARK

From the A1(M) join M18 Eastbound at Junction 35 (signposted Hull) or from the M1 and join the M18 Eastbound at Junction 32. Once on the M18, it's basically a case of following the brown tourist signs for Doncaster Racecourse as the ground is next to the racecourse, otherwise:

Leave M18 at Junction 3, taking first exit (left) at top of slip road signed Doncaster (A6182). Go over the first roundabout and at the second roundabout leave the A6182 going straight ahead onto a new road passing a McDonald's. Bear right at the next roundabout, then straight over the next two, before taking a right (second exit) at the next traffic island, which takes you onto a dual carriageway. Go straight over the next roundabout (where there is another McDonald's) and at the next roundabout turn left onto the A638. The entrance to the fair sized club car park is just down on the left, and costs £3. Otherwise some fans have informed me that they have parked at the nearby cinema and bowling complex. However, if you do this, please make sure it is legal to park there before you do so.

Thanks to Nick Pleasant for providing the directions.

By Train
Doncaster Station is just under two miles away from the ground, so you are probably best taking a taxi. If you do have time on your hands and you fancy the long walk, then it is a fairly straight route from the railway station. As you exit, turn left and walk across to the shopping centre. Walk through the centre out on to St Sepulchre Gate and turn left. Proceed up the hill and then take a right into the High Street which runs into Hall Gate. Keep straight on this road for about a mile and you will eventually reach Belle Vue on your right after crossing a large roundabout. The ground is across the road from the race course. Please note that Hall Gate Road becomes South Parade, then Bennethorpe Road and then Bawtry Road (A638). It should take around 20-25 minutes to walk this route.

Thanks to David Thornbury and Tym Honeybone for providing the above directions.

Nick Pleasant adds: 'You can also catch the No. 57 bus from Duke Street in the town centre. Exit the railway station from the front entrance and cross over the dual carriage way using the crossing. Turn right and walk for around 200 yards to the second street on the left. Go down here and walk up to McDonald's, and take the first right after McDonald's into Duke Street. The first bus stop that you reach is for the No. 57 to Cantley. Get off the bus after the large roundabout where Doncaster Racecourse is situated. The bus takes around 5-10 minutes depending on traffic. The cost is around 70p for an adult and 40p for a child.

LOCAL RIVALS

Rotherham and Scunthorpe United.

ADMISSION PRICES

The Club operate a category system (A & B) for ticket prices, whereby the more popular matches cost more to watch. Category B prices are shown below in brackets.
Seating: Adults: £18 (£15), Concessions: £12 (£10)
Terrace: Adults: £15 (£13), Concessions: £8 (£5)

PROGRAMME

Official Programme: £2.

RECORD ATTENDANCE

37,149 v Hull City
Third Division North, October 2, 1948

AVERAGE ATTENDANCE

2003-2004: 6,939 (Division Three).

DID YOU KNOW?

That the Club have played at Belle Vue since 1922.

PRIESTFIELD STADIUM, GILLINGHAM

THE RAINHAM END

Ground Name: Priestfield Stadium
Capacity: 11,582 (all-seated)
Address: Redfern Avenue,
Gillingham, Kent, ME7 4DD
Main Telephone No: 01634-300-000
Main Fax No: 01634-850-986
Ticket Office: 01634-300-000 (choose option 3)
Team Nickname: The Gills
Pitch Size: 114 x 75 yards
Home Kit Colours: Blue & Black Hoops
Official Website:
www.gillinghamfootballclub.com
Unofficial Websites:
GFC Online: www.gfconline.co.uk
Gills World: www.gillsworld.co.uk
Gills Connect:
http://gillingham.rivals.net/default.asp?sid=934
(Rivals Network)
West Country Supporters:
www.geocities.com/wheres_the_tables
Up The Gills: www.geocities.com/upthegillsuk/

WHAT'S THE GROUND LIKE?

Priestfield Stadium has been virtually rebuilt since the current Chairman Paul Scally took over in 1995. On one side of the ground is the impressive two-tiered Medway Stand, opened in 2000, with a row of executive boxes (the type which you can sit outside of) running across the middle. Opposite is the tidy all-seater Gordon Road Stand. Unfortunately though, it contains a number of supporting pillars, which may hinder your view. This also has an unusual TV gantry perched on its roof. The Rainham End has also been redeveloped, with a single-tier cantilevered stand, which replaced a former terrace. It is an open all-seated temporary stand, erected on what was the former Gillingham End terrace. It is hoped that this will be replaced with a permanent 3,200 seated stand at some point. This stand has been named the Brian Moore Stand in memory of the legendary

commentator and lifelong Gills fan.

FUTURE GROUND DEVELOPMENTS

Even though a lot of money has already been spent in transforming Priestfield, the ambitious Chairman still wants the Club to move to a new larger purpose built stadium, which could be open for the 2008/09 season. On the face of it, this would seem to be good news, but there is a catch: the new stadium is unlikely to be situated in the Medway Towns, but somewhere else within Kent. Obviously this prospect has upset some fans and it would seem that a lot of discussions need to take place before a final decision is made.

WHAT'S IT LIKE FOR VISITORS?

Away fans are housed in part of the Brian Moore Stand where around 1,500 supporters can be accommodated. Like last season, the stand is of the temporary variety i.e. the type that you would see around the 18th hole at the British Open Golf Championship, although it is of a good size and height, plus the views of the playing action are fine. Unlike most temporary stands though, the facilities are surprisingly good, being of a permanent nature behind the stand. However, it is uncovered so be prepared to get wet! One unusual aspect of visiting Priestfield Stadium is that away supporters have to walk down a very narrow terraced street to reach the away entrance or, if coming from adjacent streets, down very tight alley ways. However, there is never normally any problems with this although after the game the police sometimes close some of the surrounding streets to keep fans apart.

WHERE TO DRINK

The ground is walkable from the town centre where there are a fair few pubs to be found. Paul Kelly, a visiting Preston fan, adds: 'We have used the Will

Adams in the town centre. The pub is in the good beer guide and does good cheap food. Plus there is a very friendly crowd of football locals happy to indulge in friendly banter - the landlord is a Gill fan too!' Robert Donaldson recommends the Southern Belle opposite the railway station, which also has a café next door. Robert Phipps, a Gillingham supporter, recommends The Ship public house on the Lower Rainham Road. Away fans though should avoid The Cricketers in Sturdee Avenue.

Michelle Dixon, the landlady of the Livingstone Arms on Gillingham Road, informs me: 'Our pub is known as an Away Supporters pub and is situated approximately 100 yards from the away turnstiles. The atmosphere within the pub is both warm and friendly and there is even complimentary bar food laid on for fans. Otherwise, you can purchase a hot pie with your pint, or visit the local chip shop, situated across the road.' This pub, which also has a beer garden, is popular with both away and home supporters and, as you would expect, it gets rather busy on matchdays.

GETTING THERE & WHERE TO PARK

Leave the M2 at Junction 4 and take the A278 towards Gillingham, going straight across two roundabouts. At the third roundabout, turn left onto the A2 towards Gillingham town centre. At the traffic light junction with the A231, turn right into Nelson Road and passing the small bus station, take a right turn into Gillingham Road. The ground is down on your right. Street Parking.

By Train
The ground is about a 10 minute walk from Gillingham railway station, which is served by trains from London Victoria (every 15 minutes) and Charing Cross (every 30 minutes). Robert Donaldson provides the following directions: 'Turn left out of the station and follow the road until you come to a crossroads. Go straight on into Priestfield Road. The visitors' turnstiles are at the far end of Priestfield Road. Allow 10 minutes to get from the station and into the ground'.

To get to the home areas, turn right at the crossroads and then first left into Gordon Road for the Gillingham End Terrace home area, the Gordon Road Stand and the Rainham End. For the Medway Stand or an alternative route to the Rainham End, turn left at the crossroads and then first right. At the far end, the road turns right and then left.

LOCAL RIVALS

With a lack of other league clubs in the area, Gillingham fans have focused on Millwall.

ADMISSION PRICES

Like a lot of clubs Gillingham operate a category system (AAA, AA & A) for different games, meaning

that the most popular games cost more to watch. AAA category prices are shown below with AA and A prices shown in brackets.
Home Fans:
Medway Stand (Upper Tier Centre):
Adults: £30 (£24) (£20), OAPs & Students: £26 (£20) (£14), Juveniles: £17 (£14) (£11)
Medway Stand (Upper Tier Wings):
Adults: £26 (£20) (£15), OAPs & Students: £24 (£17) (£13), Juveniles: £17 (£13) (£10)
Medway Stand (Lower Tier Centre):
Adults: £34 (£24) (£22), No Concessions
Medway Stand (Lower Tier Wings):
Adults: £30 (£23) (£17), OAPs & Students: £26 (£17) (£13), Juveniles: £17 (£14) (£11)
Medway Stand (Lower Tier Outer Wings):
Adults: £25 (£19) (£14), OAPs & Students: £23 (£15) (£13), Juveniles: £16 (£12) (£10), Minors: £12 (£8) (£6)
Gordon Road Stand (Centre):
Adults: £30 (£23) (£17), OAPs & Students: £24 (£17) (£13), Juveniles: £22 (£13) (£10)
Gordon Road Stand (Wings):
Adults: £26 (£20) (£16), OAPs & Students: £23 (£15) (£13), Juveniles: £19 (£12) (£10)
Gordon Road Stand (Outer Wings):
Adults: £24 (£16) (£13), OAPs & Students: £22 (£14) (£11), Juveniles: £18 (£10) (£8), Minors £12 (£7) (£5)
Brian Moore Stand:
Adults: £24 (£13) (£10), OAPs & Students: £20 (£11) (£8), Juveniles: £18 (£9) (£7), Minors: £12 (£7) (£5)
Rainham End:
Adults: £26 (£20) (£18), OAPs & Students: £24 (£17) (£15), Juveniles: £18 (£13) (£10)
Away Fans:
Brian Moore Stand:
Adults: £24 (£13) (£10), OAPs & Students: £20 (£11) (£8), Juveniles: £18 (£9) (£7), Minors: £12 (£7) (£5)

PROGRAMME & FANZINE

Official Programme: £2.50
Brian Moore's Head Fanzine: £1.50

RECORD ATTENDANCE

23,002 v Queens Park Rangers
FA Cup 3rd Round, January 10, 1948.

AVERAGE ATTENDANCE

2003-2004: 8,517 (Division One).

DID YOU KNOW?

That when Anglo-Saxons tribes settled somewhere in Kent they called their place 'Gillingham', meaning 'The House of the Shouting Men'.

VICTORIA PARK, HARTLEPOOL

Ground Name: Victoria Park
Capacity: 7,629
Address: Clarence Road, Hartlepool, TS24 8BZ
Main Telephone No: 01429-272-584
Main Fax No: 01429-863-007
Pitch Size: 113 x 77 yards
Team Nickname: The Pool
Home Kit Colours: Royal Blue & White
Official Website: www.hartlepoolunited.co.uk
Unofficial Websites:
In The Net: www.inthenet.hufc.net (Rivals Network)
Monkey Business: www.bizz.hufc.net

WHAT'S THE GROUND LIKE?

The ground was greatly improved in the mid 1990s, with the construction of two new stands at one end and one side of the ground. The Cyril Knowles Stand is the newer of the two side stands. It is a small single-tier covered all-seated stand, raised above the ground level. The other side, the Camerons Brewery Stand, has covered seating to the rear and open terrace to the front. This stand does not run the full length of the pitch and has an odd mix of orange and green seating that clashes with the Club's colours. Both ends are small covered affairs. The newer end is the small Expamet Town End, a covered terrace, for home fans. The other end, the Rink End stand, is a small covered all-seated stand which houses away supporters.

Derek Hall adds: 'All real Hartlepool fans nickname the Club Pools (not The Pool). This goes back to the pre-1967 days when the boroughs of (old) Hartlepool and West Hartlepool became amalgamated as just Hartlepool. It was because of the existence of the two very separate towns that the club was actually called Hartlepools United in the first

place. That said though, I'd prefer to see us called The Monkey Hangers!'

WHAT'S IT LIKE FOR VISITORS?

Ben Fuggles advised me to 'bring a jumper even in August!'. He was right. The wind whipping from the North Sea goes right through you, so wrap up well unless there is a heat wave. Away fans are in the Rink End Stand at one end of the ground, where up to 967 can be seated. Unfortunately there are a few supporting pillars in this stand, which may hinder your view, especially if there is a large away following. However, acoustics are good even for small numbers. Look out for the biggest meat and potato pies you have ever seen being served within the ground, they are huge! Generally I found the Hartlepool supporters okay, but unfortunately my day was spoiled by some crowd trouble at the game. I prefer thinking about the opposition's culpability rather than the Pools fans, but as the saying goes: 'It takes two to tango'.

If you wonder why Hartlepool are referred to as the 'Monkey Hangers' it is because the residents of Hartlepool are famously said to have hanged a monkey that was washed up from a ship which had sunk during the Napoleonic wars, because they thought the monkey was a French spy. The Club take this to good heart and of course who else would they have as their club mascot? H'Angus the monkey of course!

WHERE TO DRINK

The Victoria Suite near the entrance to the away end is for members only. At the same end but at the opposite corner, is the Corner Flag Supporters Bar that welcomes away fans. The entrance fee is 50p, but the bar has a good pre-match atmosphere and SKY TV. Popular with away fans is the Jackson's Wharf Pub near the ground. It has good food and real ale on tap. This pub is over the road from the ASDA store, to the left of the old sailing ship. Otherwise the ground is not far from the town centre where there are plenty of pubs to be found.

Ronnie Chambers adds: 'I would recommend The Causeway, a 15 minute walk from the ground. It is located just around the corner from the brewery near the church, has real ale and is very friendly. The Engineers Club, five minutes from the ground opposite the police station, just off the town centre is okay, as is the Raglan Club just behind the visitors end. Usual club rules apply regarding entry for these'.

GETTING THERE & WHERE TO PARK

From the A19 take the A689 signposted Hartlepool. Follow the A689 towards the Town Centre. Follow Town Centre signs for 2.8 miles, over two roundabouts. Go straight over the next two sets of lights, passing Hartlepool College on your right. The next left takes you to the stadium. If you miss the turning (as I did), go past ASDA on your left, left at the next roundabout and then left at the next traffic lights for the ground. There is a fair sized car park at the ground. Otherwise there is plenty of street parking to be found behind the away end.

By Train
Hartlepool train station is a 10 minute walk from the ground. Leave the station and go straight up a short approach road. At the end of the approach, turn right and head up Church Street towards the large church. At the end of this road is a bridge and junction with the A689. Go straight across the junction and the ground is in front of you on the left-hand side of the road. Thanks to Richard Brackstone for providing the directions.

LOCAL RIVALS

Darlington.

ADMISSION PRICES

Home Fans:
Cyril Knowles Stand (Seats): Adults: £17, OPAS/Under 16s: £9
Camerons Brewery Stand (Seats): Adults: £17, OPAS/Under 16s: £9
Camerons Brewery Stand (Terrace): Adults: £15, OPAS/Under 16s: £8
Expamet Town End (Terrace): Adults: £15, OPAS/Under 16s: £8
Family Enclosure: Adults: £17, OPAS/Under 16s: £6

Away Fans:
Rink End (Seats): Adults: £17, OPAS/Under 16s: £9

Students can also qualify for a concessionary price in the home areas, providing that the ticket is purchased from the ticket office and a valid student identity card is produced on purchase.

PROGRAMME & FANZINE

Official Programme: £2.50.
Monkey Business Fanzine: £1.

RECORD ATTENDANCE

17,426 v Manchester United
FA Cup 3rd Round, January 5, 1957.

AVERAGE ATTENDANCE

2003-2004: 5,419 (Division Two).

DID YOU KNOW?

The Victoria ground was a former rubbish tip made into a sports ground in 1886 and named after the Queen, who celebrated her Golden Jubilee in the following year.

GALPHARM STADIUM, HUDDERSFIELD

Ground Name: Galpharm Stadium
Capacity: 24,500 (all-seated)
Address: Galpharm Stadium, Huddersfield, HD1 6PX
Main Telephone No: 01484-484-100
Ticket Office: 01484-484-123
Fax No: 01484-484-101
Team Nickname: The Terriers
Home Kit Colours: Blue & White
Official Website: www.htafc.com
Unofficial Websites:
HuddersfieldNet: www.thehuddersfield.net
Huddersfield Town Down Under:
http://home.primus.com.au/jthorpe/huddersfield_town.htm
Terrier Bytes: www.terrier-bytes.com
Down At The Mac: www.downatthemac.com
(Rivals Network)

WHAT'S THE GROUND LIKE?

This stadium was opened with three sides in 1995, the last stand being added a season later. The club previously played just down the road at the Leeds Road ground, now the site of a B & Q Superstore. Most new stadiums in this country are rather boring affairs with little character, but the Galpharm (I don't think I'll ever get used to that new name!) does not fall into this category. Each stand is semi-circular rather than rectangular, and is further enhanced with large white steel tubing above the contours. In fact, from the car park, I first thought it looked like a new ride at Alton Towers! It is good to see something different from the architects for a change. The ground has won many design awards and is well worth a visit. The only disappointment is that the corners of the ground are open. The North Stand at one end and the Lawrence Batley Stand at one side are both two-tiered stands, each with a row of executive boxes running across the middle. The other two sides of the ground are large single-tiered affairs. There is an electric scoreboard at the back of the away end.

WHAT'S IT LIKE FOR VISITORS?

I had an enjoyable evening at the Glapharm Stadium. I was thoroughly impressed with the stadium and its facilities. The Club try hard to whip up the atmosphere with a band in the North Stand and a drummer in the John Smiths Stand. There is also a section of the lower tier of the

HUDDERSFIELD TOWN

Lawrence Batley Stand, where the home fans continually bait the away fans, resulting in a number of police taking up positions between the two sets of supporters. I personally did not experience any problems when I went, but it is worth bearing in mind that the Huddersfield fans are passionate about their club and this can make for an intimidating atmosphere. Exercise caution around the ground and in the town centre. Away fans are located at one end of the ground in the Travelworld (South) Stand, where the facilities are good and the view of the action excellent. There is a Ladbrokes outlet and a bar at the back of the stand. Up to 4,000 away fans can be accommodated.

WHERE TO DRINK

The ground is walkable from the town centre, albeit a long one! (20 minutes). Robert Smith recommends the Peacock, Rickys Bar and the Bradley Mills Working Mens Club. They are all located on Leeds Road, about 5-10 minutes walk from the stadium. There is also a cinema and entertainment complex behind the North Stand, where there is the Rope Walk pub. However, on my last visit, all of the above bars were not allowing in away fans, although I did manage to get into the Rope Walk Pub (I was not wearing colours), where I enjoyed an excellent pint. Dougie Hames recommends the Gas Club on Gasworks Street: 'All fans and families are welcome and the club offers Bass beers and food and you can also park in the patrolled club car park at a cost of £2. The club is easy to find as it is right by the large gas holder'.

Otherwise it is probably best to drink within the ground itself, as there are open bars at the back of the away end. If you can't bear to watch your team during the game, you can always escape as the bars remain open during the first half and half-time. They even serve draught Guinness!

GETTING THERE & WHERE TO PARK

The stadium is just off the A62 Leeds Road. It can be easiest reached from Junction 25 of the M62. Simply follow the signs for Huddersfield (A62) and you will come to the stadium on your left. Alternatively, if approaching from the South, then leave the M1 at Junction 38 and take the A637 towards and then the A642 into Huddersfield. As you approach the town centre try to keep to the right-hand lane as you will turn right at the island and go onto the A62 Leeds Road. The stadium is a short distance down this road on the right. For the car parks, turn right at the traffic lights, where the Market Pub is on the corner. The stadium is generally well signposted around Huddersfield town centre.

There is a fair sized car park located at the ground (£4) and a number of unofficial car parks nearby (expect to pay around £3).

By Train
The ground is walkable from Huddersfield train station, albeit a long one (15-20 minutes). After coming out of the railway station, turn down past the front of The George Hotel. Go straight over the crossroads into Northumberland Street and walk down across the Ring Road straight on into Leeds Road. Turn right down Gasworks Street and straight over crossroads to the ground.

LOCAL RIVALS

Bradford City and Leeds United.

ADMISSION PRICES

Home Fans:
Lawrence Batley Stand (Upper Tier): Adults: £19 OAPs: £11, Juniors: £8
Lawrence Batley Stand (Lower Tier): Adults: £17.50 OAPs: £9, Juniors: £6
John Smiths Stand: Adults: £16, OAPs: £8, Juniors:£5
Panasonic Stand: Adults: £16, OAPs: £8, Juniors: £5
Away Fans:
Travelworld Stand: Adults: £16, OAPs: £8, Juniors: £5

Students can also qualify for a concessionary price in the home areas, providing that the ticket is purchased from the ticket office and a valid student identity card is produced on purchase.

PROGRAMME

Official Programme: £2.

RECORD ATTENDANCE

At Leeds Road;
67,037 v Arsenal
FA Cup 6th Round, February 27, 1932.
At the Galpharm Stadium:
23,678 v Liverpool
FA Cup 3rd Round, December 12, 1999.

AVERAGE ATTENDANCE

2003-2004: 10,528 (Division Three).

DID YOU KNOW?

That Town's first set of shirts for the 1908/09 season were red and this earned them the nickname 'The Scarlet Runners'.

MILTON KEYNES DONS

NATIONAL HOCKEY STADIUM, MILTON KEYNES

Ground Name: National Hockey Stadium
Capacity: 9,000 (all-seated)
Address: Silbury Boulevard, Milton Keynes, MK9 1HA
Main Telephone No: 01908-607-090
Main Fax No: 01908-209-449
Ticket Office: 01908-609-000
Team Nickname: The Dons
Home Kit Colours: All white
Official Website: www.wimbledon-fc.co.uk

Unofficial Websites:
It's Been Emotional: www.itsbeenemotional.com
Supporters Club: www.mkdonsclub.co.uk
Dons MK: www.donsmk.com

WHAT'S THE GROUND LIKE?

After a long running soap opera, the Club finally moved last season from their South London roots, 65 miles up the M1 to the new town of Milton Keynes, where they have taken up residence at the National Hockey Stadium. The move has upset a number of fans, who fear that the it may pave the way for future teams moving around the country, threatening the fabric of English Football as we know it. This feeling has not been dampened with the announcement that the Club has been given permission to change its name from Wimbledon to Milton Keynes Dons. So effectively as most of us thought would be the outcome, Wimbledon Football Club is now dead and a new Milton Keynes club has taken their place in their league. Which club might be next I wonder.....
    The stadium itself is fairly new, having been built

in the mid 1990s. On one side is a good sized single-tier cantilever stand. Known as the South (Main) Stand, it is covered, all-seated, with a fair sized press area located within it. Opposite is a small block of seating that straddles the halfway line. This stand, like the rest of the remaining parts of the stadium, is open to the elements (although there are rumours that a cover will be added to the East Stand for the 2004/05 season). The arrival of the football club has meant that the stadium has had its capacity almost doubled with the construction of two temporary seated stands located at each end. These small stands are almost identical, with the West Stand given to visiting supporters. The stadium used to have an artificial pitch but to meet League rules, this has been replaced with a grass surface that on my last visit looked very good.

FUTURE GROUND DEVELOPMENTS

Work is shortly to commence on clearing a site at Denbeigh North after Milton Keynes Council granted planning permission for the Club to build a new 30,000 seater stadium. If things go according to plan then the Club could be kicking off in their new home for the start of the 2006/07 season.

WHAT'S IT LIKE FOR VISITORS?

Away fans are normally located at one end of the ground, in the West Stand, where up to 2,300 fans can be housed. If demand requires it, then the North Stand can also be allocated to away supporters, further increasing the allocation by another 1,000. The West Stand has the feel of a temporary stand rather than a permanent structure, with lots of scaffolding and corrugated sheeting in evidence. There is a walkway running under the stand for its full width and if you do walk along it, you really see how the stand seems to have been bolted together, rather than being built as a permanent structure. This stand is all-seated and is open to the elements so hope that it doesn't rain. Entrance to the ground is by ticket only, so away supporters arriving without tickets need to first purchase one from the small ticket office located at the south-west corner of the stadium (at one side of the Main Stand going towards the away end). Please also note that the stadium is a no smoking one.

To be honest, I had not been looking forward to visiting the stadium as it had a negative image to me. But I was actually pleasantly surprised. There was some atmosphere being created from the home fans, the stewarding was relaxed and the facilities inside weren't that bad, plus the legroom and view from the away stand were good. My only real grumble was that on each side of the away end there were blocks of portakabin type toilets, which in the men's case seemed to have poorly designed entrances that allowed passers-by to look directly in onto the urinals. Refreshments were provided by two burger vans selling the usual array of burgers, hot dogs and chips and on my visit they did quite well in serving the sold out away end. Outside the stadium, behind the North Stand, is a McDonald's and a Burger King outlet. I and the away fans around me were quite amused with the loudspeaker request before the game for away fans to refrain from jumping up and down, in case it caused structural problems!

WHERE TO DRINK

On my visit, the police were helpfully pointing away fans in the direction of a bar called Chicagos which has been designated as an away fans pub. It is only a five minute walk from the stadium, being located above the bus station, which is just in front and to the right of the railway station. Although it was fairly easy to get served in Chicagos, the venue is more suited to being a night club and for me it was a bit soulless. A better bet if you arrive a bit earlier is to make the slightly further walk to the Wetherspoons located behind Abbey National's head office. I stress arriving earlier as this pub gets extremely busy in the hour prior to kick off. It's located just up Midsummer Boulevard (the road going up from the railway station towards the central shopping area).

Behind the East Stand across the dual carriageway is located a Staples and a Travelodge. If you look over the road to the right of these you will see a large red bricked office block which is the Abbey National head office. The Wetherspoons is located one block behind this building. Further up Midsummer Boulevard on the right is another Wetherspoons outlet called the Secklow Hundred, plus a Bar Med, and All Bar One. These latter three pubs are about a 10 minute walk away.

GETTING THERE & WHERE TO PARK

Leave the M1 at Junction 14 and take the A509 towards Milton Keynes. At the first island turn right onto the H5 Portway (signposted A509 (A5) Central Milton Keynes). Keep straight on this road crossing eight roundabouts. At the ninth roundabout, turn left. The stadium is over on the right. If you do get lost, follow the signs for the railway station as the stadium is located close to it. There is plenty of pay and display car parking around the stadium. This is mostly £1 for five hours immediately behind the home end, but other parking areas can cost as much as £5 for the same period (these areas are indicated by red markings on the roads around the car park bays, so check carefully). For evening games, the pay and display areas are normally free of charge after 6pm.

By Train
Milton Keynes Central is only a few minutes walk away from the stadium. As you come out the station entrance, turn left and the stadium is situated just behind the office block located in front of you.

LOCAL RIVALS

The nearest other League club is Northampton Town.

ADMISSION PRICES

Home Fans:
South Stand: Adults: £20, Concessions: £15
North Stand: Adults: £12, Concessions: £10, Juniors: £5
East Stand: Adults: £15, Concessions: £10, Juniors: £8
East Stand Family Area*: Adults: £10, Concessions: £7, Juniors: £5
Away Fans:
West Stand: Adults: £15, Concessions: £10, Juniors: £8
* Tickets for this area must be purchased prior to matchday.

PROGRAMME & FANZINES

Official Programme: £2.50.

RECORD ATTENDANCE

8,118 v West Ham United
Division One, November 25, 2003.

AVERAGE ATTENDANCE

2003-2004: 4,751 (Division One).

DID YOU KNOW?

That a lot of fans who originally supported Wimbledon in South London, now follow AFC Wimbledon, who were newly formed in 2002. They currently play in the Isthmian League.

CITY GROUND, NOTTINGHAM

Ground Name:	City Ground
Capacity:	30,602 (all-seated)
Address:	City Ground, Nottingham, NG2 5FJ
Main Telephone No:	0115-982-4444
Main Fax No:	0115-982-4455
Ticket Office:	0871-226-1980
Ticket Office Fax No:	0115-982-4470
Team Nickname:	The Reds
Pitch Size:	115 x 78 yards
Home Kit Colours:	Red & White

Official Website:
www.nottinghamforest.co.uk
Unofficial Websites:
Blooming Forest: http://nottinghamforest.rivals.net
(Rivals Network)
Forest@Bugcafe: www.btinternet.com/~bugcafe/
Tricky Trees Message Board -
www.trickytrees.com/forums/
Alternative Forest - www.alternativeforest.co.uk
Lost That Loving Feeling -
www.lostthatlovingfeeling.co.uk

WHAT'S THE GROUND LIKE?

From a distance the ground looks quite picturesque sitting on the banks of the River Trent. Both ends have been redeveloped during the 1990s, much improving the overall appearance. The Bridgford Stand houses away fans in the lower tier; it is odd because one third of this stand was built lower then the rest, due to a local Council planning requirement to allow sunlight through to the houses in nearby Colwick Road. Opposite, the Trent End is the most recent addition to the ground. It is a large two-tiered stand that looks quite smart. One unusual feature of the stand is that running across the middle are a number of rows of seating enclosed within a

covered shaded glass area. On one side there is a similarly impressive two-tiered stand with executive boxes in between, which was built in 1980. Once called the Executive Stand, it was recently renamed the Brian Clough Stand in honour of their greatest manager. Facing this is a smaller and much older Main Stand that now looks quite tired in the company of its shiny new neighbours.

FUTURE GROUND DEVELOPMENTS

Jon Heath informs me: 'The Club have revealed plans to increase the capacity of the City Ground to 40,000. This would involve the redevelopment of the Main Stand. However, this is dependant on Forest gaining promotion to the Premier League and the Club being able to secure the freehold of the City Ground from Nottingham City Council'.

WHAT'S IT LIKE FOR VISITORS?

Up to 4,750 away fans can be accommodated in the lower tier of the Bridgford Stand, where the facilities and view of the action are good. I personally did not have any problems at the City Ground, but I have heard of away fans getting some hassle; for example, it has not been unknown for the odd object to be thrown down on away fans from so-called Forest fans seated above. Also, don't be surprised if the stewards keep asking you to sit down if you stand in the seated areas, which can get annoying. There are also some Forest supporters in the 'A' Block of the Main Stand nearest to the away supporters, who feel it is their duty to continually berate away fans during the game, which can be unsavoury. It is also advised to keep colours covered around the ground, especially if you support another Midlands team. The good news though is that away fans can really make

WHERE TO DRINK

some noise from this stand, so make the most of it!

Michael Whitaker recommends the Larwood & Voce which is about five minutes walk from the away end, on Fox Road (off Radcliffe Road). As Michael says: 'The place is an all-round good pre-match pub. Every time I've been there it's well occupied by away and Forest fans'. Michael adds that the Southbank, very near to the ground, and the King John in the City Centre, should be avoided by away supporters. Paul Stevens adds: 'The Trent Bridge Inn (TBI) next to the cricket ground is another pub the away fans are advised to steer clear of. They have doormen at the entrance checking matchday tickets to make sure you are a home supporter'. Simon Phillips recommends the Stratford Haven, just down the road from the Larwood & Voce, where there is great beer and food, very bustling and is used by both home and away fans'. Whilst Tim Cooke, a travelling Millwall fan, has a different angle (so to speak): 'Definitely one for the lads! Hooters (on the main road A6011, on the outskirts of the City Centre, you can't miss it!) has very nice waitresses wearing just enough to cover things up, serves lovely beer, and great food. Take my advice, make a weekend of it, Nottingham is a top city!' Otherwise, alcohol is available inside the ground, including Fosters, John Smiths & Guinness.

GETTING THERE & WHERE TO PARK

From The North:
Leave the M1 at Junction 26 and take the A610 towards Nottingham and then signs for Melton Mowbray. Cross the River Trent and you will see the ground on your left. Alternatively as you approach Nottingham on the A610, you will pick up signs for 'football traffic'. Although following these seems to take you all around the outskirts of Nottingham, you do eventually end up at the City Ground along the A6011.

From The South:
Leave the M1 at Junction 24 and take the A453 towards Nottingham. Then take the A52 East towards Grantham and then onto the A6011 into Nottingham. The ground is situated by the A6011.

Rowland Lee provides an alternative route: 'Leave the M1 at Junction 21a (Leicester East) and follow the A46 dual carriageway towards Newark. After around 20 miles, take the A606 towards Nottingham. At the first roundabout that is the junction with the A52, take the fourth exit onto the A52, signposted towards Grantham. At the next roundabout turn left onto the A6011 towards Nottingham. The ground is about a mile down this road.

There is a large car park at the ground; otherwise there is some street parking. Steve Barratt informs

me: 'Regarding the parking at Forest, the council operate a car park on matchdays on the Victoria Embankment. They charge £3 but it is only a two minute walk to the ground. The car park is right on the banks of the River Trent, on the ground side of the river, but on the other side of the dual carriageway from the ground'. Gerry Toms adds: 'Bear in mind that as the one end of the ground backs onto the River Trent, you cannot drive around it, so it is probably best to park at first available opportunity or you may find yourself crossing the River Trent and having to comeback on yourself again'.

By Train
The ground is walkable from Nottingham railway station (20 minutes). As you come out of the main station entrance, turn left and then left again. Follow the road down to the dual carriageway and then turn right. The ground is about three-quarters of a mile down the dual carriageway on the left, just over Trent Bridge.

LOCAL RIVALS

Derby County and Leicester City.

ADMISSION PRICES

The Club operate a category system (AA & A) whereby the most popular matches (category AA) such as against Derby and Sunderland cost more to see. Category A prices are shown where applicable below in brackets:

All Areas Of The Ground:
Adults: £31 (£25)
Senior Citizens: £22 (£17)
Students Under 23: £16 (£10)
Under 16s: £14 (£10)

PROGRAMME & FANZINE

Official Programme: £2.50.
Blooming Forest Fanzine: £1.

RECORD ATTENDANCE

49,946 v Manchester United
Division One, October 28, 1967.

AVERAGE ATTENDANCE

2003-2004: 24,751 (Division One).

DID YOU KNOW?

That innovative Forest were the first team ever to use shin guards in 1874.

BOUNDARY PARK, OLDHAM

Ground Name: Boundary Park
Capacity: 13,624 (all-seated)
Address: Boundary Park, Oldham, OL1 2PA
Main Telephone No: 0870-753-2000
Main Fax No: 0161-627-5915
Pitch Size: 106 x 72 yards
Team Nickname: The Latics
Home Kit Colours: Blue With White Trim
Official Website:
www.oldhamathletic.co.uk
Unofficial Websites:
Oldham Athletic E-Zine: www.oafc.co.uk
Latics Supporters Club Canada:
http://latics.cjb.net/
Come On Oldham: www.comeonoldham.co.uk

WHAT'S THE GROUND LIKE?

At one end is the comparatively new Rochdale Road End, a good sized all-seater covered stand with an excellent view of the pitch. It has windshields on both sides and an electric scoreboard on its roof. Part of this stand is given to away supporters. The other end, the Seton Stand, is a medium sized all-seater covered stand. Again, there are windshields to either side, but the elderly nature of this stand is apparent from the supporting pillars running across the front of it. On one side there is an old two-tiered Main Stand, now named the Pukka Pies Stand. This used to have terracing in front, since filled with seating. There is still some old unused terracing on one side of this stand. On the other side is the

small Lookers Stand. This is a covered seated stand that doesn't quite run the full length of the pitch. Again there are a number of pillars in the upper tier, where there is also a television gantry suspended beneath its roof. The stand is unusual in giving the impression of being on a slope - the lower tier has more seats on one side than the other. Part of this stand has a Police Control Box, whilst on the other side there is a strange single storey executive box like structure, built on stilts. The ground also benefits from four large floodlight pylons, leaving the visitor in no doubt that this is a football ground. The Club has a mascot called 'Chaddy The Champion Owl'.

FUTURE GROUND DEVELOPMENTS

The Club's new owners have announced that they are looking at the possibility of replacing the present Lookers Stand with a new 6,500 capacity stand. No timescales have been announced as to when the development might take place, but it is believed that the Club will soon be drawing up plans for the new stand.

WHAT'S IT LIKE FOR VISITORS?

Away fans are housed in the Rochdale Road Stand at one end of the ground, where the normal allocation is 1,800 seats. This can be increased to over 4,000 if required. Dependent on numbers, the Rochdale Road End is either given totally to the away support or is shared with home fans. If the latter applies, away fans are kept separate from the home fans by a large moat like gap, which certainly makes for a lot of banter. The facilities in this newer stand are fairly good, as are the acoustics. If you get a chance, make sure to try a Pukka pie (£1.50). Some fans reckon that this is the best part of a visit to Boundary Park.

I found this Club to be particularly friendly. They have an unofficial motto that 'the only club we hate is Man United', everyone else is very welcome. The only complaint that I had about visiting the ground was that it always seems to be cold, with a biting wind that goes right through you. This is due to Oldham being on the edge of the Pennines.

WHERE TO DRINK

The Clayton Arms pub is on one corner of the ground. This small comfortable pub serves Lees beers, reasonably priced food and has a large screen to show SKY Television. It gets extremely busy on matchdays.

Chippy Lees, an exiled Latics fans in Cornwall, recommends the following: 'The Old Grey Mare on Rochdale Road is worth a visit. If you walk to the top of Sheepfoot Lane and turn left at the newspaper shop, the pub is about 100 yards down the road on the right. There's a varied selection of beers available, and again a warm welcome is assured. Further down on the right is The White Hart. If you turn right at the top of Sheepfoot Lane, you'll eventually come to The Queens. It's on the corner of a junction. It was frequented by several West Ham fans one night, who found the beer to be so good and cheap compared to London prices, that they decided to stay there for the rest of the evening. It was just as well, as it was the usual bone chilling night, and they lost! Across the road is The Royal, which is a cosy little local and next door is a larger more modern one, the Brook Tavern'.

If you are arriving by train, there are other pubs you can visit en route. See below.

GETTING THERE & WHERE TO PARK

Leave the M62 at Junction 20 and take the A627(M) towards Oldham. Take the second slip road off the A627(M) following the signs for Royton (A663). At the top of the slip road you will find a large roundabout which has a McDonald's and a KFC around it. Turn left at the roundabout onto the A663 towards Royton (beware though of 30mph speed cameras on this stretch). You will be able to see Boundary Park over on your right. Take the next right-hand turn into Hilbre Avenue which will take you up to the large Club car park,

situated behind the Lookers Stand. The cost of the car park is: cars £2, mini buses £5, coaches £10.

If you want to go straight to the Club main entrance, then at the roundabout take the second exit onto A627 Chadderton Way (signposted Oldham). After around 300 yards, take the first left into Boundary Park Road and at the end of the road turn right into Sheepfoot Lane.

By Train

There are three stations that you could use to get to Boundary Park. Oldham Mumps, Oldham Werneth or Mill Hills. However Oldham Mumps is a 45 minute walk from the ground and is not really practical. Better bets would be Oldham Werneth or Mills Hill. These stations are served by North West Trains on the Oldham Rochdale loop. Trains for Oldham depart from Manchester Victoria platforms 1 or 6. If you buy a ticket to Oldham and arrive from the South at Manchester Piccadilly, your fare includes travel on the Metrolink to Victoria station. As you exit the platforms at Piccadilly turn left for the Metrolink station. Take the tram for BURY only to get to Manchester Victoria.

Oldham Werneth

The station is around a 15 minute walk from the ground. Exit the station and turn right onto Featherstall Road South and walk for about three-quarter miles through one set of traffic lights and a small roundabout at Tesco until you come to a large roundabout. Turn left onto Chadderton Way (cross over at the underpass as Chadderton Way is a dual carriageway) and follow for another quarter mile until you come to Boundary Park Road (by the B&Q Warehouse), turn right and Boundary Park is ahead. You will be approaching the ground from the home supporters' end, so at the end of Boundary Park Road, turn right up Sheepfoot Lane past the main stand to the other end of the ground. It is extremely unusual for any taxis to be at Werneth station.

Chippy Lees adds: 'As you walk along Featherstall Road away from Werneth station, you will encounter quite a few Indian restaurants and pubs, which are worth a visit. Turn right from the station and walk until you come to Tesco's at the top of the road. Turn left at the dual-carriageway and Boundary Park is on the right. Again, there are several pubs on the way, the best being The Spinners across from the dual-carriageway'.

Mills Hill

Nick Archer informs me: 'Mills Hill station is on the Oldham-Rochdale loop and is also served by some trains coming from York, Leeds, Huddersfield, Halifax, Wakefield, Liverpool, Wigan and Blackpool. The only difference to the travelling arrangements from Manchester Victoria is that fans should ONLY BOARD trains going to ROCHDALE and ensure checking the train does stop at Mills Hill, as some go direct to Rochdale. Trains usually run every half an hour from Manchester. It takes about 20 minutes to walk to the ground from this station.

Mills Hill station itself is closer than Oldham Werneth station and the walk to the ground passes two very nice, hospitable pubs! As you leave the station, head towards the traffic lights. There, you will see a large pub called the Rose Of Lancaster, which is cheap and serves bar meals. Continue up the road (Burnley Lane) on which the Rose Of Lancaster is situated. On the right you will come to a school called North Chadderton Comprehensive and a set of lights. Bear to the right at these lights. Keep going until you reach another pub called the Chadderton Park Inn which is situated on a large roundabout. Boundary Park is in view from here. Then simply cross the road in the direction of the ground (using the subway is highly recommended!) and head towards the ground. This route also brings you directly to the away end!"

Jon Brierley adds: 'Alternatively, rather than getting a train from Manchester to Oldham, you may find it easier to take a bus from Manchester Piccadilly Bus Station. Services operate every 15 minutes or so on Saturday afternoon. Numbers 25, 181 and 182 make the 25 minute trip to Oldham and go past the ground. Doing this would allow you to nip into the Rifle Range pub on Burnley Lane, where the beer is both good and cheap'.

LOCAL RIVALS

Manchester United and Manchester City.

ADMISSION PRICES

Home Fans:
Pukka Pies Main Stand (Upper): Adults: £18, OAPs/Under 16s: £9
Pukka Pies Main Stand (Lower): Adults: £17, OAPs/Under 16s: £9
Lookers Stand (Upper): Adults £18, OAPs/Under 16s: £9
Lookers Stand (Lower): Adults: £14, OAPs/Under 16s: £8
SSL Stand: Adults: £18, OAPs/Under 16s: £9, Under 12s: £3
Slumberland Dunlopillow Rochdale Road End: Adults: £18, OAPs/Under 16s: £9
Away Fans:
Rochdale Road End: Adults: £18, OAPs/Under 16s: £9

PROGRAMME & FANZINES

Official Programme: £2.

RECORD ATTENDANCE

47,671 v Sheffield Wednesday
FA Cup 5th Round, January 25, 1930.

AVERAGE ATTENDANCE

2003-2004: 6,566 (Division Two).

DID YOU KNOW?

In terms of feet above sea level, Boundary Park is the third highest ground in the Premier and Football Leagues.

VALE PARK, PORT VALE

Ground Name: Vale Park
Capacity: 23,000 (all-seated)
Address: Hamil Rd, Burslem, Stoke On Trent, ST6 1AW
Main Telephone No: 01782-655-800
Main Fax No: 01782-836-875
Ticket Office: 01782-811-707
Team Nickname: The Valiants
Pitch Size: 114 x 77 yards
Home Kit Colours: White & Black
Official Website: www.port-vale.co.uk
Unofficial Website:
One Vale Fan: www.onevalefan.co.uk

WHAT'S THE GROUND LIKE?

At one end of the ground is a fair sized single-tiered all-seated stand, complete with an electric scoreboard on the roof. This stand, the Phones4U Stand, houses the away supporters and it replaced a former open terrace. Opposite is the Big AM Stand, covered and all-seated. The corners on either side of this stand have been filled. The Carling Stand (also known as the Railway Stand) on one side is fair sized, covered and all-seated. All three of these stands have a small number of supporting pillars, halfway up them, which may restrict your view. The other side, the Lorne Street Stand, is a relatively new smart looking 5,000 all-seated stand, complete with 48 executive boxes, which so far has been half built. To keep some sense of history, the original clock from the old stand has been incorporated into the new construction. Unfortunately it is unclear when

this stand will be completed as building work has been suspended due to lack of finance. A pity, as the empty predominantly concrete area really brings the ground down. Still, if this stand does get completed, it will look superb. On the opposite corner is a Police Control Box keeping a watchful eye over the crowd. The pitch is one of the widest in the League and the crowd are further set back from the playing action by the surrounding cinder track.

FUTURE GROUND DEVELOPMENTS

Port Vale's new owners hope to eventually complete the currently half built Lorne Street Stand. This would vastly improve the overall look of the ground.

WHAT'S IT LIKE FOR VISITORS?

Up to 4,500 away supporters can be accommodated in the Phones4U Stand, where the view and facilities located on the concourse behind the stand are good. Even a relatively small number of away fans can really make some noise from this stand, as the acoustics are excellent. However, the slope is quite shallow, which might affect your view should a tall person be seated in front. Normally though, you could still move to another seat if necessary.

I've been to Port Vale on a number of occasions and always found it to be a good day out. However, the experience has sometimes been a little intimidating, not due to the Port Vale supporters, but more because of the huge police presence in and around the ground. One police officer said to me as we left the ground five minutes early, as my team were losing 4-0: 'Leaving already? There's still five minutes to go! Now who said that police officers don't have a sense of humour? Still, on the plus side, the pasties on offer within the ground are among the best The P.A within the ground is quite deafening at times and there is no escape, even in the toilets, as it is piped through!

If you wonder at half-time why the Port Vale fans seem transfixed with staring at the away end, it is not intimidation, but the electric scoreboard perched on the roof of this stand! (which the away fans can't see). Vince Smith, a visiting Northampton Town fan, adds: 'I must say it was an enjoyable day out at Vale Park, with very friendly stewards, turnstile operators and very good food served by friendly staff. All in all a very pleasant experience and far more enjoyable than a visit to their near neighbours.'

WHERE TO DRINK

Bernie Mountford informs me: 'The Vine, on Hamil Road near to the ground, is certainly a good bet for away supporters. A good pint is on offer coupled with an enjoyable pre-game atmosphere'. This pub is certainly the main away fan pub, but it not for claustrophobics, as this small pub packs the fans in like sardines. Still it was friendly enough, with a range of real ales on offer.

On my visits, most of the pubs around the ground have either pretended to be shut (i.e. you can see people inside drinking but the door is locked) or do not let away supporters in. However, there are a couple in the town centre that will admit small groups if you smile nicely at the bouncer. I visited the New Inns (just along from Kentucky Fried Chicken in the town centre), which was friendly, served real ale and reasonably priced food.

GETTING THERE & WHERE TO PARK

The ground is located in the town of Burslem, one of the six towns comprising Stoke On Trent. Leave the M6 at junction 15 or 16 and take the A500 towards Stoke on Trent. Follow A500 until the A527 Tunstall/Burslem exit, where you take the A527 towards Tunstall/Burslem. At the next island just past the Price Kensington factory, turn right for Burslem town centre. Continue on this road up the hill, crossing another island and into Burslem town centre. Continue straight on over the traffic lights at the crossroads and then take the first road on the left which takes you down to the ground. There is a large car park located outside a superstore next to the ground, otherwise street parking.

By Train
Longport station is the closest to the ground, but is a good 30 minute walk away and is not well served. Most fans end up at Stoke On Trent railway station, which is over four miles away, and take a taxi (about £6) up to the ground. Tim Rigby informs me: 'To catch a bus, turn left from the station and head up towards Stoke Road. Turn right into this road and there is a bus stop on the other side of the road, opposite Signal Radio. Bus numbers 21 and 21a will take you to Burslem town centre, from which you can take the short walk up to the ground'. Whilst Ian Bannister adds: 'You can also catch bus service number 29 to Burslem. As you go out of the entrance to Stoke station, the bus stop is a short way down on the left. The destination of the bus is Bradeley (the 29 going the opposite way from across the road goes to Keele) and you can get off in Burslem town centre for the ground. The bus costs adults £1 single or £1.90 return'.

LOCAL RIVALS

Stoke City and Crewe Alexandra.

ADMISSION PRICES

All Areas Of The Ground (except Family Stand): Adults: £16, OAPs/Students: £10, Juveniles: £7
Family Stand:
Adults: £16, OAPs/Students: £8, Juveniles: £5

PROGRAMME

Official Programme: £2 - Sold from booths within the ground.

RECORD ATTENDANCE

49,768 v Aston Villa
FA Cup 5th Round, February 20, 1960.

AVERAGE ATTENDANCE

2003-2004: 5,810 (Division Two).

DID YOU KNOW?

Dave Seddon, a visiting Brentford supporter, tells me; 'The roof of the Caudwell Stand was originally that of the Main Stand at Chester City's old Sealand Road ground'. Stephen Wood adds: 'The roof of the away end was indeed bought by Bill Bell back in 1991-92 for £300,000 as Chester were moving grounds. It was installed during the 1992-93 season and the first team we played when the roof was fully constructed was, you guessed it, Chester!'

ROTHERHAM UNITED

MILLMOOR, ROTHERHAM

Ground Name: Millmoor
Capacity: 9,500 (all-seated)
Address: Millmoor Ground, Rotherham, S60 1HR
Main Telephone No: 01709-512-434
Main Fax No: 01709-512-762
Ticket Office: 0870-443-1884
Ticket Office Fax: 01709-512-775
Pitch Size: 115 x 76 yards
Team Nickname: The Millers
Home Kit Colours: Red & White With Black Trim
Official Website: www.themillers.co.uk
Unofficial Websites:
Supporters Trust: www.rufctrust.co.uk
Millers Net: www.millersnet.co.uk (Rivals Network)
Rotherham Mad: www.rotherhamunited-mad.co.uk (Footy Mad Network)

WHAT'S THE GROUND LIKE?

On one side is the partly covered all-seater Main Stand, which in common with the rest of the ground, has a number of supporting pillars. It is about two-thirds of the length of the pitch and to one side, some strange looking executive boxes/administration offices have been erected. I say strange because they look like a load of Portakabins that have been bolted together. The corner at this part of the ground is open and overlooked by a railway bridge. On my last visit, this had many supporters viewing the game for free. The other side, the Millmoor Lane Stand, has a mixture of covered and open seating. Roughly each section on this side is about a third of the length of the pitch. The covered seating in the

middle of this stand looks quite distinctive, with several supporting pillars and an arched roof. Both ends are former terraces, with several supporting pillars and have now been made all-seated. The larger of the two is the Tivoli End, used by home fans. It was noticeable that the pitch slopes up towards this end. The ground also benefits from a striking set of floodlights, the pylons of which are some of the tallest that I have come across (approximately 124 feet high, I've since been told).

FUTURE GROUND DEVELOPMENTS

Neil Uttley informs me: 'The Club have announced that they intend to replace the existing Main Stand with a new 7,000 capacity, two-tiered new stand. The will cost in the region of £4.25m to build and will look similar to the existing East Stand at Barnsley. However, no formal time scales have yet to be announced as to when this will take place'.

WHAT'S IT LIKE FOR VISITORS?

Away fans are housed in the Railway End, where just over 2,000 fans can be accommodated. This end is covered and all-seated and it doesn't take a lot of away fans to really make some noise. On the downside there are a couple of supporting pillars which could impair your view. An unusual feature is that away fans can only access this end via a small, narrow alleyway. If demand requires it, then a portion of the Millmoor Lane Stand can also be allocated to away supporters.

I enjoyed my last visit to the ground. I found the Rotherham fans fairly friendly in the pub that I visited before the game and the standard of stewarding within the ground was relaxed. There is also a great range of pies available inside the ground, with even hot pork pies available (at £1.20 each). I particularly enjoyed the Pukka Chicken Balti Pie on sale at £1.70 each, which is made with puff pastry and is different to the other brand of Balti pie available elsewhere.

WHERE TO DRINK

I had an enjoyable pre-match drink in the Butchers Arms in Midland Road. The pub had a warm welcome and a good mix of home and away supporters. There is on street parking in the surrounding streets and the ground is about an eight minute walk away. To find the pub, as you proceed along the A629 from the A6109, turn right at the first island that you reach on the A629 which appears to lead into a small industrial estate and then take the second left into Midland Road. The Butchers Arms is situated down this road on the left, opposite the bus depot.

Stuart Abbs recommends the Tivoli Club at the ground. I have also been advised that Shooters (formerly known as Queens) and the Prince of Wales are best avoided by away supporters. Wayne Hopkins recommends the Millmoor Pub on the corner of Millmoor Lane next to the ground. 'This is a great place for both home and away fans to meet before a match and is also the HQ for the Rotherham United Supporters Club'. Please note that alcohol is not available in the away end.

Neil Uttley adds: 'The Moulders Rest on Masbrough Street occasionally let away fans in depending on the opposition. Otherwise there are a good selection of pubs in the town centre, however many employ door staff on matchdays and police presence is high; some pubs operate a no club colours policy. Recommended is the Rhinoceros (a Wetherspoons pub) on Bridgegate (across the road from McDonald's) and one to avoid is the County Borough opposite the Bus Station on the corner of Corporation Street and Bridgegate'.

GETTING THERE & WHERE TO PARK

Leave the M1 at Junction 34 and take the A6109 towards Rotherham. At the large roundabout, which is the junction with the A629 turn right, proceed along the A629 crossing a small roundabout and then at the second much larger roundabout turn right and you will see the ground over on your right. You can see the floodlights of the ground for some distance away. Either street parking or there is a car park behind the Main Stand which costs £2.

There is a handy unofficial car park that away

fans can use behind the Zone nightclub on Main Street. Access to the car park (cost £2) is by a slip road off the dual carriageway and is well signposted near to the ground. From the car park a subway takes you down the back of the scrap yards to Millmoor Lane and the away end turnstiles.

By Train
The ground is walkable from Rotherham train station, about a 5-10 minute walk. Steve Orton adds: 'To get to the ground, turn left out of the railway station and walk towards the roundabout. Then follow the blue tourist type signs directing pedestrians to Rotherham United F.C.'. Otherwise if you don't fancy the walk then bus numbers 11 and 12 (to Meadowhall) stop outside Millmoor and are every 10 minutes or so on Saturday afternoons from Rotherham bus station.

LOCAL RIVALS

Barnsley, Sheffield Wednesday and Sheffield Utd.

ADMISSION PRICES

Home Fans:*
Main Stand: Adults: £17, Concessions: £11
Tivoli End: Adults: £15, Concessions: £9
Millmoor Lane Stand: Adults: £15, Concessions: £9
Away Fans:*
Railway End: Adults: £15, Concessions: £9
* These prices only apply to tickets purchased prior to matchday. Tickets purchased on matchday will incur an additional charge of £2 per ticket.

PROGRAMME

Official Programme: £2.50.

RECORD ATTENDANCE

25,170 v Sheffield United
Division 2, December 13, 1952.

AVERAGE ATTENDANCE

2003-2004: 7,138 (Division One).

DID YOU KNOW?

That the Tivoli End took its name from the Tivoli Cinema which was originally situated behind that stand.

GLANFORD PARK SCUNTHORPE UNITED

Ground Name:	Glanford Park
Capacity:	8,500
Address:	Doncaster Rd, Scunthorpe, DN15 8TD
Main Telephone No:	01724-848-077
Ticket Office No:	As Above
Main Fax No:	01724-857-986
Pitch Size:	111 x 73 yards
Team Nickname:	The Iron
Home Kit Colours:	White, Blue & Claret
Official Website:	www.scunthorpe-united.co.uk

Unofficial Websites:
Scunny Fan: www.scunnyfan.co.uk
SUFC Crazy: www.sufc-crazy.tk
Irn-Bru Net: http://iron-bru.net/ (Footy Mad Network)

WHAT'S THE GROUND LIKE?

The Club left the Old Show Ground and moved to the new Glanford Park in August 1988. It is somewhat box-like in appearance with all four stands being of equal height. The ground is totally enclosed with all four corners having been filled (with advertising hoardings). The home end is terracing, whilst the other three sides of the ground are all-seated. The main downside are the many supporting pillars which can spoil the view. The Club seem to have gone a bit over the top, with each stand having a named sponsor. Gone are East, West, North and South Stands. In are: Country Chef, Scunthorpe Evening Telegraph, Jones Electrical and Caparo Merchant Bar Stands!

WHAT'S IT LIKE FOR VISITORS?

Away fans are housed in the Caparo Merchant Bar Stand (aka the South Stand) at one end. This is all-seated and can house 1,650 supporters. If demand requires it, then extra seats can be made available in the south corner of the West Stand. I had somewhat of an uneventful day out at Scunthorpe, with no problems. However, I do have to say that the ground lacked atmosphere, possibly because there were few away supporters on my visit. Across the road from the ground there is a Retail Park with a number of eating outlets such as a Tesco's Cafe, KFC and McDonald's.

James Broadbent adds: 'The ground is very easy to find on the edge of town. Scunthorpe is generally a friendly place to visit, where you can have decent banter and a good day out. To help boost the atmosphere, the Club allows drums and musical instruments to be brought into the ground'.

WHERE TO DRINK

There is one pub right at the entrance to the ground called The Old Farmhouse, which, as Bryan Woods informs me: 'This Thwaites pub welcomes all fans but no colours are allowed'. There is another pub near the ground called the Berkeley, a favourite haunt for away supporters. To find this Sam Smiths pub, go past the ground (or park there first) and follow the main road towards Scunthorpe and it is on the left-hand corner of the first roundabout you reach. If coming by train, then the Parkinson Arms or the Honest Lawyer (on Oswald Road and good for real ale) are both recommended by John Blackman. Noel Curry adds: 'A popular haunt for away supporters is the Blue Bell Wetherspoons Pub on Oswald Road in the town centre.'

GETTING THERE & WHERE TO PARK

The ground is on the outskirts of Scunthorpe, making it easy to find from the motorway. Leave the M180 at Junction 3 and take the M181 for Scunthorpe. At the end of this motorway, you will see the ground on your right. Turn right at the first roundabout onto the A18 and right again into the large car park at the ground.

By Train
Scunthorpe station is over two miles away from the ground. Therefore a taxi is the easiest way to reach the stadium. However, if you have time on your hands and are feeling fit.... Turn left out of the station and head towards the crossroads (facing a church) and turn right into Oswald Road, going past a set of traffic lights and the Honest Lawyer and Blue Bell pubs. At the next traffic lights, turn left into Doncaster Road (where there a number of fast food outlets). Then just go straight down this road and you will eventually reach Glanford Park on your left. Otherwise catch the number 341 bus from the bottom of Doncaster Road (outside the Atlantis Chippy) down to the ground (fare £1).

LOCAL RIVALS

Hull City, Grimsby Town, Lincoln City and Doncaster Rovers.

ADMISSION PRICES

The Club operate a category system (A & B), whereby the most popular games cost more to watch. Category B prices are shown in brackets.
Home Fans:
Evening Telegraph West Stand (Exec Area): Adults: £21 (£20), Concessions: £14 (£13)
Evening Telegraph West Stand: Adults: £16 (£15), Concessions: £9 (£8)
Country Chef East Stand: Adults: £14 (£13), Concessions: £8 (£7)
Jones Electrical North Stand: Adults: £12 (£11), Concessions: £7 (£6)
Away Fans:
Caparo Merchant Stand (Away): Adults: £14 (£13), Concessions: £8 (£7)

PROGRAMME

Official Programme: £2.

RECORD ATTENDANCE

At Glanford Park:
8,775 v Rotherham United
Division 4, May 1, 1989
At The Old Showground:
23,935 v Portsmouth
FA Cup 4th Round, January 30, 1954

AVERAGE ATTENDANCE

2003-2004: 3,840 (Division Three).

DID YOU KNOW?

That the 'Lindsey' from Scunthorpe and Lindsey United was dropped from the Club's title in the mid 50s.

ROOTS HALL, SOUTHEND UNITED

Ground Name: Roots Hall
Capacity: 12,392
Address: Victoria Ave, Southend-On-Sea, SS2 6NQ
Main Telephone No: 0870-174-2000
Main Fax No: 01702-304-124
Ticket Office: 0870-174-2001
Team Nickname: The Shrimpers
Pitch Size: 110 x 74 yards
Home Kit Colours: Blue With White Trim
Official Website: www.southendunited.co.uk
Unofficial Websites:
Shrimpers Net: www.shrimpers.net (Rivals Network)
Shrimper Zone: www.shrimperzone.com
Artful Shrimper: www.artfulshrimper.com

WHAT'S THE GROUND LIKE?

At one end of the ground is the relatively new HI-TEC South Stand. It replaced a former open terrace and greatly improved the overall look. It is a small 'double decker' type of stand, the upper tier hanging over the lower. It is all-seated and covered, but unfortunately has a few supporting pillars. On its roof is a small clock, dedicated to former player, Director and Chairman Frank Walton. There are a couple of blocks of flats that overlook the ground from behind this stand. Away fans are now housed in what was originally the home end, the North Stand, which is a covered seated stand at the other end of the ground. This stand, like the West Stand at one side of the pitch, are both single-tiered and have old looking 'barrel' shaped roofs. The West Stand extends around to the North Stand so that one corner is filled with seating. It has a number of supporting pillars right at the front, which hinder views of the action for some. It also has the most precarious looking TV gantry that stands on stilts and is accessed by a long ladder. On

the other side the East (Main) Stand is another single-tiered, covered stand that has a row of executive boxes running across the back of it. At the front are some strange looking dugouts, which has the management team standing at the front leaning on a wall, with the players sitting behind. The Club have an unusual looking club mascot called 'Elvis The Eel'!

FUTURE GROUND DEVELOPMENTS

Although the Club have now secured the lease on Roots Hall until 2006, they still intend moving to a new 16,000 capacity stadium to be located at Fossetts Farm, just behind the Club's training ground in Eastern Avenue. The £12.5m stadium would be all-seated and comprise a two-tier main stand with curved roof, plus three one-tier sides and be enclosed at the corners. The Club are hoping to obtain planning permission for the scheme.

WHAT'S IT LIKE FOR VISITORS?

Away fans are primarily housed in the North Stand, which is now all-seated after being a former terrace. Like most former terraces that have had seats bolted onto them, the legroom and height distance between each row is less than desirable. The large number of supporting pillars will probably also impede your view; although this does not make for a great experience at least the Stand is covered. Around 2,000 away fans can be accommodated in the North Stand, with a further 700 seats available to away supporters in the West Stand if required. One good point for away fans in the North Stand is that comparatively few numbers of fans can really make some noise from it. On my last visit, there was quite a good atmosphere and I experienced no problems around the ground.

The Essential Football Fan

Refreshments within the away area are served from a 'Transport Café' type establishment, complete with tables and chairs. The usual range is available such as pies (£2), cheeseburgers (£2.30), hot dogs (£2) and chips (80p). Bear in mind though, that getting your drinks in one piece back to your seat can be quite a challenge. The front of the stand is below pitch level, with stairs leading up to each pitch access point where the stewards stand. Going up and down these flights of stairs, with a cup of coffee in each hand, can present a problem.

A couple of groans though... the toilets were pretty grim to say the least and for the second time I have missed the start of a game at Roots Hall, because there has been only one turnstile open taking cash (there is another one open, but for tickets only - bought from a separate booth!). Inevitably, one operator can't cope with the queue, so my advice is to head for the ground a bit earlier than normal.

WHERE TO DRINK

On my last visit away fans seemed to have made their way to the Spread Eagle and Golden Lion pubs, which are only yards apart, on the A127, just up from the car park entrance to the Main Stand. The Spread Eagle was fairly full with fans from both teams occupying different sides of the bar and the atmosphere was fairly relaxed, as was the Golden Lion pub, which is the closest pub to the ground. There is also a good fish and chip shop located across the road by the traffic lights, called the Fish House, which I found to be very good.

Henry Willard, a visiting Yeovil fan, adds: 'The Blue Boar pub, which is at the crossroads (by the traffic lights), is a very good place for away fans to congregate before the game - it was friendly and relaxed. At the ground itself (go past the club shop, then walk down the steps), is the recently opened Shrimpers Bar, which was open to both sets of fans and quite comfortable.

A little further away are two more pubs - The Bell, which you pass on your way into Southend on the A127, and the Nelson in North Road. The Nelson is a basic pub with a beer garden and is probably only worth a visit if you arrive early and want to kill time. It is about a five minute walk from the Spread Eagle. Just go past the Spread Eagle on your right, turn right at the lights and then turn left into North Road, opposite the petrol station. The pub is up on the right.

GETTING THERE & WHERE TO PARK

From the M25, take Junction 29 and follow the A127 to Southend. Continue towards the town centre, through the lights near to the Bell Pub. At the next roundabout, turn right (third turning), continuing on the A127. The ground is on the right just past the next traffic lights. If you turn right as you reach the ground, this will put you behind the away end where there is

plenty of street parking to be found. Otherwise, there is a car park at the ground behind the Main Stand which costs £5.

Bear in mind that in the fair weather months of Aug/Sep/April/May, if the weather is at all sunny the whole of East London seems to head down the A127 on a Saturday afternoon, so allow an extra 30 minutes if the temperature is above 65F.

By Train
The closest station to the ground is Prittlewell, about a five minute walk away. It is served by trains from London Liverpool Street. As you exit the station, turn right and you will then come to a crossroads with traffic lights. On your right is the above mentioned Fish House. Pass this and turn right. Walk about 100 yards and the ground is tucked away on your left. If you happen to end up at Southend Central station (served by trains from London Fenchurch Street), you're about a 15 minute walk from the ground. The main bus station is close to Southend Central and therefore a bus to the ground is the easy option.

LOCAL RIVALS

Colchester United, Leyton Orient and West Ham.

ADMISSION PRICES

Home Fans:
Online Financial East Stand: Adults: £16.50, Concessions: £7.50, Juniors: £7
HI-Tec South Stand (Upper Tier): Adults: £16.50, Concessions: £7.50, Juniors: £7
HI-Tec South Stand (Lower Tier): Adults: £13.50, Concessions: £7.50, Juniors: £7
C2C West Stand: Adults: £16.50, Concessions: £7.50, Juniors: £7
Royal Bank Of Scotland Family Enclosure: Adults: £11.50, Child: £2
Away Fans:
Universal Cycle North Stand: Adults: £16.50, Concessions: £7.50, Juniors: £7

PROGRAMME

Official Programme: £2.50.

RECORD ATTENDANCE

31,090 v Liverpool
FA Cup 3rd Round, January 10, 1979.

AVERAGE ATTENDANCE

2003-2004: 4,535 (Division Three).

DID YOU KNOW?

The ground was once the site of a house called Roots Hall, hence the name of the ground.

SWANSEA CITY

VETCH FIELD, SWANSEA CITY

Ground Name: Vetch Field
Capacity: 11,742
Address: Vetch Field, Swansea, SA1 3SU
Main Telephone No: 01792-633-400
Main Fax No: 01792-646-120
Ticket Office: 01792-633-425
Team Nickname: The Swans or Jacks
Pitch Size: 112 x 74 yards
Home Kit Colours: White & Black
Official Website: www.swanseacity.net
Unofficial Websites:
Swansea Till I Die:
http://stid.swanseawales.me.uk/home.htm
Jack Army: www.jackarmy.net (Rivals Network)
This Is Swansea:
http://www.aardvarkcymru.co.uk/swansrd.htm
SCFC.co.uk: www.scfc.co.uk

WHAT'S THE GROUND LIKE?

It is somewhat of a tired looking ground; however there are plans to move to a new stadium (see below). The West Terrace, at one end, is partly covered (to the rear) is given to away supporters. The other end, the East Stand, is a two-tiered, covered, all-seater stand that doesn't run the full width of the pitch (just over halfway). I believe the intention was for the whole ground to be similarly developed, but economics have dictated otherwise. One side is the North Bank, a large covered terrace; opposite is the smaller, all-seated Centre Stand.

FUTURE GROUND DEVELOPMENTS

Steve Edwards informs me: 'The Club intend to move to a new purpose built stadium on the present site of the existing Morfa Stadium. The former athletics stadium has now been demolished and work is well underway in constructing a new multi-purpose 20,000 capacity all-seater stadium, plus a retail and leisure park. The stadium has mostly been funded by Swansea City Council and will cost in the region of £24m to build. It will comprise four separate stands and will feature translucent roofing to allow more light onto the pitch area. The stadium has been designed by TTH, the same company who designed Sunderland's Stadium Of Light. If things go to plan, then both Swansea City Football Club and Swansea Rugby Club could be both kicking off in their new home in Autumn 2005'. The stadium has been given the provisional name of the White Rock Stadium but it is likely to attract the name of a corporate sponsor.

WHAT'S IT LIKE FOR VISITORS?

Away fans are housed in either part of the West Terrace where just over 1,000 fans can be accommodated at one end of the ground, which is partly covered (to the rear), or in the Centre Stand, depending on numbers. I found the atmosphere quite good. This is helped as the away fans can really make some noise under the cover in the West Terrace. It has been a while since I have been to the Vetch Field and on both occasions there was a little hassle with home fans. I have received reports that a day at Swansea City, in line with the general improvement in football, is now far more enjoyable. However, it is worth bearing in mind that the Swansea fans are passionate about their Club and this can make for an intimidating atmosphere. Exercise caution around the ground. As a matter of interest, most visiting teams stay in the Holiday Inn on the front, so if you are into autograph hunting....

WHERE TO DRINK

Nigel Olsen recommends the Mumbles/The Swansea Marina areas along with a new pub area on Wind Street as the best areas to indulge in a few drinks. Merv Williams adds: 'Wind Street (pronounced wine) is five minutes from the Vetch. There are plenty of pubs such as the Goose and Granite, Yates and the Bank Statement. Ask for Castle Gardens and you'll see Wind Street'. The Garibaldi and the Pantygydwr behind the North Bank are best avoided by away supporters.

GETTING THERE & WHERE TO PARK

The ground is near the sea front, so if you drive along there, you can't miss the floodlights. The A4067 is the main coast road that passes the ground. From the M4 take the A483 at Junction 42 towards Swansea. Then take the A4067 towards The Mumbles and you will eventually see the ground's floodlights on your right. Street parking or there are council car parks at the Marina on the sea front (which were useful for a quick getaway after the game). Geoff Knights, a visiting Macclesfield fan, adds: 'There is now a designated away supporters' car park at County Hall on the left of the main road coming from the east opposite the prison. It is well signposted and entrance and exit are easy as the junction is controlled by traffic lights. The parking fee for cars is £1.50 and for coaches £4.50'.

By Train
The train station is about a 10 minute walk away. As you leave the station, head straight down the High Street for about half a mile. At the traffic lights by Argos, turn right. When you get to the roundabout, take your first left after the pedestrianised area into Kingsway. Continue along the Kingsway until you get to the roundabout by the Potters Wheel. Go straight on and take the third left and then carry straight on and you get to the West Terrace away end. Thanks to David Thomas for providing the directions.
   Alex Latham, a travelling Lincoln fan, adds: 'A slightly quicker way to the ground avoiding the City Centre from the station is as follows: exit the station, turn left down the High Street, which becomes Wind Street. At the end of Wind Street, turn right at the T-junction into Oystermouth Road. Follow this road past Swansea Museum, Tesco and the HM Prison. Just past the prison, turn right into Argyle Street for the ground'.

LOCAL RIVALS

Cardiff City.

ADMISSION PRICES

Home Fans:
Centre Stand: Adults: £15, No Concessions
East Stand: Adults: £14, Concessions: £8
Wing Stand: Adults: £13, Concessions: £8
Family Stand: Adults: £13, Concessions: £8
North Bank Terrace: Adults: £11, Concessions: £6
East Terrace: Adults: £11, Concessions: £6
Away Fans:
West Terrace: Adults: £11, Concessions: £6

PROGRAMME

Official Programme: £2.

RECORD ATTENDANCE

32,796 v Arsenal
FA Cup 4th Round, February 17, 1968.

AVERAGE ATTENDANCE

2003-2004: 6.853 (Division Three).

DID YOU KNOW?

In 1912, a patch of land was secured by the name of The Vetch Field. Children would play on this dirt ground which had vetch growing on it. This was a cabbage like plant cultivated for cattle feed.

SWINDON TOWN

COUNTY GROUND, SWINDON

Ground Name: County Ground
Capacity: 15,728 (all-seated)
Address: County Road, Swindon, SN1 2ED
Main Telephone No: 0870-443-1969
Main Fax No: 01793-333-703
Ticket Office: 0870-443-1894
Ticket Office Fax: 01793-333-780
Team Nickname: The Robins
Pitch Size: 110 x 70 yards
Home Kit Colour: Red & White
Official Website:
www.swindontownfc.co.uk
Unofficial Websites:
This Is Swindon: www.thisisswindontownfc.co.uk
Swindon Town Mad: www.swindontown-mad.co.uk (Footy Mad Network)
Supporters Trust: www.truststfc.co.uk

WHAT'S THE GROUND LIKE?

At one end is the Stratton Bank Stand, a former terrace with rows of seats bolted on to it. This area is uncovered and has a clock above it as well as a small electric scoreboard. Opposite is the small covered Town End, with several supporting pillars across the front. An unusual feature is that the supporting legs of one of the floodlight pylons are actually in one side of the stand, there are even some seats situated behind them! The sides are larger, two-tiered covered stands towering above the two ends. The newest of these is the attractive Nationwide Stand, while on the other side is the older Arkells Stand. The latter has windshields on either side and a few supporting pillars.
The ground also benefits by a striking set of four floodlight pylons. Once a feature across the

country, floodlights are slowly but surely disappearing from the landscape, being replaced by rows of lights across the stand roofs. It's a shame really, if only because the floodlight pylons made it a lot easier to locate a ground in a town or city and were always synonymous with a football ground.

FUTURE GROUND DEVELOPMENTS

The Club have formally announced their intention to leave the County Ground, their home for over 100 years and move to a new purpose built stadium at Shaw Tip, in the West area of Swindon. It is hoped that the new 23,000 capacity stadium will open for the start of the 2007/2008 season.

WHAT'S IT LIKE FOR VISITORS?

Away fans are normally placed in the Arkells Stand at one side of the pitch, where up to 1,200 fans can be housed. This is an older stand with facilities to match, but at least you are under cover. If you are at the back of this stand, there is one supporting pillar which may impair your view of the goal but otherwise it is fine. You even get a view of some of the rolling Marlborough Hills beyond one corner of the ground! There is a small kiosk at the back of the stand serving, amongst other, refreshments and the delicious 'Football's Famous Chicken Balti Pie' (£2.20), but be careful when taking them back to your seat. The entrances to the seating areas are through large solid doors, and to compound matters they open out towards you!
Teams with a larger away following can also be allocated the Stratton Bank End if required. A

further 2,100 fans can be accommodated in this area, but the end has no cover and is therefore open to the elements. Fine on a nice sunny day, but on a cold wet winter's day, it can be grim. I found Swindon to be a relaxed and fairly friendly day out, although the size of police presence on my last visit seemed excessive. On a previous visit I managed to talk my way into the players' lounge and bar after the game, quite an experience!

WHERE TO DRINK

The County Hotel right by the ground did not allow entrance to away supporters on my last visit. Best to continue down County Road and seek out the Cricket Club that sits behind the Arkells Stand. Mark Osborne from Swindon adds: 'On matchdays, home and away fans can park on the cricket ground (for a small fee) and then have access to a drink in the cricket club. This is a very friendly (as well as cheap) club that always welcomes away fans'. I would echo these comments but also add that you can still get into the cricket club (there is no charge) even if you have not parked there. Alcohol is available within the ground to away fans in the Arkells Stand (but not in the open Stratton Bank End), otherwise if you arrive early Swindon town centre is 15 minutes walk away.

GETTING THERE & WHERE TO PARK

The ground is well signposted in and around Swindon town centre. Just follow signs for 'The County Ground'.

From The M4:
Leave at junction 15 and take the A345 (Queens Drive) towards Swindon. At Drake's roundabout, turn left towards the Magic Roundabout, The County Ground is on the corner of this roundabout.

From the North A419 from Cricklade/Cirencester/M5:
This must be the easiest route - follow Cricklade Road down the hill. It becomes Cirencester Way about halfway down. At Transfer Bridges roundabouts, turn left at the first and then straight over the second. The County Ground is on the left after the mini-roundabout.

Located near one corner of the ground is the Magic Roundabout. Whoever designed this must have been on something. It is a large island surrounded by five mini roundabouts, which effectively means that traffic can go round the main roundabout the wrong way! Confused? I was!

If you survive the Magic Roundabout then there is some street parking. Otherwise park at the cricket club (take County Road off the Magic

Roundabout, go past the County Hotel on your right, you will see a small sign further down on your right for football parking, just before the mini roundabout) or St Josephs School (£3 opposite Burger King) by the ground.

By Train
The ground is walkable from Swindon train station and will take you around 10-15 minutes. Leave the station, cross the road and proceed up the road between the two pubs (Great Western and Queen's Tap), continue to the end of the road. Turn left, proceed along Manchester Road, through traffic lights as far as you can go. At the junction, turn right. The County Ground is about 300 yards up this road on the left. Thanks to John Bishop for providing me with the directions.

LOCAL RIVALS

Oxford United, Bristol City, Bristol Rovers and Reading.

ADMISSION PRICES

Home Fans:
Arkells Stand**: Adults: £23, Concessions: £15, Juniors: £9
Nationwide Stand**: Adults: £23, Concessions: £15, Juniors: £9
Town End: Adults: £15, Concessions: £12, Juniors: £9
Family Area: Adults: £19, Concessions: £12, Juniors: £4
Away Fans:
Arkells Stand**: Adults: £23, Concessions: £15, Juniors: £9
Stratton Bank: Adults: £15, Concessions: £12, Juniors: £9
    ** A £2 reduction on these prices is available if the ticket is purchased prior to matchday.

PROGRAMME

Official Programme: £2.50

RECORD ATTENDANCE

32,000 v Arsenal
FA Cup 3rd Round, January 15, 1972.

AVERAGE ATTENDANCE

2003-2004: 7,839 (Division Two).

DID YOU KNOW?

That the first County Ground was on the site of the present Swindon Cricket Ground.

PRENTON PARK, TRANMERE

Ground Name: Prenton Park
Capacity: 16,587 (all-seated)
Address: Prenton Rd West, Birkenhead, CH42 9PY
Main Telephone No: 0151-609-3333
Main Fax No: 0151-609-0606
Ticket Office: 0151-609-3322
Ticket Office Fax: 0151-609-3335
Team Nickname: Rovers
Pitch Size: 112 x 72 yards
Home Kit Colours: White With Royal Blue Trim

Official Website:
www.tranmererovers.co.uk
Unofficial Website:
Rovers Rearguard: www.roversrearguard.com
(Rivals Network)

WHAT'S THE GROUND LIKE?

One end has a large newer stand (the Kop Stand) that dwarfs the rest of the ground and replaced a former open terrace. This end used to house both home and away supporters, but has now been changed to home fans only. At the opposite end, away fans are housed in another relatively new stand called the Cowshed. It has an electric

scoreboard on its roof and looks a little strange as one side has more rows than the other, giving a sloping effect. One side of the ground has a large, older Main Stand, while the John King Stand (formerly the Borough Road Stand) opposite is smaller, running the entire length of the pitch.

WHAT'S IT LIKE FOR VISITORS?

After a long campaign by Tranmere fans, the large Kop End is now purely for home fans. Away fans are housed in the opposite end, the affectionately named Cowshed. However, you will be relieved that the only connection with a real cowshed is the name, as the fairly new covered all-seated stand has good facilities and unhindered views of the playing action. It can hold up to 2,500 fans.

I found Prenton Park to be one of those unremarkable away visits, not made any better by the smallish crowd in attendance. However, I experienced no problems around the ground and found it to be a fairly relaxing day out.

WHERE TO DRINK

Jim Ennis informs me: 'The Prenton Park Hotel, which is situated about 20 yards away from the visiting supporters' turnstiles, is popular with away fans. Otherwise alcohol is available in the away end'.

There are also a number of other pubs in walking distance of the ground. The Mersey Clipper, behind the Main Stand, and The Sportsmans Arms on Prenton Road East are recommended. A little further away is the Swan Pub on Woodchurch Road, a 10 minute walk. Away fans are welcome and it has the added advantage of having 96 car parking spaces available, which are either free or have a small charge levied that can be redeemed against a drink at the bar.

All fans please note: it is a criminal offence to drink alcohol on the streets of Birkenhead, you may find yourself being arrested if you do.

GETTING THERE & WHERE TO PARK

From M6/M56, join the M53 and exit at Junction 4 and take the B5151 Mount Road from the fourth exit of the roundabout (the ground is signposted from here). After two and a half miles when Mount Road becomes Storeton Road, turn right into Prenton Road West and the ground will be visible on the right-hand side.

Sue Warwick adds: 'An easier route is to leave the M53 at Junction 3 and take the A552 Woodchurch Road towards Birkenhead. You will pass a Sainsbury's and then as you reach the Half Way House pub, turn right at the traffic lights onto the B5151 Mount Road. Take the first left for the ground'.

There is a car park at the ground, otherwise, street parking, but beware that there is a strict local residents parking scheme in operation around the ground.

I got hopelessly lost trying to find the ground and did actually end up at the Mersey admiring the views of Liverpool across the river. My frustrations were not eased when, on asking a local chap for directions to the football ground, the guy replied 'Liverpool or Everton?' After asking about another three locals, I finally found the ground after going round most of Birkenhead.

By Train

The closest railway stations are Rock Ferry and Birkenhead Central, both served by Liverpool Lime Street. Both stations are a fair walk from the ground (15-20 minutes). Philip Jackman provides directions from Rock Ferry station: 'On leaving Rock Ferry, turn right and walk up the road for a fair distance until you reach a roundabout. At the roundabout, turn right again and walk straight up until you are close to the Sportsman pub. Then turn left down Everest Road and walk straight down to the bottom where you will be standing opposite the turnstiles for the Cowshed Stand'.

Craig Skyrme informs me: 'If you get off the train at Hamilton Square instead, there is a football bus laid on just outside the station. It runs about every 10-15 minutes and if you show your train ticket you can get aboard for free of charge, otherwise it costs 50p.

LOCAL RIVALS

Liverpool, Everton, Chester, Wrexham and from a little further afield, Bolton Wanderers.

ADMISSION PRICES

Home Fans:
Main Stand: Adults: £17, Young Persons: £13, Seniors: £9, Juniors: £4
Borough Road Stand: Adults: £15, Young Persons: £11, Seniors: £7, Juniors: £4
Kop Stand: Adults: £14, Young Persons/Seniors: £7, Juniors: £4
 Away Fans:
Cowshed Stand: Adults: £16, Young Persons: £12, Seniors: £8, Juniors: £4

PROGRAMME

Official Programme: £2.50.

RECORD ATTENDANCE

24,424 v Stoke City
FA Cup 4th Round, February 5, 1972.

AVERAGE ATTENDANCE

2003-2004: 7,606 (Division Two).

DID YOU KNOW?

That the Club once wore dazzling orange and maroon halved shirts with navy blue shorts, which coincided with joining the West Lancashire League in 1889. These were abandoned for blue and white by the turn of the century.

BESCOT STADIUM, WALSALL

Ground Name:	Bescot Stadium
Capacity:	11,300 (all-seated)
Address:	Bescot Crescent, Walsall, WS1 4SA
Main Telephone No:	0870-442-0442
Main Fax No:	01922-613-202
Ticket Office:	0870-442-0111/0222
Ticket Office Fax:	0870-787-1966
Team Nickname:	The Saddlers
Pitch Size:	110 x 73 yards
Home Kit Colours:	Red & White
Official Website:	www.saddlers.co.uk

Unofficial Websites:
Up The Saddlers: http://steveroy.com/walsall/
The Saddlers: www.thesaddlersfc.tk (Sport Network)
NMFE: http://walsall.rivals.net/default.asp?sid=931
(Rivals Network)

WHAT'S THE GROUND LIKE?

The Saddlers moved to the Bescot Stadium in 1990 from Fellows Park. With the opening of the Purple Stand in 2003, the Club are finally getting a ground to match their ambitions. This new stand is for home fans and is a large two-tiered affair that completely dwarfs the rest of the ground. It is smart looking, with a glassed area running across its middle, which houses the concourse. Unusually, it has a slightly larger upper than lower tier. Before it was redeveloped, this end was previously called the Gilbert Alsop (a former Walsall playing great) Stand, but in a commercial sponsorship deal, has been renamed the Purple Stand. A sign of the times I guess The rest of the stadium is totally enclosed with three of the stands being roughly the same height, giving it a 'box-like' feel. These stands are not particularly big, around 15 rows high. The corners are filled, but only for advertising hoardings. Above the William Sharp stand there is a small electric scoreboard,

whilst on one side there is a small television camera gantry precariously perched on the roof. One unusual feature are the strange looking floodlights, which sit on the roofs of the side stands. The main disappointment is the large number of supporting pillars in each of the older stands (the new Purple Stand is pillar free). As Walsall unfortunately very rarely fill the stadium, this is not a huge problem. However, for big games, this can be very annoying if you are unlucky enough to get seated behind one.

FUTURE GROUND DEVELOPMENTS

The Club have announced that they have been granted planning permission to redevelop the William Sharp end of the ground. The new stand would look similar to the Purple Stand and add 2,300 seats, raising the overall capacity to 13,500. It would also mean that up to 4,000 away supporters could be accommodated at that end. The back of the stand will also feature a giant advertising hoarding, clearly visible from the M6. Permission has been also granted to build a hotel behind the William Sharp End.

WHAT'S IT LIKE FOR VISITORS?

Away supporters are housed in the William Sharp Stand at one end of the ground, where around 2,000 away supporters can be accommodated. There are a few supporting pillars at the front which could spoil your view. The good news though is that even a small amount of away fans can really make some noise and make a good atmosphere. A trip to Walsall can be disappointing in terms of trying to get there and the stadium itself, but is more than countered by the relaxed atmosphere around the ground and the friendliness of the Walsall fans themselves.

WHERE TO DRINK

The King George V in Wallowes Lane is okay. It is about a 10 minute walk, opposite the Morrisons Supermarket. If you are walking from the stadium, go out of the official car parks and down towards McDonald's. Go past McDonald's on your right and take a left-hand turn into Wallowes Lane. At the end of the lane, turn left onto the main road and the pub is just setback on the left.

Gary Cotterill informs me: 'At the stadium, there is the Saddlers Club, which sometimes allows small numbers of away fans in at a cost of £1'. Please note that alcohol is not served inside the stadium, but you will find the delicious 'Football's Famous Chicken Balti Pie' (£2) on offer (allegedly Walsall were the first Club to stock balti pies). Whilst, on the adjoining retail park that you pass on the way in to the stadium, there is a McDonald's to keep the kids happy.

Neil LeMilliere, a visiting Exeter City fan, adds: 'Couldn't get into the Saddlers Club at 2.10pm. It is then a long way to go to get a drink anywhere else if you don't know where you are going - in fact too far! The Balti pies were excellent but the food ran out pretty early'.

GETTING THERE & WHERE TO PARK

The ground is right next to the M6 - in fact you can see it from the motorway just north of the RAC Control Centre. Unfortunately, this stretch of motorway normally has a large traffic jam on both Saturday lunchtimes and early weekday evenings, so allow extra time.

From M6 South:

Leave the M6 at Junction 7 and take the A34 towards Walsall (beware though of speed cameras on this stretch of dual carriageway), turn left at the Bell Inn public house into Walstead Road (signposted Bescot Stadium, Bescot Station Park & Ride). Continue straight on this road for two miles, passing pub called the Tiger on your left. You will come to Bescot Stadium and the entrance to the away end is on your right.

From The M6 North:

Leave the M6 at Junction 9 and take the A461 towards Walsall. Bear right onto the A4148 (Wallowes Lane) and turn right at the second set of traffic lights. You will see the ground on your left.

Car Parking:

There is a good sized car park located at the ground (cost £3) or alternatively there is some street parking off Wallowes Lane. Ian Stevens advises: 'Avoid parking on the nearby Morrisons Supermarket car park (built on the site of the old Fellows Park), as unless you can prove that you are shopping there, you run the risk of being clamped'.

By Train

Note that if you go by train, Bescot Stadium has its own station, situated behind the away end only a few minutes walk from the turnstiles. Trains run there on a local line from Birmingham New Street and the journey time is around 20 minutes. There is a regular service on Saturdays along this line and you should not have too many problems getting away after the game.

LOCAL RIVALS

Wolverhampton Wanderers, West Bromwich Albion, Birmingham City and Aston Villa.

ADMISSION PRICES

Home Fans*:
Purple Stand (Upper Tier): Adults: £17, Senior Citizens: £12. Juniors: £10
Purple Stand (Family Tickets): 1 Adult + 1 Junior: £20, Extra Junior on family ticket £6
Purple Stand (Lower Tier): Adults: £13, Concessions: £10
H.L. Fellows Stand: Adults: £17, Concessions: £13
Banks Stand: Adults: £17, Senior Citizens: £12, Juniors: £10
Banks Stand (Family Tickets): 1 Adult + 1 Junior: £19, Extra Junior on family ticket £6
Away Fans*:
William Sharp Stand Stand: Adults: £17, Concessions: £12
* Discounts of up to £2 are available on most of these prices when match tickets are purchased prior to matchdays.

PROGRAMME & FANZINE

Official Programme: £2.20
Ninety Minutes From Europe (NMFE) Fanzine: 50p.
There is also an excellent programme shop behind the William Sharp Stand.

RECORD ATTENDANCE

11,049 v Rotherham United
Division One, May 9, 2004.
Record Attendance At Fellows Park:
25,453 v Newcastle (Div 2) August 29, 1961.

AVERAGE ATTENDANCE

2003-2004: 7,853 (Division One).

DID YOU KNOW?

It was decided around 1930 to rename the Hillary Street ground Fellows Park in honour of the then chairman H.L. Fellows.

HUISH PARK, YEOVIL TOWN

Ground Name: Huish Park
Capacity: 9,400 (5,212 seated)
Address: Lufton Way, Yeovil, Somerset, BA22 8YF
Main Telephone No: 01935-423-662
Main Fax No: 01935-473-956
Pitch Size: 115 x 72 yards
Team Nickname: Glovers
Home Kit Colours: Green & White Hoops
Official Website: www.ytfc.net
Unofficial Websites:
Cider Space: www.ciderspace.co.uk
On To Victory: www.ontovictory.co.uk
The Dutch Glover: www.dutchglover.tk

WHAT'S THE GROUND LIKE?

Yeovil is predominantly remembered for some classic giant killing deeds in the FA Cup and the famous slope of the pitch. With the move to a new ground in 1990, that slope has gone, but the team have continued to impress. Generally, the ground is a tidy looking one, in a pleasant setting, with lots of trees visible behind the stands. Both sides of the ground are similar looking stands and are of the same height. They are both cantilevered, covered single-tiered stands that are all seated. Each stand has windshields to either side. The only differences between these stands is that the Main Stand has some executive boxes running across the back of it plus the dugouts and players tunnel, whilst the Bartlett Stand has a press box suspended from beneath its roof and a small simple looking electric scoreboard. At one end is the medium sized Westland Terrace, which is covered and for home supporters and again has windshields to either side. Opposite is the Copse Road Terrace, which is given to away fans. This is smaller and uncovered. Oddly, the steel work is

in place at the back of this stand to incorporate more terrace space, but the concrete rows have so far not been added. The ground is completed with a set four modern floodlight pylons, one in each corner of the ground.

WHAT'S IT LIKE FOR VISITORS?

Away fans are situated in the Copse Road open terrace at one end of the ground. This is uncovered, so hope for a dry day. Up to 1,750 supporters can be housed in this area. Additionally, around 300 seats are allocated to away fans in the Bartlett Stand. As this stand is covered it is a better bet, especially if the weather is bad. Normally, a visit to Huish Park is enjoyable and the atmosphere good. This is boosted by a very vocal crowd in the home terrace as well as the presence of a drummer and trumpeter in that end (on my last visit the trumpeter was even imitating an ambulance siren as the trainer ran on to treat an injured player!). If Yeovil score, then Glad All Over, by the Dave Clark Five, blasts out around the ground. It is worth noting though that the local fans are passionate about their Club and caution around the ground may be required for some of the bigger games.

On my last visit, I was five minutes late getting to the game and had missed the kick off. Unbelievably the turnstiles had already closed at the away end and I, and a number of other away fans, had to run around the ground to try and find someone who could get us in. We managed this and I have to say that the stewards were particularly helpful and friendly. I found the large police presence in and around the ground perturbing. In my mind, it was not at a high profile game so I was somewhat surprised at the amount of local constabulary there. To make matters worse, they started on my pet hate - the videoing of away fans during the game. The catering offered was the usual assortment of pies, pasties and burgers (£2), but let's just say they were not the best I or my wife have ever had.

WHERE TO DRINK

I was pleasantly surprised to find a large marquee outside the ground that had been set up as a make shift beer tent. There was a large sign outside the marquee which announced: 'Everyone Is Welcome!' Just a pity that wasn't quite correct as any away fans in colours were turned away at the entrance by a couple of burly looking bouncers. Some visiting fans did refer the bouncers to the said sign, but to no avail.

There are three pubs within about a 10-15 minute walk of the ground: The Bell, The Arrow and Brewsters (which, according to Stephen Pugsley, also has a handy fish and chip shop next door called Palmers). I could only find the Arrow pub and in my efforts to locate it, ended up joining up with a number of other away fans who were also looking lost in our quest to find beer! The pub itself, when located, was quite a spacious estate type pub, which on my visit was fine and I was served quickly, although it was predominantly home to support fans with only a small number of away fans present (in colours). I did notice though that the police were watching over the pub from a squad car.

To find this pub, from the ground car park, walk back up the road past the ground to the top of it and turn right. At the end of this road, turn left onto the main road and after a short distance, take the first right. Go straight down this road through the new looking residential area and after about 10 minutes, you will see a clearing on your right and just beyond this, there are some shops with the Arrow pub in the middle.

GETTING THERE & WHERE TO PARK

The ground is located on the very outskirts of Yeovil and is signposted from the A303. Leave the A303 at the Cartgate roundabout and take the A3088 towards Yeovil. Follow the road for approximately 8-9 miles until you reach a roundabout on the outskirts of Yeovil with the Westlands Airfield directly in front of you. Turn left at this roundabout and then continue straight on, crossing a number of roundabouts. As you pass the entrance to an Asda superstore, take the next left for the ground, which can be seen from the road.

There is a fair sized car park at the ground, which on my last visit was free of charge. Otherwise, there is plenty of street parking to be had on the roads leading down to the ground.

By Train

Yeovil has two railway stations, Yeovil Junction, 2-3 miles out of town and Pen Mill junction about a mile from the town centre. Both are on the opposite side of town to the ground. From both stations, it is advised to get a taxi to the stadium or the alternative is to catch the Hopper to the bus station. However, this is still a couple of miles from the stadium and there are not many buses running to it.

LOCAL RIVALS

From non-league days, Weymouth and from a little further a field, Bristol Rovers. The nearest league club is Bournemouth, but the fans and media appear to have latched on to Torquay as a West country derby.

ADMISSION PRICES

Home Fans*:
Main Stand: Adults: £16, Concessions: £13, Under 16s: £7
Bartlett Stand: Adults: £15, Concessions: £11, Under 16s: £7
Westland Terrace: Adults: £15, Concessions: £10, Under 16s: £7
Away Fans*
Bartlett Stand (Seating): Adults: £15, Concessions: £11, Under 16s: £7
Copse Road Terrace: Adults: £14, Concessions: £9, Under 16s: £7
    *A £2 discount is available on the above tickets, if they are purchased prior to matchday. Members of the Junior Glovers Club can obtain further discounts on the Under 16s ticket price.

PROGRAMME & FANZINE

Official Programme: £2.50.
Onto Victory Fanzine: £1.

RECORD ATTENDANCE

At the original Huish Park:
16,318 v Sunderland
FA Cup 4th Round, January 29, 1949
At the current Huish Park:
9,348 v Liverpool
FA Cup 3rd Round, January 4, 2004.

AVERAGE ATTENDANCE

2003-2004: 6,197 (Division Three).

DID YOU KNOW?

That the Club was originally formed as Yeovil Casuals in 1895.

BOSTON UNITED

YORK STREET, BOSTON UNITED

Ground Name: York Street
Capacity: 6,643
Address: 14-16 Spain Place, Boston, Lincs, PE21 6HN
Main Telephone No: 01205-364-406
Main Fax No: 01205-354-063
Team Nickname: The Pilgrims
Home Kit Colours: Amber With Black Trim
Official Website: www.bostonunited.co.uk
Unofficial Websites:
Boston Fever: www.bostonfever.com (Rivals Network)
Boston United Mad: www.bostonutd-mad.co.uk (Footy Mad Network)

WHAT'S THE GROUND LIKE?

A rather picturesque ground, which is well balanced as all four stands are roughly the same height. The Finnforest Stand, on one side of the pitch, is a good sized, covered all-seated stand. Its only drawback are a couple of supporting pillars. The other side, the Spayne Road Stand, is a smaller, newer covered terrace. It is so low that house roofs behind are clearly visible. The Town End is a fair-sized partly covered terrace (to the middle). The other end, the York Street Stand, is strange. It is raised above pitch level, meaning that spectators have to climb a staircase at the front to reach the seating area (which is mostly benches). A small terrace is at the front. Unusually for a League ground, the press area is sited in the upper part of the York Street Stand, directly behind the goal. At one

side of this stand is a Police Control Box. The ground has a striking set of floodlights and, something that I haven't seen for a long time, flags fluttering in the wind on each of the stand roofs.

WHAT'S IT LIKE FOR VISITORS?

Away fans are housed at one end of the ground in the Town End terrace, where up to 1,821 fans can be accommodated. When in the Conference, this was a home terrace, but with admittance to the Football League, the Club have given it to away fans to ensure proper segregation. This has miffed a number of home fans, who now mostly congregate on one side of the Spayne Road Terrace. Still, away fans can benefit from a good sized stand that has seen a number of improvements during the closed season, such as new toilets and catering facilities being built. Further good news is that the acoustics in this stand are pretty good, meaning that a relatively small number of away fans can make some noise. Away fans are not allocated any seating within the ground.

I found a visit to York Street to be an enjoyable day out, with good facilities, atmosphere and friendly home fans. To be truthful, as the Club has only been promoted to the Football League in 2002, I didn't expect that the ground would be up to much. I was wrong on that assumption and pleasantly surprised of what I found.

Thanks to Club Secretary Colin Woodcock, for his hospitality, shown to my wife and me, on our recent visit to the ground.

WHERE TO DRINK

Ken Fox informs me: 'The Coach & Horses on Main Ridge is the nearest pub to the ground. It serves the excellent Batemans ales which are locally brewed'. On my visit, this smallish pub was very crowded. It is probably a better bet to carry on down Main Ridge to the Wellington, a larger quieter pub serving hand-pulled Mansfield Bitter. Also on the corner of this road is the Eagle Chippy, which was doing a brisk business when I passed it. Ken continues: 'There is a Social Club behind the York Street Stand, but visiting supporters are only likely to be admitted if they can show that they are members of their own Clubs' supporters club. Otherwise, the ground is only a five minute walk away from the town centre, where there are plenty of good pubs to be found. The Eagle, in West Street near the railway station, and The Still in Market Place are both recommended, as well as any Batemans pubs you come by.

GETTING THERE & WHERE TO PARK

From The North:
From the A1 take the A17 towards Sleaford/Boston. After passing Sleaford take the A1121 towards Boston and then onto the A52. On entering Boston you pass the railway station on your left and then pass the junction with the A16 Spalding Road on your right. Go over the small Haven Bridge and straight along into John Adams Way (dual carriageway) and the floodlights of the ground can be clearly seen on the right. Turn right at the next traffic lights, into Main Ridge, then take the next right into York Street.

From The South:
From the A1 take the A43 towards Stamford and then on entering Stamford Town Centre take the A16 towards Market Deeping/Spalding and then onto Boston. On entering Boston, you will go over a railway crossing. Bear right at the next set of traffic lights (signposted Boston College). Go over the small Haven Bridge and straight along John Adams Way (dual carriageway), the floodlights of the ground can be clearly seen on the right. Turn right at the next traffic lights into Main Ridge, then take the next right into York Street.

The fair sized car park behind the York Street Stand is now for permit holders only, so all other fans will need to either park in one of the town centre pay and display car parks or seek street parking.

By Train
Boston railway station is a 10 minute walk from the ground. Head down Station Street towards the large church tower. At the end of the street is a

Police Station, bear right down the right-hand side of the station and head over the river footbridge. Once across, turn right up the alleyway into Church Lane. Keep going straight on, past the Britannia Inn and then cross the street to go down South Street. Take a left turn into Spain Lane and at its end you will come to a dual carriageway. The ground is clearly visible on the opposite side of it.

LOCAL RIVALS

Lincoln City, Scunthorpe United and Hull City.

ADMISSION PRICES

Home Fans:
Seated: Adults: £15, Over 65s: £10.50, Under 16s: £7.50
Terrace: Adults: £13, Over 65s: £9.50, Under 16s: £6.50
Away Fans:
Terrace Only (Town End): Adults: £13, Over 65s: £9.50, Under 16s: £6.50

PROGRAMME & FANZINE

Official Programme: £2.80.
Town End Tales Fanzine: £1.

RECORD ATTENDANCE

11,000 v Derby County
FA Cup 3rd Round, January 1. 1974.

AVERAGE ATTENDANCE

2003-2004: 2,963 (Division Three).

DID YOU KNOW?

That the only other nickname for the Club was the 'Stumpites', which was briefly used back in the 1940s. The 'Stump' is the local name for the main church in Boston, St. Botolph's, which is the largest parish church in England with a tower that is 272 feet high.

MEMORIAL STADIUM, BRISTOL ROVERS

Ground Name: Memorial Stadium
Capacity: 12,000
Address: Filton Avenue, Horfield, Bristol BS7 0BF
Main Telephone No: 0117-909-6648
Main Fax No: 0117-908-5530
Team Nickname: Pirates
Home Kit Colours: Blue & White Quarters
Official Website: www.bristolrovers.co.uk
Unofficial Websites:
BRFC 1883: www.gashead.dial.pipex.com
Black Arab: www.blackarab.org
Bristol Rovers 1883:
www.geocities.com/bristolrovers1883/index.htm

WHAT'S THE GROUND LIKE?

The ground was formerly owned by Bristol Rugby Club (who still play there), and even though it has seen some changes since the football club moved in 1996, it still has the feel of a ground not totally dedicated to football. On one side is the DAS Stand, which, with its pavilion, looks more like a cricket stand. It has a row of hospitality boxes across the top, with a few rows of seats in front. Below is an area of terrace. Just under the roof is a television gantry and a small electric scoreboard. The stand runs for about half the length of the pitch and straddles the halfway line. On one side of it, towards the Blackthorn End, is a small covered terrace, used as a family area, whilst the other side is unused. Opposite is the Hill House Hammond Stand, taller than the DAS Stand, but similar in length. This stand has covered seating to its rear and terracing at the front. It has open terracing to either side, one of

which is given to away supporters. The team dug outs are located in front of this stand, although the dressing rooms are located behind the DAS Stand. This leads to quite a procession of players and officials at half-time and full time. At one end is the Blackthorn End, which is a covered terrace. Opposite is the unusual looking South Stand. This was originally erected as a temporary stand, to fill the previously empty end. It has now been opened for a few seasons, although it still looks, with its green seats and bright white roof, more suitable for an outdoor show jumping competition than a football ground. The stand only runs for just over half the width of the pitch, has several supporting pillars running across the front and has been nicknamed 'the tent' by Rovers fans.

WHAT'S IT LIKE FOR VISITORS?

Away supporters are housed in an open terrace in one corner of the ground so you might get wet if it rains. This area is located on one side of the Hill House Hammond and South Stands. The open terrace makes it difficult for away fans to generate noise. Up to 1,100 away supporters can be accommodated in this area. I must recommend the huge tasty Cornish pasties (£1.90) that are sold at the ground, and they also offer vegetarian ones which makes a change. Also on offer are a range of pies including the delicious 'Football's Famous Chicken Balti Pie'. I did not experience any problems on my visits; however, I noted that the Rovers fans seemed to tolerate away fans rather than being over friendly. They can still do a good rendition of their club anthem 'Goodnight Irene', when the occasion stirs.

BRISTOL ROVERS

I found it quite amusing that the Rovers fans are nicknamed gasheads. Nick Wootten of Bristol informed me that this term comes from where the old Eastville stadium in Bristol was sited. Next to a (sometimes smelly) gas works! In fact, it was rumoured that if Rovers were losing at half-time, the gas would be turned up to put off the opposition!

WHERE TO DRINK

The Wellington pub near the ground was recommended to me by Alex in Bristol. It has a good pre-match atmosphere and real ales, although plastic glasses are given out. Please note though that I have received reports of away fans getting hassle at this pub, so use your discretion. Rhys Gwynllyw, a visiting Wrexham supporter, recommends the Annexe Inn next to the Sportsmans Arms. 'The Annexe Pub is friendly and is listed in the Good Beer Guide. Last time I was there it had seven real ales on tap. I had no hassle at all in my Wrexham top'. Steve Pugh adds: 'The Annexe Inn is in Nevil Road, which is about 10 minutes walk from the ground. You can find it by following the signs for the County Cricket Ground'. Otherwise there is a bar behind the clubhouse terrace that allows away supporters in. I have been informed that away fans should avoid the John Cabot pub.

GETTING THERE & WHERE TO PARK

Exit M5 at junction 16 (signposted Filton) and join the A38 (South) towards Bristol City Centre. The ground is about five miles down the A38. You will pass the large British Aerospace works and further on, you will pass on your left the Royal George and Duke of York pubs. At the next traffic lights, the Memorial Ground is signposted to the left and is about 100 yards down this road. If you go over the lights you will see the Wellington pub on your right. There is a fair amount of street parking around the sides and back of the pub.

By Train
The nearest railway station is Bristol Parkway which is about two miles away from the ground and is a little too far to walk from, so you are probably best to jump in a taxi or buses 73 and 74 run from the station past the ground.

LOCAL RIVALS

Bristol City, Swindon Town and Cardiff City.

ADMISSION PRICES

Home Fans*:
DAS Stand (Centre Seating): Adults: £19, Concessions: £15.50

DAS Stand (Wings Seating): Adults: £16.50, Concessions: £8.50
DAS Stand (Terrace): Adults: £13, Concessions: £6
Hill House Hammond Stand (Seating): Adults: £16.50, Concessions: £8.50
Hill House Hammond Stand (Terrace): Adults: £11, Concessions: £5
Family Terrace: Adults: £9, Concessions: £4
South Stand: Adults: £13.50, Concessions: £6.50
Blackthorn End: Adults: £11, Concessions: £5

Away Fans*:
DAS Stand (Terrace): Adults: £11, Concessions: £5

* The above prices quoted are for tickets purchased prior to matchday. Tickets purchased on matchday cost £2 more per ticket.

PROGRAMME

Official Programme: £2.50.

RECORD ATTENDANCE

At The Memorial Stadium:
11,433 v Sunderland
Worthington Cup 3rd Round, October 31, 2000
At Eastville;
38,472 v Preston North End
FA Cup 4th Round, January 30, 1960

AVERAGE ATTENDANCE

2003-2004: 7,142 (Division Three).

DID YOU KNOW?

Bristol Rovers were formed under the evocative title of Black Arabs in September 1883, following a meeting of five young schoolteachers at a restaurant on Stapleton Road, in the Eastville district of the city.

GIGG LANE, BURY

Capacity:	11,669 (all-seated)
Address:	Gigg Lane, Bury, Lancashire, BL9 9HR
Main Telephone No:	0161-764-4881
Main Fax No:	0161-764-5521
Ticket Office:	0161-705-2144
Ticket Office Fax:	0161-763-3103
Team Nickname:	The Shakers
Pitch Size:	112 x 73 yards
Home Kit Colours:	White & Royal Blue
Official Website:	www.buryfc.co.uk
Unofficial Websites:	

Bury Mad: www.bury-mad.co.uk (Footy Mad Network)

WHAT'S THE GROUND LIKE?

The ground was completely rebuilt in the 1990s with the last new stand, the Cemetery End, completed in 1999. The new stands have vastly improved the overall look of the ground, whilst at the same time making it an all-seated one. The Manchester Road End is a fair sized stand that is covered and has an electric scoreboard; however, it does not run the full width of the pitch, one side ending with the edge of the penalty box. This stand is given to away supporters. The other end, the Cemetery End, is a former terrace that has been demolished and replaced with a new 2,500 seater stand. It extends around one corner to the South Stand and looks quite smart. There is a small Police Control Box suspended beneath the roof in its corner. On one side is the Main Stand, with raised seating, meaning that supporters have to climb a small set of steps to enter it. Part of the front has a small box like structure with a number of windows running along the front. It particularly caught my eye, as since the windows are almost at pitch level, I wondered just how many broken ones they get each season. Opposite is the South Stand, similar in design to the ends with a TV gantry suspended below its roof. The one open corner of the ground has a small block of flats situated behind it, but the rest of the ground has a number of trees visible behind and above the stands, making it more attractive.

WHAT'S IT LIKE FOR VISITORS?

Away fans are housed in the covered Manchester Road End at one end of the ground, where even a small amount of fans can generate plenty of noise. Just over 2,000 away supporters can be accommodated, where you will normally enjoy a good view of the action. However, there is a row of supporting pillars about a third of the way up the stand, which could cause problems if your team has a large following. The stand is also situated quite well back from the pitch and is slightly below pitch level. The catering is quite good, with a range of burgers and hot dogs (£2.20) and the delicious 'Football's Famous Chicken Balti Pie' (£2.20). My only grumble was the archaic toilets in a relatively new stand. On the whole, however, it was a relaxed and normally a good day out.

WHERE TO DRINK

There are plenty of pubs around the ground and along Manchester Road in particular. There is also a supporters' club at the ground, which sometimes allows in small numbers of away fans. My pick of the pubs on Manchester Road are the Swan & Cemetery, around a 10 minute walk from the ground. This Thwaites pub is quite comfortable, serves good hand-pulled beer and has a separate restaurant area. Nearer to the ground are the Pack Horse and the Staff of Life. On my last visit, the Pack Horse seemed to be the main pub for away fans and has a conveniently situated chippy around the corner from it. The Staff of Life is a stone's throw from the Park and is a basic pub serving hand-pulled Lee's. Also recommended on Manchester Road is the Waterloo, nearer the town centre.

GETTING THERE & WHERE TO PARK

Leave the M66 at Junction 3. Take the left-hand exit at the junction and follow this road until you come to the junction with the A56 Manchester Road. At this T-junction, which has traffic lights, turn right towards Bury. You will pass the Swan & Cemetery pub on your left and then some playing fields. At the end of the playing fields, just before the traffic lights and a couple of pubs, turn right into Gigg Lane for the ground. However, please note that Gigg Lane is normally closed on matchdays and the ground itself is not easily seen from the A56. Street parking.

By Train
Bury Metrolink is served by trams from Manchester Victoria and Piccadilly mainline railway stations. Bury Metrolink Station is about a 15 minute walk from the ground. Turn left out of the station along a pedestrian walkway going underneath the dual carriageway. On the other side of the dual carriageway, turn right towards the Town Hall. Just before the Town Hall, turn left into Knowsley Street and at the bottom of Knowsley Street, turn left onto the main A56 Manchester Road. It is then a case of going straight along Manchester Road for about half a

mile and you will reach Gigg Lane on your left. Thanks to Andy Grainger for supplying the directions.

LOCAL RIVALS

Bolton Wanderers and Rochdale.

ADMISSION PRICES

Home Fans:
Main & South Stands: Adults £15, Students: £8, OAPs: £6, Juniors: £5
East Stand (Cemetery End): Adults: £13, Students: £8, OAPs: £6, Juniors: £5
Family Stand (Cemetery End): 1 Adult & 1 Child: £12, extra Adult: £10, additional child: £2, OAPs: £6
Away Fans:
Manchester Road Stand: Adults: £13, Students: £8, OAPs: £6, Juniors: £5.

PROGRAMME

Official Programme: £2.

RECORD ATTENDANCE

35,000 v Bolton Wanderers
FA Cup 3rd Round, January 9, 1960

AVERAGE ATTENDANCE

2003-2004: 2,892 (Division Three).

DID YOU KNOW?

Gigg Lane has been Bury FC's only home since its foundation. Initially, it was a plot of land rented from the Earl of Derby, who owned the surrounding estate. Their first stand was built here in 1887.

WHADDON ROAD, CHELTENHAM TOWN

Ground Name: Whaddon Road
Capacity: 7,407 (3,139 seated)
Address: Whaddon Road,
Cheltenham, GL52 5NA
Main Telephone No: 01242-573-558
Fax No: 01242-224-675
Team Nickname: The Robins
Pitch Size: 111 x 72 yards
Home Kit Colours: Red & White
Official Website: www.ctfc.com
Unofficial Websites:
The Robins Nest:
www.thisengland.freeserve.co.uk/ctafc.htm
Cheltenham Town Mad: www.cheltenhamtown-mad.co.uk (Footy Mad)

WHAT'S THE GROUND LIKE?

Whaddon Road has greatly improved since
Cheltenham entered the League in 1999, with
half the ground being redeveloped. The latest
addition is the In2Print Stand, opened in
November 2001. This stand sits proudly at one
side of the pitch and was built by Barr
Construction. It is a covered, all-seated, single-
tiered stand containing 2,034 seats. Part of this
stand is given to away supporters. On the other
side of the pitch is the UCAS Main Stand, which
has seating to the rear and terracing at the front.
Straddling the halfway line, it does not extend
the full length of the pitch, having open spaces
to either side. At one end is the small, covered,
Cheltenham and Gloucester Terrace, while
opposite the Whaddon Road End is given to
away supporters. This end has a small covering
on one side of the terrace. A small Police

Control Box keeps a watchful eye on matters
from this corner of the ground by the away end.

WHAT'S IT LIKE FOR VISITORS?

The improvements made to the ground have also
benefited away supporters. Seating is now
available to away supporters on one side of the
covered In2Print Stand where up to 900 seats can
be allocated. Entrance to the seated area first
involves walking through the away terrace, as
there is no separate away entrance to the seated
area. Facilities and view of the playing action are
good.
A further 1,162 fans are housed in the Whaddon
Road terrace at one end of the ground. The views
of the playing action are not as good from this
section as from the seated area and it is only
partly covered on one side. Facilities have been
improved in this area with a new toilet block
being built, plus better catering is on offer. You
can choose from burgers (including, for those with
a bigger appetite, a half-pounder with cheese £3),
hot dogs, pies (including the Pukka Chicken Balti
Pie £2) and bacon baps (£2).
I found Cheltenham itself to be quite pleasant
and the supporters friendly. The picturesque
Cotswold Hills around Cheltenham can easily be
seen from inside the ground. The atmosphere is
also pretty good and there is a drummer in the
home end. I did find the P.A. to be a bit
deafening though.
Neil Le Milliere, a visiting Exeter City fan,
informs me: 'I have found some of the stewarding
to be over the top and some supporters were
ejected from the ground for little reason'. Peter

CHELTENHAM TOWN

Llewellyn adds: 'Don't go on a race day like I did - it's worse than getting away from Old Trafford!'

WHERE TO DRINK

There is a club bar at the ground called the Robins Nest which allows in small numbers of away fans for a small admittance fee. The closest pubs that I found to the ground were the Fox & Hounds and The Greyhound, but they both have more of a home feel about them. Away fans are probably better heading to the Sudeley Arms or The Conservatory on Prestbury Road on the outskirts of town. There is even a decent fish & chip shop situated in between the two. To find these pubs, turn right out of the club car park and then turn left at the end of the road. Go straight over the roundabout and The Sudeley Arms is on your left and the Conservatory is further up on your right. It is no more than a 10 minute walk from the ground.

Otherwise, there is the Parklands Social Club, where you can also park your car (£3). Simply go down Whaddon Road, passing the ground and the bowling club on your left. Take the first left-hand turn and the entrance to the social club car park is a short distance down on the left.

GETTING THERE & WHERE TO PARK

From The North:
Leave the M5 at Junction 10 and take the A4019 towards Cheltenham. Keep straight on through the traffic lights until you come to a large roundabout (there is a McDonald's on the left), at which you turn left. Continue up this road going over a double mini roundabout. Keep going for about 300 yards and then turn right into Swindon Lane. Go over the level crossing and straight over the next roundabout (signposted Prestbury) passing the race course on your left. Turn right into Albert Road (signposted Gloucestershire University) and at the bottom at the roundabout turn left into Prestbury Road (the ground is signposted from here) and then further down Prestbury Road, turn right into Whaddon Road. The ground is down on the left.

From The South:
Leave the M5 at Junction 11 turning right towards Cheltenham. Go across first roundabout - GCHQ is on your left. Turn left at the next roundabout into Princess Elizabeth Way. Go straight over the next roundabout (the exit is over at about '1 o'clock'). Keep on up this road and you will come to a big roundabout where you will see a McDonald's on the corner. Go straight across this roundabout and continue up this road going over a double mini roundabout. Then as North. There is no usable car park at the ground and nearby street parking is limited. The Parklands

Social Club does allow some parking at £3 per car (see Where To Drink). Otherwise there is a free Park & Ride service to the ground operating from Cheltenham Racecourse, which is well signposted around the town. Journey time on the Park & Ride service is obviously dependant on traffic, but is around 10 minutes on average.

By Train
Cheltenham Station is over two miles from the ground, so best to jump in a taxi.

LOCAL RIVALS

Kidderminster Harriers, Swindon Town and although not local, Cardiff City and Rushden & Diamonds.

ADMISSION PRICES

Seating:
Adults*: £16, Concessions: £12, Children: £7
Terrace:
Adults*: £14, Concessions: £9, Under: 16s: £5
 * A £1 discount is available on this price if the ticket is purchased prior to matchday.
 Concessions apply to over 65s and students.

PROGRAMME

Official Programme: £2.50.

RECORD ATTENDANCE

At Whaddon Road:
8,326 v Reading
FA Cup 1st Round, November 17, 1956
At The Athletic Ground:
10,389 v Blackpool
FA Cup 3rd Round, January 13, 1934.

AVERAGE ATTENDANCE

2003-2004: 4,116 (Division Three).

DID YOU KNOW?

Cheltenham Town changed to red and white in 1903, earning them the nickname 'The Robins'. They had previously played in a deep red playing kit, inspiring the nickname 'The Rubies'.

DEVA STADIUM, CHESTER CITY

Ground Name: Deva Stadium
Capacity: 6,012 (3,284 seated)
Address: Bumpers Lane, Chester, CH1 4LT
Main Telephone No: 01244-371-376
Fax No: 01244-390-265
Team Nickname: The Blues
Home Kit Colours: Blue & White
Official Website: www.chestercityfc.net
Unofficial Website:
Unofficial Chester City: www.chester-city.co.uk

WHAT'S THE GROUND LIKE?

The ground was opened in 1992. All four sides are covered and are roughly the same height, making the stadium look quite tidy. Each stand has perspex windshields to each side, whilst the corners of the ground are open. The stadium is a small, fairly simple affair with two sides being seated and the two ends being terrace. The East Stand is slightly taller than the facing West Stand, having a few more rows of seating and some enclosed glassed viewing areas at the back of it. The stadium is completed with a set of four thin modern floodlight pylons.

WHAT'S IT LIKE FOR VISITORS?

Away fans are mostly housed in the South Terrace at one end of the ground, where around 1,200 supporters can be accommodated. 600 seats are also made available to away supporters in part of the West Stand. The delicious 'Football's Famous Chicken Balti Pie' is available inside the ground.

On my one visit when Birmingham played there, the Blues fans were allocated the whole of the West Stand as well as the South Terrace, which made for a great atmosphere. It was a friendly and relaxed day out.

WHERE TO DRINK

Lee Wilcox provides the following information: 'There are no pubs around the ground, although there is a supporters' club in the Main Stand, where away fans are welcome (50p entry). If you venture into the City Centre (a 15 minute walk) then I can recommend the Coach and Horses and the Dublin Packet near the Town Hall. The latter was once owned by ex-Everton striker Dixie Dean. Near to the train station down by the canal is the excellent Old Harkers Arms which also serves good food'.

GETTING THERE & WHERE TO PARK

The ground is located out of town on an industrial estate. Stay on the M56 until you reach a roundabout at the end of the motorway. Follow the signs to North Wales and Queensferry A5117. After around one and a half miles, you will reach a set of traffic lights where you need to bear left onto the A550 (signposted North Wales and Queensferry). After another one and a half miles (after passing RAF Sealand and crossing a bridge), turn left onto the A548 (signposted Chester). Head straight through the first set of lights and after half a mile turn right at the next set. Head down Bumpers Lane to the end of the road and the

ground is on your right. Plenty of car parking at the ground (£3), however if you use the club car park, it can be quite difficult to get away easily after the match.

By Train
Chester railway station is over two miles from the ground, so either get a taxi or take a bus. Lee Wilcox adds: 'The No. 10 from behind the town hall passes the ground every 15 minutes. There is also a football special which also leaves from behind the Town Hall, costing 65p'.

LOCAL RIVALS

Wrexham and Tranmere Rovers.

ADMISSION PRICES

East & West Stands (seating): Adults: £15, Concessions: £10, Under 16s: £6
North & South Stands (terrace): Adults: £13, Concessions: £8, Under 16s: £5

PROGRAMME

Official Programme: £2.

RECORD ATTENDANCE

At Sealand Road:
20,500 v Chelsea
FA Cup 3rd Round, January 15, 1952
At Deva Stadium:
5,987 v Scarborough
Conference League, April 17, 2004

AVERAGE ATTENDANCE

2003-2004: 3,065 (Conference League).

DID YOU KNOW?

That most of the ground (apart from half the East Stand and the club offices) is actually situated in Wales.

THE NEW STADIUM, DARLINGTON

Ground Name:	The New Stadium
Capacity:	27,500
Address:	Neasham Road, Darlington, DL2 1GR
Main Telephone No:	01325-387-000
Main Fax No:	01325-387-050
Ticket Office:	01325-387-030
Pitch Size:	110 yards x 74 yards
Team Nickname:	The Quakers
Home Kit Colours:	Black & White
Official Website:	www.darlington-fc.net

Unofficial Websites:
Darlo Uncovered: www.darlofc.co.uk (Rivals Network)
DFC Online: www.dfc-online.tk (Sport Network)
The Tin Shed: www.the-tinshed.co.uk
DAFTS: www.dafts.co.uk

WHAT'S THE GROUND LIKE?

The stadium, which was opened in 2003, is impressive looking and a good size. It is completely enclosed with all the corners filled with seating. All the stands are single-tiered and of an equal height. There is a perspex strip that runs around the stadium, beneath the roof, to allow more light to reach the pitch. The stands look virtually identical apart from the South Stand that includes a section for the Club Directors and an executive area along the back of it. In the South East corner of the stadium is a Police Control Box.

WHAT'S IT LIKE FOR VISITORS?

Away fans are housed in East Stand at one end of the stadium, where around 3,000 supporters can be accommodated. Martin Redfern, a visiting Scunthorpe fan, informs me: 'It's a nice stadium and there seems to be plenty of parking (although I heard several grumbles about the £5 charge!). The usual food and drink are on offer inside from well run and well staffed outlets and the view from the away end is very good. I hardly noticed the stewards (which is good), but the atmosphere was a little subdued on my visit. No surprise really with just over 3,600 fans sitting in a

stadium that can seat over 20,000'. Peter Llewellyn adds: 'Although I'm not that tall at six feet, I found the legroom to be one of the tightest that I have come across at a new stadium. I was so uncomfortable that I seriously thought about leaving before the end'.

WHERE TO DRINK

The stadium is built right on the outskirts of Darlington and there are not that many pubs in the vicinity. Steve Duffy informs me: 'There is the Copper Beech Pub on Neasham Road, a 10 minute walk towards the town centre. Otherwise there is the Tawny Owl Pub, a Vintage Inn which is about a quarter of a mile the other side of the A66 roundabout. This though is more of a restaurant than pub, but decent enough for lunch'.

It may therefore be an idea to drink in the town centre, where there are plenty of pubs to be found. For the real ale buffs, there is the Number Twenty 2, in Coniscliffe Road. Other pubs of note are the Wetherspoons outlet on Skinnersgate and Humphrys on Blackwellgate. Daniel Hawkes warns: 'The Nags Head & Hogans are best avoided by away fans'. Mick Hubbard, a visiting Aston Villa fans, adds: 'We ducked down a little side street called Mechanic's Yard (which is opposite the indoor market, near the big train sculpture) and discovered a gem of a pub called the Quaker Coffee House. The small bar was an Aladdin's Cave of real ales, having nine on tap. It was a fantastic place and also has a separate café upstairs'.

At the stadium itself there is a bar called Bar 66, which does admit away fans, however, as you would expect, it gets very crowded. Otherwise, alcohol is available on the concourses inside the stadium.

GETTING THERE & WHERE TO PARK

From The South:
Leave the A1 (M) at Junction 57 and take the A66 towards Darlington/Teeside. Continue straight along the A66 going across two roundabouts. At

the third roundabout, you can clearly see the stadium just over on your left. Turn left at this roundabout into Neasham Road for the stadium.

From The North:
Leave the A1(M) at Junction 59 and take the A167 towards Darlington. Then take the A1150 towards Teeside. Turn onto the A66 towards Darlington and you will come to the stadium on your right. Although this route is not the shortest, it does avoid driving through Darlington Town Centre.

Car Parking:
There is a fair sized car park at the stadium which costs £5 per car.

By Train
Darlington train station is around one and a half miles away from the stadium. Either get a taxi or walk it by leaving the station and turning right past the taxi rank and towards the car park. Cross the covered footbridge back over the railway into Albert Road. Go right down this road and then take a right into Neasham Road. The stadium is about a mile further down this road on your left. It should take about 25 minutes to get there.

LOCAL RIVALS

Hartlepool United.

ADMISSION PRICES

All areas of the stadium:
Adults*: £15, Concessions: £7
   * A £2 discount is available on the price of this ticket providing that it is purchased prior to matchday.
   Concessions apply to over 60s, under 16s and students.

PROGRAMME

Official Programme: £2.50.

RECORD ATTENDANCE

At The New Stadium:
11,600 v Kidderminster Harriers
Division 3, August 16, 2003.
At Feethams:
21,023 v Bolton Wanderers
League Cup 3rd Round, November 14, 1960.

AVERAGE ATTENDANCE

2003-2004: 5,023 (Division Three).

DID YOU KNOW?

That Darlington's old Feethams ground was originally rented from a certain magnificently named John Beaumont Pease, a prominent member of the local Quaker community.

BLUNDELL PARK, GRIMSBY TOWN

Ground Name:	Blundell Park
Capacity:	10,033 (all-seated)
Address:	Blundell Park, Cleethorpes, DN35 7PY
Main Telephone No:	01472-605-050
Ticket Office:	As Above
Main Fax No:	01472-693-665
Team Nickname:	The Mariners
Pitch Size:	111 x 75 yards
Home Kit Colours:	Black & White
Official Website:	www.gtfc.co.uk

Unofficial Websites:
Electronic Fishcake: www.grimsby.org (Rivals Network)
International Supporters Club: www.gtisc.co.uk
Jailhouse Rock: http://jailhouserock.cjb.net/
Cod Almighty: www.codalmighty.com
Supporters Trust: www.gtst.net
Three Fish: www.three-fish.co.uk (Sport Network)

WHAT'S THE GROUND LIKE?

Both ends are small covered stands. Home fans are located in the strangely named Pontoon Stand at one end, away fans at the opposite end. One side has a small covered stand and joins the away end, so that one corner is filled. Other corners of the ground have recently been filled with temporary seating so that only one corner remains unused at one side of the John Smiths Stand. This is the tallest stand, being two-tiered and covered. However, this stand only runs half the length of the pitch, straddling the halfway line. It was previously called the Findus Stand in keeping with Grimsby's links with the fishing trade. In fact, if I

remember correctly, I believe the Grimsby fans chant 'We only sing when we're fishing!' whilst pretending to cast with imaginary rods.

FUTURE GROUND DEVELOPMENTS

The Club's intention to move to a new purpose-built stadium near Great Coates has hit a major snag, with the failure to purchase the necessary land. It is therefore now unclear as to whether the £14m pound scheme will materialize. The Club may consider applying for planning permission on a different site.

WHAT'S IT LIKE FOR VISITORS?

Away fans are located in the Osmond Stand, at one end of the ground, where 2,200 supporters can be accommodated. One downside of this stand is that there are a number of supporting pillars which can impair your view of the game. Blundell Park is a rather small ground and sometimes gets over criticised by visiting fans. But there is normally always a passionate crowd, which contributes to a good atmosphere. Remember though to wrap up warmly as there can be a biting wind coming off the North Sea.

WHERE TO DRINK

Dave Peasgood has informed me that the unofficial away fans pub is the Leaking Boot (formerly Darley's Hotel) which is halfway between Cleethorpes and Blundell Park on the north side of Grimsby Road. To get there, head down the A180 and drive past the ground. It's about 400 yards further up the road on the left. It is a large pub and car park and allows in children. The Fish & Chips in Cleethorpes are legendary and there are some good outlets located near to the ground. Josh's fish and chip shop near the Leaking Boot comes recommended. Other recommendations by Dave include the Blundell Park Hotel, which, if you arrive early, serves some good food at reasonable prices (expect to pay around £5 for a good portion of fish and chips). The Rutland Arms is also recommended for both home and away fans to mingle, however this is some distance from the ground and doesn't allow in children. (It is about half a mile before Blundell park, turn left at Ramsdens superstore and left again, and you'll see the pub at the opposite end of their car park. If in coaches, then from where you will be parked, head back the way you came, along the sea wall for 5 minutes and you'll see the pub). The Imperial pub by the ground is not recommended for away fans.

GETTING THERE & WHERE TO PARK

The ground is situated on the A180 which runs between Grimsby and Cleethorpes. Cleethorpes is well signposted from Grimsby town centre, just head towards Cleethorpes on the A180 and you will reach the ground on your left.

There is no car park at the ground, therefore only street parking. As you drive along the A180 towards the ground, the home end appears first, then after the McDonald's is the away end. From there, continue towards Cleethorpes and try any of the side streets to the left or preferably the right and you should find a parking spot okay.

By Train
Cleethorpes railway station is about a mile from the ground and takes 15 minutes to walk to the ground. As you come out of the station, turn left and walk along the sea front. Just keep going and you will eventually see the ground on your left. Thanks to David Fretwell for providing the directions.

LOCAL RIVALS

Scunthorpe United, Hull City and Lincoln City.

ADMISSION PRICES

Home Fans:
Upper John Smiths: Adults: £16, OAPs: £10, Juniors: £6
Lower John Smiths: Adults: £14, OAPs: £10, Juniors: £6
Pontoon Stand: Adults: £14, OAPs: £10, Juniors:

£6 (Students and Unemployed with ID: £10)
Main Stand: Adults: £16, OAPs: £10, Juniors £6
Away Fans:
Osmond Stand: Adults: £16, OAPs: £10, Juniors: £6

PROGRAMME

Official Programme: £2.50.

RECORD ATTENDANCE

31,651 v Wolverhampton Wanderers
FA Cup 5th Round, February 20, 1937.

AVERAGE ATTENDANCE

2003-2004: 4,730 (Division Two).

DID YOU KNOW?

That Blundell Park is not located in Grimsby but in the nearby town of Cleethorpes.

MATCHROOM STADIUM, LEYTON ORIENT

Ground Name: Matchroom Stadium (formerly known as Leyton Stadium, but still referred to by many fans as Brisbane Road)
Capacity: 4,989 (reduced due to redevelopment work)
Address: Brisbane Road, Leyton, London, E10 5NF
Main Telephone No: 020-8926-1111
Ticket Office: 020-8926-1010
Main Fax No: 020-8926-1110
Team Nickname: The O's
Pitch Size: 115 x 80 yards
Home Kit Colours: Red & Black
Official Website: www.leytonorient.com
Unofficial Websites:
LOFC Online: www.lofconline.com (Rivals Network)
O-Net: www.brisbaneroad.com

WHAT'S THE GROUND LIKE?

Following the Club's decision to sell part of the Brisbane Road site to a property developer, the ground is undergoing major works at the moment. Both the West Stand and North Terrace have been demolished and the two ends of the Main Stand have also been removed. It is intended that a new West and North Stand will be built at a cost of around £9m and in each corner of the ground, blocks for residential use will also be constructed. The new West Stand, when completed (hopefully

for the start of the 2005/06 season), will have a capacity of 2,500 and will become the headquarters for the Club. This stand will also house the changing rooms. The new North Stand will be similar in design to the existing South Stand, with a capacity of 1,500. It is intended that this will house away supporters in the future.

At one end is the comparatively new single-tiered, South Stand (capacity 1,336 seats), which replaced a former open terrace. An unusual feature of this stand is that it is raised above pitch level, meaning that you have to climb a small set of steps at the front to reach the seating area. The reduced Main Stand is still a fair size; this partly covered stand is now all-seated after having seating installed on the former front terrace. Unfortunately, it has several supporting pillars and the roof doesn't quite cover all of the front seating. It does though have an interesting gable on its roof which has Leyton Orient proudly emblazoned across it.

WHAT'S IT LIKE FOR VISITORS?

With the redevelopment works being undertaken, the ticket allocation for away fans has been reduced to 700. Away supporters are housed in one side (towards the South End) of the Main Stand, where there are a couple of supporting pillars that may impede your view. I have been to Orient a number of times and have always been impressed by the state of the pitch. Even in January it is immaculate and at the start of the season you could almost play snooker on it! The delicious 'Football's Famous Chicken Balti Pie' (£2) is available inside the ground.

I have not experienced any problems at Brisbane Road with Orient supporters, but have found the local police not so friendly. On one occasion the police filmed the crowd, right on the touchline in front of us, for most of the second half, which I found to be quite intimidating. A friend of mine almost got himself ejected from the ground, when he queried the policeman filming whether we would be on Match of the Day!

WHERE TO DRINK

The nearest pub to the ground is the Coach & Horses. To get there, take a right out of Leyton station and walk down for about half a mile. It is on your left, within sight of the floodlights. The Three Blackbirds has been recommended and it is a bit further up Leyton High Road, on the right. Stephen Harris adds: 'The best pub near to the ground is the Birkbeck Tavern in Langthorne Road, behind the tube station'.

GETTING THERE & WHERE TO PARK

Thanks to O-Net for the following directions: Approaching London you will at some point hit the M25. Use this to get to the M11 (unless you're coming from Cambridge, in which case you'll already be on it) take the southbound carriageway for about six miles and take the right fork signposted for the North Circular.

At the bottom of the flyover where the roads merge, move into the left-hand lane and turn left at the roundabout onto the A104. After about one mile at the next roundabout, take the right exit - still the A104 (a landmark here is the quaintly decorated Lamb's Café). Half a mile further on, turn left into Leyton Green Road (signposted to Leyton and Stratford), and left again into a short slip road past the bus garage entrance and left into Leyton High Road - you'll see the Leyton Leisure Lagoon opposite as you wait to make the turn. Continue until you see the floodlights and then find a side turning to park in the backstreets. Street Parking.

By Tube

The nearest tube station is Leyton (about a quarter of a mile away) which is on the Central Line. Come out of the station and turn right down Leyton High Road. Cross over the road to the other side and continue down it. You will come to Coronation Gardens on your left and the floodlights of the ground can be clearly seen behind them. Take the next left past the gardens into Buckingham Road for the ground.

LOCAL RIVALS

West Ham United and from further a field, Brighton and Southend.

ADMISSION PRICES

Executive Area: Adults: £30, Concessions: £24
Main and South Stands (Seated): £16, Concessions: £10
Away Supporters (Main Stand Seats): £16, Concessions: £10

PROGRAMME

Official Programme: £2.50

RECORD ATTENDANCE

34,345 v West Ham United
FA Cup 4th Round, January 25, 1964

AVERAGE ATTENDANCE

2003-2004: 4,157 (Division Three).

DID YOU KNOW?

In 1966 Orient opted to drop Leyton from its name but the suffix was reinstated in the early 1980s.

SINCIL BANK, LINCOLN CITY

Ground Name: Sincil Bank
Capacity: 10,130
Address: Sincil Bank Stadium, Lincoln, LN5 8LD
Main Telephone No: 01522-880-011
Main Fax No: 01522-880-020
Team Nickname: The Imps
Pitch Size: 110 x 73 yards
Home Kit Colours: Red, White & Black
Official Website: www.redimps.com
Unofficial Websites:
The Forgotten Imp: www.theforgottenimp.co.uk
Imp Net: www.impnet.co.uk
Imp Sight: www.impsight.co.uk – (Rivals Network)
Lincoln City Mad: www.lincolncity-mad.co.uk
(Footy Mad Network)
The Imps: www.sportnetwork.net/main/s261.php
(Sport Network)

WHAT'S THE GROUND LIKE?

On one side is the large all-seater CO-OP Community Stand. This large single-tiered covered stand opened in 1995 and has a capacity of 5,700. Opposite is the Lincolnshire Echo Stand, a small old looking covered stand (although in fact it is comparatively modern being built in 1987). It is seated, but only runs half the length of the pitch, straddling the halfway line and hence there are gaps at either side. One gap has now been partly filled by a tiny covered Family Stand. Both ends are small covered affairs. The Mundy South Park Stand is all seated and has a row of executive boxes running across the back. This stand has a

couple of supporting pillars at the front. The other end is the Stacey West, all-seated covered stand, for home supporters. It was named in memory of the two Lincoln supporters who lost their lives in the Bradford City Fire at Valley Parade in 1985.

WHAT'S IT LIKE FOR VISITORS?

Away fans are housed in part of the CO-OP Community Stand at one side of the pitch. The normal allocation for away fans is 1,900 and this stand is divided between home and away supporters. The facilities and view of the pitch are good and there is also a great range of food available, including the delicious 'Football's Famous Chicken Balti Pie', burgers, Lincolnshire sausage and bacon rolls. I had an enjoyable day at Lincoln. There was a good atmosphere at the ground, with plenty of noise being created by the local band in the CO-OP Stand.

Jason Adderley, a visiting West Brom supporter, adds: 'Lincoln's small band of fans are passionate about their team and are one of the friendliest bunches I've met on my travels. The atmosphere was great and the drums were rousing, leading the chants of the Lincoln supporters'.

WHERE TO DRINK

Neil Le Milliere, a visiting Exeter City fan, adds: 'Away supporters are admitted to the supporters' club (called the Centre Spot) behind the South Park Stand. The Mansfield Smooth beer and the hot pork rolls were excellent. Otherwise the

George & Dragon is well recommended'. There are plenty of good pubs to be found if you head along the High Street towards the town centre. Guy Collings recommends the City Vaults on High Street, while John Bennett, a visiting Bristol Rovers supporter, recommends the Golden Eagle on the same street. Jon Morley adds: 'The Portland pub down Sincil Bank about 800 yards from the ground and the Wetherspoons pub Ritz on the High Street both serve reasonably priced food and ales'.

GETTING THERE & WHERE TO PARK

Lincoln is not the easiest place to get to, as it is not conveniently situated next to a motorway. I had great difficulty in finding the ground and the two people that I asked directions for were unaware that Lincoln had a football team! However, I have been recently informed that the ground is now well signposted around Lincoln. Otherwise follow the A46 into Lincoln (which leads onto the High Street) and the ground is indicated from there. If you follow the signs for away coaches, this leads you onto the A158 South Park Avenue, where there is plenty of street parking to be found (although it is a 10 minute walk to the ground). Otherwise the signs lead you to the ground, where, if you arrive early, you can park behind the Stacey West Stand (cost £4), otherwise street parking. Ian Gibson adds: 'On matchdays, the South Common is open for parking, which can be found at the beginning of South Park Avenue when coming in from either the A46 or from the High Street. It's free to park and only about a 5-10 minute walk from the ground'.

By Train
Lincoln Central train station is around 15 minutes walk to the ground. Turn left out of the station and walk up to the traffic lights next to St. Mary's church. Turn left at these traffic lights onto the High Street, walking over the railway level crossing. Walk along the High Street (passing many good pubs) for approx 10 minutes before turning left into Scorer Street. Walk along Scorer Street until you come to a bridge across the Sincil Drain river. Turn right immediately after crossing the bridge onto Sincil Bank - the ground is straight ahead. Thanks to John Smalley for providing the directions.

Alternatively there is a shorter route (but you miss those fine pubs!): Come out of the station and turn right to go down the road. About 30 yards ahead on your right you will see some steps and a bridge over the railway. Go over the bridge and once on the other side follow the road down to the ground. Thanks to Ben Schofield for providing these directions.

LOCAL RIVALS

Scunthorpe United, Mansfield Town, Hull City, Grimsby Town, Peterborough and Boston United.

ADMISSION PRICES

The Club operate a category system (A & B) whereby the most popular matches cost more to watch. Category B prices are shown in brackets. This mainly applies to adult tickets only.
Home Fans:
Echo & CO-OP Community Stands:
Adults: £16 (£15), Over 60s: £11, Under 15s: £5
Stacey West, Mundy South Park & Family Stands:
Adults: £14 (£13), Concessions: £9, Under 15s: £5
Executive Area:
Adults: £30 (£28), Under 15s: £17 (£16)
Away Fans:
CO-OP Community Stand:
Adults: £16 (£15), Concessions: £11, Under 15s: £5

PROGRAMME & FANZINE

Official Programme: £2.50.
The Deranged Ferret Fanzine: £1.20

RECORD ATTENDANCE

23,196 v Derby County
League Cup 4th Round, November 15, 1967.

AVERAGE ATTENDANCE

2003-2004: 4,910 (Division Three).

DID YOU KNOW?

The ground was named after the Sincil Drain which runs behind the West side of the ground. Banks of earth were formed as part of the project to originally construct the ground – hence the ground name of Sincil Bank.

MOSS ROSE, MACCLESFIELD TOWN

Ground Name:	Moss Rose
Capacity:	6,335 (2,599 seats)
Address:	London Road, Macclesfield, SK11 7SP
Main Telephone No:	01625-264-686
Main Fax No:	01625-264-692
Team Nickname:	The Silkmen
Pitch Size:	100m x 60m
Home Kit Colours:	Blue & White
Official Website:	www.mtfc.co.uk
Unofficial Website:	
Silkweb: www.thesilkweb.com (Rivals Network)	

WHAT'S THE GROUND LIKE?

Even with recent developments, the ground is still on the smallish side, with a non-league feel about it. One side is predominantly uncovered terracing, with a small seated Main Stand sitting in the middle. This type of stand is a classic design, once common across the country, but many have since disappeared with redevelopment. On the other side is the covered, single-tiered Alfred McAlpine Stand, which was opened in March 2001. This smart looking all-seated stand, with a row of executive boxes to its rear, has greatly improved the overall look of the ground. The Star Lane End is a relatively new covered stand that is a strange mix of seating and terracing – strange and unusual in having a terrace area behind the seating area. Apparently seating was added to the terrace in this way so that the Club could fulfil the then Football League's rules concerning the number of seats that a club ground needed to be admitted

into the Football League. Opposite is the open terraced Silkman End, which is given to away supporters.

FUTURE GROUND DEVELOPMENTS

David Fenton informs me: 'The Club have outlined proposals to redevelop the Silkman End. The existing terrace will remain much the same but behind it will be a tier of seating and behind this a new four storey building housing offices and a gym. There will also be a roof over both the new seats and the terrace. However, no firm time scales have been announced as to when this will take place'. It is anticipated that after this stand is built, that away fans would relocate to the Star Lane End.

WHAT'S IT LIKE FOR VISITORS?

Away fans are primarily located in the open Silkman End, where up to 1,500 fans can be accommodated. Additionally, 403 seats are made available in the new Alfred McAlpine Stand. The seating may well be a better bet, as this stand is covered and the facilities new, unlike the Silkman End Terrace, where facilities are pretty basic and the toilets grim. There is one burger van providing refreshments in this area, although £2.50 for a less then desirable cheeseburger seemed rather over-priced for this part of the world. The view of the playing action and the atmosphere within the ground are both pretty good, with some enjoyable banter between the two sets of supporters. On the whole, I enjoyed my visit to Macclesfield as it was a nice relaxing day out.

WHERE TO DRINK

The ground is located on the outskirts of Macclesfield and therefore there is not a tremendous choice of pubs or even a handy chippy. The Golden Lion is the only close pub, about a 10 minute walk from the away turnstiles. I found the pub warm and friendly, although it didn't do any food which was surprising. There was a 50-50 mix of home and away supporters on my last visit. To find the Golden Lion, simply head down Moss Lane, which goes behind the away terrace, and then turn left at the corner of the ground and walk down behind the new stand. Keep straight on this road and you will come to the pub on the left. Geoff Knights adds: 'There are also several pubs in the town centre and others on the London Road on the way from the town centre to the ground'.

Eamonn Prendergast informs me: 'If you are travelling by train and walking to the ground then you will pass a number of pubs. I would strongly recommend The Railway View on Byrons Lane and The Sun Inn on Mill Lane. Both are on the way to the ground, have friendly atmospheres and sell a wide variety of local and other brews. You could also try The Albion and The Travellers Rest. There are several chippies and fast food outlets on the way back to the station from the ground if you fancy a bite after the game'.

GETTING THERE & WHERE TO PARK

From the South:
Leave the M6 at Junction 17 and turn onto the A534 towards Congleton. On reaching Congleton town centre follow the signs for A54 Buxton. Stay on the A54 for around five miles and then turn left on to the A523 towards Macclesfield. You will see the ground on your left after entering the outskirts of Macclesfield.

From The North:
Leave the M6 at Junction 18 and take the A54 towards Congleton. On reaching Congleton town centre follow the signs for A54 Buxton. Then as South.

Mostly street parking around and behind the ground and on the A523 itself.

By Train
Geoff Knights informs me: 'Macclesfield railway station is about one and a quarter miles from the Moss Rose ground, about a half hour walk. As you leave the station, at the bottom of the station approach, turn left onto Sunderland Street and follow until the traffic lights at Park Green (War memorial and gardens). Turn left onto Mill Lane (it

is probably better to cross onto the opposite side of the road here at the traffic lights) and follow this road which becomes London Road. Just after passing the Catholic Church on the right, the ground comes into sight ahead.

Chris Dale adds: 'From the bus station, opposite the Railway Station, you can catch a bus to the ground. It is served by Arriva Cheshire service 9 (showing Moss Rose circular) which operates every 12-20 minutes during the day. In the evenings, the buses only run hourly but are augmented by service 14A (showing Sutton/Langley circular), also at hourly intervals'.

LOCAL RIVALS

Altrincham.

ADMISSION PRICES

Home Fans:
Main Stand (Seating): Adults: £17, Concessions: £12
Main Stand (Terrace): Adults: £13, Concessions: £8
Alfred McAlpine Stand: Adults £17, Concessions: £12
Star Lane HFS Loans Stand (Seating): Adults: £13, Concessions: £8
Star Lane HFS Loans Stand (Terrace): Adults: £13, Concessions: £8
Away Fans:
Alfred McAlpine Stand (Seating): Adults: £17, Concessions: £12
Silkman Terrace: Adults: £13, Concessions: £8

PROGRAMME

Official Programme: £2.50.

RECORD ATTENDANCE

9,003 v Winsford United
Cheshire Senior Cup 2nd Round, February 4, 1948

AVERAGE ATTENDANCE

2003-2004: 2,385 (Division Three).

DID YOU KNOW?

The original Macclesfield Football Club was founded sometime in the mid 1800s by the late Col. J W H Thorpe, and in the early days played under rugby rules on a field off Victoria Road called Bowfield Lane.

MANSFIELD TOWN

FIELD MILL, MANSFIELD TOWN

Ground Name: Field Mill
Capacity: 10,000 (all-seated)
Address: Quarry Lane, Mansfield, NG18 5DA
Main Telephone No: 0870-756-3160
Main Fax No: 01623-482-495
Team Nickname: The Stags
Home Kit Colours: Amber & Blue
Official Website: www.mansfieldtown.net
Unofficial Websites:
Déjà vu: www.yellows.co.uk (Footy Mad Network)
Stags Online: www.stagsonline.com (Rivals Network)
Ollerton Stags: www.ollertonstags.co.uk
Supporters Association: www.stagsnet.net

WHAT'S THE GROUND LIKE?

During the past couple of years and at a cost of £6.5m, Field Mill has been transformed into a modern stadium, with the building of three new stands. Both ends, the North Stand and Quarry Lane End, plus the West Stand on one side of the pitch have been redeveloped. The ends are almost identical single-tiered stands, each accommodating just under 2,000 supporters. The latest addition to the ground is the West Stand, opened in February 2001. This is a cantilevered two-tiered stand, with a capacity of 5,500. On the other side of the ground is the rather small Bishop Street Stand, a covered seated stand that only runs half the length of the pitch. This now looks rather dowdy alongside its new shiny neighbours.

FUTURE GROUND DEVELOPMENTS

There are plans to redevelop the small remaining

Bishop Street Stand, but no formal time scales have been announced.

WHAT'S IT LIKE FOR VISITORS?

To confuse matters, away fans are now housed in the opposite end from last season. They are now accommodated in the North Stand, a move that has been unpopular with a number of home fans, as the North End of the ground has been the traditional home end for many years. As you would expect from a relatively new stand, the views of the playing action and facilities are pretty good. Around 1,800 supporters can be accommodated.

I had a fairly uneventful trip to Mansfield and did not encounter any problems. It seemed to be a friendly place that was quite relaxed. However, Alistair Wright, a visiting Bristol City supporter, states: 'I found the standard of stewarding at Field Mill to be particularly poor and at times they seemed almost hostile towards the away support'. The delicious 'Football's Famous Chicken Balti Pie' (£2.20) is available inside the ground.

WHERE TO DRINK

The Early Doors pub next to the ground is popular with both home and away supporters, although it can get rather crowded. It does quite good food and has an outside seating area. Pete Smith recommends The Talbot on the A60 near the Safeway Supermarket. Chris Patrick adds: 'The Sir John Cockle pub is on the A38 going into Mansfield from the M1 and again serves good food. The Lord Byron pub on Quarry Lane is also popular with both home and away fans'. Whilst Terry Gospel advises that away fans should avoid the Victoria and Red Lion Pubs.

GETTING THERE & WHERE TO PARK

From The North:
Leave the M1 at Junction 29 and take A617 to Mansfield. After six miles, turn right into Rosemary Street. Follow this road for one mile and turn right into Quarry Lane.

From The South:
Leave the M1 at Junction 28 and take the A38 to Mansfield. After 6.5 miles, turn right at the crossroads into Belvedere Street, then right into Quarry Lane.

Peter Llewellyn informs me: 'You can park at the ground at a cost of £2. Otherwise it is street parking'. Malcolm Dawson, a visiting Sunderland supporter, adds: 'I parked in the retail park (PC World, Curry's, B&Q) behind the North Stand. I assumed that there would be unlimited free parking, but when I got back after the match I had a parking ticket for £30. Be warned!'

By Train
The ground can be seen from Mansfield railway station which is no more than 10 minutes walk away. The station is on a local line and is served by trains from Nottingham. To get to the ground from the station, leave the station and turn left along the dual carriageway (away from the town centre) and you should see a retail park on the right. Go straight ahead at the first set of traffic lights along Portland Street and then right at the next lights and into Quarry Lane. The ground is a short distance down this road on the right-hand side.

Martin Monk adds: 'For away fans using the trains, take note that for midweek matches, the last train leaves from Mansfield - Nottingham at 9.45 PM and the last train leaves from Mansfield - Worksop at 9.38 PM. You should check with your train operators as both of these times fall before a 7.45 KO match finishes. Away fans have been known to have been left stranded in Mansfield and have struggled to get home. Also note the Robin Hood Line does not run on a Sunday'.

LOCAL RIVALS

Chesterfield.

ADMISSION PRICES

Home Fans:
West Stand (Upper Tier): Adults: £16, OAPs: £11, Under 16s: £8
West Stand (Lower Tier): Adults: £15, OAPs/Students: £10, Under 16s: £ £7
South (Quarry Lane End) Stand: Adults: £15, OAPs: £10, Under 16s: £7
Family Enclosure: Adults: £15, Under 10s: £5
Bishop Street Stand: Adults: £15, OAPs: £10, Under 16s: £7
Away Fans:
North Stand: Adults: £15, OAPs: £10, Under 16s: £7

PROGRAMME

Official Programme: £2.

RECORD ATTENDANCE

24,467 v Nottingham Forest
FA Cup 3rd Round, January 10, 1953.

AVERAGE ATTENDANCE

2003-2004: 5,207 (Division Three).

DID YOU KNOW?

Field Mill was first used for football sometime in 1861 making it the oldest ground in the Football League.

NORTHAMPTON TOWN

SIXFIELDS STADIUM, NORTHAMPTON

Ground Name:	Sixfields Stadium
Capacity:	7,653
Address:	Sixfields Stadium, Northampton, NN5 5QA
Main Telephone No:	01604-757-773
Main Fax No:	01604-751-613
Ticket Office No:	01604-588-338
Ticket Office Fax No:	01604-589-318
Pitch Size:	116 x 72 yards
Team Nickname:	The Cobblers
Home Kit Colours:	Claret & White
Official Website:	www.ntfc.co.uk

Unofficial Websites:
The Cobblers: http://web.ukonline.co.uk/ntfc/
The Fields Are Green:
www.stormloader.com/cobblers/

WHAT'S THE GROUND LIKE?

The Club moved from their old County Ground to the new stadium in October 1994. This neat all-seater stadium is located on the outskirts of Northampton. Sixfields has three small covered single-tier stands, and another larger single-tier covered West Stand (capacity 4,000), at one side of the pitch. Away supporters are housed at the South Stand end. The Club has received awards for the facilities provided for disabled supporters. A large hill overlooks the ground where small numbers congregate to watch the game free, even though they can only see half the pitch!

FUTURE GROUND DEVELOPMENTS

Kevin Dunn informs me: 'Following the Club's successful bid to buy a 150 year lease on Sixfields

Stadium, they have announced that the stadium is to be further developed so that the overall capacity will rise to 15,000. This will mean new North, East and South Stands as well as executive boxes being added to the West Stand. Part of the development will also feature the building of a hotel behind the South Stand. The home end at Northampton's old County Ground was called the Hotel End, so it is quite apt that the new stadium will also feature its own Hotel End. It is believed that it will take five years for the plans to be fulfilled.'

WHAT'S IT LIKE FOR VISITORS?

Away fans are located in the South Stand at one end of the pitch, where 850 supporters can be accommodated. If demand requires it, an additional 300 seats can be made available in the Alwyn Hargrave Stand. One slight inconvenience about Sixfields is that you can't pay at the turnstiles. You have to buy your ticket first from a Portakabin and then you have to queue again. Some away fans have been caught by this when arriving late. However, I have received a number of reports complementing the standard of stewarding, other club officials and the Northampton fans themselves.

Having lived in Northampton for a year and watched Northampton Town win the old fourth division, I have a soft spot for them. The fans themselves are quite passionate and this makes for a great atmosphere especially at cup games. Robert Dunkley informs me: 'Outside the West Stand there is a used programme stall stocking a wide range of programmes from different clubs and seasons'.

NORTHAMPTON TOWN

WHERE TO DRINK

The ground is built on a leisure complex on the outskirts of Northampton. This consists of a couple of fast food establishments, a cinema and the ground itself. There are two pubs on this site, Chevys, which is for home supporters only, and The Sixfields Tavern (no away colours). I managed to get into Chevys when I went to see Northampton play Gillingham. The bouncers on the door asked me which club I supported. When I replied Birmingham City, they were totally confused as they had obviously not been programmed for this response. Nevertheless they still let me in.

Steven Jones informs me: "A couple of other bars have recently opened on the Sixfields complex, both of which are better than the Sixfields Tavern and Chevys in terms of service, space, atmosphere, etc. One of them is the Old Orleans, a restaurant and bar, and the other is Sports Bar (bowling alleys, 9-ball tables, big screens for post-match scores round-ups, etc, equally popular with home and away fans)'. Whilst Carl Brown adds: 'I found myself drinking in a T.G.I. Friday's outlet opposite the Main Stand. Maybe not your stereotypical pre-match watering hole but very convenient for a drink, plus there was a wonderful array of fine waitresses on display, serving the goods!"

If you are coming into Northampton from the M1 via the A45, you will pass the Turnpike Pub, which is okay for away fans. Otherwise if you have a bit of time on your hands, then continue to walk along the A45 towards the town centre, where you will soon reach the Northampton Saints Rugby ground. Opposite is a pub called The Rover, which is family friendly and has been recommended to me.

GETTING THERE & WHERE TO PARK

From The South:
Leave the M1 at Junction 15A and take the A43 towards Northampton and you will come to the ground on your right.

From The North:
Leave the M1 at Junction 16 and take the A45 towards Northampton and, again, you will come to the ground on your right.

The Sixfields stadium is well signposted around the area. There is a fair sized car park located at the ground (which is free although in an effort to raise funds a donation, in the region of £2, is asked for). Make sure you arrive early as it has been known to get full for the more popular games. Also don't try to park at the Virgin Cinema as you will be charged £10 for your trouble.

By Train
Northampton train station is over two miles from the ground, so it is probably best to hire a taxi. However, if you feel like braving the 25-30 minute walk, then Phil Spokes provides the following directions: 'Turn right from the station and follow the road past the express lift tower (you can't miss it, a tall tower that was once used for testing lifts), passing the Wickes store on the left. Continue down to the Leisure Centre, turn left down the path beside it and then turn right onto the road. You will see the stadium in the distance in front of you.

LOCAL RIVALS

Rushden & Diamonds, Cambridge and Peterborough United.

ADMISSION PRICES

Home Fans:
West Stand Upper Tier: Adults: £17, Concessions: £11.50
West Stand Lower Tier: Adults: £16, Concessions: £10.50, Under 16s: £6
Alwyn Hargrave Stand: Adults: £15, Concessions: £8, Under 16s: £4 (as part of family)
Dave Bowen Stand: Adults: £14, Concessions: £9.50

Away Fans:
South Stand: Adults: £14, Concessions: £9.50
Concessions apply to over 60s, under 16s and students (with current NUS card, or letter from school).

PROGRAMME

Official Programme: £2.50.

RECORD ATTENDANCE

At Sixfields Stadium;
7,557 v Manchester City
Division Two, September 26, 1998
At the County Ground;
24,523 v Fulham
Division One, April 23, 1966

AVERAGE ATTENDANCE

2003-2004: 5,306 (Division Three).

DID YOU KNOW?

That at one time Northampton's principle manufacturing industry was the making of shoes. Hence the Club's nickname of 'The Cobblers'.

MEADOW LANE, NOTTS COUNTY

Ground Name: Meadow Lane
Capacity: 20,300 (all-seated)
Address: Meadow Lane,
Nottingham, NG2 3HJ
Main Telephone No: 0115-952-9000
Main Fax No: 0115-955-3994
Ticket Office: 0115-955-7210
Pitch Size: 114 x 76 yards
Club Nickname: The Magpies
Home Kit Colours: Black & White
Official Website: www.nottscountyfc.co.uk
Unofficial Websites:
Notts County Trust: www.nottscotrust.org.uk
Nottscounty.net: www.nottscounty.net (Rivals
Network)
Notts County Mad: www.nottscounty-mad.co.uk
(Footy Mad Network)

WHAT'S THE GROUND LIKE?

During the 1990s the ground was completely
rebuilt, creating an attractive all-seater stadium.
Although the ground comprises four separate
stands, it is quite smart. Both sides are single-
tiered stands, the larger of which is the Main
Stand. Away fans are housed in the large Kop End,
containing 5,400 supporters. Again this is a newer
stand with excellent facilities. The other end is the
smaller covered Family Stand, with a small
electric scoreboard on its roof.

WHAT'S IT LIKE FOR VISITORS?

I was very impressed with the new stands at the
ground and had a pleasant day out. The view from
the away end was excellent as were the catering

facilities. The local fans seemed friendly enough.
The only disappointments were that the
substantial supporters' club didn't allow in away
supporters and that the ground generally lacked
atmosphere, although away fans can really make
some noise in the Kop Stand. Christopher Bushe,
a visiting Brentford supporter, adds: 'The Notts
County stewards were a bit over the top in terms
of numbers and in attitude'.

WHERE TO DRINK

There are a few pubs around the ground that let
away supporters in and are quite friendly and serve
good real ale. Steve, from the Pie Fanzine, informs
me: 'On the main London Road, just across from
the hump-back bridge over the canal, is the newly
refurbished and renamed Globe. A comfortable
open-plan pub with good food and five ever-
changing real ales. On the other side of Trent Bridge
(although mercifully facing away from that rusting
monstrosity with a red tree painted on the side!) is
the Southbank, the Globe's sister pub. It also serves
excellent food and has sport on numerous
televisions; three real ales are offered here including
one from the tiny local Mallards brewery. Just across
from the front of the station down Queensbridge
Road is the Vat and Fiddle situated next door to the
Castle Rock micro-brewery. It offers 10 real ales and
hot and cold food. Children are welcome. At the far
end of Meadow Lane away from the ground, you
will find the Magpies pub. Named after Notts
County's nickname, it is of course painted red and
depicts two magpies on its sign - testimony indeed
that national brewers have lost touch with their
customers! It offers well kept real ales and excellent

but inexpensive meals. Get there early enough and you can even park in their car park'.

Chris Rhoades recommends the Trent Navigation (parking also available there at £1.50) and the Trent Bridge Inn. Chris claims that: 'The food is locally renowned, especially the pies!' Whilst Tim Cooke, a travelling Millwall fan, has a different angle (so to speak): 'Definitely one for the lads! Hooters (on the main road A6011, on the outskirts of the City Centre, you can't miss it!) has very nice waitresses wearing just enough to cover things up, serves lovely beer and great food. Take my advice, make a weekend of it, Nottingham is a top city!' Alcohol is also available within the ground.

GETTING THERE & WHERE TO PARK

Leave the M1 at Junction 26 and take the A610 towards Nottingham and then signs for Melton Mowbray. Turn left before the River Trent into Meadow Lane. You can park at the Cattle Market (opposite the away end £2) or in the club car park (opposite the club offices in Meadow Lane - £2.50). Otherwise there is plenty of street parking.

By Train
The ground is 10 minutes walk from Nottingham railway station. As you come out of the main station entrance, turn left and then left again. Follow the road down to London Road and then turn right. The ground is about a quarter of a mile down the dual carriageway on the left.

LOCAL RIVALS

Nottingham Forest, Mansfield Town, Chesterfield and Derby County.

ADMISSION PRICES

Home Fans:
Main Stand:
Adults: £18, Over 60s: £11, Students: £9, Under 16s: £4
Jimmy Sirrell Stand:
Adults: £16, Over 60s: £10, Students: £9, Under 16s: £4
Family Stand:
Adults: £13, Over 60s: £9, Students: £9, Under 16s: £4
Away Fans:
Kop Stand: Adults: £16, Over 60s: £10, Under 16s: £4

PROGRAMME

Official Programme: £2.50.

RECORD ATTENDANCE

47,310 v York City
FA Cup 6th Round, March 12, 1955

AVERAGE ATTENDANCE

2003-2004: 5,933 (Division Two).

DID YOU KNOW?

That County called themselves the Lambs in pre-1900 days, a provocative name derived from an infamous gang of Nottingham thugs.

KASSAM STADIUM, OXFORD

Ground Name: Kassam Stadium
Capacity: 12,500 (all-seated)
Address: Grenoble Rd, Oxford,
OX4 4XP
Main Telephone No: 01865-337-533
Main Fax No: 01865-337-555
Ticket Office: 01865-337-533
Team Nickname: The U's
Pitch Size: 112 x 78 yards
Home Kit Colours: Yellow & Blue
Official Website: www.oufc.co.uk
Unofficial Websites:
OU Exiles: www.ouexiles.org.uk
Rage Online: www.rageonline.co.uk
This Is United: www.thisisunited.co.uk

WHAT'S THE GROUND LIKE?

The Club moved from the Manor Ground in the summer of 2001 to the purpose built Kassam Stadium (named after Oxford Chairman Firoz Kassam). The stadium was built at a cost of around £15m and is located on the outskirts of Oxford. It has only three sides, with one end remaining unused. Each of the stands are of a good size, are all-seated, covered and are roughly of the same height. The South Stand, on one side of the pitch, is two-tiered with a row of executive boxes. This is a particularly impressive looking stand with Police Control and Press Boxes situated at the back. Opposite is the single-tiered North Stand, primarily given to away supporters. This has a number of strange looking floodlights protruding from its roof. At the one end is the Oxford Mail Stand, which is also single-tiered. There is a special type of pitch, one of the first to have artificial grass woven into the live turf. One disappointment is the large gaps in the corners, which sets the stands back from the playing surface and means cold winds whistling through in winter.

FUTURE GROUND DEVELOPMENTS

Foundations have been put in place for the future construction of a fourth stand at the West End of the stadium. However, it is unlikely that this will be built for at least a couple of years.

WHAT'S IT LIKE FOR VISITORS?

Away fans are housed on one side of the North Stand, towards the open end of the ground. This stand may be shared with home supporters, or as was the case on my visit, the whole stand was given to the away support. There is little around the ground in terms of pubs and eating establishments, so you may have to find such comforts within the ground itself. The refreshments on offer are okay, with a range of rollover hot dogs and pies. Bottles of Carlsberg Lager are also available at £2.20. However, I have had a number of reports that it still takes an eternity to get served in the refreshment area and/or that they have run out of hot food/drinks. One visiting supporter even suggested taking a flask and packed lunch. Please note that you are not allowed to smoke within the ground, apart from the concourses where the refreshment areas are located.

The Kassam is light years away from the old Manor Ground. The facilities within and pitch view are excellent and there is also good legroom. The atmosphere is not bad, with the Oxford fans in the Oxford Mail Stand doing their best to raise it. I did notice that they hadn't quite got used to their new home, still chanting the London Road End chant from the Manor Ground. With one end of the ground being open, there is always the remark of 'watch my car' as another wayward shot flies into the car park behind. On the whole I found the Kassam Stadium to be an enjoyable and a largely friendly day out.

Derek Fennel, a visiting Blackburn supporter, adds:

'The stewards at the Kassam seemed very helpful and accommodating which led to a feeling of watching the game in relaxed frame of mind. There was great vocal support from the home supporters in the North Stand who really got behind their team'.

WHERE TO DRINK

The nearest Public House is The Priory, which is just behind the car park at the open end of the ground. The pub is owned by Club Chairman Firoz Kassam and is quite an historic looking building. On my visit, the pub seemed fine for away fans, but can get quite crowded. It boasts a large screen for SKY TV, served hand-pulled Tetleys and offered a wide range of pies and filled rolls. Andy Wraight adds: 'There is now a Holiday Inn Hotel on the corner behind the Oxford Mail and South Stand, which has a fair sized bar. It welcomes football supporters and has Sky Television. Otherwise alcohol is served within the ground.' Kim Rockall informs me: 'A new cinema and bowling alley complex was recently opened adjacent to the stadium, called Ozone. Inside the bowling alley there is a bar, which also has SKY TV and a fast food outlet'.

GETTING THERE & WHERE TO PARK

The stadium is quite well signposted from the main routes into Oxford, with brown football signs pointing the way. The stadium can be found in between the Oxford Science Park and Blackbird Leys Estate. From the A423 Ring Road, take the A4074 towards Reading. After the roundabout with Sainsbury's on one corner, take the left turn signposted Cowley/Wallington/Oxford Science Park and you eventually come to the ground on your left.

There is plenty of car parking around and at the stadium itself. Parking is mostly free; however don't get tempted to park on a grass verge as you may well end up with a parking ticket for your trouble. John Attwood, a visiting Gillingham supporter, adds: 'When arriving at the stadium, ignore the first car park entrance that you come to and go up to the second entrance as the first will have you parking at the 'open' end. There is a roundabout by the second entrance, which will take you back to the first entrance if the other half is full. I was also heavily delayed in trying to leave the car park after the game as there were only two exits available'. An additional 300 car parking spaces are now available at the Ozone cinema and bowling alley complex adjacent to the stadium, which are also free to use.

By Train
Oxford railway station is over two miles from the ground and it is really not advisable to try to walk it. There is a bus service, Number 601, running from Oxford station to the ground. It leaves the station at 13.45 and 14.15 (Sat) and 18.30 and 19.00 (midweek). Return fares are: adults £1.60, children 80p. Buses return to the rail station from the ground 10 minutes after the final whistle.

LOCAL RIVALS

Swindon Town, Reading and Wycombe Wanderers.

ADMISSION PRICES

Home Fans:
South Stand Upper Tier (bought in advance): Adults: £17, Students: £12.50, Concessions: £11.50
South Stand Upper Tier (on the day): Adults: £20, Students: £15.50, Concessions: £14.50
South Stand Lower Tier (bought in advance): Adults: £15.50, Students: £12 Concessions: £9.50
South Stand Lower Tier (on the day): Adults: £18.50, Students: £14.50 Concessions: £12
South Stand Family Area (must be at least one adult + one under 16):
(bought in advance) Adults: £14.50, Students: £12, Over 65s: £9.50, Under 16s: £4
(on the day) Adults: £18.50, Students: £15.50, Over 65s: £12, Under 16s: £7
Oxford Mail (East) Stand (bought in advance): £13.50, Students: £10.50, Concessions: £7
Oxford Mail (East) Stand (on the day): Adults: £16.50, Students: £13.50, Concessions: £10
Away Fans:
North Stand (bought in advance): Adults: £15.50, Concessions: £9.50
North Stand (on the day): Adults: £18.50, Concessions: £12
 Students must have a current NUS Card. Concessions apply to over 65s and under 16s. Thanks to Chris Stilwell for providing the ticket price information.

PROGRAMME

Official Programme: £2.50.
Rage On Fanzine: £1.
Yellow Fever: £1.

RECORD ATTENDANCE

At The Kassam Stadium:
12,177 v Aston Villa
Worthington Cup 3rd Round, November 6, 2002
At The Manor Ground:
22,750 v Preston North End
FA Cup 6th Round, February 29, 1964

AVERAGE ATTENDANCE

2003-2004: 6,296 (Division Three).

DID YOU KNOW?

Desmond Morris, author of the epic "The Soccer Tribe" as well as "The Naked Ape", designed today's all too familiar crest.

PETERBOROUGH UNITED

LONDON ROAD, PETERBOROUGH

Ground Name:	London Road
Capacity:	15,314
Address:	London Rd,
	Peterborough, PE2 8AL
Main Telephone No:	08700-550-442
Main Fax No:	01733-344-140
Pitch Size:	112 x 76 yards
Team Nickname:	The Posh
Home Kit Colours:	Blue & White
Official Website:	www.theposh.com
Unofficial Website:	
Posh Net: www.posh.net	

WHAT'S THE GROUND LIKE?

On one side of the ground is the impressive looking South Stand. Opened in 1996, the 5,000 capacity stand replaced a former open terrace. The stand is two-tiered, covered and all-seated. There is also a row of executive boxes running across its middle. The other side, the Main Stand, is a two-tiered covered stand that is all-seated. Both ends are covered terracing that were given white roofs a couple of seasons back, in an effort to brighten up their appearance. However, they both have a number of supporting pillars at the front of them, which could spoil your view of the game.

WHAT'S IT LIKE FOR VISITORS?

Just under 4,000 away fans can be accommodated in the Reynopoly Terrace, with a further 800 seats being made available to away fans in the Main Stand. The terrace has several supporting pillars, which may obstruct your view. I found the atmosphere at London Road quite good, fairly friendly and whatever team that Barry Fry manages is always likely to provide a good afternoon's entertainment.

WHERE TO DRINK

Michael Howard, a visiting Reading Supporter, informs me: 'The Cherry Tree pub on Oundle Road is quite popular with away fans. Although small, it is a friendly pub. It costs £2 to park in their car park but you get £2 off a beer if you present the parking ticket at the bar'. Whilst Gordon Pearson recommends: 'The Peacock, which can be found as you come over the River Nene. Proceed down London Road past the ground on the left and the pub is situated on the right at the traffic lights next to a KFC drive through'. Mike Whorrall, a visiting Stockport fan, adds: 'The Charters Cafe Bar is worth a visit. It is located on a boat on the River Nene, on the opposite side of London Road walking towards the town centre. The lower deck is the Cafe Bar whilst the upper deck is a Chinese restaurant'. Otherwise the ground is in walking distance (10 minutes) of the town centre (which is very pleasant and complete with a cathedral) where there are plenty of good pubs to be found.

GETTING THERE & WHERE TO PARK

The ground is located on the outskirts of the town centre, on the A15 London Road. It is fairly well signposted around the town centre.
From the North/West:
Drive into the town centre, follow signs for Whittlesey (A605) which will lead you to the London Road. The new stand is quite visible from some distance away, so keep a lookout.

From the South:
Leave the A1 at the junction with the A15. Take the A15 towards Peterborough. You will eventually come to the ground on your right. There is a car park at the ground or otherwise there is a council pay and display car park just off London Road (on your left as you pass the ground going towards the town centre).

By Train
Peterborough station is around a mile away from the ground. Turn right out of station and follow the main road, passing an Asda store on your right. At the traffic lights near to Woolworths, turn right. Go over the bridge and you can see the floodlights of London Road, over on your left. It takes about 20 minutes to walk from the station to the ground. Thanks to Andrew Dodd for providing the directions.

LOCAL RIVALS

Cambridge United and Northampton Town.

ADMISSION PRICES

Home Fans*:
Executive Seating: Adults: £25-£35, Concessions: £15
South Stand Seating: Adults: £16, Concessions: £8
South Stand Family Area Seating: Adults: £16, Concessions: £8, Under 12s: £5
Main North Stand Seating: Adults: £16, Concessions: £8
London Road Terrace: Adults: £11, Concessions: £8

Away Fans*:
Main Stand A Wing Seating: Adults: £16, Concessions: £8
Reynopoly East Terrace: Adults: £11, Concessions: £8

* Please note that a £1 discount is available on adult tickets provided that the ticket is purchased prior to matchday.

PROGRAMME

Official Programme: £2.50.

RECORD ATTENDANCE

30,096 v Swansea City
FA Cup 5th Round, February 20, 1965.

AVERAGE ATTENDANCE

2003-2004: 5,174 (Division Two).

DID YOU KNOW?

Peterborough United were founded in 1934 at a meeting in the Angel Hotel, Peterborough, where local worthies gathered and decided it was time for the city to have a new football club. United emerged to fill the void left by the forerunners Peterborough and Fletton FC, founded in 1923.

SPOTLAND, ROCHDALE

Ground Name: Spotland
Capacity: 10,249
Address: Sandy Lane, Rochdale, OL11 5DS
Main Telephone No: 01706-644-648
Ticket Office No: As Above
Main Fax No: 01706-648-466
Team Nickname: The Dale
Pitch Size: 114 x 76 yards
Home Kit Colours: Blue With White Trim
Official Website: www.rochdaleafc.co.uk
Unofficial Website: RochdaleAFC.com: www.rochdaleafc.com (Rivals Network)

WHAT'S THE GROUND LIKE?

The ground has benefited greatly with the construction of three new stands over the last 10 years and is quite picturesque, with a number of trees being visible behind the stands. The latest addition is the smart looking Per-Fit Windows Stand at one side of the pitch, which was opened during the 2000-01 season. This single-tiered stand replaced a former terrace and has a capacity of 4,000. On the other side is another single-tier, the all-seated Motorama Main Stand. This has a number of supporting pillars and executive boxes at the back. At one end the W.M.G (Pearl Street) Stand is the third of the new stands. This is also all-seated and serves as a Family Stand. It has a couple of supporting pillars that are right at the front of the stand. The

Thwaites Beer (Sandy Lane) end is the only terraced area remaining. This small terrace has in recent seasons had a roof erected. There is a Police Control Box located in one corner, between the Main and Pearl Street Stands. Spotland is shared with the Rochdale Hornets rugby league team.

WHAT'S IT LIKE FOR VISITORS?

Away supporters are housed in the Willbutts Lane Stand (recently renamed the Per-Fit Windows Stand), where the view of the action and the facilities are pretty good. Up to 4,000 supporters can be accommodated and normally away fans are confined to the centre of the stand. If required, then this stand can be split between home and away fans. The acoustics are excellent, so away fans can really make some noise. This, coupled with both home ends singing and the obligatory drummer, makes for a good atmosphere. If Rochdale do score, then 'Tom Hark' by the Piranhas blasts out around the ground from the P.A. system.

In my opinion, Spotland is one of the best footballing days out in the country. Friendly and knowledgeable fans, good stewards, good facilities, three pubs located at the ground, a great range of pies on offer and not a bad atmosphere to boot. In other words, all the right elements to make for a great day out. Add a pretty lady on my arm, my team winning 6-0 and I'll think that I have been transported to heaven!

WHERE TO DRINK

At the ground, there are two bars to choose from, Studds and the Ratcliffe Arms. Studds is located underneath the Pearl Street Stand and is worth a visit, if only to sample the large range of tasty pies and pasties on offer at £1.50 (which are also available inside the ground). You can even have a pie and peas for £1.80. No real ales here, but the bar has some lovely looking barmaids which softens the blow. The Ratcliffe Arms is located at the car park entrance to the ground, on Sandy Lane. This pub has SKY TV and on my last visit had a mixture of home and away fans. A couple of minutes walk along Willbutts Lane is the Church Pub, which seemed to be the favoured haunt of away fans. Also on Willbutts Lane is a small chip shop, with lengthy queues.

If you arrive early, the Cemetery Hotel, located at the bottom of Sandy Lane and on the corner with Bury Road, is also worth a visit. This comfortable historic pub has a range of real ales on offer and again friendly clientele. Otherwise alcohol is available inside the ground, although it is cans poured into plastic glasses.

GETTING THERE & WHERE TO PARK

Exit the M62 at Junction 20 and take the A627(M) towards Rochdale. At the end of the A627(M), you should be in the left-hand lane to turn left at the traffic lights. Go straight on over the roundabout (approach in the middle lane) into Roch Valley Way. At the next crossroads (where the Cemetery pub is on the corner) go straight onto Sandy Lane, where the ground can be found on the right after approximately three-quarters of a mile.

Car parking at the ground is very limited (£2) so unless you arrive very early, it is mainly street parking. Be wary of the residents only parking - the police are clamping down on the unwary. Otherwise on the way up Sandy Lane, there is also matchday parking at Oulder Hill School which you will see on your left (it is then a 10 minute walk uphill to the ground).

By Train
Rochdale is served by trains from Manchester and Leeds and is around two miles away from the ground. I would recommend you take a taxi, but if you do decide to walk it will take you around 30-35 minutes to do so.
Immediately as you leave the station, there is a roundabout in front of you. Cross it, keeping to the left and take the second left into Lower Tweedale Street. Follow this street until its end where it meets Manchester Road. Turn right along Manchester Road (which is a dual carriageway). Pass Drake Street and then cross the Manchester Road via the pedestrian crossing, now the left-

hand side of the dual carriageway. Carry on in the same direction as before. Turn left into Dane Street (where you will see a large ASDA store) and this leads into Mellor Street (A6060). At the end of Mellor Street turn left along Spotland Road (A680) and then left again into Willbutts Lane for the ground. Thanks to Björn Sandström for providing the directions.

LOCAL RIVALS

Bury, Burnley, Oldham, Manchester United and Manchester City.

ADMISSION PRICES

Home Fans:
Thwaites Beer Stand (Terrace): Adults: £10.50, Concessions: £6.50
Motorama Main Stand: Adults: £15, Concessions: £9
W.M.G Stand: Adults: £12.50, Concessions: £6.50
McDonald's Family Stand: Adults: £12.50, OAPs: £6.50, Under 16s: £2.50 (maximum two under 16s per accompanying adult)
Away Fans:
Per-Fit Windows: Adults: £15, Concessions: £9

PROGRAMME

Official Programme: £2.20.

RECORD ATTENDANCE

24,231 v Notts County
FA Cup 2nd Round, December 10, 1949.

AVERAGE ATTENDANCE

2003-2004: 3,277 (Division Three).

DID YOU KNOW?

That Rochdale haven't been out of the bottom division since 1974-75, the longest consecutive run of any team in the bottom league.

NENE PARK, RUSHDEN & DIAMONDS

Ground Name: Nene Park
Capacity: 6,441 (4,641 seats, 1,800 terracing)
Address: Irthlingborough, Northants, NN9 5QF
Main Telephone No: 01933-652-000
Main Fax No: 01933-650-418
Ticket Office: 01933-652-936
Ticket Office Fax No: 01933-652-638
Team Nickname: Diamonds
Home Kit Colours: White, Blue & Red
Official Website: www.thediamondsfc.com
Unofficial Websites:
RDFC.net: www.rdfcnet.co.uk
The 2 Diamonds: www.the2diamonds.tk

WHAT'S THE GROUND LIKE?

The ground was completely rebuilt during the 1990s. What emerged was not only a modern stadium, but one of quality in terms of workmanship and materials used. The ground is totally enclosed, with all stands covered and roughly the same height. Three sides of the ground are all-seated, with terracing behind one goal in the home end. The Air Wair Stand at one end is particularly pleasing to the eye, having a semi-circular roof. The corners of the ground, although enclosed, do not house supporters. One corner has an electric scoreboard, apparently bought from Millwall FC. An unusual feature is the owl statues on the roofs brought to deter other birds from the area.

WHAT'S IT LIKE FOR VISITORS?

Away fans are housed at one end of the ground,

in the all-seated Air Wair Stand where the normal allocation for away supporters is 1,000. This end is normally shared with home supporters but if demand requires it then the whole of this stand can be given to visiting fans, increasing the number to 2,372.

I was thoroughly impressed with the ground and facilities and on my last visit, there was a good atmosphere generated. It still has a new feeling from when it was built and from what I can judge no expense has been spared. The legroom and views from the away end are excellent. I also found the stewarding to be okay and the Rushden fans to be amicable. If you are feeling hungry, then the refreshment areas offer large Diamond double burgers at £2.60, as well as the delicious 'Football's Famous Chicken Balti Pie'. You may also want to have a look in the Club Shop which carries a range of discounted Dr Martens clothing and footwear.

WHERE TO DRINK

There are no pubs within the immediate the vicinity of the stadium. However, there are bars within the ground and away fans are treated to their own bar, called the Airwair bar. If you want a proper pub, you can either take the 15 minute walk into Irthlingborough or drive down the A6 for another couple of miles to Higham Ferrers.

At the traffic island by the entrance to the ground, you will find a road leading up to Irthlingborough. If you walk up this road, you will first come to a pub on your right called The Bull, which is quite popular with away fans. If you continue straight on past this pub, then you will reach another on your left called The Horseshoe, a small comfortable pub serving real ale. A little further on from this pub is Mai's Chinese take away & chippy, which we found to serve good food that we happily munched on the way back down to the ground!

Roger Paterson adds: 'If you go into Higham Ferrers heading towards Rushden itself, you will find a pub called the Green Dragon (located just before Higham market square on the left-hand side). Here you will find a large selection of beers. They specialise in real ales and often have a good range of guest ales. An assorted food menu is also available. A little further up the High Street is The Griffin, with a smaller selection of beers but the restaurant is excellent and good value. The Queens Head (located on the opposite side of the road) is more basic, offering regular lagers and bitters.

Alternatively you can drive to the Needle and Awl. This is probably the best place for away fans, as it offers a vast amount of ales, beers and lagers as well as good food. Driving there will take five minutes. When you exit the ground, turn left towards Rushden (on the A6), then right at the roundabout (this will have you heading towards Wellingborough on the A45). Proceed along the A45 for approx one and a half miles then take the first exit of the next roundabout and there will be the Needle and Awl. You will find the supporters of Rushden a friendly lot'.

GETTING THERE & WHERE TO PARK

So where are Rushden & Diamonds located? Well they are in Northamptonshire. The ground is located in Irthlingborough, just off the A6 between Bedford and Kettering. It is a little strange as the ground basically seems to be in the middle of nowhere, on the outskirts of Irthlingborough and surrounded by green fields. Travelling down the A6 it just seems to appear out of nothing!

From The North/Midlands:
Leave the motorway at the M1/M6 intersection and take the A14 towards Kettering. On just passing Kettering take the A6 towards Irthlingborough/Rushden/Bedford, you will reach the ground on your left.

From The South:
Leave the M1 at Junction 15 and take the A508 towards Northampton. At the junction with the A45, turn right towards Wellingborough. Follow the A45 past Wellingborough and then towards Rushden. At the junction with the A6, turn left towards Irthlingborough. You will come to the ground on your right.

There is a fair sized car park at the ground, which is free! However, it is normally full within an hour of kick off and this leads to a number of cars parking on grass verges along the A6. It is

also worth noting that it can take some time to exit the official car park after the game (one Cambridge fan informed me that it took him 45 minutes and suggested that this was another reason why fans parked along the A6).

By Train
The nearest railway station is in Wellingborough, which is six miles away! Therefore definitely take a taxi to the ground and at the same time book one for the return.

LOCAL RIVALS

Kettering Town, Northampton Town, Peterborough United and from a little further a field, Luton Town.

ADMISSION PRICES

Home Fans:
North Stand: Adults: £17, Concessions: £12, Under 16s: £6
South Stand: Adults: £17, Concessions: £12, Under 16s: £6
Airwair Stand: Adults: £17, Concessions: £12, Under 16s: £6
Peter De Banke Terrace: Adults: £14, Concessions: £9, Under 16s: £5

Away Fans:
Airwair Stand: Adults: £17, Concessions: £12, Under 16s: £6

PROGRAMME

Official Programme: £2.50.

RECORD ATTENDANCE

6,431 v Leeds United
FA Cup 3rd Round, January 2, 1999

AVERAGE ATTENDANCE

2003-2004: 4,457 (Division Two).

DID YOU KNOW?

With a capacity of 6,441, the ground holds more that the entire population of the town of Irthlingborough where it is located.

GAY MEADOW, SHREWSBURY TOWN

Ground Name: Gay Meadow
Capacity: 8,000
Address: Gay Meadow, Shrewsbury, SY2 6AB
Main Telephone No: 01743-360-111
Main Fax No: 01743-236-384
Team Nickname: The Shrews
Pitch Size: 114 x 74 yards
Home Kit Colours: Blue & Amber
Official Website:
www.shrewsburytown.com
Unofficial Websites:
Blue & Amber: www.blue-and-amber.co.uk (Rivals Network)
Swedish Supporters Club:
http://home.swipnet.se/shrews/

WHAT'S THE GROUND LIKE?

The ground has not had any new developments for some time. However, it is full of character and picturesque, with a number of trees visible around the ground. Both ends are primarily open terraces, one of which, the Station End, is given to away supporters. The away terrace does have a small covering at the back, but it doesn't cover much of it. Both ends are very close to the pitch. One side is a small covered terrace, called the Riverside Terrace, which has a number of supporting pillars and a strange television gantry perched in the middle of it. The other side is a small, covered, all-seater Main Stand, the corner of which is given to away supporters. One unusual aspect of this stand is that one side of it is higher then the other.

There are again a few supporting pillars in this stand.

FUTURE GROUND DEVELOPMENTS

Andrew Davies informs me: 'On October 8, 2002, planning permission was granted for the building of a new stadium. The New Meadow, as it is known, at the Oteley Road site (on the outskirts of town, near Meole Brace by the A5) will be a 10,000 all-seated state of the art stadium, which will cost £10m to build'. However, this is dependant on the Club being able to turn the current Gay Meadow site into luxury apartments, for which planning permission has yet to be granted. Once this hurdle has been overcome, then the Club can commence with the building.

WHAT'S IT LIKE FOR VISITORS?

Up to 2,000 away fans can be accommodated in the largely open Station Road terrace. Best to try and obtain one of the 500 seats that are allocated to away supporters in the covered Main Stand. I found the stewards to be not the friendliest in the world, however Shrewsbury is quite a pleasant town to spend some time and along with the picturesque ground, you should find Gay Meadow to be one of your better away days. Unless of course it is pouring with rain!
Jer from Largs adds: 'Shrewsbury is a cracking ground to visit if you are a neutral fan who likes visiting different grounds. The town itself has loads of character and architecture, whilst the ground is

a throwback to the good old days of terracing and tasty pies'. This included the delicious 'Football's Famous Chicken Balti Pie' available inside the ground.

One game I witnessed at Gay Meadow was particularly boring. In fact, part way through the second half of a dull 0-0 affair, someone shouted from the away end to the Shrewsbury goalkeeper: 'Do you have to watch this s**t every week?' To which the keeper replied that he wasn't bothered as he was on loan and that he would soon be returning to his home club!

WHERE TO DRINK

Pete Davies recommends the two closest pubs to the ground in Abbey Foregate: 'The Crown, which is two minutes from the ground, is a good pub for pre-match banter. A little further up the road is The Dun Cow. Quality ales (Ushers), food (Desperate Dan Pies) and barmaids (nice!). If you are walking down to the ground from the town centre then the small Nags Head pub is worth a stop. If the Desperate Dan pies don't fill you up, then there is the Flaming Great chip shop, conveniently situated next to the entrance road to the ground!

GETTING THERE & WHERE TO PARK

At the end of the M54 continue onto the A5. After about seven miles, there is a traffic island which is at the junction with the A49. Bear left at this island still following the A5. At the next traffic island, turn right towards Shrewsbury (signposted A5064 town centre/crematorium). Follow this road past Shrewsbury College and up to another island. At this island there is a large Nelson Column like statue on your right. Take the third exit (the football ground is signposted at this point) and this will take you down into Abbey Foregate. Follow the road down until you come to the Abbey (passing the Dun Cow pub on the left). The ground is further down on the right. Just before this on the left is the Abbey Foregate pay & display car park, which, if you arrive early enough, should have plenty of spaces. If you continue past the ground and under the railway bridge, you will pick up signs for other town centre car parks.

By Train
The ground is walkable from Shrewsbury train station, which is served by trains from Birmingham New Street and Crewe. Walk over the bridge across the station and turn right out of it. Go right again down a path to the river. Go right again and along the river footpath and you will soon see the ground on the other side. This should take about 10-15 minutes to walk. If you decide to wander around the town centre before

making your way up to the ground and you lose your bearings, just follow the pedestrian signs for the Abbey as this is quite near. Thanks to Simon Rogers for providing the directions.

LOCAL RIVALS

Telford, Wrexham and Walsall.

ADMISSION PRICES

Home Fans:
Main Stand (Members Only):
Centre: Adults: £17, Juniors/OAPs: £11
Wakeman: Adults: £14, Juniors/OAPs: £9
Family: £14 (one adult + one child) Extra Adult: £14, Extra Child: £5
Riverside Terrace/Wakeman End: Adults: £12, Juniors/OAPs: £7
Away Fans:
Station End (Terrace): Adults: £12, Juniors/OAPs: £7
Main Stand (Seating): Adults: £14, Juniors/OAPs: £9

PROGRAMME

Official Programme: £2.

RECORD ATTENDANCE

18,917 v Walsall
Division 3, April 26, 1961

AVERAGE ATTENDANCE

2003-2004: 4,007 (Conference).

DID YOU KNOW?

That the Club have played at their Gay Meadow ground since 1910.

EDGELEY PARK, STOCKPORT

Ground Name: Edgeley Park
Capacity: 11,000 (all-seated)
Address: Hardcastle Road, Stockport, SK3 9DD
Main Telephone No: 0161-286-8888
Main Fax No: 0161-286-8900
Team Nickname: The Hatters
Pitch Size: 111 x 71 yards
Home Kit Colours: Royal Blue & White
Official Website:
www.stockportcounty.com
Unofficial Websites:
Hatters Matters: www.hattersmatters.com (Rivals Network)
Independent Supporters Association: www.hisc-online.co.uk
Stockport County Trust:
www.stockportcountytrust.com
County Hatters:
www.freewebs.com/countyhatters/

WHAT'S THE GROUND LIKE?

At one end is the large Robinsons Brewery Stand, which is the newest addition to the ground and is the home end. This stand towers over the rest of the stadium, which looks rather small in comparison. Opposite, the Railway End is a former open terrace converted to a seating area. It is usually unused on matchdays and has a small electric scoreboard above it. Both sides are quite old looking stands, that are both covered and all-seated. The Main stand is only about two-thirds the length of the pitch and straddles the halfway line. It was recently renamed the Stockport Express Stand. On the other side is the Vernon Building Society Stand, allocated to away supporters. The ground is shared with Sale Sharks Rugby Club.

FUTURE GROUND DEVELOPMENTS

Paddy Dresser informs me: 'The Club still hope to redevelop the Railway End, with a two-tier 5,200 seated stand, which will be similar in design to the existing Robinsons Brewery Stand. However, no time scales have been announced as to when this will take place'.

WHAT'S IT LIKE FOR VISITORS?

Away fans are predominantly housed on one side of the Vernon Stand, where the normal allocation is 800 seats. This stand is covered; however, there are a number of supporting pillars which may impede your view. If this happens, the stewards do allow you to stand at the back of the stand to get a better view. You can access the entrance to this stand by walking behind the large Cheadle End and through the car park. Strangely then you have to walk across the front of the home fans section to reach the away area. However I have not received any reports of this causing problems.

The Railway End, where most of the away fans used to be housed, is now normally not open for most games. It can still be allocated to away fans if demand requires it, increasing the allocation by another 1,500 seats. However, this end is uncovered, so if you do end up in there, be prepared to get wet.

The facilities within the ground are pretty good, with modern toilets, whilst the refreshment kiosk, staffed by friendly faces, offers a good range of pies, including the delicious 'Football's Famous Chicken Balti Pie' (£2).

Stockport is another club that has become tolerant towards away supporters in recent years and is now a more pleasurable away trip than it used to be. If you are a plane spotter, then this is your ground, as during the game many large airplanes fly over the ground having taken off from nearby Manchester Airport!

WHERE TO DRINK

There is a small Labour Club (C.I.U. Affiliated) right by the entrance to the Railway End that allows visitors in, for a small entrance fee. It is a small club that could do with modernising, but I found it both comfortable and welcoming. Otherwise, there are a number of pubs along a shopping area, across the main road from the away end. Probably the best is the Royal Oak just at the end of Castle Street. Very friendly, away supporters are welcomed and there's always a bit of good natured banter flying about.

John Keane adds: 'Away fans will get a warm welcome in the Sir Robert Peel halfway up Castle Street. One pub to avoid is John Jo Greens'. Steve Johnson recommends The Armoury, a Robinsons pub situated by the roundabout at the top of Castle Street, which is very good for away fans. The Landlord is very friendly, the Robbies beer is excellent and the home fans there are very welcoming. Whilst Vaughan Skirrey, a visiting Sheffield Wednesday supporter, recommends The Grapes. As you come up the hill from the station, the pub is on the left at the top of Castle Street. Otherwise, Paul Turner, a visiting Oldham fan, recommends The Swan which is by the roundabout going towards the town centre. Good beer, atmosphere and away fan friendly.

Please note that alcohol is not available in the away end. If you chose to drink in Stockport town centre, it is worth looking out for a Robinsons pub, as the beer is excellent and is actually brewed in Stockport itself.

GETTING THERE & WHERE TO PARK

From The North/South:
M6 to junction 19. Take the A556 towards Manchester/Altrincham. Then join the M56 towards Manchester Airport. After a few miles leave the M56 and join the M60 towards Stockport. Leave the M60 at Junction 1 and head towards Stockport. Turn right at the second set of traffic lights to go onto the A560 towards Cheadle. Then turn left into Edgeley Road (there is a pub on the left-hand corner at the lights at this junction). The ground is down this road on the right.

From The East:
M62 to junction 18. Take the M60 towards Stockport. Leave the M60 at Junction 1 and head towards Stockport. Turn right at the second set of traffic lights to go onto the A560 towards Cheadle. Then turn left into Edgeley Road (there is a pub on the left-hand corner at the lights at this junction).

The ground is down this road on the right.

The ground is well signposted around the area. Street parking.

By Train
Stockport railway station is in walking distance of the ground (around half a mile). Come out of the station and turn left up Station Road and continue up the hill towards the roundabout. Go straight over the roundabout and turn left into Caroline Street for the ground. Thanks to Andy Harris for the directions.

LOCAL RIVALS

Manchester City, Crewe Alexandra, Oldham, and a little further afield, Burnley.

ADMISSION PRICES

Home Fans:
Stockport Express Stand: Adults: £19, Concessions: £11, Juniors: £7
Vernon Building Society Stand: Adults: £19, Concessions: £11, Juniors: £7
Robinsons Brewery Cheadle Stand: Adults: £16, Concessions: £11, Juniors: £6
Away Fans:
Vernon Building Society Stand: Adults: £19, Concessions: £11, Juniors: £7
Railway End: Adults: £16, Concessions: £11, Juniors: £6

PROGRAMME

Official Programme: £2.50.

RECORD ATTENDANCE

27,833 v Liverpool
FA Cup 5th Round, February 11, 1950.

AVERAGE ATTENDANCE

2003-2004: 5,315 (Division Two).

DID YOU KNOW?

Following the success of Argentina in the 1978 World Cup, Stockport County adopted sky blue and white striped shirts, until the Falklands war caused them to rethink.

PLAINMOOR, TORQUAY

Ground Name: Plainmoor
Capacity: 6,000
Address: Plainmoor, Torquay, Devon, TQ1 3PS
Main Telephone No: 01803-328-666
Fax No: 01803-323-976
Team Nickname: The Gulls
Home Kit Colours: Yellow With Blue & White Trim
Official Website: www.torquayunited.com
Unofficial Websites:
Capital Gulls:
http://homepage.ntlworld.com/peter.sellars/cgulls/index.html
Barnstaple Gulls: www.barnstaplegulls.co.uk
Torquay Fans MSN Group:
http://groups.msn.com/torquayfans
Fans Forum: www.torquayunited.net

WHAT'S THE GROUND LIKE?

The ground is basic and small, but has steadily improved over the years. Differing from other clubs, the Directors' Box is situated behind one goal, in the Westward Family Stand, rather than being to the side of the pitch. This is a neat, attractive, covered all-seater stand. The other end is a small covered terrace, built in 2000 to replace a former open terrace. It also boosted the atmosphere within the ground. A new Police Control Box has been constructed to one side of this stand. Both sides are covered. At one side is the seated Main Stand, with a small amount of terracing to the front. It runs for just over half the length of the pitch. The other side is a newer, small covered terrace, called the Carlsberg Popular Terrace. It looks slightly odd, having a

television gantry perched on its roof. Thanks to Simon Primmer for helping me out with some of the information on this page.

FUTURE GROUND DEVELOPMENTS

Dan Morton informs me: 'Plans have been drawn up to replace the existing Main Stand with a new 2,500 capacity all-seater stand. However, the development has been put on ice as the Club have been so far unable to buy the freehold to the ground from Torquay Council'.

WHAT'S IT LIKE FOR VISITORS?

Around 1,100 away supporters can be accommodated in the Sparkworld Away Stand, at one end of the ground. The Club also makes 200 seats available to away supporters in the covered Main Stand. Additionally, there is a small terraced area that can be made available adjacent to the Main Stand, but this area is open to the elements. The Sparkworld Away terrace is covered and the acoustics are good, meaning that relatively few away supporters can still really make some noise from this area. When I went, the weather for autumn was superb, so I thoroughly enjoyed the visit. Torquay is a good place to go for a night out, so I would recommend staying and making a weekend of it.

WHERE TO DRINK

The supporters' club Boots & Laces, behind the main stand, allows away supporters in and I found it quite pleasant and friendly. Simon Blogg recommends O'Connors near the ground. Neil Le

Milliere, a visiting Exeter supporter, adds: 'The George Inn on Babbacombe Road was extremely welcoming, both before and after the game. The pub is around a 10 minute walk from the ground and also has an excellent fish and chips place next door (restaurant and take away) that has won national awards'.

GETTING THERE & WHERE TO PARK

At the end of the M5, follow the A38 and then turn left onto the A380. On reaching Kingskerwell, take the first exit at the large roundabout (there is a McDonald's and Sainsbury's on one side) onto the A3022 towards Torquay. After one mile, turn left towards Babbacombe (A379). After one mile, turn left into Westhill Road for Warbro Road. Torquay United is signposted on nearing the ground. Street parking.

By Train
The ground is over two miles away from the main Torquay railway station and so a taxi (around £4) may well be in order. Neil Le Milliere adds: 'Torre station (one stop before Torquay station, but not all trains stop there) is closest to the ground. Walk up the hill opposite the station and it's 10-15 minutes away.

Alex Latham, a visiting Lincoln supporter, adds: 'As I arrived over two hours before kick off and with time on my hands, I decided to walk from Torquay station to the ground. It took me a good 35 minutes. Here are the directions: exit the station down to the seafront and turn left towards the town – it is the B3199 Torbay Road. Stay on this road as it becomes The Strand, Torwood Street and then Babbacombe Road. After passing Ilsham Road on the right and Westwood Avenue on your left, take the next left-hand turn into Warberry Road. At the top of the hill turn into Windsor Road. The ground can be clearly seen from the bottom of Windsor Road'.

LOCAL RIVALS

Exeter City and Plymouth Argyle.

ADMISSION PRICES

Home Fans:
Family & Main Stands (Seating): Adults: £15, OAPs: £12, Under 16s: £5
Carlsberg Popular Terrace: Adults: £14, OAPs: £11, Under 16s: £5

Away Fans:
Sparkworld Away Stand (Terrace): Adults: £14, OAPs: £11, Under 16s: £5
Main Stand (Seating): Adults: £15, OAPs: £12, Under 16s: £5
Students can also have the concessionary OAP

ticket, but you first need to register with the Club.

PROGRAMME & FANZINE

Official Programme: £2.00.
Capital Gulls Fanzine £1.

RECORD ATTENDANCE

21.908 v Huddersfield Town
FA Cup 4th Round, January 29, 1955.

AVERAGE ATTENDANCE

2003-2004: 3,460 (Division Three).

DID YOU KNOW?

That the Club was founded in 1899 by school leavers of Torquay College and Torbay College under the guidance of Sergeant-Major Edward Tomney.

RACECOURSE GROUND, WREXHAM

7Ground Name: Racecourse Ground
Capacity: 15,500
Address: Mold Road, Wrexham, LL11 2AH
Main Telephone No: 01978-262-129
Main Fax No: 01978-357-821
Ticket Office No: 01978-366-388
Team Nickname: The Robins or Red Dragons
Pitch Size: 111 x 74 yards
Shirt Sponsors: Gap Personnel
Home Kit Colours: Red & White
Official Website: www.wrexhamafc.co.uk
Unofficial Websites:
Red Passion: www.red-passion.com
Manchester Reds: www.manchesterreds.co.uk
Red Army: http://www.btinternet.com/~redarmywxm/

WHAT'S THE GROUND LIKE?

For a number of years the ground had only three sides, with one side being open, following the demolition of the old Mold Stand. In 1999, this situation was rectified with the opening of the Pryce Griffiths Stand (named after the former Wrexham Chairman). This is a single-tiered all-seater stand that has greatly improved the overall ground appearance. It is semi-circular in design with a capacity of 3,500 seats. The other side, the

Sainsbury's Stand, is a fair sized two-tiered covered stand, which is now all-seated, having previously had terracing at the front. One end, the Kop End, is a medium sized partly covered (to the rear) stand and is for home supporters. The other end, the Roberts Builders Stand, is covered and again is two-tiered and all seated. There is an electric scoreboard on the roof of this stand.

WHAT'S IT LIKE FOR VISITORS?

Away fans are housed in the upper tier of the Roberts Builders Stand, holding just over 2,000. If demand requires it, a further 1,000 can be accommodated in the lower tier. There are a couple of small supporting pillars in the upper tier of this stand. On my last visit, I found Wrexham to be relaxed and friendly, with both sets of supporters mixing freely in the pubs beforehand. The atmosphere was generally good, although there were a section of Wrexham supporters in the Pryce Griffiths Stand who seemed to be permanently baiting the away fans. Inside the ground, the delicious 'Football's Famous Chicken Balti Pie' (£2.20) is available.

WHERE TO DRINK

There is one pub right on the corner of the ground at the Kop End called The Turf. It is a Marstons pub which does allow away supporters, but only in small numbers. It can get extremely busy, so arrive early. Before the new Pryce Griffiths stand was built, this pub used to have a balcony that overlooked the ground. Otherwise, the town centre is about a 10 minute walk, where there are plenty of good pubs to be found. A favourite haunt of away supporters is the Wetherspoons pub in the town centre, called the Elihu Yale (named after a local man who founded Yale University in the USA). To find it, walk along the road from the ground towards the town centre. After about half a mile, go through the double set of traffic lights. After the next road junction, it is located in the row of buildings on your left, in Regent Street. Apparently Wrexham has more pubs in ratio to the population than any other town in Britain - sounds a good place to me!

GETTING THERE & WHERE TO PARK

From The North:
Take the A483 towards Wrexham (this is the Wrexham bypass). Leave the A483 at the junction of the A541 Mold Road. The ground is 300 yards from this junction (on the A541) towards Wrexham town centre.

From The South:
Take the M54 from the M6 (Junction 10A Northbound). Follow the M54 to the end of the motorway and join the A5 towards Shrewsbury. Continue on the A5 past Shrewsbury and Oswestry and then join the A483 towards Wrexham. Stay on the A483 as you reach Wrexham (this is the Wrexham bypass). Then as above. Street parking.
If you arrive early (around 1-1.15pm), there is some street parking to be had on the other side of the road from the car showroom by the Turf Pub. Otherwise, there are a couple of private car parks, charging in the region of £2.

By Train
Wrexham general train station is located next to the ground.

LOCAL RIVALS

Chester City, Cardiff City, Swansea City, Tranmere Rovers, Crewe Alexandra and Shrewsbury Town.

ADMISSION PRICES

Home Fans:
Sainsbury's Stand Executive Area: Adults: £20, No Concessions
Sainsbury's Stand (Upper): Adults: £15, Concessions: £10
Sainsbury's Stand (Lower): Adults: £14, Concessions: £9

Pryce Griffiths Stand: Adults: £16, Concessions: £11
Kop Terrace: Adults: £13, Concessions: £7
Family Ticket (Sainsbury's Stand & Kop Terrace)
1 Adult & 1 Child: £17
1 Adult & 2 Children: £21
1 Adult & 3 Children: £25
Away Fans:
Roberts Builders Stand: Adults: £16 Concessions: £11 (OAPs, Juniors)

PROGRAMME

Official Programme: £2.50.

RECORD ATTENDANCE

34,445 v Manchester United
FA Cup, 4th Round, January 26, 1957.

AVERAGE ATTENDANCE

2003-2004: 4,440 (Division Two).

DID YOU KNOW?

In 1876, Wales played their first international, a match against Scotland at the Racecourse Ground.

CAUSEWAY STADIUM, WYCOMBE WANDERERS

Ground Name: Causeway Stadium
(but still referred to by many fans as Adams Park)
Capacity: 10,000
Address: Hillbottom Road, High Wycombe, HP12 4HJ
Main Telephone No: 01494-472-100
Main Fax No: 01494-527-633
Ticket Office: 01494-441-118
Pitch Size: 115 x 75 yards
Team Nickname: The Chairboys
Home Kit Colours: Navy & Light Blue
Official Website:
www.wycombewanderers.co.uk
Unofficial Website:
Chairboys On The Net:
www.chairboys.ndirect.co.uk

WHAT'S THE GROUND LIKE?

On one side of the ground is the impressive looking Frank Adams Stand, opened in 1996. This was named in memory of the man who originally donated the Club their previous ground at Loakes Park. It is a large two-tiered stand, complete with a row of executive boxes and it dwarfs the rest of the stadium. The other three stands are smaller affairs, but are at least all covered. Only the Valley Stand, at the home end, remains as

terracing. Opposite is the Dreams Stand, housing away supporters, which is a medium sized single-tiered stand with windshields to either side. Along the other side of the ground is the Main Stand. This single-tiered stand has a raised seating area, meaning that fans access it by climbing a small set of stairs in front of it.

Jon Wood adds: 'As the local council have stipulated that the capacity of the Causeway Stadium cannot rise above 10,000, the additional seats have meant that certain areas of terracing, such as the paddock area of the Seymour Taylor Stand, have been made out of bounds to fans'. The ground is currently shared with Wasps Rugby Club.

WHAT'S IT LIKE FOR VISITORS?

Away fans are mostly located at one end of the ground in the Dreams Stand, where just over 2,000 supporters can be accommodated. I personally had an enjoyable day at Wycombe. The Club has a relaxed friendly feel about it. The ground is situated in a nice setting with a wooded hill overlooking the ground (this normally has a small contingent of supporters watching the game for nothing) and with green fields surrounding the other sides. The standard football ground fare of burgers (£2.30), pies (£2), pasties and hot dogs are available from the refreshments area.

David Abbott, a visiting Northampton Town supporter, adds: 'I have to say what an excellent ground the Causeway Stadium is. Good signposting around the ground, good organisation, excellent view from the away end and friendly fans. It was a very pleasant visit and if all grounds and supporters were as welcoming and well-behaved as Wycombe, the game would be all the better for it'.

WHERE TO DRINK

As the ground is on the edge of an industrial estate, there aren't many pubs around. Neil Young informs me: 'The nearest pub to the Causeway Stadium is the Hourglass in Sands (about a 15 minute walk, from the end of the road up to the ground). Away fans are normally okay in small groups except for big games or local derbies'.

GETTING THERE & WHERE TO PARK

The stadium is located on the outskirts of Wycombe on the Sands Industrial Estate. Leave the M40 at Junction 4 and take the A4010 towards Aylesbury. Turn left at the fourth roundabout into Lane End Road and then continue straight down this road. Cross another roundabout and into Hillbottom Road. The ground is down at the very bottom of this road. On my last visit I noticed that there were a number of AA road signs labelled London Wasps, which also pointed the way to the ground.

There is a fair sized car park located at the ground (costing between £2-£5 depending on how many occupants are in the car - the more people there are the less you have to pay), or some of the industrial units provide matchday parking (around £3). As there is only one road that leads from the stadium, I have heard that it can be a nightmare leaving the official car park at full-time. I would recommend therefore parking in one of the industrial units that line Hillbottom Road towards the ground. I did this and got away alright.

By Train
If coming by train into Wycombe station, then either take a taxi (costs about £5) or get the football special bus that runs from the station to the ground on matchdays. The Football Special (No. 501) departs the railway station for the stadium at 13.55 on Saturday matchdays and 18.40 for midweek games (cost about £2.50 return). The Special returns 10 minutes after the final whistle.

Paul Willems, a visiting Bristol City supporter, adds: 'If you have the energy, then a walk from the station to the ground along the West Wycombe road takes in several pubs and can make the three-quarters of an hour it takes feel a lot less!! Those in the know will cut across a park just after the last pub on the West Wycombe Road and be there 10 minutes sooner'.

LOCAL RIVALS

Reading and from a little further afield, Colchester United.

ADMISSION PRICES

Home Fans:
Frank Adams Stand (Upper Tier Centre): Adults: £18, Concessions: £14
Frank Stand (Upper Tier Wings): Adults: £16, OAPs: £13, Under 16s: £12
Hypnosis Family Enclosure: Adults: £14, OAPs & Students (under 22yrs): £12, Under 16s: £6
Main Stand: Adults: £18, OAPs: £14, Under 16s: £12
Valley Terrace: Adults: £14, Concessions: £6
Away Fans*:
Dreams Stand: Adults: £16, Concessions: £14, Under 16s: £12
  * A £2 discount is available on these tickets, providing that it is purchased prior to matchday.

PROGRAMME

Official Programme: £2.50.

RECORD ATTENDANCE

At Adams Park:
9,921 v Fulham
FA Cup 3rd Round, January 8, 2002
At Loakes Park:
12,000 v Middlesbrough
FA Cup 3rd Round, January 4, 1975

AVERAGE ATTENDANCE

2003-2004: 5,256 (Division Two).

DID YOU KNOW?

That Wycombe Wanderers Football Club, originally called North Town Wanderers, were founded around 1884 by a group of young furniture trade workers.

MILLENNIUM STADIUM, CARDIFF

Capacity: 73,434 (72,500 for football)
Address: 101 St Marys Street, Cardiff CF10 1GE
Main Telephone No: 08705-582582
Main Fax No: 0292-023-2678
Stadium Tours: 0292-082-2228
Official Website:
www.millenniumstadium.com
A Useful Site About Cardiff In General:
Net Cardiff: www.netcardiff.co.uk

WHAT'S THE STADIUM LIKE?

Simply stunning. Built on the site of the Cardiff Arms Park by Laing, the stadium was completed in October 1999 at a cost of £130m. The stadium features a fully retractable roof which takes about 20 minutes to close and is the first of its kind to be constructed in Britain. The stadium is completely enclosed with curved corners and is mostly three-tiered with an additional row of 125 executive boxes. Add to this two huge screens, suspended beneath the roof at each end of the stadium, and you have a sight to behold. Unfortunately one end, the North Stand, is only two-tiered as it backs

onto the neighbouring Cardiff Rugby Club. Efforts were made to persuade the rugby club to move, but to no avail. Hence the stadium is built directly onto the rear of one of the rugby club stands and as there was insufficient space, a third tier could not be built. Another unusual feature of this stadium is that the grass pitch is grown outside of the stadium and is brought in when needed, allowing the stadium to be used for other events. Periodically, a falcon is flown around the stadium to keep Cardiff's pigeon population at bay.

WHAT'S IT LIKE FOR VISITORS?

The facilities are first class and there is plenty of legroom and height between rows, ensuring a good view of the action. Although the stadium is huge, one pleasant surprise is that you don't feel that you are that far away from the playing surface. One slight complaint is that at the back of the lower tier, you do feel a little cut off from the rest of the stadium as the second tier overhangs the first. You still get a good view of the playing surface, but you can't see the whole stadium. To compensate for this, huge

TV screens are suspended beneath the roof above you so that you can see what is happening. Also, the incline of the top tier (level six) is quite steep, needing some effort to climb to the top. On the plus side, the acoustics and P.A. as you would expect are first class and a great atmosphere can be generated within the stadium. Add friendly stewards, relaxed police and a generally welcoming local population, and you have all the ingredients for a great day out. In many respects, I'll be sad to see the finals return to Wembley when it is completed in 2006.

If you are lucky enough to see a game with the roof of the stadium closed, then prepare yourself for quite a spectacle. The stadium looks totally different and the atmosphere is boosted within it. You wouldn't want to see every game under cover, as it seems somewhat artificial, but as a one off it is a fantastic experience.

TICKET PRICE BANDS EXPLAINED

Excluding Executive Areas, there are normally four categories of tickets available for football games:
The most expensive tickets are for the middle tier of the stadium.
The second band of tickets is for the very front rows of the upper top tier, just above the row of executive boxes.
The third band of seats is in the mid-price category and is located around the middle of the bottom and top tiers of seating.
The cheapest seats are located in three areas where, although the views are acceptable, they are not as good as the other areas. The three areas are: 1) the very front rows of seats in the lower tier; 2) the rows of seats at the back of the lower tier. Although the view is okay from this area, you feel a little cut off from the rest of the stadium, as you are sitting under the second tier; and 3) seats right at the back of the top tier, where you are furthest away from the pitch. Again the view of the playing action is fine (unless you have sight problems as you are far away from the pitch), but some of the rest of the stadium is obscured by the tubular steelwork and large video screen hanging down from the roof.

WHERE TO EAT & DRINK

The good news is that unlike most other new stadiums frequently built on the edge of town, the Millennium is right in the centre of Cardiff. There are loads of bars and eating establishments to choose from. In fact, there are over 70 bars within a quarter of a mile radius of the stadium that can accommodate around 60,000 supporters! However your choice of pubs will more than likely be restricted to which end of the stadium your team has been allocated, as fans then tend to congregate in the pubs around each end.

The South End of the stadium has the larger bars centred around it in St Marys Street, where the usual names of Wetherspoons, Walkabout and O'Neils can be found. My pick in this area were the Wetherspoons outlet, the Prince Of Wales (a former theatre where you can now have a pint in the royal box!) and, if you are looking for a good pint of Brains, The Albert is just in front of the brewery. However, these pubs fill up quickly so aim to get there for opening time. Gareth Baglow recommends The Cottage on St Marys Street.

At the North End, Danny Boy recommends the Owain Glyndwr by the market and the Angel Bar beneath the hotel of the same name. Whilst Bob Kurac, a visiting Liverpool supporter, adds: 'The City Arms is a cracking good pub, right opposite the entrance to gates 2 and 3. Two small bars, excellent ales (Brains) and a big screen for sports.' Mark Tyler recommends: 'The Cayo Arms on Cathedral Road. It is only five minutes walk from the stadium, has a beer garden in front of it, so if the weather's good you can have a pre-match pint while sharing some banter with the opposing fans and soaking up the atmosphere as fans stream past on their way to the match. Directions: walking away from the City Centre, cross the river Taff on the bridge just North of the stadium and take the first right. You are now in Cathedral Road and The Cayo is the first pub you reach, a couple of hundred metres up on the right'.

Just off St Marys Street is Caroline Street, nicknamed locally as chip alley. The street is home to a number of kebab shops and chippies.

Alcohol is also served from one of 23 bars within the stadium, although please note that you are not allowed to take alcohol back to your seat. The bars are open until 15 minutes before kick off. Prices inside the stadium were par for the course with pasties and pints being around £2.50. It was reasonably easy to get served before the game started, although for some reason the bars are closed at half-time. Programmes retail normally between £4 and £5.

GETTING THERE & WHERE TO PARK

The stadium is well signposted from the M4 and surrounding routes, with electronic signs advising which junction to take. The junction exiting the M4 into Cardiff (up to four junctions are used 29-33) will depend on which Park & Ride scheme you will be getting, as separate ones are set up for opposing supporters, and depending on whether you are going by coach or car. Unless you are going to be at the stadium several hours before kick off, then due to traffic restrictions put in force on matchdays, you will not be able to drive near to, let alone park by, the stadium. You will therefore have to use the Park & Ride service. The Park & Ride scheme is not free: it costs £5 to park and there are huge queues waiting after the game to go back to the car parks. I would advise that you allow plenty of time for your journey as traffic congestion along the M4 and going into Cardiff can be quite bad. Alternatively I would advise either stopping in Cardiff the night before, or driving part of the way and then getting a train into Cardiff (see below).

By Train
Cardiff Central station is only a few minutes walk from the stadium, directly behind the South Stand. As you come out of the station, the stadium is across the road in front of you. Fans may also consider driving to Newport station and getting the train for the 15 minute ride into Cardiff Central. The cost of an off-peak adult return from Newport to Cardiff is £3.30 and the trains run regularly before and after the game. You can't park for long periods at Newport Station itself, but there is a large shoppers' car park on the other side of the dual carriageway to that of

the station entrance. Although advertised as a short term car park, you can park there all day and on my last visit this cost £3.90. I also noted that on Sundays the barrier to the car park exit is not in place, so you can park for free. Alternatively there is a smaller car park, just past the entrance to the shoppers' car park, or if you continue up to the traffic island and turn right, there is another car park located over the bridge.

STADIUM TOURS

The stadium offers regular tours on most days throughout the year. The tour itself costs:
Adults: £5
Children 5-16 years: £2.50
Children Under 5s: Free
Concessions (OAPs Students, Unemployed, Proof required): £3
Family Ticket: 2 Adults + 3 Children: £15
I have been on the tour myself and would definitely recommend it. It lasts around 45 minutes and is one of the better tours that I have been on, full of interesting facts, coupled with a sense of humour. You can book your tours on: 02920-822-228.

DID YOU KNOW?

That the pitch is not a permanent feature of the stadium. It is grown in another location and then brought into the stadium on 7,400 individual pallets, which are then connected together. The pitch can then be removed from the stadium allowing it to be used for other non-sporting purposes such as exhibitions and pop concerts.